Extraordinary
TOGETHERNESS

Extraordinary TOGETHERNESS

A WOMAN'S GUIDE TO
Love, Sex, *and* Intimacy

BY SARÍ HARRAR AND JULIA VANTINE

Medical Advisor, Barbara D. Bartlik, M.D.
Weill Medical College of Cornell University

RODALE

Prevention Health Books for Women is a trademark of Rodale Inc.

Printed in the United States of America on acid-free ∞ , recycled paper ♻

"Are You (or Is Your Husband) a Workaholic?" on page 255 was adapted from *He Works, She Works: Successful Strategies for Working Couples* by Jaine Carter, Ph.D., and James D. Carter, Ph.D. © 1995 by Jaine Carter, Ph.D., and James D. Carter, Ph.D. Reprinted by permission.

Library of Congress Cataloging-in-Publication Data

Harrar, Sarí.
    Extraordinary togetherness : a woman's guide to love, sex, and
intimacy / by Sarí Harrar and Julia VanTine.
        p.   cm.
    "Prevention Health Books for Women."
    Includes index.
    ISBN 1–57954–025–2 hardcover
    ISBN 1–57954–325–1 hardcover reissue
    1. Women—Sexual behavior.   2. Sex—Popular works.   3. Sexual
excitement.   4. Women—Psychology.   I. VanTine, Julia.
II. Prevention Health Books for Women.   III. Title.
HQ29.H365   1999
306.7—dc21   99–23939

Distributed to the book trade by St. Martin's Press

     4   6   8   10   9   7   5   3   hardcover
  2   4   6   8   10   9   7   5   3   hardcover reissue

Visit us on the Web at www.rodalebooks.com, or call us toll-free at (800) 848-4735.

WE **INSPIRE** AND **ENABLE** PEOPLE TO IMPROVE
THEIR LIVES AND THE WORLD AROUND THEM

Sex and Values at Rodale Press

We believe that an active and healthy sex life, based on mutual consent and respect between partners, is an important component of physical and mental well-being. We also respect that sex is a private matter and that each person has a different opinion of what sexual practices or levels of discourse are appropriate. Rodale Press is committed to offering responsible, practical advice about sexual matters, supported by accredited professionals and legitimate scientific research. Our goal—for sex and all other topics—is to publish information that improves people's lives.

About Prevention *Health Books*

The editors of *Prevention* Health Books are dedicated to providing you with authoritative, trustworthy, and innovative advice for a healthy active lifestyle. In all our books, our goal is to keep you thoroughly informed about the latest breakthroughs in natural healing, medical research, alternative health, herbs, nutrition, fitness, and weight loss. We cut through the confusion of today's conflicting health reports to deliver clear, concise, and definitive health information that you can trust. And we explain in practical terms what each new breakthrough means to you, so you can take immediate, practical steps to improve your health and well-being.

Every recommendation in *Prevention* Health Books is based upon interviews with highly qualified health authorities, including medical doctors and practitioners of alternative medicine. In addition, we consult with the *Prevention* Health Books Board of Advisors to ensure that all the health information is safe, practical, and up-to-date. *Prevention* Health Books are thoroughly factchecked for accuracy, and we make every effort to verify recommendations, dosages, and cautions.

The advice in this book will help keep you well-informed about your personal choices in health care—to help you lead a happier, healthier, and longer life.

Notice

Extraordinary Togetherness Staff

EDITOR: Sharon Faelten

WRITERS: Sarí Harrar, Julia VanTine

CONTRIBUTING WRITERS: Alisa Bauman, Robin DeMattia, Judith Lin Eftekhar, Selene Yeager

ART DIRECTOR: Darlene Schneck

BOOK DESIGNER: Carol Angstadt

ASSOCIATE RESEARCH MANAGER: Anita C. Small

BOOK PROJECT RESEARCHERS: Jennifer A. Barefoot, Lori Davis

EDITORIAL RESEARCHERS: Molly Donaldson Brown, Grete Haentjens, Bella Hebrew, Karen Jacob, Jennifer L. Kaas, Sherry Kiser, Terry Sutton Kravitz, Elizabeth B. Price, Jennifer P. Reimert, Staci Ann Sander, Elizabeth Shimer, Lucille S. Uhlman

SENIOR COPY EDITOR: Amy K. Kovalski

PRODUCTION EDITOR: Cindy Updegrove

LAYOUT DESIGNER: Keith Biery

MANUFACTURING COORDINATORS: Brenda Miller, Jodi Schaffer, Patrick T. Smith

Rodale Healthy Living Books

VICE PRESIDENT AND PUBLISHER: Brian Carnahan

VICE PRESIDENT AND EDITORIAL DIRECTOR: Debora T. Yost

EDITORIAL DIRECTOR: Michael Ward

VICE PRESIDENT AND MARKETING DIRECTOR: Karen Arbegast

PRODUCT MARKETING MANAGER: Tania Attanasio

BOOK MANUFACTURING DIRECTOR: Helen Clogston

MANUFACTURING MANAGERS: Eileen F. Bauder, Mark Krahforst

RESEARCH MANAGER: Ann Gossy Yermish

COPY MANAGER: Lisa D. Andruscavage

PRODUCTION MANAGER: Robert V. Anderson Jr.

ASSOCIATE STUDIO MANAGER: Thomas P. Aczel

OFFICE MANAGER: Jacqueline Dornblaser

OFFICE STAFF: Julie Kehs, Suzanne Lynch, Mary Lou Stephen

Board of Advisors for
Prevention Health Books for Women

Jean L. Fourcroy, M.D., Ph.D.

Past president of the American Medical Women's Association (AMWA) and past president of the National Council on Women's Health in New York City

Clarita E. Herrera, M.D.

Clinical instructor in primary care at the New York Medical College in Valhalla, associate attending physician at Lenox Hill Hospital in New York City, and president of the American Medical Women's Association (AMWA)

JoAnn E. Manson, M.D., Dr.P.H.

Associate professor of medicine at Harvard Medical School and co-director of women's health at Brigham and Women's Hospital in Boston

Mary Lake Polan, M.D., Ph.D.

Professor and chair of the department of gynecology and obstetrics at Stanford University School of Medicine

Elizabeth Lee Vliet, M.D.

Founder and medical director of HER Place: Health Enhancement and Renewal for Women and clinical associate professor in the department of family and community medicine at the University of Arizona College of Medicine in Tucson

Lila Amdurska Wallis, M.D., M.A.C.P.

Clinical professor of medicine at Weill Medical College of Cornell University in New York City, past president of the American Medical Women's Association (AMWA), founding president of the National Council on Women's Health, director of continuing medical education programs for physicians, and master and laureate of the American College of Physicians

Carla Wolper, R.D.

Nutritionist and clinical coordinator at the Obesity Research Center at St. Luke's/Roosevelt Hospital Center in New York City and nutritionist at the Center for Women's Health at Columbia Presbyterian Eastside in New York City

Foreword

Nearly two years ago I began consulting with the authors of *Extraordinary Togetherness: A Woman's Guide to Love, Sex, and Intimacy* as they launched the book. The final product has completely exceeded my expectations. I never imagined that the book would be so comprehensive, so well-balanced, and so complete. The authors have created an encyclopedic work encompassing all stages of long-lasting relationships—how they begin, how to nurture them, and how to handle the twists and turns along the way. As a result, the book is the relationship counterpart of a standard home health encyclopedia, a 544-page reference book to refer to again and again as issues arise throughout a lifetime together.

Written by a team of skilled women writers, *Extraordinary Togetherness* approaches lasting relationships from a woman's point of view. Women's feelings are addressed in a commonsense, problem-solving manner, offering factual information, advice, and solace. Concepts are brought to life with personal anecdotes from real people. Women of all ages will find something for themselves and for their loved ones. A teenage girl, for example, will find essential information about birth control and sexually transmitted diseases as well as guidance on making smart choices. A married woman who is concerned that her sex life is becoming too predictable and staid will find novel suggestions. A woman whose mate is overly jealous or unfaithful will find essential advice. A divorced woman who is dating again or managing a reconstituted family will find effective strategies. And a mature woman coping with the loss of a spouse will find support.

Other important areas covered in the book include the importance of forgiveness; how to improve communication, enhance intimacy, and fight fairly; how to know when you are drifting apart; cures for commitment phobia; how to handle in-laws, dual careers, and money; and what women need to know about dating safely.

The chapters on sexuality and love-making techniques are handled particularly well, tackling even taboo subjects with tact and taste. Thus, women of all ages can benefit, whether they are young women learning about their own bodies for the first time, or mature women adjusting to the changes in sexual physiology that normally accompany aging. The book covers such areas as differences in the time required for men and women to get aroused; ways to enhance orgasm; massage and other pleasuring techniques; ways to bring passion back into marriage; the importance of afterplay; sexual aids; lubricants; aphrodisiacs; videos; and ways to address the more common sexual problems.

The chapters on gynecology are medically sound and as good as the best textbooks available, but they are written in a clear, straightforward manner that nonmedical readers will appreciate. Tough medical decisions, like whether or not to have a hysterectomy or take hormones, are dealt with particularly well. Even men's sexual anatomy and sexual problems are covered. That's essential because women often assume responsibility for the couple's sexual problems, even when the man is experiencing a primary sexual disorder, such as premature ejaculation or problems with erections. As renowned sex researchers Masters and Johnson emphasized, sexual dysfunction almost always results from the couple's interaction, not one person's problems only.

The writers spoke with hundreds of practicing therapists, authors, medical researchers, and other experts regarding specific problem areas in relationships. Thus, the text is more focused and up-to-date than if the writers had simply quoted published studies and books on love, sex, and intimacy.

The overall effect has been to produce a comprehensive work, containing a wealth of accurate information, that passed a rigorous system of review. The legions of experts who contributed to this book essentially comprise a "Who's Who" guide to the self-help literature on love, sex, and intimacy. As a result, the reader is given information she can trust.

As a psychiatrist and sex therapist, I will keep *Extraordinary Togetherness* on hand and refer to it frequently as I counsel women who struggle with relationship problems. I will also make it available in my office and recommend that patients read it themselves. The book offers an abundance of helpful, straightforward, well-thought-out advice.

I also plan to share *Extraordinary Togetherness* with my colleagues who provide therapy—it's an extremely valuable resource.

Barbara D. Bartlik, M.D.
Weill Medical College of Cornell University

Contents

PART FOUR
Extraordinary Dating

PART FIVE
Extraordinary Marriage

PART SIX
Extraordinary Sexual Health

WOMEN'S SEXUAL HEALTH

PART SEVEN
*Extraordinary
Problem-Solving*

Introduction

M y husband and I have been married 25 years—a long-lived union by today's averages. When acquaintances ask me the secret to our long-lasting marriage, I always say, "It's simple. We have separate bathrooms."

"No, really," they implore. "What keeps you two together?"

"Okay," I confess. "We each do our own laundry. And oh, yeah—we each have our own television set. And we work in totally different professions."

"So you're saying the secret to staying together is to lead completely different lives?"

Quite the contrary. People often remark that John and I seem inseparable—the Velcro Twins, clinging snugly to each other through thick and thin. We have many, many strong bonds: We both love to hike, bicycle, and ski—and do so together, often. We both come from large, outgoing families. We love good food. And we love to grow things around the house.

The list goes on. But lest you assume we think in lockstep, or that we've never had a fight, think again. We don't always agree. Marriage has been the full tour—we laugh, we cry, we grit our teeth. But somehow, by trial and error, we figured it out. Twenty-five years after saying "we do," we're still together and more in love than ever. It's extraordinary.

As the authors researched and wrote *Extraordinary Togetherness*, they asked women who had been married 30, 40, or 50 years or more the same questions people ask John and me. What keeps you together? What was your biggest challenge and how did you resolve it? What is the secret of *your* extraordinary togetherness?

Those couples are profiled throughout this book. Their stories vary somewhat, but nearly everyone credited the same two factors with their success: trust and communication. Couples who stayed together supported each other. And they shared their thoughts, feelings, ideas, and yes, even their criticisms.

When we asked experts what they deemed the key ingredients to long-lasting love, they, too, cited communication. Time and again, their advice was to talk things through.

Talking, it seems, is to a healthy relationship what exercise is to physical health—without it, the relationship atrophies. With it, the two of you thrive.

The benefits of staying happily together go beyond a more peaceable home life (and more money available to spend on vacations instead of divorce attorney fees). Research done at the University of Chicago attributes several important and substantial benefits to marriage. Compared with people who have never married or whose previous marriages have ended, men and women who are married:

- Deal with stress better
- Are less likely to drink, smoke, or engage in other risky habits
- Are more likely to take care of their health
- Have more frequent and satisfying sex
- Have a greater sense of meaning in their lives
- Live longer

Men and women benefit from marriage equitably, but in different ways, according to Linda J. Waite, Ph.D., professor of sociology at the University of Chicago, who conducted the study. Marriage increases material well-being—income, assets, and wealth. These, in turn, give the couple access to better medical care, better diet, and safer surroundings—things that are especially important to women. Marriage also works as a mutual support group, which Dr. Waite says is of special benefit to men. And, she points out, marriage provides both partners with an on-site, readily available sex partner. But she emphasizes that it's the emotional investment of marriage, not just availability, that leads to more frequent and satisfying sex.

Whether you're married, in a committed relationship, or still looking for "Mr. Right," *Extraordinary Togetherness* can help you achieve ultimate emotional and physical intimacy. The advice is fresh, candid, practical, and inspiring. And it's not just for newlyweds. Even if you've been married for years, you can benefit. I know: In editing this book, I learned much about how to make my marriage last another 25 years.

Sharon Faelten

Sharon Faelten
Editor
Prevention Health Books for Women

PART ONE

Extraordinary Love

Attraction

The sexual energy generated by people who find each other attractive may be so subtle that they don't even realize they like each other . . . at first. Or it can be so strong that sparks jump and dance when they touch.

Whether it starts as a spark or a simmer, there is no mistaking the power of attraction, says Helen Fisher, Ph.D., research associate at the Rutgers Center for Human Evolutionary Studies and an anthropologist at Rutgers University in New Brunswick, New Jersey, and author of *Anatomy of Love*. "Attraction is that 'magnetic' force that takes all your sexual energy and focuses it on one particular person," she says. And once it kicks in, there's no keeping our eyes (or our hands) off of each other.

"When a man and a woman first meet and find themselves attracted to each other, their behavior is quite predictable," says Timothy Perper, Ph.D., a Philadelphia-based researcher and author of *Sex Signals: The Biology of Love*. "When a man sees a woman he's interested in, he doesn't want to take his eyes off of her. Women notice this and decode a man's behavior very quickly."

Say Romeo and Juliet were alive today, and they first meet at a party (as they do in the play). Here's a play-by-play look at what happens.

Juliet signals her interest. "She'll begin to stand more erect," says Dr. Perper. "Her eyes will flicker, and she'll brush her hair with her hand." (Not surprisingly, an uninterested Juliet will simply turn away.)

Romeo subconsciously notices Juliet's preening. "He now knows he has passed the first traffic light," Dr. Perper says. "Some guys, if they're aren't experienced at this, will now try to run the light. They'll go over to her right away, for example. Bad idea. She's still not sure about him yet. He needs to give her some time."

Juliet notices the host or hostess talking to Romeo. Juliet sees that he's "safe."

"The next step is universal in all female animals," says Dr. Perper. "Once she determines that he's okay, she's going to initiate a meeting. If he's standing by the hors d'oeuvres, she'll approach the table, pretending that she wants some hors d'oeuvres, too."

Either Romeo or Juliet begins to talk about how delicious the weenie rolls are. At this point, Juliet should never wait for, or rely upon, Romeo to speak first.

And regardless of who speaks first, the initial overture may be awkward. "I've watched thousands of couples go through this, and I'm telling you, they mess it up. They agonize," says Dr. Perper. "It's pretty funny."

Next, Romeo and Juliet discuss the merits of turkey dogs over regular beef frankfurters. "This is called escalation response," Dr. Perper explains. "They are escalating toward greater intimacy. It's a very sensitive time, because if he turns away out of shyness or insecurity, she won't get over it."

But, assuming that Romeo wants to talk, he will start to look from the weenie roll to Juliet's face, back and forth, back and forth. "They're going to begin to stand closer and closer and move in synchronicity," Dr. Perper says.

One of them—probably Juliet—then touches the other for the first time. "Oh, that's so interesting," she'll say.

Romeo is aroused at this point, Dr. Perper adds, but not sexually. "It's more a type of focused attention and alertness," he says. "At this point, virtually everyone uses the same words to describe the feeling: I found her fascinating. Or riveting. Or entrancing. And they just want more and more and more."

The Chemistry of Love

Most of us studied *Romeo and Juliet* in English class, but the play makes a great chemistry lesson. During this mating pas de deux, all kinds of hormones and powerful brain chemicals are at work.

"This feeling of attraction isn't called chemistry for nothing," says Theresa Crenshaw, M.D., a certified sex therapist in San Diego and author of *The Alchemy of Love and Lust*. When you and the guy to whom you're attracted first meet, you both produce certain hormones, including phenylethylamine (PEA) and dehydroepiandrosterone (DHEA). You also secrete pheromones, which are chemical substances that produce subtle odors that trigger a reaction in others.

"The sight of this new love will raise the PEA levels in your brain, while the smell of him will raise the pheromones," Dr. Crenshaw says. "Other chemicals, such as oxytocin, are fueled by touch," she adds. "That's one reason why our feelings of attraction compel us to be affectionate in the beginning of a relationship.

"These hormones and chemicals are addictive," says Dr. Crenshaw. "When the levels start to drop, we begin to crave them more and more."

He Notices, She Notices

What do you first notice about a guy? His eyes? His smile? His clothes?

When men and women meet someone, they first notice facial features, according to one survey by Opinion Research. Both take less notice of clothes and hair. As for bodily attraction—well, see for yourself.

Feature First Noticed	Percent of Men	Percent of Women
Eyes	39	35
Smile or teeth	25	40
Body	14	4
Clothing	12	11
Hair (or lack of hair)	3	4
Shoes	1	2
Hands	1	1
Don't know	7	3

That's why being separated from a lover or mate resembles withdrawal. "We then look for ways to feed our now-dependent brains with these hormones," says Dr. Crenshaw. "We can't stop thinking about our beloved because we're desperate to keep those sense-memories alive in order to receive the benefits of our love drug."

As the relationship continues, these "attraction" hormones are eventually replaced with other, more commitment-minded chemicals, says Dr. Crenshaw.

Whom Do You Love?

Why we feel attraction is no mystery, says Dr. Fisher. It's Mother Nature's way of getting us to make babies. Why one guy makes your knees melt but another leaves you colder than a penguin on New Year's Day is one of nature's riddles. The answer appears to lie in what scientists call our love maps, says Dr. Fisher.

Your love map is basically a mental blueprint of everything that you find enticing and exciting—or revolting and dull—about a potential mate, explains Michael Mills, Ph.D., associate psychology professor and researcher at Loyola Marymount University in Los Angeles. Most of this blueprint is drawn during your formative childhood years. But the foundation is laid before you're even born, he says.

"Evolutionary research shows that men are born with a natural tendency to be attracted to women with maximal fertility," says Dr. Mills. "That's why men traditionally gravitate toward younger women with curvaceous figures—these qualities signal childbearing capability," he says. "Women, on the other hand, have evolved to find men who can protect and provide. So they're generally attracted to men who are tall, well-muscled, and somewhat older."

Yet there's more to attraction than hips and pecs, procreation and protection. That's where the rest of the love map comes in. "Ultimately, everything from cultural preferences to how our families treated us while we were growing up helps determine who makes our hearts flutter," says Dr. Fisher. "From the time we were small children, we unconsciously built this list of what we like, what we don't like, and what we're looking for."

But what's really important is not so much *why* you feel attraction, but that you do, says Dr. Fisher. "Attraction leads to infatuation, which eventually leads to attachment, which usually leads to having children and perpetuating the human race."

Reignition, Blastoff

Unfortunately, once matchmaker Momma Nature has you and your beloved starry-eyed and smitten, you're left to your own devices, says Patricia Love, Ed.D., a licensed marriage and family therapist in Austin, Texas, and coauthor of *Hot Monogamy*. And almost inevitably, that raw attraction you had for each other during the early years of your relationship begins to wane. "It is entirely natural that as you become more familiar with one another, the strong pull you once felt weakens somewhat," says Dr. Love. "Yet many couples panic when this happens. They think it means they are no longer attractive to each other, or worse, no longer in love. And most often neither is true."

The secret to keeping your bond strong through the years is to jump-start your interest in one another in some way, says Dr. Fisher. "Even if you've been together for years, there are plenty of ways to reignite your attraction." The following strategies can help.

Adorn yourself. Too often, we stop trying to be attractive for each other, says Dr. Love. "Both men and women tend to stop trying to make themselves attractive just because they already have a mate," says Dr. Love. "Pay attention to your style and grooming much as you did during your courting years. Put on some jewelry. Get a new haircut. Update your wardrobe. Sure, you probably have a few more pounds and a few more wrinkles than when you first met. But pay attention to your appearance, and you'll project the same positive qualities that attracted your husband in the first place. He'll notice. And it will encourage him to do the same."

Get a room. One of the things that helps keep attraction intense is the mystery, novelty, and discovery that surrounds it, says Dr. Fisher. When you live with the same person in the same house and dress the same way day in and day out, the novelty wears off. "Get a hotel room, just for a night. Dress up. Have fun. The novelty will help spark that old attraction."

Do something radically different. Again, the more commonplace everything becomes between the two of you, the less powerful the attraction may become, says Dr. Fisher. So pick up new hobbies and pastimes, both together and separately. "Anything that can renew your interest and curiosity in one another can help spark attraction. Learn a new sport, like scuba diving. Join a volunteer group. Just engage in something different. You'll start noticing each other again."

Reacquaint yourselves. Remember that it's not just your physical appearance that triggers your attraction to each other, but all those other parts of your love map, including your interests, personality, thoughts, and feelings, says Larry Hof, a certified marriage and family therapist, vice president of relationship consulting at Advanta Corporation, and a United Methodist minister in Spring House, Pennsylvania. "It's important to continue talking to one another, sharing your most recent ideas and thoughts. The more you strive to get to know one another, the stronger your attraction can become."

Communication

C ecil and Harold Waite have been married for more than 60 years. They have three daughters, six grandsons, and 11 great grandchildren. Both in their eighties, they still get a kick out of holding hands. In fact, Cecil finds her husband "more lovable" today than when they first married. How have they weathered the storms of six decades and come through still so in love? "We always talk about whatever feelings we have," Cecil says plainly.

Could it be that something as simple as talking is that critical to a successful relationship? Yes, according to Cecil and 29 other couples featured in the book *Living Happily Ever After: Couples Talk about Lasting Love*, by Laurie Wagner, Stephanie Rausser, and David Collier. Clear, honest communication is the staple of lasting love—the unifying bond holding all 30 tightly knit couples through more than 30 years of life's ups and downs. No matter how bad things got, the couples talked.

"Nothing is more important for holding a relationship together than communication," says Ruth Jacobowitz, trustee for the National Council on Women's Health, member of the Woman's Advisory Board at the University of California, San Diego, Women's Health Center, and author of *150 Most-Asked Questions about Midlife Sex, Love, and Intimacy*. "Every aspect of your relationship from paying the bills to having sex hinges upon communication. Talking and listening to each other is how you know what each of you wants and needs in this life," says Jacobowitz, of La Jolla, California, who has surveyed more than 2,500 women on relationship issues.

Same Language, Different Expressions

Though communication is the most important aspect in lasting love, it is also the one we most commonly have trouble maintaining, says Sarah Ossey, a certified social worker in New York City. Good communication happens when both you and your husband are expressing yourselves clearly and honestly and both of you are listening and understanding, says Patricia Love, Ed.D., a licensed marriage and family therapist in Austin, Texas, and co-author of *Hot Monogamy*. Where we run into trouble is that though we learn the same words and the same language, men and women are taught to express themselves differently, she says.

"Women are socialized to open up emotionally and to communicate by talking about our thoughts and feelings," explains Ossey. "Men learn to socialize by talking, too, but not about their emotions. They learn to interact by talking about events, like sports," she says. "Probably the most common complaint I hear in couples therapy is that the woman doesn't feel like her husband really talks to her, and that he feels overwhelmed by her demands to 'open up.'"

That's not only the most common complaint but also one of the most serious, adds Jacobowitz. "Nothing can put a strain, and even an end, to a relationship more quickly than a shutdown in communication, especially when you need to discuss sensitive issues like your sex life, raising your children, or problems with your in-laws."

Constructive Conversation

The trick is not to force men to communicate like women or vice versa, says Dr. Love, but for men and women to learn ways to express themselves that work for both. Here's what experts suggest.

Speak up. This seems very, very basic. But the first step toward good communication is opening your mouth and speaking to each other, says David Schnarch, Ph.D., director of the Marriage and Family Health Center in Evergreen, Colorado, and author of *Passionate Marriage*. "When things get rough, couples often don't talk to each other. And they think that means they're not communicating. Well, couples *always* communicate. When they don't talk to each other, they're communicating their anger or indifference," he explains. "And that won't get you very far. When you speak up, at least you're showing that you care. That's an important first step."

Speak for yourself. When either men or women are unhappy about something, we often don't speak up because we're afraid that our partners will be unhappy with us or reject us for what we're saying, says Dr. Schnarch. "Instead of worrying about how he'll react, just tell your husband what's on your mind, simply so he knows you better," he says. "You'll find it much easier to approach almost any discussion if you go into it with the sole objective of having your husband understand where you're coming from rather than placing the weight of the discussion on having him agree with you in the end. In return, offer him the same courtesy. Ask him to tell you what he's thinking just so you understand him better, not to determine if he feels the same way you do."

Say "I." "Always take responsibility for what you say," says Dr. Love. "It's a golden rule of relationship communication." Avoid pointing fingers at your partner during a discussion by saying things like, "You make me so mad!" or "You never listen to me!" Instead, try more "I"-centered statements like, "I'm angry" or "I don't feel like you listen to me." Your husband will be much more sympathetic to your grievance and more open to having a mutual problem-solving discussion if he doesn't feel attacked, she says.

Make conversation, not war. "Couples often block good communication by approaching a discussion more like a war than a conversation," says Dr. Love. "We try to dominate the conversation. We interrupt each other. Or worse, we 'fire' at one another and then mentally 'reload' while the other person is talking without ever hearing a word they've said. Clearly, this is not the way to constructive communication," she says.

If you're prone to military talk tactics, Dr. Love recommends what she calls a mirroring exercise, where you and your husband agree to take turns speaking and paraphrasing each other until you both feel you're understood. It works like this.

1. Make a brief statement, like "I want us to spend more time together, but I want it to be quality time, not just doing the bills together."

2. Ask your husband to paraphrase what you just said and then ask if he completely understood, as in, "So, you want us to spend more time together doing things we enjoy, not just everyday maintenance activities. Is that right?"

3. Next, say, "Yes, that's right," then add a thought. Or clarify, if necessary.

4. Your husband again paraphrases and asks for confirmation, showing he understands.

5. Next, it's his turn to make a statement.

"At first, this is tedious," says Dr. Love. "But it slows down the conversation and forces you to listen closely and respond to one another. That prevents your conversation from turning into an argument. You also benefit by

Women Talk Face to Face, Men Talk Side by Side

Don't be surprised if the man in your life is easier to talk to while you're driving somewhere together in the car. According to communication consultant Mary Mitchell, men prefer to talk things over sitting side by side, while women prefer to talk face to face.

understanding each other better," she says. "The next time you sense that you're entering a verbal battle, ask your partner to try this approach instead."

Skip the opening lines. Do not preface a discussion with "We have to talk," says Patricia Evans, an interpersonal communication expert in Walnut Creek, California, and author of *The Verbally Abusive Relationship*. "When you open a discussion with that phrase, you are essentially saying, 'I know what your problem is, and I'm going to tell you,'" she says. "People are naturally defensive to that. Besides, just the fact that you're saying, 'We need to talk' implies that you're not comfortable talking and sets the stage for an awkward conversation." Instead, simply go right into the discussion. "Start with, 'By the way . . .' and say what you need to say," she suggests. "If it's a very sensitive issue, you can say, 'There's something on my mind. I know you're busy right now, but can we set aside some time on Wednesday night?'"

Take a hike. If you've reached a stalemate in your discussion, lace up your cross-trainers and take a walk together, suggests Dr. Love. "Many couples find it easier to communicate while walking," she says. Just the movement of walking releases tension, which can help relax you both and let you talk more freely and comfortably. "Walking out in public places also keeps the discussions more civil, too," adds Dr. Love. "You're both more likely to keep angry outbursts in check."

Form a union. "One of the barriers we have to good communication in Western cultures is the incredibly high priority we put on our individuality," says Paul Brocklehurst, founder of the British Society for the Promotion of Unconditional Commitment in Relationships (SPUR) in Cheshire, England, which helps promote the value of family and marriage relationships. Sometimes couples won't meet in the middle on issues because each person is stuck in the mindset that compromise means losing some of his or her individuality, he says. The next time you're engaged in a discussion, especially one involving conflict, focus on how you and your husband are alike, not how you're different. "The lines of communication run much better when you're on common ground," Brocklehurst says.

Talk about it today. You might expect that the longer you and your husband are together, the easier it will be to talk to each other, says Dr. Schnarch. Well, the opposite is actually true, he says. "The longer partners are together, the more they have at stake in a relationship and the less willing they are to risk rejection," he says. "I always advise people to begin opening up right away. Start today. It won't get any easier with time."

Break the myths. Don't fall into the trap of believing that if you really love each other, you won't have to tell each other what you're thinking or how you're feeling, says Larry Hof, a certified marriage and family therapist, vice president of relationship consulting at Advanta Corporation, and a United Methodist minister in Spring House, Pennsylvania. "There is this romantic notion that husbands and wives should be so in tune with each other that they just know what the other is thinking and feeling," says Hof, who has authored seven books on marriage and family. "That's completely ridiculous. Even couples who have been happily married for decades can't read each other's mind. As the years go by, we change. What we want changes. It is dangerous to the relationship to expect that you and your husband will know how you're feeling unless you talk."

Keep pillow talk pleasant. There's a right place and a right time to discuss any problems you may have with family, friends, and finances. When the two of you are lying together in bed is rarely one of them, says Jacobowitz. "If there's an issue in the relationship you need to discuss, you should do it in a place where you feel on equal terms with your partner, like while you're in the car or while you're making dinner together," she says. "Bed should be a place that is pleasant—a place where you don't talk about the troubles between you. And never, ever discuss sexual problems in bed. You need to feel free to be open and vulnerable while lying between the sheets. You won't feel that way if you're subject to criticism while you're there."

Savor your silence. "Words can be so clumsy," says Brocklehurst. "As healthy and important as talking is, sometimes the best communication comes when there are no words at all. Sometimes there is more value in just 'being' with each other for a while. Sit down and hold each other; savor the quality of the silence and become sensitive to the communication that can take place within it. You might even find that taking time to enjoy your silence will make the time you talk even more worthwhile."

Conflict and Anger

F orget champagne and caviar, dining and dancing. One memorable Valentine's Day, Lucille Gibbs and her husband gave each other a gift that made their 30-year-old marriage bloom again: a weekend conflict-resolution class.

"We learned to really listen to one another and tune in to each other's needs," says Gibbs, 49, a social worker in San Francisco. "It has made a huge difference."

Attentive listening. Joint problem-solving. Coping with anger. Knowing when to discuss a "hot-button" issue and when to back off. These skills, Gibbs says, have helped them resolve issues small and large—from reducing clutter in the family car to Lucille's decision to move back to the couple's San Francisco home after holding a good job in a town three hours away for four years.

"I used to think a good relationship was easy and happened just because people loved each other. But now I know that's not real," she notes. "I've realized that you really have to choose every day to make your marriage great, by working out the conflicts in a loving way."

End the Blame Game

Lucille's right. Good conflict does make for good—and lasting—marriages. When researchers at the Catholic University of America in Washington, D.C., and the University of Denver in Colorado tracked 135 couples for a decade, they discovered that the best predictor of marital happiness and longevity wasn't compatibility, personality traits, or even how much in love a couple felt on their wedding day. It was a couple's ability to handle everyday disagreements.

"Conflict is inevitable in marriage," says Susan Heitler, Ph.D., adjunct professor at the University of Denver School of Professional Psychology and author of *The Power of Two: Secrets to a Strong and Loving Marriage*. "Two people cannot live side by side for years without having disagreements. After all, there are so many decisions to make in family life, from what time to eat dinner to how to manage the finances. How the two of you handle all those natural differences of opinion will determine the destiny of your relationship."

All too easily, the simplest discussion—say, whose turn it is to haul the trash to the curb—can turn a peaceful home into a scene from *Roseanne*. We're talking about bickering. Blaming. Accusations. Tears. Icy silence. Stormy battles. Threats. Insults. Even physical violence. "Trouble often happens because couples haven't learned the simple techniques that turn disputes into collaborative problem-solving," Dr. Heitler says. "Without these techniques, we revert to handling differences the way our parents did, or we may fall back on old patterns from earlier relationships. We start out with the best of intentions, but something goes wrong. And so we end up frustrated, angry, discouraged, and confused."

Exploding the Myths

Conflict doesn't have to end in frustration and anger. You can turn painful disputes into respectful, productive "fix-it" talks by learning a handful of simple skills, psychologists say. But first, it's helpful to explore a few myths about marital bliss that can actually perpetuate squabbling.

Myth: The better a marriage, the less conflict there will be.

Reality: Constructive conflict is healthy. One hallmark of a good relationship is the freedom both partners feel to voice differences of opinion, notes William Bailey, Ph.D., associate professor of human environmental sciences at the University of Arkansas in Fayetteville. "You can't squelch disagreement and have a healthy marriage," he says. "In fact, research shows that women who expect conflict in marriage will be more successful in long-term relationships than women who expect marriage to be a smooth, disagreement-free ride."

fascinating

Top Skirmish-Starters

What gets your goat, ticks you off, gets under your skin? When researchers asked 947 adults who were engaged, married, or living together to name the issue that couples argue about most, the following were the top problems reported (listed in order of importance).

1. Money
2. Children
3. Chores

4. Communication
5. In-laws
6. Careers

Myth: Anger is destructive. It's good to let it all out, or ignore it.

Reality: Anger is an essential human emotion that can help you pinpoint problems and propel you toward solutions, says Harriet Lerner, Ph.D., a staff psychologist at the Menninger Clinic in Topeka, Kansas, and author of *The Dance of Anger.* Consider anger a signal that something needs changing, she recommends. Then use problem-solving skills to reach your desired goal.

"This requires courage for women, who are taught by society not to get angry," Dr. Lerner notes. As a result, some women avoid anger and try to be "nice ladies." Others vent anger ineffectively and may be dismissed as irrational or crazy, she notes. "Neither approach uses anger productively."

Using anger productively also requires patience and a little restraint. "When you're feeling anger, you may be working out of the brain's ancient, reptilian limbic system. It wants to rant, rave, and attack," Dr. Lerner says. "You have to remind yourself to calm down enough to focus on the problem at hand. Simply venting anger only makes us feel angrier—it doesn't resolve anything."

Myth: Marital problems, such as unproductive fighting, only improve when both partners work it out.

Reality: Sure, it's better if you both agree to learn new skills, Dr. Heitler says. But either partner alone can make small changes that will still vastly improve the climate of a marriage, psychologists say. "You, alone, can do a lot," says Dr. Heitler. "If a woman is clear about the steps in conflict resolution and

Secrets of Long-Lasting Love

Patience and Compromise:
A Winning Combination

Mary Jane Fanuka and her husband Anthony of Cherry Hill, New Jersey, met in the summer of 1947. It was the Fourth of July, and Mary Jane and her girlfriends as well as Anthony and his pals had traveled from Philadelphia to spend the holiday at the beach. The two groups of friends collided, and Mary Jane and Anthony hit it off. When they returned to Philadelphia, they continued to see each other. Two years later, on February 5, 1949, they married. Mary Jane says that more than four decades of marriage have taught her the importance of patience and compromise.

The first year Anthony and I were married was difficult for us. We were very young and short on money, so we moved in with his parents until we could afford our own place. Living with in-laws was quite a challenge: They had established their lifestyle; we were newly married and trying to set our own life in order. But we made it through the year, and then we moved into a place of our own.

Once we were settled, Anthony and I started a family. We both wanted to have a large family—we would have eight children together—and we worked hard so we could afford to do so. My husband worked outside of the home to support us financially, and I worked in the home to raise the

can stay on that route, then the odds go way up that her husband will join in. It's as if one person knows the path through the forest. Then the odds are better that both of you will find your way out, together."

Beyond Quarreling

Dr. Heitler suggests this five-step approach for fixing the problems that crop up almost daily in married life.

1. First listen to your own feelings, so that you understand the problem and your ideas for solutions. For example, you might say to yourself, "Gee, I feel re-

kids and take care of the house. With only one of us bringing home an income, and eight kids in the house, we had to plan our finances carefully. Money was never a problem, but sometimes it was tight.

As you can imagine, there has always been a lot of action in our house and, inevitably, a lot of arguments. But it's amazing. Even with 10 different people who thought 10 different ways, disagreements were resolved fairly quickly between us. All of us learned that if you weren't patient enough to listen to each other so that you could reach some sort of compromise, you'd never get anywhere. So we all became masters at giving a little so that we could get a little.

Our family has always been very important to Anthony and me. When the kids were in the house, all our energies focused on them, and now we have our grandchildren to focus on as well. Some of our favorite times have been when our kids bring their families for a visit. When they aren't around, the house just seems empty.

Anthony and I are very comfortable with each other. And we've been married for so long that I think we've become almost habit to each other. At this point in our lives, I don't think we could live without each other. Besides, being together just makes everything in life so much better.

ally angry and frustrated when I come downstairs in the morning to a kitchen full of dirty dishes. I can barely find room to make coffee and the kids' lunches."

2. Calmly describe the problem to your husband. Focus on how it affects you, rather than blaming your spouse. For example, "Arthur, when the kitchen is untidy in the morning, it's hard for me to make breakfast and put together lunches. Last night's dirty dishes take up all the counter space."

3. Suggest a solution—and ask his point of view. Tactfully tell him what you would like to see change. Then ask how that solution would work for him. For example, "I'd like it if you could do the dishes before bed at night. How would that be for you?"

4. Listen to his response. This makes his views and feelings an important part of the discussion, and it ensures that you're not simply forcing him to do something he may not want to do. For example, he might respond by saying, "Sometimes I'm just too tired to do the dishes alone at night."

5. Together, craft a solution that accommodates both of you. Spend time brainstorming. To solve the dirty-dishes dilemma, a couple might decide to do the dishes together with some lively music playing—or to use paper plates on busy nights. "The important thing is to listen to each other and find a solution that fits the needs of both partners," Dr. Heitler says. "That way, you're collaborating. One person isn't dictating and blaming, and the other doesn't have to defend and apologize."

Squabble Squashers

Here's more expert advice for couples who are fine-tuning their conflict-resolution skills.

Understand Mars and Venus. Women and men handle conflict differently. While you may want to discuss a problem for hours, he may want to retreat by leaving the room or hiding out behind a magazine. "That's called pursuit and withdrawal," Dr. Bailey says. "The goal of good conflict-resolution is to strike a balance. A pursuer may have to be satisfied with less talk. Someone who withdraws may have to listen and talk a little more than he would like."

Talk about yourself—and about solutions. When stating a problem, avoid below-the-belt tactics such as complaining, blaming, accusing, name-calling, and threatening, Dr. Heitler says. "Focus on what you would like, on how a problem affects you, on positive steps that you would like to see," she suggests. "Remember that you and your partner are on the same team. You wouldn't want to attack a team member."

Really listen. Once you've voiced your concern and offered a solution, pay full attention to your partner's point of view, Dr. Heitler says. "That's hard," she notes. "When we feel irritated about a problem, we tend to feel that our needs are sacred and our partners' are insignificant."

Know when to back off. Tired? Hungry? Overwhelmed? Angry? Lonely? Then postpone problem-solving discussions to a time when you'll be more productive, Dr. Heitler suggests.

Evolution of a Relationship

Ask Betsy Price about the "success secret" of her 26-year marriage, and her answer is at once honest and romantic. "Relationships evolve and change, especially when you have children," says Betsy, whose husband, Bill, was her high-school sweetheart. The Prices, who make their home in Reading, Pennsylvania, run a window-treatment business together and enjoy mutual interests including cooking, gardening, antiques, and home renovating. "When your partner and the circumstances surrounding your relationship change, so does your love, which can only grow stronger with acceptance," she says.

"When we first got married, it was easy and fun," she recalls. "When we had our two daughters, things changed a little. Children definitely put stress on a marriage—you can get so caught up in them that you can forget about your partner. But we made sure we made time for just the two of us. We'd sit down to a nice dinner, with candles and wine, after putting the children to bed. Time alone has kept us very close."

Six Stages of Love

Whether it's children or the demands of your job, an interest you just have to pursue or a need to spend time with your old friends, *something* invariably cuts short the honeymoon phase of every long-term relationship, says Liberty Kovacs, Ph.D., former head of the Center for Marriage and Family Therapy in Sacramento, California, and former assistant clinical professor of psychiatry at the University of California at Davis, who studied the evolution of long-term relationships for three decades.

"Our society romanticizes marriage, which leads people to believe that the sweet honeymoon phase will go on forever," Dr. Kovacs says. "But it never works that way. Conflict is natural. It's healthy. I believe there's an innate drive inside us that propels us forward and that uses marriage as a vehicle for individual growth as well as the growth of the partnership."

Secrets of Long-Lasting Love

Their Love Grew As Demands Increased

Gail Coenen met her future husband when she and her girlfriend doubled-dated with Ted Coenen and his navy buddy in 1967. Ted was with Gail's girlfriend, but he paid more attention to Gail than he did to his date. It was a disaster. A few nights later, Ted and Gail went out alone and hit it off. They started dating steadily, got engaged two months later, and married on May 28, 1968. Today the Coenens live in Mosinne, Wisconsin. In the course of their marriage, Gail and Ted have faced two major tests—raising children and overcoming a major health problem.

Ted and I married just a short time after we met, but we knew we were right for each other. The truth of the matter is that we were probably more in lust than in love with each other back then, and over the years we've worked to develop that lust into a deep friendship and loving partnership.

It's that love and friendship that have gotten us through the most trying times in our relationship. In the mid-1970s, things were so tense that I wasn't sure our marriage would make it. We had just started our family, and we decided that I would stay home and raise our two young children and take care of the house. My husband was working several jobs so that we could afford for me to be at home. There wasn't a whole lot of time left for the two of us. But we pulled through.

In her research, Dr. Kovacs identified six stages that partners may experience over the course of a lifetime of marriage. "Not every marriage goes through all phases," she notes. "Some stop at an earlier phase. Others go back and forth, as new stresses bring up new issues for each partner to address, and create new conflicts for a couple to negotiate. A couple may spend years and years in one stage. There are no rules. Every marriage is different." Here are the stages Dr. Kovacs identified.

Stage 1: I only have eyes for you. Brimming with romance and passion, Stage 1—the honeymoon phase—feels like a delicious romp. But this

More recently, our love was again put to the test when my doctor found a tumor between two vertebrae in my spinal column. The doctors operated right away, and fortunately the tumor wasn't cancerous and there was no injury to my spine.

Still, it was a difficult time. Ted was dealing with his emotions and my emotions as well as managing to take care of me and our house. For several months, he had to feed me, dress me, and do all the housework. It was a lot of pressure.

But there is always good that comes out of trying situations. My surgery had a positive effect on our family. My husband's side of the family had never been that close, but my operation really brought them together. And my parents, who had always been tough on Ted, eased up on him after seeing him take care of me. Things would have been a lot more difficult for Ted and me without the love and support we had from each other and our families.

After that scare, our priorities changed. We don't measure our happiness by material things like our car or how much money we have in the bank, but by the time we have together. We enjoy a trip to the grocery store or taking our nightly walk because it gives us plenty of quality time together.

intense "just-the-two-of-us" stage also allows a man and a woman to cement a caring, supportive bond—and lay the groundwork for a satisfying sexual relationship, Dr. Kovacs notes.

Stage 2: Romance meets reality. The honeymoon's over. You begin to realize that your beloved can't satisfy all of your needs. This may sound like common sense, but it can come as a shock and sometimes even feels like betrayal, Dr. Kovacs says. What triggers this stage? Something as simple as times when the two of you want to do different things (you want to visit your family Saturday afternoon, he'd rather golf with his buddies, for example).

Stage 3: Showdown at the OK corral. Power struggles erupt. Both of you may feel that the other isn't doing what he or she should. Many divorces happen during this disagreement-filled phase, Dr. Kovacs notes. Underneath, something important is stirring: Partners are just beginning to learn how to meet their individual needs and nurture a marriage at the same time.

Stage 4: I've got to be me. This is the classic seven-year-itch—which Dr. Kovacs says can happen at any time. You and your husband move toward independence. Each partner now focuses on "me"—on satisfying personal needs, rather than battling over who's right and who's wrong in the relationship.

Stage 5: We can work it out. Emotional storms subside. Couples who make it this far are secure about who they are as individuals and can share their deepest selves freely, instead of battling, fleeing, or making unrealistic demands. Intimacy deepens.

Stage 6: Friends and lovers. Warmth and acceptance prevail, as both partners master the balancing act between "me" and "we." The couple learns to collaborate, supporting each other's strengths while each satisfies individual needs.

Navigating Your Marriage

The following tips can help you and your mate at any stage of your relationship.

Negotiate, don't attack. Learn to express your individual needs without criticizing or blaming your partner. Then make decisions and solve problems as a couple, Dr. Kovacs says. (For more information on communication and conflict resolution, see pages 8 and 13.)

Don't make him over. Recognize that you can't change your partner, Dr. Kovacs says. Try to use conflicts and disagreements as a way to learn about your partner—and yourself.

Resist the seven-year-itch affair. Dr. Kovacs says that it may be especially tempting for a man or a woman to have an affair during Stage 4, when couples focus on individual needs, as a way to create emotional distance and declare independence. But, she says, real independence is gained by developing your true self—and sharing yourself with your spouse.

Forgiveness

Maybe it was something relatively small, like a critical remark at the wrong time. Maybe it was monumental, like lying to you about a tryst he had five years ago. First degree or third degree, you've been burned. You're angry. And it hurts.

The worst part is that every little thing reminds you of the incident, triggering the pain, embarrassment, and burn of betrayal all over again. Now it's like the Berlin Wall has been resurrected between the two of you, and you haven't the ability or the energy to get over, around, or through it.

"You can try going about your life, pretending nothing happened," says Michael E. McCullough, Ph.D., researcher with the National Institute for Healthcare Research in Rockville, Maryland, and coauthor of *To Forgive Is Human*. "Or, you can try firing a shot of your own at him to get even. But the only way you can really free yourself from the pain is to forgive him."

Forgiveness is one of the most essential elements in any successful relationship, says forgiveness researcher June Tangney, Ph.D., clinical psychologist and professor at George Mason University in Fairfax, Virginia, and coauthor of *Self-Conscious Emotions*. "Frankly, if you are unable to forgive, neither the relationship nor you have much hope of moving forward," she says. "You can't love, enjoy, or really even communicate with one another if you can't forgive."

To Begrudge Is Human

The hardest part about forgiveness is getting to the point where you *want* to forgive, says Dr. McCullough. "We have a natural desire to punish people when they hurt us. We also don't want to set ourselves up to be hurt again." But as tough as it is, forgiving actually appears to be in your own best interests as much as it is in the interests of others. "Forgiving doesn't just keep your relationships intact. Research also suggests that it might reduce your own feelings of depression, anxiety, and hostility," he explains.

"When you don't forgive, it is you—not the person with whom you're angry—who is being eaten up inside," says Dr. Tangney. Forgiveness enables

Secrets of Long-Lasting Love

Anger Is a Waste of Time

Mary and Patrick Clark of Kario, New York, were first introduced by a mutual friend. They dated on and off for several years before they started going steady in 1961. Two years later, on August 31, 1963, they married. Mary says their marriage is successful not only because they had common life goals that stemmed from their similar backgrounds but also because they've learned to forgive.

Patrick and I were a bit older than most of our friends when we married. I was 32 and he was 36, so both of us were mature and positive that marriage was what we wanted. We were ready for long-term commitment, and we were ready to raise a family.

That doesn't mean that our relationship didn't have some tough times. For Patrick and me, having a family was very important, and we had five children together. Balancing our own lives as well as the lives of our five children was difficult at times. There was also a lot of us to support financially, so money was usually tight, especially when my husband's carpentry work was in a lull.

We had to sacrifice a lot when the kids were young in order to raise them and save for their college educations. But it was worth it, and it was what Patrick and I wanted to do. As a family, we tried to stick with activities that were fun but didn't cost a great deal of money. In the summer, we took trips

you to think about your partner and what he did to hurt you without being angry, she says. "Forgiveness frees you from the hold that anger has over you."

Giving Him a Pardon

Not sure where to begin the process of forgiveness? Here is what the experts recommend.

Take a healing time-out. Think of forgiving like nursing a broken bone. The surface heals more quickly than the core. You wouldn't expect to go out running on a broken leg right away. Likewise, don't expect that you'll

to the beach or went on picnics, and all of our children participated in athletics, so there were sporting events to attend regularly.

Fortunately, Patrick and I had similar values on how money should be spent and invested. We also agreed on how to handle problems between the two of us and within our family. I think a lot of that agreement stems from our similar upbringings. We are both Irish, and we both grew up on farms in Ireland. We have the same religious faith and similar educational backgrounds. With all of that in common, it's inevitable that most of our objectives and ideals are the same.

But similarities alone can't always hold a marriage together. Patrick and I have a great deal of trust, respect, and love between us that keeps our relationship strong. We also really enjoy each other's company.

Our marriage is a romantic partnership in which responsibilities are split 50/50. If one of us isn't doing his or her part, the relationship falls off balance and things don't work. We just have to communicate to discover what it is that's throwing things off. That's why Patrick and I discuss differences as they arise and before they evolve into something larger than they should. And we are also very quick to forgive each other because neither one of us wants to waste time being angry.

be able to dive right back into the relationship where you left off just because you decided to forgive, says Dr. McCullough. "Forgiveness is a process, not an event. Give yourself as much time as you need."

Forget about forgetting. "Saying 'forgive and forget' sounds nice, but the event happened. Forgetting is impossible," says Dr. Tangney. "Instead, when you remember the event, acknowledge that you got hurt. Then recall the reasons why you need to forgive. Repeat this process each time the offending event pops into your mind."

Walk in his shoes. The better you are at considering your husband's transgression from his point of view, the better you'll be at forgiving him, says

Dr. Tangney. "That means instead of viewing him as an evil man who set out to hurt you, be empathetic and consider the circumstances that affected his behavior. Realize that his intention was probably not to cause you pain."

Cancel your debts. If you have trouble with empathy, think of forgiveness as a canceling of debts, says Dr. Tangney. "Recognize that you are not perfect and that you often require forgiveness. Remember mistakes you've made for which friends and family have forgiven you. Forgiving someone else makes up for times when people needed to forgive you."

Don't try to even the score. "People often feel that it is incumbent upon them to enact revenge when they've been wronged," says Dr. McCullough. "Though it initially may be satisfying to get even, the long-term consequences are enormous. Revenge is a never-ending trap, as you and the other person continue hurting one another in the name of 'evening the score.' Do you really want to continue in endless retaliation?"

Give forgiveness as a gift. "Finally, consider offering forgiveness as an unconditional gift," suggests Dr. Tangney. "It is something you're giving your partner because you love him."

Intimacy

Intimacy is like success—something we claim to want. But exactly what does it mean?

Ask five of your closest friends to define *intimacy*, and you'll get five different answers. Same goes if you query their husbands.

"When I ask women what they think intimacy is, they say, 'It's sharing your emotions and feelings with each other,'" says Larry Hof, a certified marriage and family therapist, vice president of relationship consulting at Advanta Corporation, and a United Methodist minister in Spring House, Pennsylvania. "Ask men, and they'll say it's sex." The real answer? It's both . . . and neither.

"Intimacy simply means that you and your husband know each other completely," says Hof, who is author of seven books on marriage and family therapy. "You have intimacy when you both see each other as you really are—no defenses, no masks, no games. It means looking at each other over your morning Cheerios and seeing someone you know and someone who knows you better than anybody else in the world."

Making love and conversation are two ways to achieve intimacy. But they aren't the only ways, nor are they necessarily the best ways, adds David Schnarch, Ph.D., director of the Marriage and Family Health Center in Evergreen, Colorado, and author of *Passionate Marriage*. "I know couples who have been talking and copulating for 20 years without truly being intimate. Becoming intimate takes time and effort. But the payoff is enormous," he says.

"True intimacy can create a bond between you and your husband like nothing else," says Dr. Schnarch. "We each have a deep, inherent desire for someone else on this Earth to really know us before we die. Intimacy fulfills that need."

Getting to Know *You*

Before you can begin working on intimacy with someone else, however, you need to really know and accept yourself, says Hof.

"I was counseling a man engaged to be married to a wonderful, beautiful woman, for instance. But he just wasn't happy," explains Hof. "Why? Because he was trying to fit her ideas of who he was and how they should share themselves with each other, which was by discussing their emotions. I asked him what he really wanted. He said, 'I want someone I can play chess with, discuss the *New Republic* with, and have sex with.' Guess what? He didn't marry his fiancée after all. Eventually, he found someone he could share those things with, and they have an incredibly intimate, nine-year relationship, because they are able to share with each other who they really are."

Realize, too, that there's almost always room for improvement. You don't remain the same over time, and neither does your connection to one another, says Hof. You may have achieved a certain level of intimacy when you first married. But as years go by, you change. He changes. And unless you make the effort to stay connected, you can look across the dinner table after 10 years together and no longer know who's looking back. Or you can end up clinking glasses with a man you know—and who knows you—inside and out, says Hof.

Secrets of Long-Lasting Love

Intimacy Is Based on Honesty and Respect

Throughout more than six decades of marriage, Evangeline and John Bicknell have openly loved and supported each other. Today, the Bicknells, who live in Little Deer Isle, Maine, still are growing together and, says Evangeline, adapting to whatever life hands them.

John and I felt sparks between us the first night we met. We were on a double date, and I was with the other fellow, not John. The four of us went dancing. He and I had a chance to dance together, and we just clicked.

That dance was magical, and I wanted to see John again. On the ride home, I mentioned that I planned to bake brownies and listen to the opera the following Saturday afternoon, and if anyone wanted to join me, they were welcome. I hoped John would take me up on my offer. He didn't let me down.

The following Saturday, John came over and ended up staying for dinner. After dinner, we sat in front of the fire and talked. We were having such a good time that we didn't realize how late it was. John had missed the last trolley back to school, so my father had to drive him. But before he left, we made plans to see each other again.

After about three weeks of regular visits, we decided we wanted to get married. My parents encouraged me to take my time, to be sure marriage

"That's the benefit of intimacy," says Dr. Schnarch. "You can deepen your connection over time, instead of growing apart as couples often do. As long as the two of you continue to grow, which should be for the rest of your lives, you can continue to know each other more deeply."

One final word of advice: Remember that intimacy is about *knowing* one another, not necessarily *agreeing* with one another, cautions Dr. Schnarch. "Worrying about whether or not our loved ones will accept us for who we are is a huge barrier to intimacy. We often fear that if people really knew us, they wouldn't like us. But you have to get past that and approach intimacy as what I call a self-validating experience. Open up to your husband with the attitude that you don't expect him to always agree with you. He wasn't put on this

was what I wanted. John and I continued to visit each other, and with each visit we grew closer—we were quite compatible. Finally, we were engaged and then married on June 16, 1936.

Our life together has been a long and wonderful trip. I said to myself when we were married that this is the man I'm going to live the rest of my life with, and I meant it. John and I have loved each other, including everything about each other, no matter what has come our way.

Not that there haven't been some challenges. If my parents hadn't helped us out financially when we first got married, we might have been living on the streets. And during World War II, John was stationed in Texas for two years with the Navy, while I was living in New York State with the first two of our seven children. Frequent, lengthy letters kept our marriage flourishing. What happened, happened. We had to deal with it, and we always made the best of it.

It's been easy for us to make the best of things because we cherish each other. John and I are quite comfortable together and respectful of one another. We've always been very honest, and when we disagree, we manage to find a compromise. But what has really made it work for us is that we enjoy just being—being ourselves and loving each other openly.

Earth to validate and reinforce you. You just want him to love you, and he can't do that if he doesn't really know you."

Building Blocks

How do you begin to become intimate, if not by sitting down and pouring out your soul? "There are hundreds of ways to express who you are to each other and to deepen your intimacy," says Hof, who has devoted much of his 25 years in counseling to intimacy. "And they're not necessarily what you'd expect."

Hof offers his clients a dozen techniques for deepening intimacy that involve everyday activities including, of course, sex and talking. "These techniques give you a vast array of opportunities to discover each other and to build new and stronger levels of intimacy with your partner, no matter how many years you've been together," he adds.

Play show and tell. Take turns choosing a museum, play, or cultural event to attend together each month. Share with each other the things you find beautiful in nature, music, even movies, as you experience them, suggests Hof. "By sharing what I call aesthetic intimacy, your knowledge of and appreciation for each other, and what the other one appreciates, will grow."

Take a stand. "Passion doesn't have to be just about sex," says Hof. "You can be equally passionate (and intimate) about politics or a charitable cause, and you can find intimacy through mutual commitment." Consider joining a volunteer group or political organization that interests you. Encourage your husband to do the same, if he's so inclined. You don't have to agree on your politics or your causes, adds Hof. "The common passion is what's important."

Build each other up. Take turns discussing and helping each other reach your personal goals, advises Hof. "You get a dual benefit here. You not only come to understand what each of you hopes to achieve in this life but you also combine your imaginative efforts to make it come true."

Form a united front. Trite but true: United we stand, divided we fall. The next time conflict or a crisis arises, deepen your intimacy by exploring what is causing each of you pain, advises Hof. Then create a united front to solve the conflict. "Conflicts are actually great learning and intimacy-building experiences if you allow them to be, because you learn more about what's important to each of you," says Hof. Practice when the two of you have a conflict with a third party, like an auto mechanic, not when the conflict is a personal issue between the two of you.

Express yourself. You have hundreds of thoughts and feelings a day. Don't keep them all to yourself. Or worse, don't assume that your husband can guess what you're thinking or feeling. Simply expressing how everyday things make you feel, like how you enjoy sharing the morning paper and coffee with your husband, deepens your intimacy.

Read a book. Pick a novel that you both want to read. Read it, and discuss it. No need for book reports. Just enjoy hearing how each other's mind works. You'll learn volumes about each other.

Go for a spin. Clean up your bikes and go out for a spin. Or go hiking. Whatever recreation you enjoy, playing together is highly intimate behavior, says Hof. "When are you more relaxed than when you drop your guard and you're out playing like you did when you were a kid?"

Look to your spiritual beliefs. There's another familiar saying: The family that prays together stays together. The same can be true for couples, says Hof. "If you are both interested and active in spiritual or religious activities, take the time to do some religious study together," advises Hof. "Too often couples go about their routines and rituals without ever discussing how they really feel about their spirituality. Understanding one another on this level can create an enormous bond between you. If you both pray, praying together can be particularly intimate," says Hof. Same goes for meditation, yoga, or other calming or spiritual rituals.

Wash, rinse, and repeat. Remember how you liked doing even mundane things like the laundry together when you first met? Go back to that time, and join forces to get the daily tasks done quickly and in the pleasure of each other's company, says Hof. "These may never be your favorite activities, but the act of sharing housework, home maintenance, raising a family, and generating income can create closeness. I also advise people to share in some kind of reward when the chore is done, so they can reflect on a job well done."

Begin now! The more years we spend together, the more dependent we become upon each other and the less willing we are to risk rejection, says Dr. Schnarch. "That's why affairs are so prevalent, because there's less to lose revealing yourself to a stranger. So start working on building your intimacy right away."

The Ultimate Intimacy

Intimacy may not necessarily begin in the bedroom, but with the proper "technique," it can come to a roaring crescendo between the sheets, says Dr. Schnarch, who also runs couples' retreats. Dr. Schnarch believes you have reached one of the pinnacles of intimacy when you can make love, and come to an orgasm, with your eyes open looking deeply into one another.

"Most people can't tolerate it, because we're accustomed to tuning each other out when we're having sex so we can feel our own sensations. But with this approach, we focus on our partners, not just the feeling in our loins," says Dr. Schnarch. "It's very shocking to let your partner see into your eyes while you're having sex with him, but it's worth it. I see couples who have been having sex for 20 years, and the first time they accomplish this, they end up crying in each other's arms."

To reach this point requires considerable work. But the payoff is great, says Dr. Schnarch. "How much you can open your eyes during sex is a good barometer of your intimacy," he explains. It brings intimacy to the forefront of your relationship, so you work on becoming closer. When you finally reach the eye-opening conclusion, you'll not only have the best sex of your life but also intense, profound intimacy with your partner, he says.

To try this for yourself:

Kiss and see. A safe place to warm up to eyes-open intercourse is eyes-open kissing. Dr. Schnarch recommends starting with what he calls *kissus interruptus*, which means taking little pauses while kissing your husband to make eye contact. "This can be a sexy way to start exploring this level of intimacy."

Take a look inside. The idea is not to open your eyes and stare at your partner's eyeballs, but rather to try to look inside your husband and allow him to look inside of you, advises Dr. Schnarch. "What you'll find is that when you open your eyes, you may be more aware of *yourself* than of your partner," he says. "This self-consciousness can be a little uncomfortable at first, but if you work through it, you'll achieve a wonderful connection."

Play peekaboo. Just can't get up the nerve to look your lover right in the eyes during sex quite yet? Try lying naked side-by-side in bed, with each of you opening your left eye. "That way you can see each other without the sense of being seen," says Dr. Schnarch. "Some people even play a bit of peekaboo, where they close or cover their eyes and then open them again. This can be a great way to take the serious edge off of the event," he says. "After all, the road to intimacy is supposed to be enjoyable. Smile and have some fun."

Jealousy

❦

You call him at home or work and the line is busy. Or you answer your phone and the caller says, "Sorry, wrong number" and hangs up. Do you feel jealous? Probably not. But what if the two of you go to a party and he spends a lot of time dancing with someone else? Or you catch him behind the hors d'oeuvres table fooling around with somebody else? So much for cool and calm.

Situations like these are practically guaranteed to get most people's jealousy juices churning, says Ayala Malach Pines, Ph.D., professor of psychology at Ben-Gurion University in Israel and author of *Romantic Jealousy: Symptoms, Causes, Cures.*

"Jealousy is a perfectly natural human emotion that arises when a person perceives a threat to a valued relationship," says Dr. Pines, who has surveyed more than 1,000 people about what makes them jealous and how they react. Jealousy can range from the occasional problem (your back goes up when he talks about an attractive woman at work) to chronic and extreme possessiveness (he demands to know everything you're doing and who you're doing it with 24 hours a day).

Feelings of jealousy can also kick in when we feel that a thing or a situation that we want, be it a new car or a great job, isn't available to us but is available to someone else, says Sunny Shulkin, a licensed social worker and psychotherapist in Philadelphia. That kind of jealousy rarely threatens a relationship, though.

Jealousy is normal. An out-of-proportion response is not, says Dr. Pines. "For example, discovering an extramarital affair is one of the most painful and devastating experiences a person can have, and intense jealousy is perfectly normal," she says. "But if there is no real threat—if the threat exists only in the imagination of the jealous person—then jealousy is not normal." (Neither is feeling little or no jealousy over a clear and obvious threat, she adds.)

Keys to Your Emotional Composure

Unbridled jealousy can wreak havoc on relationships and lead to bitter fights and even domestic violence. A nationwide survey of marriage counselors in the United States indicates that jealousy is a problem for one-third of all couples coming for marital therapy, reports Dr. Pines. But handled well, jealousy can be a teacher, an opportunity to learn more about yourself and your relationship, experts say.

"People who suffer the pains of jealousy can learn something valuable," says Dr. Pines. "Jealousy can help answer important questions, such as 'What does this experience tell me about myself?' and 'Is this the kind of relationship I want for myself, and if not, what can I do to change things?'"

What Makes Men (and Women) Jealous

Men get jealous as often and as intensely as women. But they differ in what they get jealous about and how they respond, says Ayala Malach Pines, Ph.D., professor of psychology at Ben-Gurion University in Israel and author of *Romantic Jealousy: Symptoms, Causes, Cures*. Knowing the difference can help you anticipate jealousy in your mate (or yourself).

Her trigger: an emotional threat. Knowing or suspecting that her man is working with or talking to another woman on a deep emotional level can get a woman going. If she discovers that her mate has had an extramarital affair, she'll ask him questions like, "Do you feel close to her? Do you love her? What did you tell her about us? About me?"

How she reacts: Women tend to blame themselves, get depressed, and ask themselves questions like, "What did I do wrong to make this happen?"

His trigger: a sexual threat. A man will get riled up seeing his partner being flirty or sexual toward another man. Upon discovery of an affair, he will ask her questions like, "How good was he in bed? Was he better than me?"

How he reacts: Men tend to externalize their feelings when their jealousy is provoked, lashing out in anger, blaming their partners, and leaving—either the house or the relationship.

Here's what experts suggest to cope with jealousy—yours and your mate's.

Normalize outside attractions. "So much of jealousy comes out of an irrational belief that you and your partner should never have any feelings of attraction toward anyone else," says Peggy Vaughan of La Jolla, California, who conducts workshops and seminars on recovering from extramarital affairs and is the author of three books, including *Making Love Stay*. If either of you finds yourself attracted to someone else, acknowledge it.

Create a jealousy checklist. Together. If jealousy is a problem in your relationship but the situation is too explosive for conversation, Dr. Pines suggests this approach. You and your partner will each need three pieces of paper.

On page one, write "behaviors that trigger my jealousy." Then list things such as "When you're nauseatingly sweet to every woman on the street after being indifferent to me." If it's your partner who's jealous, list behaviors that seem to make him angry and hurt, such as "You get so suspicious about every man I happen to bump into."

On page two, write "needs behind my jealousy." You might list things here such as "I need to feel I'm your one and only." If your spouse is the jealous one, title the page "needs behind my annoyance." These might include items such as "I need for you to trust me instead of being suspicious."

On page three, write "wishes." Then list things your partner can do to fulfill your basic needs. List specific and concrete actions, not "make me feel special" or "show me that you trust me," but "put your arm around me while we walk down the street" or "give me a kiss when I get home late from work instead of questioning me suspiciously."

Discuss your completed lists with each other and decide which of your wishes you can both follow through on. Then do it.

Consider your jealousy history. If feelings of jealousy crop up again and again, take a close look at yourself and your family history, suggests Dr. Pines. "Ironically, if you grew up in a family where one parent was unfaithful to the other, you're likely to have chosen a partner who is like your unfaithful parent," she says.

Possessiveness runs in families, too, Dr. Pines says. If your parents acted like they should belong to one another, never letting one out of the other's sight, you likely grew up believing that's the norm in relationships.

"Becoming self-aware isn't going to instantly resolve the situation," says Dr. Pines, "but this information can help guide you and is a good first step."

Pretend you're not jealous. Stuck in a nonstop cycle of jealous interrogation, whining, and fault-finding? Do your best to act as if you're not jealous at all, says Dr. Pines. You'll help yourself in two ways: First, you will gain some actual control over your jealousy. And second, you'll evoke a much more positive response from your partner. "By behaving more reasonably and positively, despite feelings to the contrary, couples can reverse their downward spiral of interaction and start resolving the situation," Dr. Pines explains.

True Love Is Not Possessive

Jealousy can stem from the feeling that we don't have what we really need on a very deep emotional level, says psychotherapist Shulkin. "The most basic of human needs is a relationship with a person who is totally attuned to us, totally committed to our well-being," she says. "When that's missing, you feel like you're missing out." This is a common issue for people whose parents weren't there for them when they were children, which left them with a feeling of insecurity and neediness.

Neediness, in turn, leads to possessiveness.

"Possessiveness often stems from the false assumption that a lot of togetherness is a good thing," says Vaughan. "The truth is, possessiveness is not a sign of love. Love is wanting the best for your partner, not wanting to entrap her and prevent her from living her own life. Freedom and commitment are not mutually exclusive."

If your mate is overly possessive and constantly prying for information, experts offer these remedies.

Reverse the situation. Behave as if you were the possessive one and crank up the attention. "Call him at work every hour to ask him what he's doing, whom he's talking to, everything," says Dr. Pines. "This works like magic. All of a sudden, the person who's normally jealous relaxes because he's getting this new kind of attention from you."

Flood him with information. Another approach to dealing with a prying partner is to flood him with information about everything that's going on with you, down to the last puny detail. "Flooding not only inundates the jealous person with so much information that his anxiety and insecurity are dispelled," says Dr. Pines, "but one day, he's going to say, 'Enough!'"

Get a life. Each of you needs independent activity, Vaughan says. Not just one of you, Vaughan stresses, but both of you. "So often the man goes out with his friends or goes and plays sports while the woman stays home and doesn't do anything for herself. That's when she really starts feeling jealous and possessive." So find things you enjoy doing on your own or with people other than your partner, and encourage your partner to do the same.

Love and Passion

*Love is a romantic designation for a most ordinary biological or,
shall we say, chemical process.*
—Greta Garbo to Melvyn Douglas in *Ninotchka*

Actually, Garbo was only about half right. Love *is* a chemical process. But ordinary? On the contrary. Love is extraordinary.

Love makes your heart dance when the phone rings when you're dating. Love makes you sit up until sunrise fretting after your first fight. It's what compels a man and a woman to stand at the altar and profess their devotion "as long as you both shall live."

And love is extraordinarily important: It drives us to unite and create another person together, says Michael Mills, Ph.D., associate psychology professor and a researcher on love at Loyola Marymount University in Los Angeles.

"Love is really our ancestors whispering in our ears," Dr. Mills is fond of saying. It was part of Mother Nature's grand plan that you would meet your husband, fall head over heels in love, have a baby or two, and perpetuate the human race, he says. "We are simply programmed to fall in love."

That's the easy part.

The hard part is staying "in love," explains Dr. Mills. "You're bowled over with these overwhelming sensations that come with being in love. You feel like you're going to be walking on air forever. And suddenly, you hit the ground. That's because while love itself is completely natural, our expectations of it are decidedly unnatural," he says. "Evolution defined love as the force we need to produce children. That's all. We have defined love as something that will give us companionship and happiness for the rest of our lives. And we're not quite designed for that."

That's why as years of marriage go by, you may have periods when you don't exactly feel "in love" with your husband all the time, says Helen Fisher, Ph.D., research associate at the Rutgers Center for Human Evolutionary Studies and an anthropologist at Rutgers University in New Brunswick, New Jersey, and author of *Anatomy of Love*. "Falling in love is natural. Staying in love is not always natural."

Secrets of Long-Lasting Love

Separate Interests Keep Love Fresh

Eleanor Plevin and her husband Robert of New Port Beach, California, were destined to be married. The couple met at a children's camp in New York State, where they were both counselors during the summer of 1938. At first glimpse, Eleanor knew Bob was the one; she pointed toward him and declared to her friend, "I'm going to marry that man." Three years later, on May 11, 1941, they did marry. Eleanor says the difference in their family backgrounds has been the biggest hurdle in their marriage.

Bob and I spent that entire summer together while we were working at the children's camp. By the time fall rolled around, we were pretty serious about each other, but we both had to go back to college. I was living at home in Brooklyn, New York, and attending Hunter College, but Bob was living on his own clear across the country, studying at the University of Wisconsin at Madison. We were only able to visit each other once that year, but our romance continued to thrive through letter writing. After Bob graduated in 1939, he returned to New York and we dated steadily until we married two years later.

By far, the biggest challenge has been adapting to each other's family backgrounds. I truly believe that seeing how your own parents and family interact lays the groundwork for how you will interact in your marriage and

That's not to say that staying in love can't be done, however. Fortunately, love is one of those rare areas where you *can* fool Mother Nature. You just need to know how she works.

Anatomy of Love

Certain animals do what scientists call pair bonding, says Dr. Fisher. And in humans, love is part of that process. "Humans have evolved three emotion systems of brain activity that compel us to go out and find a mate."

with your children. My family was very open and loving. Growing up, I never spent much time away from home, so I was accustomed to regular interactions with my family. Bob, on the other hand, didn't have the comfort of a close-knit family. By the time we met, he'd had many experiences on his own, which made him rather independent.

When I married, I expected things to be like they were between my parents. It took me a few years to realize that even though we were married, Bob wasn't going to give up his independence. He was the type of guy who wanted to go and play golf or attend some social event after he finished up at the office. And I knew that if I continued to sit at home and wait for him, the loneliness I was feeling was only going to get worse, and our relationship wasn't going to last. So I took classes at the local schools, started teaching music lessons, and volunteered to be a Braille transcriber. Bob and I also started having children, and between raising our two kids and taking care of the house, I certainly didn't have much free time on my hands.

Finding my own interests has helped strengthen my marriage with Bob. Because we have our individual activities, we really treasure the time we have together. Separate interests also help keep things exciting and fresh between us. We always have things to share with each other—the opera, theater, and athletic events—and we always have a good time together.

The first is lust. "Lust is driven by testosterone, a hormone that both men and women produce, although women have less than men," says Dr. Fisher. Lust's sole purpose is to get you out there looking for someone.

The next emotion is attraction, or romantic love. Attraction is activated when you find Mr. Right. When you feel romantic attraction, your brain is flooded with natural amphetamine-like uppers such as dopamine, which cause the punch-drunk exhilaration, giddy energy, and reduced appetite associated with passionate love.

Next comes attachment. Often, after about one year, the high begins to wear off, perhaps because your brain steps up production of what could be called cuddle chemicals: vasopressin and oxytocin (chemicals that produce feelings of relaxed satisfaction and attachment).

So what goes stale?

"Sometimes after about four years, those feelings of serenity and attachment begin to turn to boredom," says Dr. Fisher. "This is what people go through when they feel like they've fallen out of love," she says. "It's no coincidence that around the world, divorce occurs most often at the four-year point in a marriage."

The Labor of Love

The key to keeping yourself a little bit lovesick rather than a little bit sick of love? Recognize the natural patterns of a new relationship as they occur. And work with them, rather than against them, says Dr. Fisher. "Clearly half of the population doesn't end up in divorce court. They've found a way to make it work."

You can, too, says Dr. Fisher. Whether you've been married for 4, 14, or 40 years, there are ways to keep love alive and interesting with the same man for a lifetime. "You just need to give your brain a little jolt to feel some of the passion you felt when you first fell in love." Here's what experts recommend.

Do it once a day. No, we don't mean sex (though that's not such a bad idea). We mean "connect," says Patricia Love, Ed.D., a licensed marriage and family therapist in Austin, Texas, and coauthor of *Hot Monogamy*. "Every couple needs to develop connecting rituals that they practice every day. It can be dinner. It can be sex. It can be five minutes on the sofa reading the newspaper to each other," she says. "Pick an activity that takes you back to good times together," says Dr. Love. "These rituals act as a gateway for reminding you why you are in this relationship and for maintaining and deepening love and intimacy over time."

Get fresh. "Sure you're both busy, but there are plenty of opportunities during the day to connect and express your interest in each other," says Dr. Love. "You might want to touch each other every time you pass by. Pat each other on the behind. Kiss each other before you leave for the day. Hug when you come home. These activities help reignite interest in your partner, no matter how long you've been together."

Play the dating game. "The exhilaration of infatuation depends upon mystery, novelty, and variety. After so many years, you have to create those things," says Dr. Fisher. "Do the things you liked to do when you were dating. Dress up for each other. See a matinee." The same goes for sex, adds Dr. Love. "Make out again. Lie on the couch and kiss and stroke each other," she says. "You'll feel like teenagers again, only this time you can go all the way." Pressed for free time? "Take one afternoon off from work while the kids are at school, and come home and make love on the living room floor," says Dr. Fisher. "An encounter like this now and again can work wonders."

Color your hair. It may sound frivolous, but you'll likely be pleasantly surprised by the results. Making a few small, fun changes to your appearance like coloring your hair or trying some new fashions can help rekindle that old chemistry, says Dr. Mills. "Men are designed to be attracted to sexual variety," he says. "And when women change their hair color or their clothes, there's a little part in men's brains that says, 'Whoa, I have a new woman here.'"

Take your vacations. "Passion depends upon variety and spontaneity, both of which are hard to maintain from day to day," says Dr. Fisher. "Take some time off and go somewhere completely different. Vacations let you break out of the rut and prevent both of you from becoming bored."

Do things together. Sounds kind of obvious. But often when couples have been together for a while, they stop doing things together, says Dr. Fisher. Researchers have compiled a list of "love behaviors," or things we do together that signify we're in love. Topping the list are going to the movies together, dining out, taking walks, playing sports or engaging in outdoor activities, and lounging around together. If you haven't done any of the above for a while, now might be a good time to start, says Dr. Fisher.

Renew your commitment. You can make love last longer by making a commitment to it, says Larry Hof, a certified marriage and family therapist, vice president of relationship consulting at Advanta Corporation, and a United Methodist minister in Spring House, Pennsylvania. "The best way to think of love is as a triangle. One arm is passion. One arm is intimacy. And the base that holds it together is commitment," says Hof, who is the author of seven books on marriage and family therapy. "Consider making a commitment not only to your husband but also to keeping passion and intimacy in your life."

Recycle that energy. "Just because we're not necessarily built for fidelity doesn't mean we have to cheat," concludes Dr. Fisher. "I believe in free will, and that means that when you reach the point where your eyes start roving, you can say no to infidelity. Take that energy and put it back into your marriage."

Self-Image

A tiny catering hall. A sweltering July night. Ear-splitting music played by a wedding-reception disc jockey. And then . . . *she* stepped onto the dance floor.

She wasn't a slim woman, or conventionally pretty—yet her every movement radiated joyful, high-voltage sexiness. She swayed her ample hips. Tossed her glossy black hair. And her husband looked into her eyes, a sweet smile spreading across his face as he held her waist.

It was an unexpected lesson in the seductive power of a positive self-image. For a moment, every woman in the room wanted to be her. And every man longed to be with her.

First, Love Yourself

"When a woman loves her body and projects deep-down confidence in herself, she'll reap significant rewards in her marriage or long-term relationships," says Rita Freedman, Ph.D., a clinical psychologist in Harrison, New York, and author of *BodyLove: Learning to Like Our Looks—And Ourselves*. "It sounds like a cliché, but it's true that you have to love yourself before you can really love someone else."

Experts in couples therapy say that a positive self-image not only helps you enjoy life and cope with day-to-day ups and downs but also is crucial for a healthy relationship with your partner. Healthy self-esteem promotes:

A deeper, more honest relationship. Psychologists and marriage counselors say that women (and men) who feel good about themselves and their partners have the happiest, healthiest marriages. "The more self-esteem you have, the more loving you feel toward yourself and toward your mate," says psychotherapist Carole Rako, a licensed social worker and marriage counselor in Norfolk, Massachusetts.

Why? When your attitude is "I'm okay, you're okay," you feel confident about sharing who you really are—emotionally, intellectually, spiritually, and physically, says Rako. You respect and enjoy your partner as an individual. "High self-esteem gives you resilience—you don't take every little word, every gesture or action as a rejection," she says. "When you value yourself, you stand up for yourself. Instead of being a people-pleaser who hides her true self, you can just be who you are, without fear. And that's the basis for real intimacy."

Better sex. In one survey done by Thomas Cash, Ph.D., professor of psychology at Old Dominion University in Norfolk, Virginia, and author of *The Body Image Workbook*, women with good body images and little physical self-consciousness told researchers that they had orgasms 73 percent of the time, while women who were physically self-conscious achieved orgasm only 43 percent of the time.

Why? Perhaps because it's easier to get swept away by pleasure and passion when you're not busy trying to hide your thighs under the covers or keep your stomach muscles clenched so your tummy looks flat. And when you project confidence and joy, it's easier to kindle a spark with your partner. "Confidence in the bedroom is like confidence in the boardroom," Dr. Freedman notes. "It commands attention, allows connections to occur, and creates a positive mood."

Talk Yourself Up

Often, the source of low self-esteem lies buried in the past—the legacy of a critical or even abusive parent or other family member, says Susan Heitler, Ph.D., adjunct professor at the University of Denver School of Professional Psychology and author of *The Power of Two: Secrets to a Strong and Loving Marriage*. Their negative messages live on in the form of critical "self-talk"— a destructive internal dialogue that can sap your self-confidence. Dr. Heitler notes that negative self-talk can also be the result of short- or long-term depression.

The good news is that you can replace these messages of gloom and doom with self-talk that's supportive and loving, relationship experts say. Here's an expert-endorsed strategy for nurturing yourself from the inside out.

First, tune in. Pay attention to any negative messages you give yourself, Rako suggests. It may be painful at first, but remember that the goal is to replace specific criticisms with the right positive messages. "Notice the words and the tone of voice. Is it harsh and critical, or gentle and loving?" she asks. Notice how you feel after listening to your internal critic, too. "If you feel bad, that's a sign that you need to make a change."

Change the tape. When you catch yourself in self-criticism, consciously substitute a positive message, Rako suggests. It could be an affirmation such as "I love and honor myself at all times." Or it could be a specific rejoinder to an oft-repeated barb. For example, if your internal critic derides your brainpower, try this: "The truth is, I'm an intelligent and competent woman. I finished that report on time and my boss loved it."

Treat yourself like good company. At a loss for positive messages? Imagine the way you would talk to a close friend, a sister, a favorite aunt, or a child you love, suggests Rako. "Then act it out. Give yourself the same love and support."

Confront the critic. Stand up for yourself by refuting negative messages, Rako suggests. "You could say, 'I hear you, and that's not true.'" Don't let negative self-talk bully you. "You need to respond to it, acknowledge it, and then move on," she says.

Do a reality check. If you've been held hostage by internal criticism, you may be ignoring or downplaying the compliments and positive experiences that should be boosting your self-esteem in small ways every day, Rako says. "From now on, actively notice all the positive things about yourself—anything and everything you like about your body, your mind, your personality. Write down compliments. Keep track of small victories," she says. Flood yourself with irrefutable proof that you're a person of value.

Evaluate your progress. Good self-esteem is a habit—one that can take months to build, Rako says. "Try techniques for boosting your self-esteem on your own for two months or so, and see if you notice a difference. Ask yourself, 'Do I feel better?' and 'Am I acting differently, more assertively, with my partner and others?'" If you do experience improvement, keep using your successful techniques.

Call in reinforcements. If you don't notice any difference after working on your own for at least two months, seek professional help, says Rako. And if low self-esteem has brought your life to a halt, making it difficult to function at home or at work, or if you find yourself caught up in addictive behaviors related to low self-esteem such as an eating disorder, substance abuse, or compulsive spending, you may want to work with a counselor or psychotherapist from the start.

Don't Worry, Be Sexy

From television screens and magazine pages comes another challenge to a woman's healthy self-image: views of society's current female "ideal," complete with mile-long legs, slinky hips, ample breasts, and full, come-hither lips. (Not to mention perfect hair, perfect skin, and perfect nails!) Small wonder that in one body-image survey done by *Psychology Today* magazine of nearly 3,500 women, 56 percent admitted feeling dissatisfied with their appearances—citing frustration most often with their tummies, hips, muscle tone, and weight.

"Cultivating a positive body image when you're confronted with these impossibly perfect bodies in the media requires concentration, but women can do it," Dr. Freedman says. "The benefits are tremendous. You feel freedom to enjoy your body and to feel how strong, capable, graceful, and sexual you really already are."

Afraid your mate is judging your all-too-human thighs, tummy, or hips? The good news is that in another study, though women consistently expected men to choose a thin female body as the most attractive, in reality the men preferred a heavier, curvier female form. "I don't think men are as caught up in perfect bodies as women fear," says psychologist Robert Mielke, Ph.D., psychology professor at McComb Community College in Mount Clements, Michigan, and a certified sex therapist. "When he can look into her eyes and she smiles and shows interest and enthusiasm, nothing could be more exciting or comforting during intimacy. He feels loved and accepted. And she feels free to be herself, to be loved for who she is."

Befriending the Woman in the Mirror

You can take the following steps to boost your body image, says Dr. Freedman.

Accentuate the positive. First, stand before your mirror dressed in your underwear and slowly scan your body from your feet to the top of your head. Chose one feature you like—for example, a well-defined waist—and admire it. Then, think of a positive word that best describes it. (For example, you might choose *curvy* or *sexy*.) Close your eyes and imagine your chosen feature becoming even more like this description. Next, open your eyes and imagine superimposing this ideal image over the real one.

"The idea is to create a compassionate ideal image, to play up your positive aspects so that you really enjoy and appreciate them," Dr. Freedman explains. "This isn't unrealistic. It's just healthy optimism."

In addition, you can create a positive view of body parts you now dislike—and probably exaggerate as a result. Repeat the mirror exercise outlined above, but this time focus on a body part you find unattractive. Close your eyes and imagine this feature becoming more attractive—smaller, firmer, or more shapely. When you open your eyes, superimpose this new ideal over the real image. The goal is to reduce the negative feelings that can make slightly wide hips feel as enormous as a city block and, in so doing, overcome self-consciousness, Dr. Freedman says.

Check your progress. Try the following once a week or so to monitor your changing feelings about your body, Dr. Freedman suggests.

Stand, nude, in front of a well-lit, full-length mirror. Gaze at yourself for about 30 seconds, focusing on your whole body, not on any individual feature. Then, rate your level of comfort or discomfort on a scale of 1 to 100, with 1 being very comfortable and accepting and 100 being extremely uncomfortable. "Your rating may go up and down depending on your mood, your health, and the kind of day you've had, but over time it will go down as you make progress toward loving your body," Dr. Freedman notes.

Indulge your sensuality. Tune in to all five senses, Dr. Freedman suggests. Stop long enough to experience the way a silk nightgown slips coolly over your breasts, the slow melt of chocolate on your tongue, the play of light on summer leaves, the way music can make you want to shake your hips, the scent of a freshly mowed lawn. "Practice sensuality," she says. "The more you tune in to the aesthetic experience of your body and really feel the connections between your body and the world around you, the more you'll enjoy your body—during lovemaking, and all the time."

Time Apart

ackpacking on the rocky Appalachian Trail with her sister-in-law for a
week. Organizing a regular "girls' night out" with nine other women
friends. Jogging after work. Tarin Mullan, an environmental science teacher
in Leverett, Massachusetts, has always built "time away" into her 16-year relationship with her husband, Tad.

"When you get into a relationship, and especially when you have children,
you can start kind of losing the individual person you were," Mullan notes.
"And that individual person is who your partner found and was interested in
and loves. You have to find ways to keep experiencing your own individuality.
In the end, you're responsible for yourself—you have to know who you are."

Tad feels the same way, she says. "He knows I feel happy when I've made
time to do the things I love," she says. "Conversely, I feel happy when he has
time to go off and pursue his interests."

With rare exceptions, we all need time away from the intense togetherness of a long-term relationship. Whether it's a half-hour conversation over
cappuccino with a friend or a two-week wilderness canoe trip, a solitary
morning stroll or an uproarious girls' night out, time apart lets us unwind, explore new interests, and reconnect with ourselves and the world around us,
notes Elaine Wells, a licensed mental health practitioner at Marriage Magic
in both Omaha, Nebraska, and Council Bluffs, Iowa, who specializes in relationships. Ideally, each partner schedules some time to be alone every day in
order to process all the input of daily life.

Time apart can be especially important for women. "Women tend to be the
caregivers, to put everyone else's needs before their own," Wells says. "When
you try to please everyone else first, it can leave you feeling overwhelmed and
stressed. Just recently, I've been working with a couple whose relationship has
blossomed since the woman has started taking time out for herself."

Good for Me, Good for Us

A little separateness offers double rewards for couples, relationship experts say.

First, it allows women and men to grow as individuals. "People sometimes forget that even after marriage, you have to devote time and energy to yourself first," Wells says. You have to keep taking care of your own needs—attending to your social, intellectual, emotional, physical, and spiritual growth in ways both large and small—so that you'll feel deeply satisfied as a human being, she notes.

Second, time apart can strengthen your relationship. "Nobody can be all things to their partner," says Ester Schaler Buchholz, Ph.D., professor in the applied psychology department at New York University and author of *The Call of Solitude: Alonetime in a World of Attachment.* "You have a wide variety of needs, and some of those various needs can sometimes be filled by friends—not by your mate. This takes some of the pressure off the marriage and reduces the chances that you'll feel disappointed and angry because your spouse isn't meeting all of your expectations."

When Time Apart Is Dangerous

While time apart is almost always beneficial, three kinds of separateness can spell trouble for your relationship, notes Elaine Wells, a licensed mental health practitioner at Marriage Magic in both Omaha, Nebraska, and Council Bluffs, Iowa.

Singles'-bar separateness. "If you or he hangs out with friends who frequent singles' bars and who encourage you to make connections with the opposite sex there, even just to dance or share a drink, you could be heading in a dangerous direction," Wells notes. Instead, seek out friends who support your marriage.

Mate-hating separateness. If you spend your time apart with a friend who always severely criticizes your mate when you disclose marital problems, find someone new to talk with, Wells suggests. "You want someone who will listen, sympathize, and encourage the two of you to work out your problems," she says.

After-midnight separateness. If your husband regularly comes home late at night after spending time apart, beware, Wells says. It could be a sign he's having an affair.

But time apart is only beneficial for your relationship if both partners feel good about it—and if the two of you also spend quality time together as a couple, says Sylvia Weishaus, Ph.D., a marriage and family therapist in Studio City, California, and a clinical director of "Making Marriage Work," a marriage preparation course given all over the world. "Balance is critical," she says. "If spouses are already so busy that they barely have time for one another, then they probably don't need more time apart. And agreement is critical, too. Both partners have to feel comfortable with the other going off for an hour or an evening or a Saturday to do his or her own thing."

How to spend this precious separate-time? Think renewal and recreation, Dr. Weishaus suggests. "Staying late at work or doing housework doesn't really count," she notes. "This is a special time for rekindling an old interest, learning something new, rejuvenating your mind, body, and spirit."

The options? Night classes. A girls' night out. Gardening. An investment club. Music lessons. Volunteer work. An exercise class—or a half-hour walk around the neighborhood. The possibilities are endless, Dr. Weishaus says.

When Solitude Beckons

Sometimes the most healing kind of separateness is the quietest: time spent alone. "Solitude gives us fuel for life," says Dr. Buchholz. "It restores our energy, allows us to rest, shows us we can satisfy our own needs, and frees us to sort out thoughts and feelings."

Not loneliness or the chill of isolation, true solitude nurtures body and soul—yet it is often misunderstood, Dr. Buchholz says. "Men and women feel guilty or as if something's wrong if they want to be alone, away from their partners," she says. "But even in the happiest relationships, we can suddenly feel tired, bored, or irritable—emotions we may brush off, but all signs that we may need to be off by ourselves for a little while."

A time-out can reenergize your passion for your partner. "It even improves sex," Dr. Buchholz notes. "Remember old-time relationships in movies? People would be separated for months or years, then meet again with a bang—an exciting, romantic spark. By being alone and then coming back to your partner, you see each other anew. You're eager to be together again, emotionally and physically."

Getting There

Follow this expert advice for adding some constructive "time away" to your life.

First, check your twosome time. Before adding a separate interest to your weekly schedule, make sure you're spending quality time with your spouse on a regular basis, Dr. Weishaus says. "If you don't have that, you really don't have a relationship," she notes. "Quality time for the two of you should take precedence over time alone."

Reassure your partner. If you want to build some time apart into your relationship, broach the subject in a warm and upbeat way, Wells suggests.

Start the conversation by telling him how much you value your relationship. "I suggest starting any potentially touchy conversation this way," Wells says. "Remember, you're going to talk about something you need as an individual, not something that's a rejection of your partner. Build in lots of reassurance."

Don't use clichés like "I need some space," which can easily be misinterpreted as a desire to get *away* from your partner.

Accentuate the positive. "Explain that a little time away will make you more emotionally available in your relationship," Dr. Weishaus suggests. "This is true whether you need a 15-minute break while shifting gears at the end of the work day, or you need a night a week to take a class."

Reveal your true self. When you tell your partner what it is you'd like to do during your time apart, tell him why it's important to you, Wells says. Use this as an opportunity to share your dreams, desires, and needs.

Encourage your guy to do the same. Support the idea that spending time apart from each other can be a rewarding experience for both of you, Wells suggests. "Men can find it more difficult to maintain friendships with other men, even though the relationships are very beneficial," Wells says. "Friendships support their masculinity, their sense of identity, and give them a little fix of 'guyness' that they won't get at home."

PART TWO

Extraordinary Sex

Afterplay

I magine that the movie *Rocky* ended right after our hero, the Italian Stallion, finished the fight. No "Adrian!" No teary embraces. Instead, Mr. Balboa just hunkered down in the corner of the ring and took a nap. That's just how sex without afterplay feels—incomplete.

Sure, you've had your big toe–curling climax. But now you need an ending. Something to make you smile. Something to embrace as you drift back to reality. Something that will keep you looking for a sequel. That "something" is the kisses, caresses, and soft words that are afterplay.

Yet, all too often, just as women are cooing, their husbands are snoozing. It's as though as men climax, they fast-forward to the credits, and it's "Good night, Gracie."

The Descent

The problem is a difference in what we call detumescence—the "coming down" after climaxing, explains Barbara D. Bartlik, M.D., clinical assistant professor in the department of psychiatry at Weill Medical College of Cornell University, and assistant attending psychiatrist at the New York Presbyterian Hospital, both in New York City. For women, it takes just as long to come down as it did to reach the summit. This means that your vagina and clitoris can remain swelled for up to 15 minutes after orgasm, and even longer—two to six hours—if orgasm does not occur.

"Many women still feel turned on during this time," says Dr. Bartlik. Your husband, on the other hand, sinks like a stone. He's flaccid within a minute after orgasm. His penis may become supersensitive, so he doesn't want to be touched. And all the tension that built up in his muscles prior to climax floods out in a mighty *whooosh*, carrying him off to Dreamland.

Savory Follow-Through

What happens after sex can be the most important part of sexual intimacy. "Afterplay lays the groundwork for the next encounter," says Dr. Bartlik. So it's important that he try to keep you company if you remain awake.

> ### Why Males Sleep—Or Flee—After Sex
> Human women tend to get a little riled by a lover who is comatose, or worse, bolts from bed after a round of lovemaking. But maybe it's just a leftover natural instinct. Male bees actually fall dead after sex. Tarantulas have to flee for their lives after mating, lest their hungry lovers suck all their blood. And even cats are known to attack their Toms when the act is done.

That doesn't mean poking and prodding your husband to keep his eyes open, however. It means gentle persuasion. With a few simple techniques, you can make this period worth staying up for—for both of you.

Accentuate the positive. "Take this time to thank your lover for the pleasure and to build his confidence," suggests Dr. Bartlik. "By telling him how much you enjoyed him, you'll not only build his self-esteem but he'll also be more excited about doing it again . . . and about staying awake afterward to hear the nice things you have to say."

Keep it light. Now is not the time to discuss finances or, worse, critique your husband's love-making technique, says Dr. Bartlik. "There's no better way to have a man distance himself from you than critiquing him in bed. Tell him what you'd like different sometime over dinner, instead."

Meet in the middle. Because of differences in men and women, couples must meet halfway regarding their needs after sex. Some men want to sleep; some women want to talk and be held. "Talk about what each of you wants after sex, then work on finding common ground," says Joan Frazier, a clinical sex therapist, licensed marriage and family therapist, and director of Interface Marriage and Family Counseling in Jacksonville, Florida. "Maybe have him talk to you and caress you sometimes, and you snuggle up against him while he sleeps other times."

Make love in the morning. You can vary your afterplay by varying your sex play, says Frazier. "If you always make love in the evening, when you're already a little tired, try making love in the morning or in the afternoon, if you can. You're both more likely to stay awake and do different things afterward, which can help enrich your sex life as well."

Arousal

On the road to sexual intercourse, arousal is what happens right after you think, "Oooo, he looks nice in those jeans." It's arousal that makes your husband's penis rise with an erection and your vagina lubricate and expand to accept him. In short, without arousal, there would be no sex.

But that's only half of the story. The fact that we get aroused by one another does more for us than just allow us to have intercourse. Psychologically, arousal is what makes a man and a woman lovers as well as friends, and it helps keep their bond strong as a couple, explains Joan Frazier, a clinical sex therapist, licensed marriage and family therapist, and director of Interface Marriage and Family Counseling in Jacksonville, Florida. "Sexual arousal is part of the glue that holds us together in a long-term romantic relationship."

His and Her Satisfaction

To make the most out of how arousal can bring you and your husband together, it helps to understand the ways in which each of you becomes aroused, because sexual arousal is not only different for men than it is for women, but it also changes over time.

"First and foremost, couples should realize that it usually takes women at least three times as long to reach full arousal as it does men," says Barbara D. Bartlik, M.D., clinical assistant professor in the department of psychiatry at Weill Medical College of Cornell University, and assistant attending psychiatrist at the New York Presbyterian Hospital, both in New York City. "Men younger than 30 may take as little as 10 seconds to have a full erection and be ready for sex. Though their arousal time gets longer with age, men still don't usually take as long as women, who may need 15 to 20 minutes to reach full arousal. If couples want a satisfying sex life, they need to understand and respond to these differences."

Making matters more complicated is the fact that how you get aroused changes over the years of the relationship, says Mark Temple, Ph.D., assistant professor of health at Illinois State University in Normal, where he teaches

Chocolate Takes the Cake

According to performance artist Karen Finley, star of the show "The Return of the Chocolate-Smeared Woman," the best chocolate to spread on your body for sex play is double dark chocolate frosting.

human sexuality. "In the beginning, everything happens very instinctively. The first time you hold hands, you feel aroused. Then your first kiss is very arousing. But over time, those things do not trigger the same flood of sex hormones they once did and do not feel as arousing."

This is where the flames can cool. "After years of having sex in a long-term relationship, it's not uncommon for men and women to start having trouble reaching the same high level of arousal as easily," says Frazier. "It can be the result of boredom, unresolved expectations of frequency, buried resentment, or low or declining sex hormone levels. Or, it can be a combination of these or even other factors," she says. "But when it happens, we start worrying that the relationship has gone bad or that maybe we're not attracted to each other anymore."

Keeping the Fires Burning

The solutions are often simple, says Frazier. "As you grow, both individually and together, you need to put just a little more effort into building arousal. It becomes more of a skill. But it's one you can develop. And it's definitely worth it." Here are some suggestions for fanning those inner fires.

Write a new script. Over time, many couples develop what is known as a sexual script of the acts and behaviors that they find arousing, says Dr. Temple. "Couples will hug, kiss, pet, have oral sex, have vaginal sex, then, bam, it's over—every time. That's the way they've always done it, and that's the way they believe it should be done," he says. "Though this script works just great for a few years, eventually you can get bored with it and find yourself feeling less aroused. Abandon the script and try a whole new pattern. Maybe begin with oral sex. Or throw in a massage. Small changes can be refreshingly arousing."

Practice the three A's. An important part of maintaining your arousal as a couple is maintaining your closeness as a couple, says Gerald Weeks, Ph.D., director of the Institute of Sex Therapy at the Penn Council for Relationships in Philadelphia, a board-certified sex therapist, and author of 11 professional textbooks on sex and marital therapy. "It's easy for couples to get tied up in everyday tasks and to forget the basic niceties that keep them close. That's dangerous because arousal begins to die when you take each other for granted," he says. When couples feel themselves drifting apart, Dr. Weeks tells them to practice what he calls the three A's.

- Affirmation. Say, "I love you, and I'm glad I found you," every day.
- Appreciation. Always thank each other for the things you do for one another.
- Affection. Touch each other in affectionate, but not necessarily sexual, ways throughout the day. "Women sometimes feel that the only time they're touched is when their husbands want sex," says Dr. Weeks. "As a result, they feel pressured and become less responsive. Touch each other often, without sexual intent."

Ride your natural rhythms. The male hormone testosterone (produced by both sexes) makes you actively hunger for sex. Estrogen (a key female hormone that is present only in small amounts in men) makes you softly receptive to it. Both influence how easily you are aroused, and both ebb and flow throughout the month, says Theresa Crenshaw, M.D., a certified sex therapist in San Diego and author of *The Alchemy of Love and Lust.*

Though it can be difficult to tell when your hormones are "just right," most women can sense their sexual peaks and valleys throughout the month. You'll likely find yourself more easily aroused if you have sex during those high points, Dr. Crenshaw says. "Many women's most intense peak is right before their periods, when testosterone is prevalent. Midcycle, during ovulation, is another peak time because both testosterone and estrogen are surging. And many women even experience heightened arousal during menstruation, when they're feeling some boosts from testosterone."

Talk about love. "Part of the arousal we feel early on in a relationship is fueled by how much emotional and intellectual intimacy we establish just by talking to each other, often for hours on end," says Dr. Weeks. "Then we

Bake Your Guy a Pumpkin Pie

Each year, billions of dollars are spent on perfumes, colognes, and scented soaps. Traditionally, scientists didn't believe that odors had much of an effect on sexual arousal. Then they discovered something: When men and women lost their sense of smell, they often lost their sexual arousal as well.

"Today we know that certain scents have a dramatic effect on our sexual response," says Alan R. Hirsch, M.D., director of the Smell and Taste Treatment and Research Foundation in Chicago and author of *Scent-sational Sex*. To identify the smells that humans found the sexiest, Dr. Hirsch exposed men and women to a host of odors and then measured the blood flow to their penises or vaginas—benchmarks for sexual arousal. Surprisingly, colognes, perfumes, and other stereotypical sexy scents ranked pretty low on the arousal scale. What ranked highest? Food.

Following are the top three turn-on scents for men and women.

Top Scents for Men	Percent Increase in Penile Blood Flow
Lavender mixed with pumpkin pie	40
Doughnut mixed with black licorice	32
Pumpkin pie mixed with doughnut	20

Top Scents for Women	Percent Increase in Vaginal Blood Flow
Good and Plenty candy mixed with cucumber	13
Baby powder	13
Lavender mixed with pumpkin pie	11

Though some of those scents may be hard to introduce into your lovemaking, others are quite easy. The best way to use them? Try setting up scented candles in your bedroom. "Judging by the results of our study, lavender or pumpkin pie aromas could be quite arousing for both men and women," says Dr. Hirsch.

enter a relationship, and suddenly much of our discussion turns to problem-solving—solving problems with the house or the kids or the in-laws. There's very little to arouse anyone in that. Sit down for just 20 minutes one night a week for some romantic, intellectual discourse," suggests Dr. Weeks. It can be about a book or movie, or even just about a beautiful meadow you noticed on your drive home. "This simple exercise can build and enhance closeness and arousal."

Say, be my guest. Sometimes women think they have a problem with arousal when what they really have is a low sex drive, explains Dr. Crenshaw. "Some women have low levels of the sex-drive hormone testosterone, especially during certain times of their monthly cycles. That means they're not particularly interested in sex, but they would still respond and become quite aroused if they engaged in sexual activity. For these women, I recommend taking the 'Be my guest' approach. That is, don't immediately spurn your husband if he's in the mood and you aren't. Tell him, 'I'm not really in the mood, but I'll happily loan you my body and see what happens.' Her hormones will respond to his sexual touch, and she'll likely become very aroused. Some of the best sex happens when you just let it happen."

Work up a sweat. "We know that women who exercise report feeling more sexual," says Dr. Temple. "Doing something like jogging, cycling, or strength training several times a week not only makes women feel better about themselves but can also increase testosterone, which heightens their sexual drive and response," he says.

Be an explorer. Many couples are sexually adventurous and explore many different ways to arouse each other in the beginning of their relationships. Then a few years go by and they stop, says Dr. Bartlik. "It's not surprising that they aren't as aroused then. You can break out of sexual ennui and heighten your arousal simply by experimenting again. Buy some videos. Use erotic toys together. Read erotica. Unless there is a particular problem, you'll be aroused again in no time."

Check your pills. Finally, if you've tried everything and you still find that your arousal levels are flagging, check your medications. Some antidepressants, like Prozac, can affect your sex drive. And because they change your hormone profile, oral contraceptives can also diminish arousal and vaginal lubrication in some women, says Dr. Crenshaw. If you suspect that your pills are the problem, check with your doctor about lower doses or other options.

Erogenous Zones

༚

The essential rule of erogenous zones is that they start at the top of your head and end at the tip of your toes. Miss a spot, and you could be missing out on a world of pleasure.

"Erogenous zones aren't limited to the breasts and the genitalia," says Barbara D. Bartlik, M.D., clinical assistant professor in the department of psychiatry at Weill Medical College of Cornell University, and assistant attending psychiatrist at the New York Presbyterian Hospital, both in New York City. "They are any nerve-rich area on your body that you find sexually arousing. And they can be very different from person to person."

Some women, for example, can have an orgasm just by having their breasts caressed. A fortunate few may climax from simply having their earlobes stroked. "Those are the exceptions, of course," says Dr. Bartlik. "But there are plenty of unexpected places that may do nothing for one person but may drive another wild. You can even find new places on a long-time lover. You simply have to explore."

Mapping New Territory

"Try whole-body caresses," says Gerald Weeks, Ph.D., director of the Institute of Sex Therapy at the Penn Council for Relationships in Philadelphia, a board-certified sex therapist, and author of 11 professional textbooks on sex and marital therapy. "One partner lies down, while the other touches, caresses, and rubs them from head to toe, discovering which areas are most arousing. I've seen conservative, middle-aged couples start touching each other in whole new ways once they start exploring." Eager to map new erotic territory? Pay special attention to the following areas.

The mouth. The mouth is one of the most sensitive areas on a woman—the lips are very responsive to touching, kissing, and licking, says Miriam Stoppard, M.D., in her book *The Magic of Sex*. Stimulating a woman's mouth can "set her whole body alight," she notes.

The neck. In her book *Sex for Dummies*, Dr. Ruth K. Westheimer says that nuzzling and nibbling the nape of the neck can be highly arousing for both men and women.

The underarms. "Any area that is ticklish is rich with nerves and can be arousing when stroked," says Dr. Weeks. This is especially true of the underarms. In Dr. Alex Comfort's *The New Joy of Sex*, he calls the underarms a classical site for kisses.

Behind the knees. Bet this is one you never thought of. Like the underarms, this ticklish spot can be a real turn-on for some men and women, says Dr. Bartlik. Use a light touch on this soft, thin skin.

Inner thighs. Most men and women enjoy having their inner thighs caressed, especially if their partners sweep their hands up to where the thigh meets the crotch, says Dr. Bartlik.

The buttocks. The buttocks can be very stimulating for both men and women. But since they contain muscle as well as fat, they may require a firmer touch, like kneading or gentle "spanking," says Dr. Comfort in *The New Joy of Sex*.

The perineum. "The strip that runs from the anus to the vulva on women and the scrotum to the anus on men is a big-time sensitive area," says Dr. Bartlik.

Toes. Toe sucking has become very popular, says Dr. Weeks. "Couples seem to be discovering how pleasurable the whole foot area is." Try kissing and caressing the entire foot.

Rediscovering Familiar Ground

Of course, we all have those spots that work every time, like our breasts and genitals. But even these tried-and-true erogenous zones can elicit dramatically different sensations depending on how they're touched, says Joan Frazier, a clinical sex therapist, licensed marriage and family therapist, and director of Interface Marriage and Family Counseling in Jacksonville, Florida.

"Too often, couples get stuck rubbing each other the one way that was successful early in the relationship, and they don't try different touches," she says. "It's important to experiment, not just for the thrill of variety, but because how we like to be touched can change over time."

The Second Most Popular Erogenous Zone

Five thousand women surveyed by *Men's Health* and *New Woman* magazines ranked the neck second only to the clitoris as the spot that makes them tingle the most.

Once you locate all of your erogenous zones, you can explore new ways to stimulate them, says Dr. Weeks. "Couples can watch erotic videos together to get ideas," he says. "Try tickling each other with feathers. Trace sensitive spots with an ice cube. Rub each other with fur mittens," he says. "Mapping out erogenous zones should be a lifelong journey."

The following are the most popular erogenous zones, and some new ways to approach them.

Breasts or chest. Though women's breasts get the lion's share of attention, men's chests can be very sensitive, says Frazier. "Men and women should try rubbing around the entire chest area, not just the nipples. It can be very erotic."

Nipples. Nipples are tricky because, though both men and women usually enjoy being touched here, some people like having their nipples pinched and nibbled, while other people find the area so sensitive that they want only the lightest of touches, Frazier says. "You and your partner should definitely make it clear what you like, preferably with positive words and body language, not criticism of each other."

Genitals. Like the nipples, the genitals are very sensitive, and everyone responds to a different approach. "Generally, men like firm, direct touches," says Frazier, "while women prefer a lighter, more indirect approach." For men, the most sensitive part of the penis is the head, especially the underside, right below the opening. For women, the clitoris is the pleasure center, but the inner labia are also rich with nerves. Gentle stroking of the area just inside the vaginal opening can be very pleasurable, says Frazier, but in general, a slow and indirect approach to the "genital hot spots"—even a "touch-and-go, then return" approach—is more arousing to women than constant or direct stimulation of the genital area, at least until a woman is fully aroused.

Foreplay

❦

The biggest problem with foreplay is in the name itself. Foreplay implies that kisses and caresses are no more than brief warmups for the main event. Or optional—like appetizers or pregame shows, you can take them or leave them. Perhaps we'd all be better off if we called foreplay loveplay or sexplay. Because, without it, love and sex just wouldn't be the same.

"I tell people to call foreplay intimate caress," says marriage counselor Harry Croft, M.D., a psychiatrist and licensed sex therapist in San Antonio. "I tell them that they should kiss and hug and pet and stroke, and if it leads to intercourse, wonderful. And if it doesn't, they've still made a loving, enjoyable connection with each other."

"If you are planning on having intercourse, you will maximize your pleasure if you start with ample amounts of foreplay, doing whatever suits your pleasure," says Barbara D. Bartlik, M.D., clinical assistant professor in the department of psychiatry at Weill Medical College of Cornell University, and assistant attending psychiatrist at the New York Presbyterian Hospital, both in New York City. "One of the most common complaints we hear is that the couple is engaging in intercourse before the woman is ready," she says. "Men and women have very different sexual response cycles. It takes most women about three times as long to reach full arousal as it does men." Plus, a lot of women reach orgasm during the sex acts that are usually considered foreplay, not during intercourse itself, Dr. Bartlik points out.

If your husband is currently a dive-right-in kind of guy, it's probably not because he doesn't enjoy foreplay or because he's insensitive to your needs, adds Dr. Croft. "It's usually a matter of conditioning. Women tend to learn about sex in romantic contexts, like dating, romantic movies, and books. Men learn about sexual arousal by masturbating, where the quicker he gets it up and over with, the less likely his mom will knock on the door and ask what the heck he's doing in there."

Not Just for Intercourse

Now that you can lock the door in your own house, you should be sure to take advantage of all the joys these intimate acts can provide, says Dr.

The French Kiss Really Did Come from France

Engaging the tongue in amorous kissing was originally known as *maraichinage*, a French term used to describe the deep, prolonged kissing favored by Maraichins, peasants living in Brittany, France.

Croft. The following are some tips on slowing down and spicing up your foreplay.

Take a back-seat approach. As teens, you could turn the back seat of the old Buick into a sauna without getting past third base. Just because your "parking" days are over, however, doesn't mean your making-out days have to be, says Dr. Croft. In fact, in a *Men's Health* and *New Woman* magazine survey asking readers about their sexual likes and dislikes, women overwhelmingly ranked kissing and petting as two of their favorite forms of foreplay. "Act like kids again and make out for hours," suggests Dr. Croft.

Touch everywhere but. To get more in tune with what kind of foreplay feels good to you without the pressure of worrying whether you're satisfying your partner or if you'll have an orgasm, try taking turns at "loveplay" exercises a few times a week, suggests Domeena Renshaw, M.D., professor in the department of psychiatry and director of the Sexual Dysfunction Clinic at Loyola University of Chicago, and author of *Seven Weeks to Better Sex*.

Sit toward one another, touching each other's faces. Then either lie against one another back to chest or lie down as if you're being massaged. Take turns exploring each other without touching the breasts or genitals. If either of you becomes very aroused, take a break. Hold each other. Let it subside. Then begin again. "Your loveplay should be a pleasurable break that lets you reintroduce yourselves physically," says Dr. Renshaw. Doing these exercises a couple of times a week for several weeks will refocus your attention on the sheer sensual pleasure of touching one another without rushing into intercourse.

Be selfish. Too often, both men and women concentrate so much on touching to arouse their partners that they lose sight of their own pleasure, says Joan Frazier, a clinical sex therapist, licensed marriage and family therapist, and director of Interface Marriage and Family Counseling in Jacksonville, Florida. "I tell couples to practice 'selfish' touching," says Frazier. "Touch your partner for your own enjoyment. Take pleasure in how his muscles feel against your fingertips. Ask him to enjoy your body to his liking. You'll both be surprised at how excited you'll become." She explains that these exercises are usually assigned outside regular lovemaking sessions in order to reduce the possible pressure to "perform."

Be more direct. Though it's usually men who get most of the lessons in foreplay, women could use a little direction, too, says Frazier. "Women often hold back and touch the way they like to be touched, gently and meanderingly. But, frankly, men tend to enjoy a more direct approach. He wants you to touch his penis; he wants you to be firm." So unless you're practicing loveplay exercises, don't neglect touching where he likes to be touched most.

Be more than a bedflower. Another common foreplay wish among men is for women to participate more, says Patricia Love, Ed.D., a licensed marriage and family therapist in Austin, Texas, and coauthor of *Hot Monogamy*. "Men often wish that they felt their wives desired them as much as they desire their wives," says Dr. Love, who once heard a man describe himself as a bee buzzing around his wife, who was like a flower on the bed waiting to be pollinated. "You can make your husband feel wonderful, and may ultimately make your foreplay more gratifying for both of you, if you lavish more attention on him," she says. "If you're honestly not sure what he would like, ask him! Believe me, he'll be happy to tell you."

Add a new dimension. Perhaps the sexiest, most intimate thing you can do during foreplay is to look at one another, says David Schnarch, Ph.D., director of the Marriage and Family Health Center in Evergreen, Colorado, and author of *Passionate Marriage*. "That doesn't mean opening your eyes and looking at body parts. It means opening your eyes and looking into each other during foreplay," he says. "So often, couples tune each other out during sex. They shut out intimacy and aim for sexual stimulation. Try looking deep into your partner's eyes while you touch each other. It's challenging because we get self-conscious. But if you break through that barrier and share yourself in that way, it can be the most delightful, poignant sexual experience of your life."

Freezing Him Out

When it happens in sitcoms, it's funny. The husband plans a Super Bowl party on his 10th wedding anniversary. The angry wife threatens to banish him to the couch. He bags the bash in the name of good sexual graces. They kiss and make up, until next week.

When using sex as a bargaining chip happens in real life, however, it can be deadly to the relationship. "You don't see women physically pushing their men out of bed as much as just turning away sexually over conflicts," says Richard Meth, Ph.D., director of the Humphrey Center for Marital and Family Therapy at the University of Connecticut in Storrs. "It's a power play that satisfies anger in the short run. But in the long run, it can really destroy the relationship."

Unfortunately, bringing sex into the battle is not uncommon, says Louanne Cole Weston, Ph.D., a marriage and sex therapist in San Francisco and Sacramento. "When you want total control of a conflict, you go for what's most effective. And though women don't usually concoct a Machiavellian list of what will hurt their husbands most, they know denying sex will get his attention."

Men can be guilty of withholding sex, too. But women tend to use this tactic more often than men, says Dr. Meth. "Generally, women are less able than men to temporarily put aside things that are bothering them and be intimate. Conversely, men are able to enjoy physical and sexual intimacy regardless of most emotional issues and conflicts. And often, after they've made the physical connection, then they feel ready to open up and talk."

Warm Up to Reconciliation

What's a battle-weary couple to do? Here's how experts recommend meeting in the middle.

State your case. It's perfectly okay not to feel sexy when you're upset, says Larry Hof, a certified marriage and family therapist, vice president of relationship consulting at Advanta Corporation, and a United Methodist minister in Spring House, Pennsylvania. "But instead of turning away or, worse, threatening to withhold sex, just tell the truth. Say, 'I'm feeling too angry and

hurt to have sex. But I'd like to work this problem out so we can be close again.' That way, you're making intimacy a common goal instead of using it as a bargaining chip."

Stow the small stuff. Your sex life won't suffer nearly so much if you learn to stow away everyday frustrations, says Dr. Meth. "Compare the positive and negative consequences of not being intimate with your husband because of little things that are bothering you," he suggests. Then stow them in a mental drawer marked "later." Clear your mind. Let down your guard. And enjoy some intimate time with your husband. "When you bring out those little things later, you'll both be in a better frame of mind to resolve them," he says.

Kiss and make up instead. Sometime when you're not having a heated discussion, agree that you'll use a kiss or some other mutual expression of physical closeness to celebrate the end of your next argument, suggests Hof. That way, you'll see physical, even sexual, intimacy as a legitimate and helpful outcome of working through a problem. It'll also get you close again right after the conflict, so you'll be less likely to continue to harbor bad feelings, he says.

Improve your sex life. Women who don't have orgasms often use sex as a bargaining chip because it's no big deal to them if they lose it, says Dr. Weston. "If you really enjoy sex, you're less likely to give it up. Instead of shutting down that part of yourself, try to expand it. Ask your husband to help." Use all types of stimulation—oral, manual, bodies pressing together, outercourse (where lubricated genitals rub together without insertion). Experiment with new positions or creative techniques that enhance arousal and satisfaction. Masturbate to orgasm, if it helps you tell him what you like. "These things will take time and effort. But they won't only be good for your relationship, they'll be good for you."

Listen to those wise folks. "The old folk saying 'Don't go to bed angry' is great advice," says Hof. "Save conflicts for outside the bedroom. And resolve them—at least to the point where you're not angry with each other—by the time you lie down together at night. You may stay up later than you'd like, but in the long run, it's worth it."

Frequency

This probably won't come as any big surprise, but the more sex people have, the more likely they are to say that they have a happy life and a happy marriage. This is especially true if you're a woman, according to the General Social Survey (GSS), which surveyed thousands of Americans about their sex lives and was sponsored by the National Science Foundation at the University of Chicago.

"It's a big myth that women don't care how often they have sex," says Barbara D. Bartlik, M.D., clinical assistant professor in the department of psychiatry at Weill Medical College of Cornell University, and assistant attending psychiatrist at the New York Presbyterian Hospital, both in New York City. "Sex not only makes many women feel loved and cared for, but let's face it, sex also satisfies a basic physical need. Women crave sexual pleasure as much as men do. The problem is that life often gets in the way of couples having as much sex as they'd like."

So how much is enough? "That's really hard to answer," says marriage counselor Harry Croft, M.D., a psychiatrist and licensed sex therapist in San Antonio. "For some couples, regular sexual intercourse is extremely important for the health of the relationship. For others, it's not," he says. What's more important is that you both get as much as you'd like from each other.

Newer, Faster, or More Often

If you're both having sex as often as you'd like, read no further. If not, these tips can help you turn up the frequency on your lovemaking.

Make it quick. One of the easiest ways to have more sex is to incorporate the quickie into your love-making repertoire, says Dr. Croft. "Quickies are especially great if you have a relationship where one partner wants sex more frequently than the other," he says. "If he wants sex several times a week and she's fine with sex on the weekends, they can agree to have a couple of quickies during the week. For her, it can be an act of love. For him, it's a physical connection and release."

Add novelty. Often a couple will stop having sex as frequently as they'd like because they've gotten a little bored with their sexual routine, says Gerald Weeks, Ph.D., director of the Institute of Sex Therapy at the Penn Council for Relationships in Philadelphia, a board-certified sex therapist, and author of 11 professional textbooks on sex and marital therapy. "Novelty is the best aphrodisiac. Trying something different helps keep up your sexual interest

fascinating FACTS

Who's Having the Most Sex?

Think it's all those crazy single kids having all the sex? Think again. Single people swing less often than couples who are married or living together. Here's a close-up of who else is having the most (and the least) sex in America, according to the General Social Survey (GSS), which was sponsored by the National Science Foundation at the University of Chicago.

- About 15 percent of adults engage in half of all sexual activity.

- Jazz aficionados are 30 percent more sexually active than other people.

- Catholics have more sex than Protestants on average, but both report about 20 percent less sex than their Jewish and agnostic counterparts.

- Folks who put in 60 (or more) hours a week at the office have 10 percent more sex than those who work less.

- One in five adults hasn't had sex at all during the past year.

and, consequently, your frequency. Buy something different each month. Try new videos, erotic literature, or sex toys. Try different times, places, or activities from time to time. Don't get into a sexual rut. Even planning a regular vacation ensures that there will be some newness in your sex life."

Keep an open date. Sex can only happen if you leave enough time for it to happen, reminds Richard Meth, Ph.D., director of the Humphrey Center for Marital and Family Therapy at the University of Connecticut in Storrs. "If you're way too busy to have sex, then you should take a good hard look at your schedule and cut out the unnecessary appointments. Your sex life is important enough to make it a priority. Leave one night a week to yourselves. If you have children, find someone who can watch them regularly."

Prime your pump. Masturbation can be a great way for women to increase their interest in more frequent sex, says Dr. Bartlik. "Sometimes a woman has a dip in her sex drive because of a change in her hormones, or maybe there was some trouble in the relationship, and she still hasn't gotten back into the swing of things. Masturbating a few times a week can help her get back in touch with her sex drive."

Enjoy Saturday night sex. Despite your best attempts to steal away together, you'll inevitably hit a stretch when life gets too crazy to make love as often as you would like. So enjoy the occasions you *can* be together, while working on solutions for your schedules, suggests Dr. Meth. "Too often, couples get angry with each other when sex gets squeezed out during the week, and instead of working toward a solution, they stop having sex entirely," he says. "Saturday night sex is better than no sex. And if you enjoy it enough, you'll keep working on ways to make time for more."

Intercourse and Positions

W hen couples in ancient India got a little bored with sex, they could turn to the *Kama Sutra*, a 1,600-year-old Indian love manual that detailed numerous variations for intercourse. It even counseled lovers to study the procreative efforts of domestic animals, wild beasts, birds, and insects to pick up some spicy new techniques.

Though modern sex therapists won't shuffle you and your husband off to the zoo to buoy a sex life that's stuck in a rut, the basic recommendation will likely be similar: Try something new. "Variety is undoubtedly the best way to keep things alive," says Barbara D. Bartlik, M.D., clinical assistant professor in the department of psychiatry at Weill Medical College of Cornell University, and assistant attending psychiatrist at the New York Presbyterian Hospital, both in New York City. "As my mentor, the late Helen Singer Kaplan, once said, 'Sex is best when it's never the same way twice.'"

Of all the ways you can add variety, experimenting with positions is one of the simplest, adds Joan Frazier, a clinical sex therapist, licensed marriage and family therapist, and director of Interface Marriage and Family Counseling in Jacksonville, Florida. You don't have to buy anything or go anywhere. You just need a little imagination. It can also bring back that feeling you had when the relationship was new and you were experimenting and discovering all the time, she says.

Don't worry, therapists aren't talking about hanging from the rafters or tying your bodies into a yoga knot. Just making slight changes can bring completely new sensations to your tried-and-true positions. Here's a guided tour.

Man on Top

Deriving its name from nineteenth-century missionaries, who believed it was the only proper way to have sex, the missionary position, or man on top, allows for maximum male thrusting as well as close intimate contact between lovers.

Though the missionary position has taken some heat for not providing enough stimulation to the clitoris to be equally enjoyable for women, it puts us face-to-face during sex, which both men and women find enjoyable. Plus, women can vary this position for more direct clitoral stimulation. (See the pelvic tilt, below.) Here are a few new twists to this classic position.

Seated missionary. He sits with his legs spread on either side of you as you lie on your back with your knees bent, and he eases you onto his penis. Though thrusting power is limited, he has more direct penetration.

Knees to chest. Start by lying on your back and lifting your knees to your chest as he lies down on top of you. Hook your ankles over his shoulders while he supports his weight on his hands. This allows maximum penetration.

Cross buttocks. As you lie on your back, he enters you while lying on top across your pelvis, slightly askew with his weight on his elbows, so your bodies form an X. You'll feel a new sensation as his penis rubs against the sides of your vagina.

On the edge. While lying on your back on a bed, slide down so your pelvis rests on the edge. Your husband then leans over you while he inserts his penis. This is particularly good if your husband is heavy, because it relieves some of the weight.

The pelvic tilt. Many women find the standard lying-down missionary position more pleasurable if they spread their legs, bend their knees, and tilt their hips up. This allows your husband's pubic bone to rub against your clitoris.

Woman on Top

Though now second fiddle to the man-on-top positions, woman-on-top positions were a favorite among our ancestors. The earliest-known cave drawing, from 3,200 years ago in Mesopotamia, shows cavefolk making love with the woman on top.

Woman-on-top positions are great for a number of reasons, says Dr. Bartlik. "The woman not only can control the thrusting, but her clitoris receives more stimulation. Either partner can also use his or her hands to stimulate her clitoris and breasts. Plus, many men last longer in these positions."

Here are a few variations you might enjoy.

Reverse missionary. This is just like the male-on-top missionary, but this time you're on top, with your legs spread over his, which are closer together. You can make the fit more snug by closing your legs. Or open them wide for more clitoral stimulation.

Woman astride. Start in the reverse missionary, then draw your knees up so you're kneeling, straddling his pelvis. Men love this position because they have full view of your body and access to your breasts and clitoris. Women enjoy it for this same reason, and because you can easily control the depth of penetration. For extra spice, you can lean backward, which stimulates the front of your vagina.

Woman astride, backwards. Same as above, but you're facing away from instead of toward your husband. You lose some of the intimacy, but he has full access to stimulate or hold your buttocks.

How to Avoid a Pregnant Pause

Sure, sex can be a little tricky when you're pregnant. But as long as your doctor says it's okay, there's no need to go without until the baby's born, according to Barbara D. Bartlik, M.D., clinical assistant professor in the department of psychiatry at Weill Medical College of Cornell University, and assistant attending psychiatrist at the New York Presbyterian Hospital, both in New York City. The choice positions for pregnant women are:

Rear entry. Either lie on your side or position yourself up on all fours. These versions are great all the way through pregnancy.

Side entry. Lie on your back, perpendicular to your husband, with both legs draped across his pelvis. Then he enters you from the side, while you hold your legs close together to grasp his penis.

Sitting. These very intimate positions are comfortable and put no pressure on the abdomen.

Sitting up. He sits in bed, or on a chair. (If you're feeling particularly adventurous, try a rocking chair.) Straddle him, either kneeling or with your legs pointing forward, wrapped around his waist. Thrusting is sometimes limited, but this position is very intimate.

Sitting up, away. You can vary the seated position by mounting your husband facing away instead of toward him, so he has total access to your breasts and clitoris.

Side by Side

More languorous than adventurous, side-by-side positions are ideal for slow Sunday morning lovemaking. "What these positions lack in thrusting potential, they make up for in the opportunity to cuddle and caress," says Frazier. They're especially good for pregnant women, or heavier men or women, because neither partner must bear any weight.

Spoons. With both of you lying on one side facing the same direction, and your husband cuddling your back, draw your knees up slightly, so he can tuck up behind your pelvis and enter you from behind. You can adjust the angle of thrusting by leaning closer into or away from each other. He can also rub your breasts and clitoris in this position.

Face-to-face spoon. For this face-to-face variation, begin in one of the missionary positions and roll onto your sides, without breaking your connection. Or lie on your side facing him and lift a leg to allow him to enter you.

The wrap. To increase the penetration in side-by-side positions, try wrapping both legs around him. Bend your top leg and place it high on his hip as he pushes his thigh between yours, then lie back as he leans into you, allowing you to wrap both legs around his waist.

Rear Entry

Often indelicately called doggy style, rear-entry positions allow for deep penetration and vigorous thrusting. The downside of these positions is that they don't stimulate your clitoris at all. The upside is that it's very easy for you or your husband to stimulate your clitoris manually during rear-entry intercourse, and some women find that these positions provide pleasant pressure on the area of the front wall of the vagina, or G-spot, says Dr. Bartlik.

Classic kneeling. This position is most widely practiced with you on your hands and knees and him kneeling behind you. He then enters you, either remaining upright or draping over your back. Begin with slow thrusting since it's easy for him to hit your cervix in this wide-open position, which some women find painful, particularly if his penis is very large.

Standing. This is just like the kneeling position, only that both of you are standing up, with you bending at the waist, supporting yourself on a bed or a table. He enters you standing upright from behind. To compensate for differences in height, he can bend at the knees, or you can stand on something stable.

Lying flat. You lie flat on your stomach and chest, legs open, while he enters you from behind, arching his back and holding most of his weight on his hands. You can get deeper penetration in this position by lifting your bottom slightly off the bed. You can also close your legs for more stimulation to your inner vaginal lips and clitoris.

Just Plain Adventurous

Finally, there are some positions that you can try just for kicks, says Dr. Bartlik, but that don't necessarily lend themselves to marathon lovemaking. If you're feeling adventurous, try these on for size. Just don't feel too bad if they don't make it on your list of favorites.

Standing face-to-face. Though it looks easy in the movies, standing, face-to-face sex is one of the more complicated positions to achieve since women are usually shorter than men. Your best bet is to find a wall or a door to lean against. And don't try it in the shower!

Wheelbarrow. You can do this athletic position sitting or standing. For standing, have him enter you as in the standing rear-entry position. Then have him lift you at the pelvis as you grip his waist with your legs, so you end up in an adult's version of the position you used for wheelbarrow races in school. For a break, he can sit on a chair or the edge of the bed. Keep your sense of humor for this one.

Position X. You can last forever in this leisurely pose. Start on top of him in a woman astride position. Then clasp hands and lean back between his legs. You should end up holding hands out to the sides, connected at the genitals, with both of you facing the ceiling.

Kissing

Ask any woman about her first kiss, and she'll tell you the day, year, and place—plus how the weather was and what she was wearing.

Kisses are monumentally important to women. As little girls, we hear that a kiss can awaken a spellbound maiden or transform a frog into a handsome prince. We anxiously await our first kiss. And when it happens, we don't forget it—ever.

"Kissing is almost always our first expression of love," says marriage counselor Harry Croft, M.D., a psychiatrist and licensed sex therapist in

San Antonio. Even after they've "gone all the way," many women say kissing is not only their favorite kind of foreplay but also a favorite act of sex play, period.

It's little wonder: Our lips are rich in nerve endings that make the mouth one of the most arousing parts of the body for both men and women. "When couples first get together, they kiss and kiss and kiss for hours on end," notes Dr. Croft.

Bad Breath Remedies That Won't Let You Down

It's the quintessential night of romance. Flowers. Dinner. Wine. You and your sweetheart lean toward each other to smooch, then suddenly, garlic breath! Alcohol aroma! Coffee mouth!

Bad breath is a surefire romance squelcher, says Gary Herskovits, D.D.S., a halitosis expert in Brooklyn, New York. (He has saved marriages threatened by unpleasant exhalations.) "And some people are much more prone to it than others, which can be really hard on a relationship."

Everyday bad breath stems from ordinary oral bacteria in the mouth that produce volatile sulfur compounds that smell like rotten eggs. These bacteria thrive in a dry environment. During the day, saliva helps reduce the odor, but at night, saliva production slows. Hence the "morning mouth" phenomenon. Eating foods like garlic and onions, which also emit smelly volatile gases, and gum disease make matters worse, says Dr. Herskovits.

A minty or otherwise aromatic mouthwash or spray kills a few surface bacteria and provides a quick cover-up—for no longer than 30 minutes, says Dr. Herskovits. Mouthwash containing alcohol further dries out your mouth, making the problem worse, not better, he explains. So try an alcohol-free rinse instead.

Here's what else you can do to control bad breath.

Rinse out the real stinkers. Besides garlic, onions, and coffee, foods like milk and sweets—which ferment in your mouth—are also powerful bad

Kisses Rekindled

Just as kisses are the first sparks in an intimate relationship, they are often the first thing to fizzle when the relationship grows familiar, says Dr. Croft. "Though men enjoy kissing, they're conditioned to think of kissing as a gateway to sexual intercourse. Once men are married and can have sex anytime, they often forget about kissing."

---

breath producers. Rinse your mouth well after consuming odor-producing food or drink, says Dr. Herskovits. If you and your partner both eat garlic, you'll smell it less on each other's breath.

Don't drink—or drink just a little. Alcoholic beverages dry out the tissues in your mouth, giving bacteria full reign to stink things up, says Dr. Herskovits.

Stimulate saliva flow. Chewing gum (sugarless to avoid tooth decay) and foods like fruits and vegetables stimulate saliva production, which helps to keep bacteria in check, says Dr. Herskovits. For people with persistently dry mouth from reduced saliva flow, he recommends a saliva-boosting product called Salix, which is available at health food stores. Increasing your saliva flow becomes more important after the age of 50, when saliva production slows, he notes.

Replace your toothbrush every three months or even sooner if it becomes frayed. Use it after every meal. And remember to floss daily, too.

Brush and scrape your tongue. Crevices in the top of your tongue collect all sorts of odorous organisms. Clean them off with your toothbrush, or use a tongue scraper, which is even more effective. Tongue scrapers are available at drugstores.

Make a date with a bad breath specialist. If you've done everything right and still have bad breath, consult a dentist who specializes in treating stubborn halitosis. He or she may be able to customize a treatment that solves your problem when nothing else works.

Ten Ways to Kiss — And More

The *Kama Sutra*, a fifth-century Hindu sex manual, describes 10 types of kisses, 64 different caresses and acts of foreplay, 8 variations of oral sex, and 84 positions for intercourse. So chances are, the book offers something you haven't tried yet.

Women, too, may let kissing fall by the wayside as they become preoccupied with raising children and running a house. "But it's women who usually say they miss kissing the most," says Dr. Croft.

Rediscovering the simple pleasure of kissing can draw you closer and bring you both back to a good place in your relationship, says Dr. Croft. To make your next kiss as good as, if not better than, your first, try the following tips.

Make out — again. The next time you go to give your husband one of those perfunctory goodnight kisses, grab his head, hold it, and kiss him like you mean it, suggests Ruth Jacobowitz, trustee for the National Council on Women's Health, member of the Woman's Advisory Board at the University of California, San Diego, Women's Health Center, and author of *150 Most-Asked Questions about Midlife Sex, Love, and Intimacy*. "You'll both be pleasantly surprised at how those old passionate feelings come flooding back."

Open your eyes. "People who always close their eyes while they kiss are missing out on a very special connection," says David Schnarch, Ph.D., director of the Marriage and Family Health Center in Evergreen, Colorado, and author of *Passionate Marriage*. "Kissing with your eyes closed is really rather impersonal." Opening your eyes and looking deep into each other while you kiss can be enormously intimate and erotic, he says.

"People find it very intimidating to have their spouses look at them while kissing," Dr. Schnarch says. We get shy. We get self-conscious. "So work up to it. Try what we call kissus interuptus," he suggests. "Kiss each other for a moment. Pause. Look at each other. And kiss again."

Kiss *Kama Sutra* style. The famous ancient love manual the *Kama Sutra* suggests making kissing fun by playing kissing games, like "capture the lips." Try to see who can use their lips to capture the other person's lips first.

You inevitably end up planting lots of kisses on cheeks and chins before one of you "wins."

Don't stop at the lips. Though lips are perfect kissing targets, you needn't stop there, says Dr. Croft. "Anywhere your partner likes to be touched, he'll probably like to be kissed," he says. Try kissing every inch.

Oral Sex

Despite what veterans of the sexual revolution might think, oral sex wasn't invented in the 1960s. Rather, it's a time-honored expression of passionate love. Tantric sex guides from ninth-century India include references to oral sex, for instance.

Today, many men and women rank oral sex as one of their favorite sex play activities. According to the *Sex in America* survey conducted by University of Chicago researchers, 83 percent of men ages 18 to 44 say they enjoy receiving fellatio, or oral stimulation of the penis. And in a *Men's Health* and *New Woman* magazine survey, more than one-quarter of the women surveyed ranked cunnilingus (having the labia, clitoris, or vaginal opening stimulated with the mouth, lips, or tongue) as their favorite form of foreplay.

"For a lot of women, oral sex is the only way they have an orgasm," says Barbara D. Bartlik, M.D., clinical assistant professor in the department of psychiatry at Weill Medical College of Cornell University, and assistant attending psychiatrist at the New York Presbyterian Hospital, both in New York City. "As for men, most really love oral sex."

The Pleasure Principle

So what's the problem? For some couples, nothing. For others, trouble arises when one partner is doing more giving and not as much receiving, or when the technique leaves something to be desired.

"Though it can certainly go both ways, most often, you hear from men that they would really enjoy more oral sex than they are receiving," says Patricia Love, Ed.D., a licensed marriage and family therapist in Austin, Texas, and coauthor of *Hot Monogamy*. "These kinds of discrepancies can create tension between partners. And often they can be cleared with a little communication and understanding of each other's needs and concerns," she says.

Both men and women sometimes object to oral sex because they're concerned that the genital area is unclean. Or they're not sure what they're supposed to do down there, Dr. Love says. Others have religious objections.

If hygiene is an issue, simply shower together as part of your foreplay, says Dr. Love. And with regard to technique, it's not one of the great mysteries of the world, says Anne Semans, coauthor of *The New Good Vibrations Guide to Sex*, who has surveyed women and men on what they like and don't like regarding sexual technique.

"Good oral sex is all about being in tune with your partner's response," says Semans. Experiment. When your husband moans with pleasure, tilts his pelvis forward, and opens his legs further, you know you've done something he likes. (The same, of course, holds true for you.)

Not sure where to begin? Here are some techniques that can provide pleasure for both men and women. "Feel free to improvise as you see fit," says Semans.

The Fine Art of Fellatio

Despite what Linda Lovelace led a generation of women to believe, you do not have to "deep throat" a penis to give good fellatio. "Women have this image of bobbing up and down really fast, swallowing the whole penis. And that's just flat out not necessary," says Semans. The most sensitive area of the penis is the head, particularly the soft underside. So while he might enjoy the sensation of your lips running down the shaft, most of what drives him wild is right at the top—hence the lay term "giving head." Here are a few things men say they like best.

Treat it like ice cream. Dr. Ruth K. Westheimer's classic fellatio advice is to treat the penis like an ice cream cone. Hold the shaft like a cone, shield your teeth with your lips, and then just lick and suck around the head. It's that simple.

Add a stroke. To add to his pleasure, wet the entire penis with your mouth for lubrication, then stroke the shaft of his penis while your mouth is encompassing the head. This technique also lets you take a break and just stroke him if your mouth gets tired.

Use a little suction. Take as much of his penis in your mouth as is comfortable and make a seal around his shaft. Then suck some of the air out of your mouth. He'll feel a vacuumlike sensation as you pull your head back.

Let your hands roam. Many men like having their scrotums cradled, their nipples teased, or even their anuses stroked while they receive fellatio. To see what he likes, experiment.

Hum a tune. He may like a little vibration during oral sex. Low humming can sometimes enhance the pleasure of fellatio.

Sip a soda. Once you're comfortable with oral sex, you can get creative by sipping cold soda or warm tea, or even sucking on ice cubes, between performing fellatio. Men often like the change in temperature and sensation.

Enjoy yourself. More than anything else, men report that the best oral sex they've ever had was from women who enjoyed pleasing them. "If you're into it, he will be, too," says Semans.

Spit or swallow—your choice. "Some women don't mind swallowing ejaculate," says Semans. "Others genuinely dislike it." If you're giving oral sex as part of foreplay, then it's a moot point. But if you plan on "finishing the job," keep a towel nearby to spit the ejaculate into. Or, when you sense that he's close—his erection strengthens and his breathing intensifies—you can simply take your mouth away and help him climax with your hand.

Choice Cunnilingus

It's little wonder that many women love receiving cunnilingus (Latin for "licking the vulva"), says Dr. Bartlik. "Men's hands can be too rough or awkward, but tongues are soft, yet firm. It can be just the direct stimulus women need."

Yet some women hesitate. "In our society, many women have grown up with the idea that their genitals are dirty, and they worry that their natural taste and aroma would be a turnoff to even the most enthusiastic lover," says Robert W. Birch, Ph.D., a sex therapist in Columbus, Ohio, and author of *Oral Caress*.

"In reality, if she just showered, she's fresh as a daisy," says Dr. Birch. If she practices good personal hygiene, within a few hours after washing, she'll acquire a natural musky scent that many men find to be a turn-on. Dr. Birch cautions, however, that "after eight hours working in the hot sun, forget it! Head for the shower!"

Women typically find that some areas are more sensitive than others and certain forms of stimulation will work best. You will most likely have your own unique preferences. Whatever they are, it's very important that you're open in communicating them to your partner.

It is always more effective to communicate erotic desires and give gentle direction during the encounter, Dr. Birch suggests. "To do so before the episode may sound like a demand, and to do so after the encounter may sound like criticism. The sensual art of sharing erotic verbal feedback may take some practice, but it's 'pillow talk' of the best kind."

Ease into it. Most women need time to get in the mood and do not appreciate an impulsive premature dive for their genitals, says Dr. Birch. Couples should take the time to give and receive gentle caresses and share the mutual pleasures of kissing. You may need to remind your partner to slowly make the transition from manual to oral stimulation. Your husband may begin by rubbing your thighs, abdomen, breasts, or buttocks. He may then progress to stroking, or he may gently pinch the outer labia and mons pubis and massage the shaft of the clitoris through the skin of the mons. When you show signs of readiness (such as moaning, opening your legs, tilting your pelvis, and thrusting), he may gently run his tongue from the back to the front, along with the outer border of the inner labia. He can use his tongue to encircle the clitoris, which in most cases will be covered by the clitoral hood. He can gently lick along the side of the clitoris, lifting the hood gradually, but he should be careful. The clitoris is the most sensitive part, and too much direct touch may be uncomfortable. He can also caress the clitoris with his lips, rhythmically press on the clitoral shaft, and gently suck.

Focus on the clitoris. A woman's clitoris is composed of a short shaft and a head, covered (at times completely) by the clitoral hood. It is located above the vaginal opening, at the peak of the vulva (or genital area), where the large outer labia come together in her pubic region. Most women know where the clitoris is, but they may need to point it out to the most well-intended partner.

Before total arousal, you or your partner might find it helpful to part the labia to allow greater access to the tender membrane and sensitive clitoris. Once aroused, however, a woman's vulva will be naturally open, and the man will have no difficulty gaining access to his partner's most erogenous genital areas.

Vary the speed or pressure. Couples should experiment with the location, speed, and pressure of the oral stimulation. "There can be the gentle caress of the tip of the tongue like the tip of the soft eraser on the end of an artist's pencil. But there can also be the long, firm strokes with the flat surface of the tongue, applied like the broad brush of the housepainter," Dr. Birch says.

Add a finger or two. Lots of women love when their husbands insert a finger or two in their vaginas during cunnilingus. Some enjoy gentle finger thrusting, like intercourse. Experiment and let your husband know what you like. Have him first moisten his finger, so that it is not uncomfortable. He should massage what's generally assumed to be the G-spot, which is about two to three inches inside the vagina on the anterior wall, with the soft side of his finger, not his nail.

Try suction. It can be particularly pleasurable for a woman to have her husband lightly suck her clitoris, pulling it in and out of his mouth. This may be especially nice as you get closer to climax, because the clitoris often retracts before orgasm, which can cause a break in your pleasure if he loses contact with it. The area is so sensitive that sometimes it is barely necessary for him to move his lips or tongue to give you extreme pleasure, says Dr. Bartlik. While maintaining direct contact with the vulva, your husband can gently apply pressure or shake his head back and forth.

One important caution: Your partner should *never* forcefully blow air into your vagina. You risk developing an embolism—a tiny air bubble that could be fatal if it reaches the bloodstream.

Consider mutual lip service. Many couples who enjoy both the giving and receiving of oral stimulation not only take turns, but often find themselves moving into a position where simultaneous stimulation is possible. Playfully referred to as the 69 position, the creative couple can find several ways to orally pleasure each other at the same time. Most lay on their sides, facing opposite directions. Others might prefer having the man position himself over the woman or, conversely, the woman on top of the man. If you like giving and receiving, experiment with the 69 positions. While some folks love it, it is not for everyone.

"Some people find simultaneous oral sex too distracting to really enjoy either the giving or the receiving," says Dr. Birch. "Mix and match. Move from taking turns to a 69 position and then back again if you wish. Just have fun doing what feels good!"

Orgasm

T hey've been compared to tidal waves, volcanoes, and fireworks. They're said to cause eruptions so powerful the earth moves, or at least you swear it did. Steamy movies, TV shows, and even advertisements show scores of sweaty men and women in various states of orgasmic bliss. Yet more than 70 percent of women still aren't regularly having orgasms during sex, while more than 75 percent of men are.

It's time to close that pleasure gap.

"Every woman is born with the physical capacity to have an orgasm," says Nancy Gambescia, Ph.D., a marriage and family therapist in Bryn Mawr, Pennsylvania, who teaches at the Penn Council for Relationships in Philadelphia. "But only about one-third of women can orgasm through the thrusting of sexual intercourse alone. It's important that men and women not only understand that, but that they learn other ways to give her an orgasm. Otherwise, sex, which should be a very pleasurable event, can become a source of anxiety and frustration."

The Pleasure Zone

Before you go out in quest of more or better orgasms, it helps to know how orgasms happen and why we have them to begin with.

An orgasm is a release of built-up sexual tension that gives us a series of about a half-dozen intensely pleasurable rhythmic contractions through our pelvic regions. But it also tends to be a whole-body experience. When we orgasm, our breathing quickens, our pulse races, and sometimes our faces grimace and even our toes curl.

But while those are generally the benchmarks of orgasm, it's important to realize that orgasm is a completely unique experience. It varies from person to person, and your orgasms and your husband's can be longer or shorter and more or less intense depending on everything from your moods to how much sleep you got last night.

"Orgasms vary so much from experience to experience that sometimes women really aren't sure if they've had one or not," says Carol Rinkleib

---

Don't Fake It

The reasons vary, but the fact remains: Women fake orgasms. In a *New Woman* and *Men's Health* magazine survey of more than 2,600 women, about one-third of the women surveyed admitted to sometimes faking orgasms, while 11 percent said they routinely put on an act. Though you may think this is making your lover feel better, it's actually detrimental to both of you.

"If you fake it, you're sealing your own fate," says Barbara D. Bartlik, M.D., clinical assistant professor in the department of psychiatry at Weill Medical College of Cornell University, and assistant attending psychiatrist at the New York Presbyterian Hospital, both in New York City. "The man will repeat what he thinks is phenomenal technique, and you'll be stuck wondering how you can tell him what you really want," she says.

If you've already been faking and don't feel that you can come clean, try learning how to give yourself an orgasm, then suggesting that you and your partner try the ways you've learned. That way, you won't have to fake orgasms, because you'll really have them.

Ellison, Ph.D., a clinical psychologist and sex researcher in Oakland, California, who has surveyed more than 2,600 women ranging in age from 18 to 88 about their orgasms. "Sometimes orgasms are dramatic. But sometimes they're softer and gentler. Generally, you can tell you've had an orgasm by the feeling afterward. You'll feel more relaxed and peaceful."

Why do we have them? On the most basic level, they're for procreation. Orgasms make sex feel good, so men and women keep seeking each other out, having sex, and having orgasms. As a result, the human race keeps rolling. Men almost always ejaculate during orgasm, so their orgasms are very closely tied to reproduction. And there's even some evidence that a woman's orgasm may help her pull in and retain a greater amount of semen, which would also increase the couple's chances of reproducing.

But most important for your relationship, orgasms are a tie that binds, says

Theresa Crenshaw, M.D., a certified sex therapist in San Diego and author of *The Alchemy of Love and Lust*. "Orgasms create a loving, bonding union between you and your partner," she says. "And it's not just the pleasure of sex. During orgasm, you physically produce a chemical called oxytocin, which is known as the touch hormone, that makes you want to nuzzle and be close. So even if you're not trying to have children, touch and orgasms are important for the strength and intimacy of your relationship."

His and Hers Orgasms

Generally, men's and women's orgasms are pretty much the same. Both sexes report feeling the intense sexual buildup before them, the rhythmic release during them, and the peaceful descent afterward. But while a man climaxes easily when his penis is stimulated inside the vagina, a woman has a trickier time coming to orgasm, especially through intercourse alone.

"By and large, a woman's orgasms come from her clitoris, which doesn't receive much stimulation during the thrusting of intercourse," says Barbara D. Bartlik, M.D., clinical assistant professor in the department of psychiatry at Weill Medical College of Cornell University, and assistant attending psychiatrist at the New York Presbyterian Hospital, both in New York City. "That's one of the biggest reasons why women have a hard time having orgasms—they're not receiving enough stimulation."

Most women usually need to concentrate more to come to orgasm, says Dr. Crenshaw. "Women tend to be more distractible during sex. When the phone rings or a baby cries, a woman may lose her orgasm entirely whether she wants to or not. A man, on the other hand, will continue to ejaculate once he's begun, no matter what happens."

Finally, a woman has a complex cycle of hormones, including estrogen, testosterone, and dehydroepiandrosterone (DHEA, a hormone that helps produce our sex hormones), that makes it easier or more difficult for her to climax at any given time during the month, says Dr. Crenshaw. "She can learn to manipulate this cycle, but it takes a little time and skill."

But just because it takes women longer to reach orgasm doesn't mean that women's orgasms are any less valuable then men's, says Dr. Ellison. "You don't have to have an orgasm every time you have sex. But orgasm is important for sexual satisfaction on a physical and psychological level for both men and women." In fact, in a *New Woman* and *Men's Health* magazine survey of more than 2,600 women, more than one-third cited "not waiting for me to come to orgasm" as the worst sex habit a man can have.

Orgasm Helpers

For more frequent and intense orgasms, try these practical suggestions.

Lend yourself a hand. The easiest way to bring yourself to climax during intercourse is with "clitoral assistance," says Dr. Bartlik. "Massaging the clitoris directly is often necessary to achieve the optimal physiological sexual response. Either you or your husband can rub your clitoris in almost any position. Most men enjoy seeing a woman touch herself, so don't feel self-conscious. And it will make the experience more pleasurable for both of you."

Let him use his mouth. "Oral sex is a very, very underappreciated form of sexual stimulation," says Dr. Bartlik. For women who have difficulty coming to orgasm during intercourse even with clitoral assistance, oral sex is often the answer. "For a lot of women, oral sex is the only way they have orgasms," she says. "Men's hands can be rough and awkward, and sometimes women have trouble masturbating in front of their husbands. Have him perform oral sex either as part of foreplay or after intercourse."

Fantasize. You don't need to conjure up a mental movie of you and Mel Gibson on a Caribbean beach, but when it comes to having orgasms, the more sexual thoughts and fantasies you can have, the better, says Dr. Gambescia. "Sexual fantasies are one of the most important parts of reaching orgasm. Your brain is responsible for triggering the sexual release of orgasm," she says. As long as you keep the sexual fantasies flowing, you will continue along the sexual response path, ultimately leading to orgasm, explains Dr. Gambescia. "It can be as simple as replaying your sexual episode as it happens."

Exercise your orgasm muscles. Your pubococcygeus (PC) muscles, the muscles surrounding your vagina, are the ones that contract to produce the pleasant feeling of orgasm. When you make these muscles stronger, you can also increase the pleasurable sensation during intercourse, says Dr. Ruth K. Westheimer in her book *Sex for Dummies*. Kegel exercises are the best way to strengthen these PC muscles. Simply concentrate on the muscles you use to "hold it" when you have to urinate; contract them for 6 to 10 seconds, then relax and release them for 3 seconds. Start with 10 contractions, then gradually build up the number of repetitions and the length of each squeeze. You should begin to feel a difference during intercourse in about six weeks, she says.

Time it right. A monthly series of events, called the ovulation cycle, is responsible for the maturation of an egg. The cycle is divided into two consecutive phases: phase one—the period from the 1st to the 14th day of the cycle; and phase two—days 14 to 28. This cycle usually repeats itself at intervals of 28 days, with ovulation occurring at midcycle—your most fertile period. Become familiar with your ovulation cycle, and be sure to plan some sexual escapades during the first two weeks of it, suggests Dr. Crenshaw. "Up until midcycle, estrogen dominates while testosterone focuses attention on the drive for genital sex, leaving you feeling sexually aggressive," she says. Women also are more likely to desire orgasm during this time of the month, she says.

Wear something sexy. You can increase your sexual thoughts and thereby increase your chances of having an orgasm by slipping into something you find sexy before your next tryst, says Dr. Gambescia. "The sexier you feel, the more responsive you'll be. Try different lingerie; slip into something black; shave your pubic hair. Just think sexy."

Keep yourself in the moment. Nothing can stifle an orgasm more quickly then negative thoughts, says Dr. Gambescia, and women are notorious for it. "Women often mentally pull out of sex and begin critiquing themselves," she says. "They become anxious that they don't look good enough, or they smell bad, or a host of other troubling concerns. There is no way a woman can have an orgasm through that. Concentrate instead on the pleasure of the moment. Think how good your husband feels in you. Watch how excited he becomes by you. Hear his breath quicken. You'll be able to relax and climax much easier."

Practice on yourself. When it comes to having orgasms, practice truly does make perfect, especially if you practice with yourself, says Dr. Bartlik. "Masturbation gets women in touch with their bodies. It teaches them what kind of stimulation is the best for bringing them to orgasm."

In addition, having orgasms during masturbation boosts hormone levels that make you more sexually receptive, responsive, and probably more orgasmic, notes Dr. Crenshaw.

Eat right. Here's another reason to eat a low-fat diet: increased sex drive. Higher levels of DHEA, a hormone that enhances sex drive and may lead to more orgasms, are noted in people with low body fat, says Dr. Crenshaw. "But the key is eating healthfully, so you're not fatigued and cranky from dieting."

Take up walking. Like eating a low-fat diet, exercising can boost your sexual pleasure by lowering your body fat and pumping up your levels of the sex-drive hormone DHEA. It may also boost levels of testosterone, which can make you feel sexier, says Dr. Crenshaw. "Just be sure to exercise consistently for 30 minutes every day." Don't be foolish, however. "If you're regularly going out for a run during the only time you could be having sex, that's counter-productive," she says.

Meditate on it. Giving yourself several minutes in the morning and the evening to just close your eyes, breathe, and relax may increase your sexual pleasure by increasing your DHEA levels, says Dr. Crenshaw. "Studies show that people who meditate regularly and seriously over time have significantly higher levels of this important hormone. Plus, meditation helps relax you so you're better able to enjoy a sexual encounter."

Give yourself time. It's just a fact of life that most women don't get aroused or achieve orgasm as quickly as most men, says Dr. Bartlik. "In fact, women take about three times as long. So I tell couples to relax and be creative with their foreplay. If you need a rule of thumb, most women need at least 15 to 20 minutes of some kind of stimulation in order to achieve orgasm. So take your time and enjoy!"

The Myth of the Simultaneous Orgasm

Whether they've been going at it for 3 minutes or for 30, stars in cinema sex scenes inevitably come at the same time. It looks so beautiful and passionate that some couples strive for simultaneous orgasm as the pinnacle of sexual achievement.

"This is a mistake," says Dr. Bartlik. "Simultaneous orgasms are rare at best. And it is almost impossible for a woman to climax when she's preoccupied with timing. If it happens, great. But I wouldn't strive for it."

That said, if you still want to give it a try, it's probably easiest if the man brings himself just to the point of coming and then changes his stimulation slightly, so he maintains arousal just at the edge of orgasm, Dr. Bartlik advises. Then, when she begins to climax, it may send him into orgasm as well, she adds.

Go for Two

Once you learn how to have one orgasm, you can often learn to have two or more in the same sexual episode, says Patricia Love, Ed.D., a licensed marriage and family therapist in Austin, Texas, and coauthor of *Hot Monogamy*.

"Masters and Johnson found that some women could bring themselves to six or more orgasms in a matter of minutes," says Dr. Love. "Certainly, no one should feel inadequate if they can't have a string of orgasms, especially since one large one is every bit as good as several smaller ones. But it can be fun for you and your partner to try."

Simply have your partner stimulate your clitoris until you reach orgasm. Then he can use his fingers to massage your front vaginal wall, where the G-spot is said to be located, keeping you aroused, Dr. Love says. Then when your contractions have subsided and your clitoris is no longer hypersensitive, he can try to give you piggyback orgasms by massaging your clitoris again, she says.

Performance Anxiety

Two hundred years ago, when a man had trouble keeping an erection, doctors told him to go home and have six "amatory experiences" with his wife without making a "coital connection." Today, our language has changed, but when it comes to performance anxiety, the advice to put intercourse on hold while you relax and make out may still be the best.

As sexual problems go, performance anxiety is pretty common—just a case of sexual nerves, really. You get so worried that you won't be able to perform well that you can't perform at all. It's more noticeable in men, who tend to lose or not be able to get erections. But women get it, too. They may become too nervous to get aroused, become lubricated, or have an orgasm.

Though performance anxiety is more common among new lovers who are naturally jittery about their first sexual encounters, it also can happen among long-time married couples. Often, it's brought on by one bad encounter that snowballs into a case of persistent performance anxiety.

"Maybe he was stressed after a hard day and couldn't maintain an erection that night with his wife," suggests Nancy Gambescia, Ph.D., a marriage and family therapist in Bryn Mawr, Pennsylvania, who teaches at the Penn Council for Relationships in Philadelphia. "If he worries about it too much, it could affect their next sexual encounter, and the one after that, and the one after that. . . ."

Women, on the other hand, tend to get performance anxiety when they don't think their bodies look as good as they should, Dr. Gambescia says. "Many women get so preoccupied worrying about their breasts sagging or their behinds being too big that they can't become aroused no matter what their husbands do."

More Pleasure, Less Pressure

No matter the cause, performance anxiety can not only dampen your sex life but also drive a big wedge between you and your mate. "When performance anxiety strikes, people often avoid sexual encounters altogether rather than face the stress of trying again," says Dr. Gambescia. "After a while, both partners start feeling angry and resentful. It can spill into the whole relationship."

To stop performance anxiety from stealing the romantic show for both of you, experts offer this advice.

Build, don't blame. "Women can put a lot of pressure on their husbands without meaning to by making a big deal out of a failed erection," says Judy Kuriansky, Ph.D., of the Center for Marital and Family Therapy in New York City, host of the syndicated call-in advice radio show *LovePhones*, and author of *The Complete Idiot's Guide to a Healthy Relationship*. "Questions like, 'What happened?' or 'Aren't you attracted to me anymore?' can exacerbate performance anxiety by putting pressure on your husband to 'fix it,'" she says. Instead of looking for blame, build up your sexual confidences, advises Dr. Kuriansky. "Hug and kiss each other all over your bodies. Tell him how much you enjoy simply being with him. It happens to everyone sometimes. Don't make a big deal out of it."

Consider the obvious. "If you or your husband has been drinking, hasn't had much sleep, or has been under a lot of stress, you can't expect peak sexual performance," says Joan Frazier, a clinical sex therapist, licensed marriage and family therapist, and director of Interface Marriage and Family Counseling in Jacksonville, Florida. "If he fails to get an erection or you fail to get aroused under those circumstances, chalk it up to bad conditions, get some sleep, and have fun the next time you're both fresh and awake." (For advice on dealing with stress, see page 452.)

Have sex without intercourse. Instead of rushing right back into bed to "prove" everything is fine, take some time to enjoy sexual contact without intercourse, advises Frazier. "Take away erections and intercourse and orgasms as the 'goal' of sex, and just enjoy how good it feels to touch and kiss one another," she says. "Try taking a week off from having intercourse. Touch and explore each other for as long as you like, focusing on each new sensation moment by moment, without a goal. Make it fun, or tender. By the end, you'll see how much you've increased your levels of arousal, and you'll know you can enjoy each other without the pressure to perform."

Watch the real thing. Women with performance anxiety often can benefit from watching erotic videos that feature ordinary people enjoying sex, says Barbara D. Bartlik, M.D., clinical assistant professor in the department of psychiatry at Weill Medical College of Cornell University, and assistant attending psychiatrist at the New York Presbyterian Hospital, both in New York City. "You can find videos today, like the Better Sex videos from the Sinclair Institute in Chapel Hill, North Carolina, that show sex in a more realistic, woman-friendly light," she says. "Watching these can make women think, 'Hey, I'm normal. I can be sexy, too.'"

Accentuate the positive. If your self-consciousness about your thighs is keeping you from enjoying sex, concentrate instead on the features you like best about yourself, and your husband will, too, advises Dr. Bartlik. "If only women could see themselves through their husbands' eyes. Men tune in to what they find attractive about their wives—her curves, her hair, how expressive she is during orgasm. They don't notice a couple of pounds, a few dimples, or any little imperfections during sex. If you wear sexy lingerie that shows off what you like most, you can be sure he'll notice that, too."

See a doc. Occasional bouts of lost erections or missed orgasms are normal. But if the problem persists despite your efforts to relax and enjoy one another, a trip to the doctor is in order, says Dr. Gambescia. "All kinds of things from medications to depression can cause sexual dysfunction. A doctor can help you get to the bottom of it, so you can start enjoying sex again."

Privacy

Of the more than 100 million households in America, more than one-third have at least one child living at home. And as the elderly population continues to grow, more and more of those households are also shouldering the care of an elder parent. Then, of course, there are the millions of cats and dogs that we call part of the family.

With so many kin milling about under the same roof, togetherness can be a problem. Exactly when (not to mention where) are husbands and wives supposed to have sex?

"This is a question that many couples ask themselves today," says Larry Hof, a certified marriage and family therapist, vice president of relationship consulting at Advanta Corporation, and a United Methodist minister in Spring House, Pennsylvania. "Couples feel so guilty about spending time working away from the family that they don't spend any time together alone without the children present. And if an older parent lives in the house, the problem becomes even more complicated."

That's a problem that needs to be fixed—and soon—because nothing is more important to the health of a family than for husbands and wives to find time just for each other, says Hof. "And though part of that time alone is certainly for sex, private time is also important for couples just to be able to talk to and connect with one another," he says. "The quality of the marriage is the indicator of how strong the family relationship will be. Not only will you and your husband be better off in the long run, but so will your children."

The Great Escape

Saying you need more time alone together is one thing. Finding it is another. "You have to prioritize—and even make a few sacrifices—in order to be alone together," says Richard Meth, Ph.D., director of the Humphrey Center for Marital and Family Therapy at the University of Connecticut in Storrs. "But these changes really aren't as big as you may think. And making them will improve, if not save, your marriage." Here's what experts recommend.

Secrets of Long-Lasting Love

Connect When You Can

Marti Livingston, a nurse, met her husband, Lee, now a retired air force officer, on a blind date. A friend set them up because of their height: Lee measures in at 5'5" and needed a woman who wouldn't tower over him, and Marti, who isn't quite 4'11", met his height qualifications. Their courtship lasted two years, and they married on June 15, 1963. Today, the Livingstons live in Merritt Island, Florida. Until a few years ago, when their last child went off to college, their life was very hectic. She says adaptation made it work.

When we first met, I was working at a hospital in Philadelphia, and Lee was in town for a few weeks of training with the Naval Academy. We saw each other as much as we could while he was in Philadelphia, and when he returned to the Academy in Annapolis, we visited every other weekend.

About two months into the relationship, I headed to Europe to continue my education in France, even though it meant putting more distance between Lee and me. While I was in France, Lee continued to pursue me through lots of letters.

When I returned to the United States, the romance picked up right where we left off. I took him to meet my parents, we got engaged over the Christmas holiday, and we married in June just one week after Lee graduated from the Academy.

Create a family privacy policy. If your children are old enough to be left unsupervised, tell them that when they need to be alone for a while, they can go to their room and close the door, and you won't bother them unless it's important. Then establish the same rules for yourself, suggests Sari Locker, a certified relationship and sexuality educator, relationship correspondent on CBS television News 2 in New York City, and author of *Mindblowing Sex in the Real World.*

"Sit down with your family and establish 'closed door rules,'" advises Locker. "Say, 'Sometimes Mommy and Daddy need time alone. When we shut the door, everything is fine; we just need some privacy. We won't be

I would say the beginning of our marriage was probably the most challenging. We thought that once we were married, we would have all this time together. Boy, were we wrong. Lee's first assignment was to attend the Air Force Institute of Technology full-time. For the first two years of our marriage, he was buried in schoolwork. And I was busy caring for our child—we had our first of three children one week before our first wedding anniversary. So from the beginning, our time together was rather limited.

Between balancing our children and our careers, we had little time to talk one-on-one. Lee worked days, and I worked nights. That schedule made it easy for one of us to be around for the kids, but it also left a small window of opportunity for Lee and me to have time just for us. In between our shift changes, we started a ritual of watching the nightly news together, followed by dinner with the family. The news was our time, and over dinner we caught up with the kids. Intimacy? Well, we just fit that in whenever we could.

Our marriage works because we accept and adapt to each other "warts and all," as Lee says. Sure, we've hit some difficult times, but we get through them and forget them. It's the good times we enjoy and choose to remember.

away long, so unless it's an emergency, don't knock.' This mutual respect of privacy is healthy for the whole family."

Put a lock on the door . . . and use it. Door or no door, some people aren't able to relax knowing that their children or other family members may unwittingly barge in. "If it increases your peace of mind, buy a doorknob that locks, and use it. Sure, somebody might still knock on the door, but they won't open it," says Hof.

But if we lock the door, won't everyone know we're having sex, you may wonder? "Maybe. But if you routinely go into your room when you need some

privacy, it won't be seen as a big deal. Maybe you're watching the news. Maybe you're having sex. The bottom line is that the other members of your family know you need time together," says Hof. "And husbands and wives have a right to be alone."

Hang a sign. You can further take stress off of your "closed door" time by posting a sign that says, "Be back at such and such a time," like store-keepers do, says Judy Kuriansky, Ph.D., of the Center for Marital and Family Therapy in New York City, host of the syndicated call-in advice radio show *LovePhones*, and author of *The Complete Idiot's Guide to a Healthy Relationship.* "Explain to your family that you and your husband don't want to be disturbed until that time," she says. "Then, if one of your family members wants you for something, they know exactly when you'll be available and will be less likely to bother you in the meantime. You or your husband can also use this technique when you want some time for just yourself."

Soundproof your room. If the master bedroom is tucked off in a remote corner of the house, a securely closed door is all you need for an amorous encounter. In some homes, however, the bedroom may be well within earshot of the kids' rooms or common areas, leaving some couples worrying that even if they're not seen, they may be heard. "All you need is some very simple soundproofing," says Locker. "First, put down some carpeting on the floor to absorb sound. Then, set up a small radio or CD player, so you can put on some music to mask your voices." And if you make a habit of playing music in the bedroom, even when you're just folding laundry, your family won't automatically associate hearing music with sex.

Be a little less involved. If you and your husband are never alone together because you're never home at the same time, your problem is one of priority, not privacy, says Dr. Meth. "I see couples where the husband and the wife have their own separate activities going almost every night of the week. All these activities may bring you extra income or establish your place in the community, but you're doing them at the expense of your intimacy," he says.

"Find the one or two activities that are most important, drop the rest, and spend some relaxed private time with your family instead."

Let them be happy campers. Summer camp is a great chance for your kids to get away, socialize with other children, and learn skills like sports and crafts. "It can also mean anywhere from one to six weeks of blissful privacy for you and your husband," says Locker. "Pick up some brochures from your local school on camps in your area and let your kids pick the ones they like best."

Time Out!

Most often, couples are trying to figure out how to find time alone with each other. But occasionally, we feel like we need time *away* from each other.

"Finding time apart can be more difficult than finding time together, because conventional wisdom teaches us that we're not supposed to want to be away from the man or woman we love. When we do, feelings get hurt," says Judy Kuriansky, Ph.D., of the Center for Marital and Family Therapy in New York City, host of the syndicated call-in advice radio show *LovePhones*, and author of *The Complete Idiot's Guide to a Healthy Relationship*. But sooner or later, everyone needs some private time. Here's how to find a piece of solitude.

Don't say, "I need time away from you." Instead, explain that you are feeling a little overwhelmed and would be a more pleasant person to be around if you had some time by yourself to read, think, listen to music, or whatever it is you do to decompress.

Set boundaries. There are certain times of the day you might always want some privacy, says Dr. Kuriansky. "Some people like privacy when they're getting dressed or during personal grooming activities like shaving and showering. Discuss how you feel about being together during these times, and establish the times and activities that are 'me only.'"

Give him some space, too. If you want to get privacy, you have to be willing to give it, adds Dr. Kuriansky. "Don't barge in on your husband, kids, or other family members when you know they want to be alone. Healthy families respect each other's boundaries."

Preserve family time. It may seem contradictory, but if you and your husband want more time alone from your family, you should spend more time *with* your family, says Dr. Kuriansky. "Your family doesn't want to be around you to disturb your privacy. They want to be around you because they enjoy your company," she says. "Set aside one day or a couple of nights a week as family time, when you spend time with them and only them. Then they'll understand and you won't feel as guilty when you and your husband want time alone."

Quickies

Think about sex. How your husband's back curves as he moves against you. His deep moans. The warm tension that runs from your throat to your loins when he cups your breast in the palm of his hand.

You have just practiced the art of "quickie" foreplay. Combine this with quickie sex. Then wrap it up with quickie afterplay, and you have a recipe for a charged sex life filled with lots of lusty encounters, both long and short, says marriage counselor Harry Croft, M.D., a psychiatrist and licensed sex therapist in San Antonio.

"The quickie can be a wonderful way for busy couples to have some fun, add variety, relieve stress, and keep connected between less frequent, lengthier sexual episodes," Dr. Croft says. "It's also perfect for couples with different sex drives. Maybe he wants sex every day, but she's more of a weekend lover. So, he can say, 'How about a quickie today? Then Saturday night we'll spend hours.' Both of them end up satisfied and happy."

"Plus, the more sex you have, the more sex you want," adds Tara Roth Madden, author of *Romance on the Run: Five Minutes of Quality Sex for Busy Couples.* "Quickies are a perfect way to keep the pump primed."

Ready, Set, Go!

Interested in a quick encounter of the most intimate kind? Try Madden's recipe for a sexy five-minute tryst.

The Foreplay. "Start thinking about the encounter a few minutes before," suggests Madden. "This will help you get mentally and physically ready.

If you're concerned about lubrication, the sexiest thing to do is to use your mouth on him right before penetration. But a little K-Y Jelly stashed in your purse can work just as well."

The Strip. No need to get naked. Just strip off the bare essentials. "One leg out of the panty hose is plenty for you," Madden says. "For him, just unzip."

The Act. Hit the floor, the kitchen counter, a door frame, or any support for penetration, says Madden. "Because you don't have to hold the position for an hour, you can do quickies almost anywhere."

The Afterglow. A big hug, a sweet kiss, and you're on your way. Women may get a "reminder" of the encounter some time later as her husband's semen exits her vagina. "Think of that as the 'afterglow,'" says Madden. "If you dislike the wetness, keep some panty liners in your purse for afterwards."

Repeat as needed. If either one of you doesn't climax during a quick sex encounter, don't sweat it, says Madden. "That's the beauty of quickies. If you don't have an orgasm during one, it's not like you've missed the last train to Paris. Another encounter is just right around the corner."

Sensual Massage

"Woman is like a fruit which will not yield
its sweetness until you rub it between your hands."
—Sheikh Nefzawi, *The Perfumed Garden*

Eastern cultures have been extolling the virtues of massage for the past 5,000 years. To them, it's not only a way to rejuvenate muscles weary from a day's work but also the perfect way to prime the body for a night's play. Now, as the interest in massage in this country steadily grows, we, too, are discovering just how nice it is to reach out and touch one another.

Powerful Foreplay

Touching does a lot more than just make you feel good. The rubbing of hands on skin literally unlocks an arousing cocktail of chemicals and hormones that makes touching one of the most potent forms of foreplay you can try.

Spice Up Your Massage with Oil

Sure, hand lotion works fine. But for sensuous massage, sexy scented oils are even better. Visit a department store cosmetic counter to check out the many scents available, such as cedarwood, sandlewood, and ylang-ylang, and choose one that appeals to you.

Many people find that the smell of massage oil acts as an aphrodisiac, says Collin Brown, director of the Body Electric School in Oakland, California, which runs massage workshops and retreats for men, women, and couples nationwide.

Caution: These oils are not meant for the sensitive genital area, because they might irritate this area.

With every stroke of your husband's hands, your body pumps out a natural "bonding chemical" called oxytocin that soaks your brain and sex organs, increasing your craving for skin contact, according to Theresa Crenshaw, M.D., a certified sex therapist in San Diego and author of *The Alchemy of Love and Lust*. Each lingering touch makes your levels of estrogen, a primary female hormone, rise, flushing your skin and lubricating your vaginal walls. Every firm caress sends your testosterone (also a sex hormone in women) upward, piquing your desire to, well, feel more than your husband's hands.

What's more, neither of you needs to be a licensed massage therapist to practice this kind of sensuous massage, says Collin Brown, director of the Body Electric School in Oakland, California, which runs massage workshops and retreats for men, women, and couples nationwide.

Get Started

To begin, establish a sensuous, relaxing environment, suggests Brown. The bed or a mat on the floor is fine. Put massage oil or lotion nearby. Light the room softly. "Candles are perfect lighting. Their soft, warm glow is great for every body," he says. Also consider playing some music. "Music relaxes you and moves you. It opens your heart and makes you more receptive to receiving pleasure," Brown notes. "Pick something soft and soothing, the kind of music that helps you surrender to the occasion."

Start by agreeing that each of you will be giving the other pleasure for 20 minutes at a time, suggests Brown. "Too often, a couple will start a massage and 2 minutes into it, they're moving toward sex." Or they're both worried if the other is enjoying it. "Don't even talk if you can help it. Just signal your pleasure with moans and nonverbal communication." He stresses that there should be an agreement from the beginning that this is a reciprocal arrangement; both partners should derive pleasure from the experience. It is essential to tune in to each other's feelings before starting, says Brown. Every massage should emphasize the combination of physical pleasure and spiritual togetherness that comes from both of you being aware of each other's pleasure thresholds. Find the pressure points that are just right for your partner, he says.

As you begin, think of the whole body as an erogenous zone and rub from head to toe, giving certain areas special attention, says Dennis Shankland, a licensed massage therapist from Phoenix. Rather than doing one part at a time, you should approach massage as a routine. You should do the entire body, like a complete symphony, says Shankland, who runs "Intimate Touch for Couples" workshops through his company, A Massage for Life. By all means, use body oil. You should use enough to get a gliding effect but not so much that it becomes too slippery.

The face. "The face is a highly erogenous area," says Shankland. "Try stroking up from the chin, along the side of the face to the ears and back," he suggests. "Then stroke between the eyes down over the bridge of the nose."

Neck and shoulders. The neck and shoulder area is a favorite spot for massage because this is where we carry so much of our daily stress, says Brown. With your hands on the tops of both shoulders, use firm but gentle upward strokes with your thumbs to relax those tight muscles. Then move your hands up to the neck and use your thumb and fingers to knead it.

Hands and arms. To soothe your mate's hands, knead his palm with the ball of your hand, then gently rub each finger. Then stroke each arm up, then down.

Chest. Facing your partner, rub his chest in light, circular motions. If his chest is hairy, use more oil to lessen the friction. Both men's and women's nipples are very sensitive, Brown says, and the right touch can cause deep pleasure. He can cup your breasts with his hands and fingers, circling your nipples with light strokes.

Stomach. "Though you shouldn't really massage the delicate stomach area, both men and women enjoy having their tummies rubbed," says Shankland. "Run your hands lightly down the sides and over the hips as well. That area is very erotic." He emphasizes that you should always rub the stomach with a circular motion because that is the way the intestines coil.

Legs. Both the backs and fronts of the legs respond well to deep rhythmic rubbing and kneading. "Just remember to sweep your hand along the entire thigh muscle all the way up to the groin for the most pleasurable, relaxing results," says Shankland.

Back. A simple, soothing stroke for the back is for your partner to lie facedown while you straddle him with your knees and sit lightly on his buttocks, suggests Brown. Then place both palms on the small of his back, on either side of his spine, with your fingers pointing toward his head. Make long, slow strokes up either side of his spine to his shoulders. Then sweep across the top of his shoulders and back down the sides of his body to the beginning. Avoid massaging the spine itself, as that could cause injury, cautions Brown.

Buttocks. "If every man had his butt rubbed every day, we'd have a better chance for world peace," says Shankland. Try deep kneading as well as circular sweeps from the top of the butt, around the sides to the base, and back up the center with the palms of your hands.

Feet. Finally, pamper your partner's feet by rubbing up and down the soles with firm thumb pressure, says Shankland.

Genital Massage for Him

"When it comes right down to it, the penis is perfect for massaging. It's responsive. It's accessible. It fits in your hands. And a man's penis doesn't have to be rock hard for him to enjoy a sensuous massage," says Selah Martha, director of the women's programs at the Body Electric School in Oakland, California, which teaches traditional as well as erotic massage to men, women, and couples. "Some of these strokes feel even better when he's soft."

What is most important is the attention you are giving, says Brown. "All people need compassionate, aware touch to feel genuinely erotic and to feel full sensation in their genitals," he says.

Although many American men are circumcised, if your partner has a foreskin, be aware that the head will be very sensitive. Note his reactions to these strokes, Brown says. Some men love having their foreskins played with, and many also like having their nipples and penises played with at the same time.

Here are a few strokes to try. Before beginning, however, you should re-

---

Mind/Body Massage Music

The right music can heighten the pleasure of sensuous massage, says Selah Martha, director of the women's programs at the Body Electric School in Oakland, California. "The selections you choose should be sexy, erotic, and quietly energizing." Here are some CDs that the school recommends.

- *1492: Conquest of Paradise* (Vangelis)
- *Migration* (Peter Kater/R. Carlos Nakai)
- *Passion* (Peter Gabriel)
- *The Cross of Changes* (Enigma)
- *Natives* (Peter Kater/R. Carlos Nakai)
- *Lorenzo's Oil* (soundtrack)
- *Music to Disappear in II* (Raphael)
- *Spirit of India* (Terry Oldfield)
- *The Sky of the Mind* (Ray Lynch)
- *The Mask and Mirror* (Loreena McKennitt)
- *Soul to the Pleasure* (Ring)

---

alize that the goal of any genital massage is not to make the other person achieve orgasm, says Brown, but to raise his or her erotic energy and then spread it throughout the entire body. You're just using varying strokes to relax your partner.

Gliding stroke. With his penis resting on his belly, cup his scrotum with the hand that's closest to his feet. Then use the heel of your other hand to glide up and down the underside of the penis.

Penis rub. Douse your hands liberally with oil. Rub the penis between both palms, as if your hands were two sticks trying to create fire.

Stroking the penis. Squeeze the penis with one hand. With the thumb and forefinger (or the palm) of the other hand, stroke up the penis in a corkscrew motion. You can then reverse the stroke to create a different sensation.

Circular penis stroke. Place the back of your hand on his stomach, with his penis resting on your hand. Put your other hand on top to create a "basket" and stroke or make circling motions with your hands.

Rotation. Using a well-oiled hand, turn it around the head of his penis like you're trying to open a doorknob coated with grease. Now try turning the other way. Remember that the head of the penis is very sensitive. Repeat.

Genital Massage for You

Erotic massage is a wonderful opportunity for men to explore all the ways to stimulate their lovers' genitals, says Martha. Again, remember that this is not intended to lead to orgasm. It is an exploration of sensation and pleasure. Your partner should be striving to increase your sensation of pleasure with slow, deep, lingering strokes. Most women have never had the experience of just surrendering to the sensation without the necessity of sex, says Brown.

"A woman's vulva is like a mysterious flower or grotto, to be explored with wonder and respect," Brown says. "As a general rule, your partner should start with a light touch and let you ask for more. Touching of the clitoris should be especially feather-light and teasing. Let him know what feels right."

Here are techniques for your partner to try.

Circling. With a lubricated finger, he makes soft, rhythmic circles around the clitoris, continuing until he finds a stroke that you like best.

Labial stroke. He runs his forefinger in circles between your inner and outer labia, from the perineum (the area around the urethra) to above your clitoris, or he rubs the outer labia between his thumb and forefinger.

Vaginal rub. He inserts one or two lubricated fingers in your vagina, with the pads of his fingers over the raised, ridged spot on the front wall of the vagina behind the pubic bone, sometimes called the G-spot. He rubs it by making rhythmic gestures inside the vagina, similar to the hand signal for "come here."

Press. He presses very firmly on your G-spot, like he's ringing a doorbell. Press, release, repeat.

According to Dr. Crenshaw, you needn't have sex every time you touch. If you do, however, you'll probably enjoy it better because of the higher level of trust and bonding you've achieved.

Sex in the Tub or Shower

I f you're married to a guy long enough, sooner or later he's going to say, "Hey, let's have sex in the tub!" So "Have Sex in the Tub (or Shower)" ends up on your to-do list. You hope to get around to it some day. But you aren't sure how to go about it without putting out your back—or cracking your skull—and having to call the paramedics.

Well, procrastinate no longer. There *are* safe, comfortable ways to fulfill your fantasy.

Why the allure? Quite simply, water is a primal pleasure. "We're conceived and born in water," says Stella Resnick, Ph.D., a psychologist in Los Angeles and author of *The Pleasure Zone: Why We Resist Good Feelings and How to Let Go and Be Happy.* "It's sensuous. It's slippery and slidy and relaxing. It feels good trickling over our bodies."

It's also a unique form of foreplay, with the emphasis on play. "If you're playful and creative, you can start things off in the tub or shower and then kind of roll out of the water to get a better grip on things, so to speak," says Dr. Resnick.

"That said, you can't just jump into the water and have intercourse. It's just not going to happen," Dr. Resnick says. Water washes away a woman's vaginal lubrication, which can make penetration uncomfortable, she says.

Moreover, hot water can damage a latex condom and wash away spermicidal foams, jellies, and creams.

To make your experience safe, comfortable, and satisfying, follow these suggestions.

Tub Lovin'

Unless you're fortunate enough to have a hot tub in your home, you're most likely to encounter a hot tub in a hotel. Even the so-called portable varieties cost $3,000 or more. And while it's sometimes possible to rent portable models, they're a breeding ground for bacteria.

Some catalogs and home-shopping channels such as QVC offer portable whirlpool units for under $200. These units, which attach to the side of a bathtub, pump and recirculate the water, turning your bathtub into a whirlpool. Of course, with the device installed in the tub, there's less elbow-room for the two of you.

The following tips apply to hot tubs or regular bathtubs.

Set the scene. Light scented candles and place them around the bathroom. As you run the tub, add fragrant bath salts or fresh flower petals. If you drink, pour two glasses of wine or champagne to sip while you splash. (Use plastic glasses only.) Slip Marvin Gaye or Barry White into the portable CD player placed a safe distance from the water. Presto: You've created your own erotic spa.

Be childish. Water encourages our return to our childlike passion for play. "When we were little kids, we played in the bath," says Dr. Resnick. "We had toy duckies and windup toys that chugged through the water. We splashed." So when you and your partner step into the bath, allow your inner seven-year-old to emerge. Buy some tub toys. Let the bubble bath flow. Scrub between each other's toes. Engage in a splashing duel. The more fun you have with your mate, the more intense—and loving—the sex will be.

Use the woman-on-top position. It's the simplest way, anatomically speaking. "The buoyancy helps you achieve a nice rhythm, particularly if you move slowly and sensually," says Dr. Resnick.

Expect a flood. Bathtub sex is messy sex. If mopping the bathroom floor isn't your idea of afterplay, place a few folded towels on the floor by the tub. Also, remember that naked bodies are slippery when wet. To prevent accidents, place a towel or bath mat a few steps from the tub, for exiting the room safely.

Shower Power

If your partner dislikes baths, surprise him in the shower. While having actual intercourse in the shower requires a good sense of balance—and risks a nasty accident—it's a great opportunity for sex play. Read on.

Seduce him. The next time he's showering solo, climb in wearing a silky camisole, suggests Glenn Wilson, Ph.D., a well-known psychologist in England, in his book *Creative Loveplay*. The thin fabric will cling to your body, which he's bound to appreciate.

Full steam ahead, Matey. When your husband arrives home from work, take him by the hand and pull him, fully dressed, into a warm, waiting shower. "Afterwards, the struggle to get free of wet clothing can be highly stimulating," writes Dr. Wilson. But use common sense. Don't try this if he's wearing a good suit, or if you know things are tense for him at work.

Whip him into a lather. The next time you're showering together, thoroughly "wash" his body, suggests Dr. Wilson. Lather up his chest, stomach, and legs. Turn him around and lather his back and shoulders. Kiss. Rub your body against his. Then slowly zero in on his testicles. Massage them, using gentle but insistent pressure. Finally, "wash" his penis. Thoroughly. For at least five whole minutes. He'll love it.

Put down some traction. To reduce your risk of slipping, invest in tub decals or, suggests Dr. Resnick, just sit down on the floor of your shower. Let the water cascade over you. Pretend you're both in a waterfall on some exotic tropical island.

Sex on the Beach

You've probably thought about it. Maybe you've even done it. Next to skinny-dipping, surfside sex is one of those cherished acts of naughtiness that tempts everyone sooner or later.

Don't Get Caught

If sex on the beach is on your romantic agenda, follow this advice from Isadora Alman, a certified sexologist in San Francisco and a syndicated sex advice columnist.

Pick a private place. "The smell of the ocean and the sound of the surf can be aphrodisiacal," concedes Alman. "But getting caught *in flagrante delicto* on a public or private beach is not at all as thrilling in real life as it may be in fantasy." While police are more likely to tell you to get dressed and move on, you could get arrested and fined for "lewd and lascivious behavior," public nudity, or trespassing, depending on local ordinances.

Don't burn your booty. Most seaside trysts take place at night, when sunburn isn't a concern. But during the day, areas of skin not usually exposed to the sun can burn in the time it takes to disrobe and make love. Even if you apply sunscreen to vulnerable areas, it takes at least 30 minutes before you're protected. To maintain spontaneity, find a shady place under a swaying palm tree or canopy.

No rough stuff. If you have your choice between soft Hawaiian Islands–type sand or the granular type more common to a place like Cape Cod, go for the smoother, less abrasive version. "Either way, though, you're in for a sandy ride," says Alman, "so using a blanket is even better."

Wipe sand away. Even with a blanket between you and the elements, sand plus sweat rubbing between your skin and his can cause problems, according to Yvonne S. Thornton, M.D., clinical professor of obstetrics and gynecology at the University of Medicine and Dentistry of New Jersey in Newark. Sand in your vagina (and in and around the opening of his penis) can be excruciatingly painful, akin to making love to a piece of sandpaper. There is also the potential for abrasions to the skin around and in your vagina, which increases the risk of contracting a sexually transmitted disease (STD) or other infection. Sand can also tear a condom, upping STD risks and the potential for pregnancy. Wiping sand away during lovemaking with a damp cloth or a towelette can help. If there's a lavatory nearby, use it: Urinating after sex is the easiest way to wash sand out of your urethra.

Stay out of the water. Having intercourse in water introduces water into the vagina, and water in the great outdoors is laden with bacteria. This puts you at risk for urinary tract and other infections, Dr. Thornton says.

What's more, if you're using a condom with spermicidal gel, foam, or jelly, water can wash the spermicide out. So stick to dry land.

Sex Talk

I f your brain is your biggest sex organ, your mouth is its best outlet. Because while there are only so many sexual positions with which to express your love, there are hundreds of words you can use to enhance your sexual encounters for the rest of your life.

When most people think of sex talk, the first thing that comes to mind is the kind of "dirty" talk you get from calling 900 numbers, says Bonnie Gabriel of San Francisco, who offers workshops on erotic talk and verbal romance and is the author of *The Fine Art of Erotic Talk: How to Entice, Excite, and Enchant Your Lover with Words.* "Though using explicit language can be part of it, it's only one small aspect. Erotic talk can also be reading poetry or whispering sweet compliments. Erotic talk can range from the most romantic and devotional expressions to the most outrageously playful and explicit," she says. "It's all about bringing couples closer together."

Couples who can talk about sex, both in and out of bed, almost inevitably have a more enjoyable sexual connection, says marriage counselor Harry Croft, M.D., a psychiatrist and licensed sex therapist in San Antonio. "At the very least, when you communicate, no matter what kind of language you prefer, you learn what the other person really likes. So sex is more pleasurable for both of you."

Plus, erotic talk is just plain arousing. In a *Men's Health* and *New Woman* magazine survey that asked readers about their sexual likes and dislikes, 12 percent of women ranked talking dirty above kissing, petting, and even cunnilingus as their favorite form of foreplay.

The Language of Sex

What stops people from speaking their sexual minds? "Performance anxiety, for one," answers Gabriel. "People are afraid of sounding inept or silly. Expressing sexual wants and needs is often more intimate than physical sex. So it makes them feel very vulnerable." But even the shyest of the shy can learn to speak up, she says. It just takes a little practice. Here's how to get started.

Find a common language. If you've never tried erotic talk with your husband before, finding a common "love language" is a good way to start, says Patricia Love, Ed.D., a licensed marriage and family therapist in Austin, Texas, and coauthor of *Hot Monogamy*. Make a list of the clinical names, like vagina and penis, for the highly erogenous zones of both the male and female anatomies. Then each of you write down all the vernacular terms, like "love garden" and "member," that you like and compare notes. "The goal is to find words that are arousing for both of you," says Dr. Love.

Enjoy erotic questioning. Caress your partner's body in two different areas, or alternate the rhythm and pressure of your touch. Ask him, "Which feels better when I touch you? This . . . or this?" This is a gentle, easy way to get started using words in a nonthreatening manner. As an added benefit, it helps you learn what your partner likes and dislikes, explains Gabriel. It is much more comfortable to answer a question than to express your needs, she says. You can use the information to tailor your love-making techniques to better please your partner, she adds.

Give yourself permission. The biggest barrier for some women is giving themselves permission to be overtly sexual, says Dr. Croft. "Many women have been taught that nice girls don't do this, or married women don't talk that way, when in fact their husbands would love them to do and say very sexy things," he says. "Read erotic literature. Talk to trusted friends. Realize that other people engage in sexy behavior and that you can, too."

Give a solo performance. Like anything, sex talk takes practice. And sometimes you're more comfortable practicing by yourself rather than in front of others, says Anne Semans, coauthor of *The New Good Vibrations Guide to Sex*. "We recommend that women practice during masturbation. That way you can hear yourself saying the words. You can get used to talking during arousal and orgasm. So it will feel more natural when you're with a partner."

Give erotic feedback. Let your partner touch and caress you, Gabriel says. As his hands wander over your body, let him know when he hits a delicious spot. Take this opportunity to give him important feedback on what you like and dislike, on what feels good or whether he should apply more or less pressure to the area.

Give praise. If you do no other sex talking, try giving each other plenty of compliments on your lovemaking both in and out of bed, suggests Dr. Croft. "Too often, we just don't talk about sex. We just assume we're each pleased, and that can lead to frustration and insecurity. Compliment your lover when something feels good. Tell him later, 'I especially liked it when you did this . . . mmm.' You'll both feel happier about your sexual relationship," he says. "When you reward each other with praise, you're also bound to get more of what you really like."

Graduate Lessons

Once you have mastered the tips above, try these advanced techniques that are guaranteed to steam up your sex life, courtesy of Gabriel.

Be outrageous. Sometimes a fun way to beat performance anxiety is to act way over the top, says Gabriel. If you can't muster up the nerve to say, "Your hard cock against my leg is turning me on," try being outrageous and playful, like "I can feel your magnificent charger spring to life against my burning body," suggests Gabriel. It's funny in a playful, sexy way. And it will break the ice for more erotic talk of all kinds.

Make it an all-day affair. You don't have to restrict your sexy talk to when you're between the sheets, points out Gabriel. "I have people practice 'erotic afterglow,' or what I call take-out fantasies. Basically, it means keeping the sexual flow going long after the actual encounter is over," she explains. "When you're leaving in the morning after a night of intimacy, give each other a sexy thought to carry throughout the day," she suggests. If you have a break at lunch, you can call and tell your husband something you're imagining doing to him later, like unbuttoning his shirt and kissing his chest when he walks through the door, says Gabriel.

Playact. You can try out all types of sex talk by role-playing or acting out fantasies, says Gabriel. "You can say things as a hooker, a pirate, or a police officer that you wouldn't normally say as yourself. You can even add foreign accents, which many people find particularly sexy."

Sex Toys

ccording to *The New Good Vibrations Guide to Sex*, the first steam-powered "massager" was invented in 1869 to treat "female disorders." By the late 1800s, a British doctor developed portable, battery-operated "vibrators" to treat "hysteria." Quite simply, the good doctor would practice genital massage to induce "hysterical paroxysm" (that's orgasm to you and me), and the damsel in distress would be cured. By the 1920s, coy advertising copy was marketing vibrators in magazines, promising to make women "tingle with the joy of living!"

Later, sex toys evolved from medical devices to the butt of jokes.

"Sex toys have had this stigma of being for losers, for people who don't have real partners, or for people who have problems," says San Francisco–based Cathy Winks, coauthor of *The New Good Vibrations Guide to Sex* and coeditor of *Sex Toy Tales*. "But sex toys are simply a way to enrich your sexual encounters. They're no different from champagne, scented candles, or silk sheets."

And yes, plenty of healthy, happy heterosexual couples use them, assures Patricia Love, Ed.D., a licensed marriage and family therapist in Austin, Texas, and coauthor of *Hot Monogamy*. "Sex toys add variety to a long-term relationship," she says. "They're great for women who have difficulty reaching orgasm. And if you snuggle close, touch, explore, or look into each other's eyes when you use them, they're not mechanical or impersonal."

Lots of women seem to agree. In a *Men's Health* and *New Woman* magazine survey, 40 percent of women said they either had or would use a dildo, and the overwhelming majority approved of sex toys of some kind. A full 60 percent of the customers at the sex merchandise shop Good Vibrations are women.

It's Playtime

Okay, your interest is piqued. That's the easy part. The hard part for some women is making the next jump from wanting to try sex toys to actually buying them. The process can be a little intimidating, but catalog shopping makes it easier. You can take your time, giggle over names

---

Bestsellers

Having trouble deciding which toys to try? Here are the top three sellers at Good Vibrations, a women-owned, San Francisco–based sex merchandise company.

1. Hitachi Magic Wand. An electric vibrator with a long handle and soft round head.
2. Smoothie. A simple, straight, lipstick-shaped battery-operated vibrator.
3. Pocket Rocket. A four-inch, one-speed, battery-operated vibrator.

These toys are available nationwide at most sex toy stores.

---

like "the Humdinger," and read about what each toy does. You and your partner can even go through the catalog together, circling items that interest you.

Here's a little sex toy primer to help with your selection.

Vibrators. You'll find vibrators in all shapes and sizes. Some lifelike. Some not. Some insertable. Some not. They're usually designed for a specific kind of stimulation, like for your clitoris or G-spot. The biggest decision you'll face is whether you want a battery-operated or an electric vibrator. Battery vibes are probably the best bet for beginners. Though they're less durable and less powerful than the electric kind, they're also less expensive, so if one style isn't exactly what you want, you can try another. "Vibrators also make a nice 'couples' toy," says Winks.

Dildos. Dildos are sex toys designed exclusively for penetration. They get their odd name from the Italian word *diletto*, meaning "delight." "Both men and women enjoy the fullness and pressure of having a dildo inserted in the vagina (for women) or the anus (for either) during sex play," says Winks.

Choose from an infinite variety of sizes and styles in either rubber or silicone. Rubber toys are considerably less expensive, so they're great for experimentation. But because they're porous, they're harder to keep clean. Put a condom over the dildo to prevent bacteria from collecting in the pores in the rubber coating. Silicone toys are more expensive, but they're easy to clean (you can boil silicone), and they come in a greater range of styles.

Rings, clamps, and more. Sex toy catalogs also offer an array of nipple clamps for people who like their nipples squeezed; "love" rings, which a man can wear around his penis and scrotum to restrict blood flow from his erection and create pleasurable pressure; and fur-lined handcuffs, blindfolds, and other toys for light bondage.

Caution: It's important that sex toys be thoroughly cleaned after every use with hot water and soap, says Dr. Love. And never use a toy on the vagina that has been used in the anus without sterilizing it first. To avoid transferring bacteria, some people keep separate toys for the vagina and the anus, says Dr. Love.

"Once you start playing with sex toys, you and your partner can expand your fantasy lives, role-play, learn new things that turn each other on, and bring an element of playfulness into your relationship," concludes Winks.

Sexual Anxiety

I'm not good enough."

"I'm not pleasing him."

"I don't know what I'm doing."

"If I don't have an orgasm, he'll think something is wrong with me."

"There are times when I can't stand him touching me."

Sound familiar?

This is the sound of what sex therapists call sexual anxiety. And it's among the most painful problems that keep a couple from achieving extraordinary togetherness.

It's painful because both partners suffer in silence. If you're the anxious one, you may find it difficult, or impossible, to explain why sex provokes so much tension. Your partner may sense that something's wrong but say nothing. If it's your partner who brings his anxieties to bed, you don't want to cause him pain or embarrassment by bringing it up.

Don't Anesthetize Sex

In the movie *Annie Hall*, Diane Keaton has to smoke a joint before she can have sex with Woody Allen. "It relaxes me," she says. That's the movies. In reality, pot—along with alcohol and other recreational drugs—dulls sexual desire and physical arousal, says Barbara Andersen, Ph.D., professor in the department of psychology at Ohio State University in Columbus.

More than one or two drinks depresses the central nervous system, particularly the sympathetic nervous system, which governs sexual arousal. A woman will take longer to reach orgasm, and her climax will be less intense. A man may not get fully erect. It may also take a man longer to ejaculate, or he may not be able to ejaculate at all.

Recreational drugs, such as marijuana and cocaine, have a reputation for reducing inhibitions and thus spurring sexual desire. But chronic use of marijuana inhibits sexuality, disrupts hormonal balances, and interferes with fertility in both sexes. With sustained use of cocaine, women may find it difficult to lubricate or experience orgasm, and men may find that they can't get or keep an erection.

Just as important, chronic, heavy use of drugs and alcohol distances people from their true feelings, says Dr. Andersen. This chemically induced distance won't bring you closer to your partner. And it certainly won't unleash your potential for loving, satisfying sex.

Sexual anxiety—and the silence that surrounds it—reaches far beyond the bedroom. It keeps a couple from bonding emotionally, says Richard A. Carroll, Ph.D., director of the sex and marital therapy program at Northwestern University Medical Center in Chicago. To keep from getting hurt, anxious people tend to withdraw. When you expend so much energy protecting yourself, it's hard to let someone else in, even someone you love.

But fears about sex don't have to drive couples apart. Like toddlers who fear monsters in the closet or bogeymen under the bed, grown-ups can learn to confront their anxieties and chase them away. Sometimes a couple can banish the "monsters" themselves. Sometimes, sex therapy is necessary. But Dr. Carroll says that in both cases, the treatment is the same: talking. Revealing fears to a loving partner gives him or her the chance to show concern and support. It's this kind of openness that builds mutual trust and enriches a relationship.

The Roots of Anxiety

Women's anxieties tend to center around pleasing their partners, while men's center around their sexual performance, says Dr. Carroll. The root of sexual anxiety, however, is often the same for both genders: low self-esteem. "Men or women who have an underlying sense of inadequacy often feel sexually inadequate as well," he explains.

There are other contributing factors as well. If we received negative messages about sex as children, we may feel sinful or guilty about our behavior, which raises our anxiety about sex. People who have been sexually abused or raped as children may be so anxious that they avoid sex completely.

But often, we don't know why sex makes us anxious, says Dr. Carroll. That's because our attitudes and beliefs about sex are largely unconscious—ideas we formed when we were young. To take charge of sexual anxiety, it's crucial to make these ideas or memories conscious and to talk about them until they lose their power, he counsels.

Women's Sexual Fears

Women who are anxious about sex are often anxious in other areas of their lives, says Barbara Andersen, Ph.D., professor in the department of psychology at Ohio State University in Columbus. But there may be specific fears that contribute to anxiety. These include:

Fear of not measuring up. In performance anxiety, a person becomes overly concerned with how well he or she performs a certain task. We usually associate it with concert pianists, sports figures, or public speakers. But performance anxiety pops up in the bedroom, too. While sexual performance anxiety is most often associated with men, women also experience it. In one landmark sex study reported in the book *Sex in America*, 11 percent of women said they experienced anxiety about their sexual performance, compared to 17 percent of men.

In a woman, performance anxiety centers around whether she's pleasing her partner. She is so busy worrying about whether she's "doing it right" that she often feels that she's outside herself, watching herself. This spectatoring, as sex therapists call it, can reduce a woman's vaginal lubrication and keep her from reaching climax. A woman with performance anxiety may try to force herself to have an orgasm, says Dr. Carroll. But the harder she tries, the more elusive it becomes.

Fear of letting go. More common in women than in men, "the in-ability to let go usually presents itself as inhibited orgasm," says Dr. Car-roll. Simply put, when you climax, you're temporarily out of control, like going over the top on a big roller coaster. But you can't climax if you're looking for the emergency brake. Most women with this fear are perfec-tionists with a powerful need to control their bodies and their feelings, says Dr. Carroll.

Fear of rejection. Women pour a vast amount of emotional energy into their relationships, so the idea of our partners rejecting us is frightening. But on the whole, we trust our partners and we're not afraid to reveal our feelings. Some women, however, don't have this sense of trust. They fear that if they reveal their emotional or sexual needs, their partners will abandon them, says Dr. Carroll. So they say that they've had orgasms when they haven't. They endure sexual practices they don't like (and that their partners may believe they enjoy). They say that the sex is great when it's not. The sad fact is, it is the women who express no needs—who can't reveal their true selves—who are ultimately rejected.

Men's Sexual Fears

Men have the same fear of rejection and of not pleasing their partners as women, says Dr. Carroll. But some fears seem to plague men more than women.

Fear of failure. As adolescents, men learn that sex is an automatic process—when they're aroused, they get an erection, says Barry McCarthy, Ph.D., a psychologist and certified sex therapist in Washington, D.C., and coauthor with his wife, Emily, of *Male Sexual Awareness* and *Couple Sexual Awareness*. But as they grow older, men fear the waning of this "automatic" response, because to them, real men get erections on demand. If they can't, they may avoid sex as a way to avoid the shame and humiliation of failure, says Dr. McCarthy.

Fear of not pleasing their partners. An enduring myth about men is that they're selfish brutes, concerned only with getting their own needs met. This myth is badly out of date, says Dr. Carroll. In reality, most men in committed relationships are anxious about their sexual skills. To them, pleasing their women is a job real men perform flawlessly. "Men fear that if they don't please their partners sexually, their partners will find other men who will and leave," he says.

Fear of intimacy. No big surprise here. But what you may not know is that this fear can affect a man's performance. "Plenty of men are ardent and responsive during the courtship phase of a relationship," says Dr. Carroll. "But when they get to the commitment phase or start talking marriage, they suddenly start losing their erections or desire." That's because many men still think of sex and love as separate things. "Many men still think that sex is for bad girls, and emotional closeness and marriage are for good girls," says Dr. Carroll. So the closer to a woman they feel, the more likely they may feel that sex with her is "bad," which triggers anxiety.

Breaking the Anxiety Barrier

The most important thing to remember about sexual anxiety is that it's not "his problem" or "your problem." The problem belongs to *both* of you, says Dr. Carroll. And it's up to you to work it through—together. Here's how.

Get to ground zero. Anxiety thrives on the unknown. So if you or your partner is tense about sex, pinpointing the source of the fear makes it less frightening, says Dr. Carroll. Some questions to ask yourself: At what point does sexual anxiety hit? Before making love? During the act itself? Do specific thoughts or memories trigger the anxiety? Do you "pose" when you make love, so that you're too distracted to let yourself go? "Just making your unconscious attitudes conscious can in itself be helpful," explains Dr. Carroll.

Talk it through. In a truly intimate partnership, there's very little that can't be shared. So after you've pondered your fear or thought about what might be triggering his, ask your partner if he'd be willing to discuss the issue with you. (Asking, not demanding, is key.) For tips on talking about sexual matters, see Communication on page 8. But here's some general advice, says Dr. McCarthy: Broach the subject only when both of you are well-rested and relaxed, *not* right after sex. And as you tackle this difficult subject, ask for his support, or let him know that he has yours.

Face your anxiety. In the short run, talking about sex can raise your anxiety level. But if you keep talking, the anxiety goes away, says Jeanne Shaw, Ph.D., a certified sex therapist and director of the Couples Enrichment Institute in Atlanta. Also, acknowledge how difficult it is for you to talk about your anxiety. Dr. Shaw suggests saying something like, "I'm so anxious right now that I'm about to jump out of my skin. So just bear with me while I get my words out. I really want to talk about this with you."

If it's your partner who's struggling, hold on to your composure in the face of your partner's anxiety. Calm or soothe yourself so that you don't fall apart or get defensive, says Dr. Shaw. If you do lose your cool, compose yourself by taking some deep breaths and feeling the ground supporting you, and then listen to him and try to understand.

Consider therapy. Couples who have a difficult time communicating about sex or other areas of their relationship, or are in relationships in which one partner has been sexually abused, may need the help of a sex therapist. "Sex therapy can help people examine their beliefs about sex and help them develop healthier attitudes," says Dr. Carroll. A sex therapist can also help people who were abused face the trauma they may have experienced. For more information on sex therapy, see page 494.

Sexual Desire

Any woman who has been in love knows the feeling: All her husband has to do is walk through the room and she tingles with desire. Every woman who has been in love also knows, however, that her libido doesn't sing "I'm in the Mood for Love" all the time. In fact, sometimes, no matter how desirable her husband looks and acts, the only song her sex drive seems to sing is "Hit the Road, Jack!"

It's not that women aren't sexual creatures. It's just that, while men's libidos rev close to the red much of the time, women's engines generally idle at a cooler level and require a little priming to get pumped into full gear, says Patricia Love, Ed.D., a licensed marriage and family therapist in Austin, Texas, and coauthor of *Hot Monogamy*. "Men think about sex more often, are more easily aroused, and want sex more frequently. It's a biological fact. This discrepancy in sexual desire is the most common complaint sex therapists hear. It can really drive a wedge between couples."

Testosterone and Time

The biggest reason why men tend to hang around sexual overdrive while women switch gears is that men have more of the petrol that fuels passion—testosterone, says Barbara D. Bartlik, M.D., clinical assistant professor in the department of psychiatry at Weill Medical College of Cornell University, and assistant attending psychiatrist at the New York Presbyterian Hospital, both in New York City.

"Testosterone is the hormone responsible for sex drive," Dr. Bartlik says. "And men have 10 to 20 times more of it than women. Making matters more complicated, as women reach menopause and beyond, their hormone levels decline. So they produce less estrogen, which is the hormone that helps them become physically aroused and receptive to sex, and less testosterone, which makes them want sex in the first place," she says.

Then there's the fact that life just gets in the way as we move through adulthood, Dr. Bartlik says. "Women tend to have a decline in sexual interest from their mid- to late thirties through menopause," she says. "Some of that is hormones, but a great deal is also because their lives become more complicated with careers and children and the usual conflicts that occur during marriage. We've found that after 65, women start to show a lot more interest in sex again."

Fire Up the Libido

The fact that many women put sex on the back burner for a while in no way implies that you should sit back patiently and wait for your wayward sex drive to arrive with your first Social Security check. With a little time, understanding, and hormonal manipulation, there are plenty of ways to fire up your libido and have you and your husband dancing in the sheets again.

Give yourself a hand. Stimulating yourself is often the best way to jump-start your libido, according to Dr. Bartlik. "Masturbation helps a woman get back in touch with her sex drive. When she rediscovers those sexy feelings without the pressure of a partner, she is better able to rekindle those feelings later with her husband." Plus, masturbation increases testosterone levels, which will also liven up your longing for sex. "We tell women to masturbate an hour or two before they know they'll be having sex," Dr. Bartlik says. "If that's not possible, even the day before can help prime the pump."

Boost your body. Sex drive often slumps when self-esteem is low, says Dr. Love, especially when the problem is a negative body image. "Becoming more physically active is a wonderful way to improve both problems," she says. "Regular exercise not only improves the way you look but it also improves the way you feel about your body, which is most important."

And if looking and feeling better weren't enough, exercise also gives your testosterone levels a boost, says Mark Temple, Ph.D., assistant professor of health at Illinois State University in Normal, where he teaches human sexuality. "Studies show that when women begin to work out, their sex drives often increase," says Dr. Temple. "Part of that is probably due to the increase in testosterone through the physical exertion. And part of it is probably because when a woman thinks she looks sexier, she begins to feel sexier."

Watch *The Lover*. Sex begets sex, says Dr. Bartlik. And that includes thinking about sex, reading about sex, or watching sex. "Getting turned on this way is like mental foreplay," she explains. Reading or watching erotica floods your body with the same hormones that actual sex play does. These hormones include phenylethylamine, an amphetamine-like substance (also found in chocolate) that creates love-struck euphoria; estrogen, which enhances arousal; and testosterone, which boosts sex drive. So you'll feel more sexually charged as a result. "And it certainly doesn't have to be porn," says Dr. Bartlik. Companies like San Francisco–based mail order retailer Good Vibrations offer erotic movies and books by women for women. You can also find sections on erotica at most major chain bookstores.

Have sex in the backyard. Okay, maybe playing doctor on the deck isn't a keen idea if the neighbors are barbecuing 10 yards away. But routine love-

Secrets of Long-Lasting Love

Romancing the Marriage

Linda Greenwald and her husband Joel of Harriman, New York, met on the job at a geriatrics facility in 1973. They started dating and immediately clicked. Three months later, on April 21, they married. After more than 25 years of marriage, Linda says that making time for romance has been the key to maintaining their loving relationship.

Joel and I entered marriage sort of naive. Back then, we didn't fully grasp all the work and the time that it takes to nurture a relationship. Now, our marriage is something we work at every day.

Some days, working at our marriage is more difficult than others, particularly with our schedules. My husband is a musician who often performs at night, and I'm a nurse who prefers the day. It's not unusual for him to just be getting his third or fourth hour of sleep by the time I'm out of bed and ready to face the day.

Because of our schedules, romance is not something either one of us takes for granted. For both my husband and me, romance is equated with the time we spend together. It's not about material things like flowers or jewelry, but it is about being together and exchanging ideas with each other.

We spend lots of time sharing with each other because we know communication is an important process that we can't stop working at if we expect our marriage to last. It has been during those times that we haven't

making can lead to less interest in lovemaking, so it's important to shake it up, says Ruth Jacobowitz, trustee for the National Council on Women's Health, member of the Woman's Advisory Board at the University of California, San Diego, Women's Health Center, and author of *150 Most-Asked Questions about Midlife Sex, Love, and Intimacy.* "If you always do this and he always does that, there isn't much to excite you or make you want to do it again and again," she says. "Sex doesn't have to happen at 11:00 P.M. in bed. Try making love outside. Or do it in the laundry room. The variety will help bring the excitement of novel sexuality back into your relationship, and you'll want more."

communicated or we've communicated poorly that we've hit some rocky spots. And you know, for as long as we have been together, we're still learning from each other and still surprising each other with what we think and feel. I attribute that surprise to the constant change and growth we've had both in our lives and our relationship.

To keep our relationship fresh, my husband and I recently started weekly dates in which we alternate planning something that the other person has to go along with without complaint. That way, we both get to do what we want, and we aren't at odds with each other. For example, on one of our first dates, my husband took me out for Thai food. I don't care much for Thai food, but it was a new experience and both of us enjoyed the evening. It has been fun to try new things as well as things we've tried before and didn't think we liked. Your tastes definitely change over the years.

One other trick that keeps the romance intact for us is scheduling sex. We certainly do have spontaneous sexual activity on occasion, but for the most part, we make dates and appointments with each other. That way, neither party feels vulnerable to rejection. It's also kind of exciting because it's like an affair within our marriage.

Romance is very important to Joel and me. And although it's work, it's also so much fun that you forget you're actually working.

Check the baggage at the door. Sure, a leaky roof and berating boss can dampen your sexual spirits, says Richard Meth, Ph.D., director of the Humphrey Center for Marital and Family Therapy at the University of Connecticut in Storrs, but once you're an adult, there will always be one problem or another weighing on your mind. So unless you want to wait until the kids are gone and you're retired, you have to develop a knack for compartmentalizing, he says. "Mentally gather the things you're fretting about and stash them in the back of your mind, out of conscious thought, for the next hour. You can promise yourself you'll return to them later, if that helps. Then close the bedroom door—leaving those worries outside—and enjoy yourself. It takes a little practice. But it's well worth it."

Talk yourself into it. Many women talk themselves out of sex without even knowing it, says Gerald Weeks, Ph.D., director of the Institute of Sex Therapy at the Penn Council for Relationships in Philadelphia, a board-certified sex therapist, and author of 11 professional textbooks on sex and marital therapy. "People will say things to themselves like, 'It's been so long since we've had sex, why bother?' or 'I probably won't have an orgasm, anyway,' so they basically talk themselves out of it," says Dr. Weeks. Instead, he recommends countering your negative self-talk with positive self-talk. By saying things like, "My husband looks sexy tonight," or "Sex would feel good right now," you can talk yourself into a state of sexual desire, he says. "Thinking positively is counter to what many of us do, but it can work just as well—and yield better results—than thinking negatively."

Get back in touch. When couples first get together, they can't keep their hands off of each other, says marriage counselor Harry Croft, M.D., a psychiatrist and licensed sex therapist in San Antonio. And usually their touches and caresses lead to intercourse. "The problem is that the couple starts to think touches and caresses are a signal for intercourse, and they stop touching and stroking when they don't have time for sex or aren't in the mood," he says. Before they know it, they're not touching or having sex anymore, because touching wasn't just a signal for intercourse, it was what helped them want sex to begin with.

Touching doesn't just feel nice. It actually sends oxytocin (a compound that is so powerful that it's sometimes referred to as Cupid's arrow) coursing through your brain and reproductive system. Oxytocin encourages cuddling and is largely responsible for the contractions and pleasure of orgasm. "You feel relaxed and bonded with your lover after orgasm because your body is flooded with oxytocin," says Dr. Temple.

The take-home advice: "Touch each other as much as possible," says Dr. Croft. "It doesn't have to end in intercourse. But it will probably put you in the mood more often."

Find a fantasy. Fantasy and sex drive go hand in hand, says Dr. Bartlik. "Very sexually active women have lots and lots of fantasies, which in turn lead to more sex and, of course, more fantasies," she says. "Don't worry if your fantasies aren't about your husband. They can be about anyone or anything that makes you feel aroused. That's why they're fantasies."

If you need help fueling your erotic imagination, there are plenty of books of erotic stories on the market today that are written especially for women, says Dr. Weeks. "My *Secret Garden* is a classic book of both men's and women's fantasies. Try reading one or two stories a day to spark your fantasy life," he says.

Examine your meds. You can try every technique in the book and not see a lick of lift in your libido if you're taking a medication that dampens sex drive, says Dr. Bartlik. "Antidepressant medications often inhibit sexual desire and excitement," she says. "But so does depression, so you shouldn't stop taking your medication because your sex drive is low." Instead, she recommends talking with your doctor about improving the situation by changing your medication, reducing the dosage, or trying some "antidotes" like ginkgo biloba that may counteract the libido-dampening effects.

Laugh it up. Too often, we start taking life so seriously that we lose our senses of humor, says Domeena Renshaw, M.D., professor in the department of psychiatry and director of the Sexual Dysfunction Clinic at Loyola University of Chicago, and author of *Seven Weeks to Better Sex.* The same is true in our sex lives, she says. We get this idea that sex is supposed to have all the drama and passion that it does in the movies, and we're disappointed when it doesn't. This kind of pressure can dampen your sex drive. Instead, try sharing a good-natured laugh when things don't go as planned. "Humor relieves the 'Woe is me' syndrome," says Dr. Renshaw. "And it brings you closer together."

Sexual Needs

You wish he'd use more foreplay. You wish he'd take you more slowly. You need, really need, him to hold you after you've made love, not just kiss your cheek and switch off the bedside lamp.

Whatever you need, the question is, have you told him?

Even in the best of relationships, it can be hard to tell our guys what we want in bed. We may be shy about discussing sex, or think our partners should "just know." We may fear we'll hurt his pride. Or maybe we just haven't given our needs much thought—which isn't surprising, since many of us were raised to satisfy men's needs rather than our own.

But keeping silent "is like going to a restaurant and expecting to tell the waiter to guess what you want," says Michael Seiler, Ph.D., a certified sex therapist and associate director of the Chicago-based Phoenix Institute, which specializes in sexual and emotional intimacy problems.

Telling our partners what we need—and listening to what they need—bonds us more strongly, both in and out of the bedroom. It builds trust. It shows we care. It opens the door to all sorts of exciting possibilities. "Speaking up can be the beginning of a transformation in a relationship," says Gina Ogden, Ph.D., a certified sex therapist in Cambridge, Massachusetts, and author of *Women Who Love Sex*.

If telling your partner what you need can improve unsatisfying or so-so sex, ongoing discussions about your love life can make good sex extraordinary, says Barbara Levinson, Ph.D., a licensed marriage and family therapist and owner of the Center for Healthy Sexuality in Houston. "Your sexual needs evolve over time, so sexual communication should be ongoing," she says. The payoff is enormous and can enrich every aspect of your relationship.

What We Need: Emotional Safety

Our sexual needs are as unique as our fingerprints. But generally speaking, women want the whole package—sex that's deeply emotional *and* physically mind-blowing. Read on to decide if you're getting that package deal.

Sex with "soul." "Good sex is more than physical," says Dr. Ogden. Orgasms aren't enough; we need to feel loved and understood, and we need to feel special. That's why most of us enjoy cuddling and being stroked and caressed before sex. Loving gestures like these satisfy one of our deepest needs: to feel connected to the partner we love.

For the same reasons, many of us need this emotional closeness after we've made love—what sex therapists call afterplay. We've shared ourselves, body and soul, and we want to know that he was right there sharing with us.

Trust in our partner. Trust is the cornerstone of intimacy. When we trust, we open our hearts and allow our partners in, literally and figuratively. "Women are at their most vulnerable during sex," says Dr. Levinson. "They need to know that their partners care about them, not just the sex."

His and Hers Wish Lists

The exercise below can help couples start talking about their sexual needs, says Michael Seiler, Ph.D., a certified sex therapist and associate director of the Chicago-based Phoenix Institute, which specializes in sexual and emotional intimacy problems.

Get a notebook and tear out six pieces of paper—three for you, three for him. At the top of the first sheet, write "Things we do in bed now." At the top of the second, write "Things that we don't do in bed now that I would love to try." Label the third sheet "Things we don't do in bed now that I don't want to try, now or in the future." Repeat with the three remaining sheets.

Retreat to separate rooms to fill out each sheet. Rank each item from 1 to 10 (with 1 being the most enjoyable). Give yourself plenty of time, at least 30 minutes.

Make your lists as specific as possible, says Dr. Seiler. For example, on sheet two, don't write "I need more oral sex." Rather, write "Before we have intercourse, I need at least 10 minutes of oral sex, which would include stroking and kisses on my inner thighs."

When you're done, exchange lists. Note the similarities and the differences. You're bound to find some common ground—and a few surprises.

His to-do list might include activities that are on your never list, or vice versa. For example, if he wants you to perform oral sex and swallow his semen, and the very thought makes your heart sink, ask him if you could perform oral sex longer but not swallow, or stimulate him manually. "Negotiate, as you negotiate everything else in a relationship," says Gina Ogden, Ph.D., a certified sex therapist in Cambridge, Massachusetts, and author of *Women Who Love Sex.*

What if he refuses to play the game at all? To borrow a phrase from *Cool Hand Luke* (a film beloved by most men), what you've got here is a failure to communicate. A certified sex therapist is trained to help couples talk about such issues, says Dr. Seiler.

To feel emotionally safe, we need to feel physically safe. Men who are physically abusive destroy the possibility of intimacy. Many women have sex and even climax in such abusive relationships, says Dr. Levinson. But while their physical needs may be satisfied, their emotional ones are not.

Power. Not power over our partner, but "an inner power that fills us with energy," says Dr. Ogden. This power tells us that it's okay to ask for what we want; it allows us to experience pleasure, not just give it; it lets us be playful and spontaneous and bold between the sheets.

Women who feel this inner power are also able to speak up when there's a problem. "They're able to say, 'This is what I need. This is what I like,'" says Dr. Levinson.

What He Needs: Our Understanding

Men are less likely to wonder "Does she really love me?" than "Is my penis hard enough?" But men, too, need to feel desired and loved. "Many just don't know it," says Dr. Levinson. Here's what your partner would tell you if he could.

Your desire. An enthusiastic partner is the most potent aphrodisiac known to man—any man. "Men want their partners to be involved and aroused, because her arousal feeds his arousal," says Barry McCarthy, Ph.D., a psychologist and certified sex therapist in Washington, D.C., and coauthor with his wife, Emily, of *Male Sexual Awareness* and *Couple Sexual Awareness.* "This is especially true as a man ages and it becomes more difficult for him to get or maintain an erection."

If you tend to be the passive partner, initiate sex on a regular basis, says Dr. McCarthy. Taking the lead makes him feel desired and lets him be the pursued, rather than the pursuer. Most couples have a special "signal" that they use when they want to make love. If you don't have one, try these: Take a shower before bed. Put on a special nightgown on the nights you're feeling amorous. Once you're in bed, stroke his thigh under the covers. Your special signal should say, "I'm willing if you are." Don't worry: He'll catch on.

The option of saying "no." While we like knowing that our partners desire us, sometimes job pressures or sheer fatigue leaves us too wiped out for sex. And sometimes we'd just rather read.

Surprise: Men feel this way, too. Yet turning down an offer of sex is difficult for them, says Dr. McCarthy. "It's not manly to turn down sex," he says. Plus, your partner thinks it's his job to please you. So if you ask, he feels he must deliver. Right away.

Of course, this belief is so much silly male machismo. But he believes it. So if you initiate sex but he's too tired or preoccupied to accept, don't insist. Respect his feelings. Let him know that he may have to perform for his boss or his golfing buddies, but he doesn't have to perform for you.

Requests, not demands. Many men say they hate Valentine's Day because they feel their wives or girlfriends expect—no, demand—the flowers and candy. And demands make men resentful. If you issue sexual requests like a drill sergeant—"Stop that, now do this, a little to the left, hold it!"—he's more likely to feel like a trained seal than a lover. And such micromanaging of the sex act will only reinforce his idea that sex is performance art.

To get your needs met, "take a softer, gentler approach," says Dr. Levinson. Murmur into his ear, "I'd love it if you'd. . . ." Gently slide his fingers where you want them. Sigh with satisfaction when he does it right. Such enthusiastic appreciation will make him even more eager to please you.

Getting in Sexual Sync

Good sexual communication is honest, specific, and considerate of a partner's feelings. These guidelines can help you broach the subject, tell him what you need in bed, and focus on solutions, not blame.

Talk at the right time. No one wants to hear that the sparks aren't flying anymore. To broach such a delicate subject, you should both be relaxed—during a quiet walk, a weekend away, or just sitting in the living room with a glass of wine, says Dr. McCarthy. The worst time to talk sex is immediately after sex. "Especially after mediocre sex," he says. "You're just too vulnerable."

Be a sexual diplomat. Telling your partner that he's a lousy lover is not going to make him eager to please you. In fact, it will erode intimacy rather than enhance it. So rather than telling him what he's doing wrong, brainstorm with him about ways to make it right—even great. Try something like, "While I've felt a lot of pleasure, I haven't been having the kind of experience I'd really like to. I'd like to talk about ways that we could enjoy sex more," Dr. Seiler suggests.

If you're feeling angry or hurt, you may not feel like being all that considerate of his feelings. It's important to tell your partner how you're feeling, especially if you're angry, says Dr. Seiler. But the overall message should be that you love him and want to reach a solution together.

Deal with problems ASAP. Many of Dr. Levinson's patients wait for years before seeking help. By that time, this tiny seed of a problem has grown deep roots. "When a problem comes up, you need to talk about it immediately," says Dr. Levinson. You might say something like, "I might have seemed distant when we made love last night. I'd like to tell you why." Or, "You seemed a little preoccupied. Did you agree to sex just to please me?"

Cheer him on. We don't mean you have to wear a short skirt and carry pom-poms. (Unless you want to.) But the kind of cheerleading you should do all the time is the verbal kind. "If the sex was great, tell him so," says Dr. Levinson. "Tell him how close to him it made you feel. Sexual communication isn't just about criticism. You need to celebrate each other, too."

Sex with the Lights On

They say the eyes are the mirror to the soul. But they're also the gateway to our hearts, brains, and, frankly, our sex drives.

They don't call them bedroom eyes for nothing, says Helen Fisher, Ph.D., research associate at the Rutgers Center for Human Evolutionary Studies and an anthropologist at Rutgers University in New Brunswick, New Jersey, and author of *Anatomy of Love*. "The eye, not the heart, the genitals, or the brain, is the initial organ of romance," she says. "Eye contact has an immediate sexual effect. There's even a term for the arousing stare men and women engage in before sex: the copulatory gaze."

Our eyes not only spark our arousal but they can also fan the flames of passion, especially for men, adds Patricia Love, Ed.D., a licensed marriage and family therapist in Austin, Texas, and coauthor of *Hot Monogamy*. "Men are very sensitive to visual stimulation. The sight of his partner's body, the sight of their bodies joining, and the sight of her arousal are enormous turn-ons for most men."

Unfortunately, all these turn-ons can be turned off with the flick of a switch—a light switch, that is. And very often, women are doing the flicking, not because they don't like the way their husbands look, but because women tend to feel a lot more self-conscious about their bodies, says Nancy Gambescia, Ph.D., a marriage and family therapist in Bryn Mawr, Pennsylvania, who teaches at the Penn Council for Relationships in Philadelphia. "They worry about looking fat or undesirable," she explains.

In addition to short-circuiting some of their husbands' pleasure, complete darkness also prevents women from getting the most out of lovemaking, says Dr. Love. "Gazing into each other's eyes while making love is incredibly intimate and arousing. If the room is pitch-black, you miss out on that important connection."

Decent Exposure

The trick is to shed a little light on the situation without ending up feeling totally exposed. Here's what experts recommend.

Light a candle. You needn't make love under the blast of a 100-watt bulb for visual pleasure, says Dr. Love. "A single candle is often all you need to illuminate a room in a soft, sexy way that both men and women enjoy. Skin glows beautifully in candlelight."

See yourself through his eyes. Despite your insecurity, chances are your husband truly enjoys how you look, says Dr. Gambescia. Really. Even if you're carrying a few more pounds than you would like. In fact, in a *New Woman* and *Men's Health* magazine survey of 11,000 men, 60 percent said they would still find their mate sexy even if she gained 10 or 20 pounds.

Bask in his pleasure. Instead of worrying about yourself, try focusing on your partner's arousal, suggests Dr. Gambescia. "Women love to see their partners' sexual responses. Take advantage of the lighting to watch him

fascinating
FACTS

Sex in Rome: At Night, in the Dark, in Your Pajamas

In ancient Rome, proper citizens were not to have intercourse in a lighted room or before nightfall, and Roman women were not to fully disrobe for sex.

become aroused and enjoy you, and you'll find that you're enjoying yourself more, too."

Keep the fantasies rolling. To distract yourself from negative thoughts, find thoughts that are pleasurable to you, says Dr. Gambescia. "Fantasies can be about anyone or anything; just keep those sexual fantasies running."

Sex with Your Ex

They say that breaking up is hard to do. But finding someone new may be even harder. As we mature into adulthood, the pool of available men grows smaller. The fear of AIDS and other sexually transmitted diseases looms large. And, frankly, after developing a relationship history and sexual repertoire with one man, it's mighty hard to start over.

It's little wonder, then, that many women fall back into the arms of their exes once or twice after a separation or divorce. "Our bodies are complex; familiarity is relatively easy," says Patricia Love, Ed.D., a licensed marriage and family therapist in Austin, Texas, and coauthor of *Hot Monogamy*. "We spend years getting into a rhythm with one person, learning likes and dislikes. It takes a lot of time and energy to reestablish that with another person. Just the process of trying to find someone new can be exhausting."

The question is, even if sex with your ex-husband or former lover is comfortable and convenient, is it any good for you or the relationship?

Reality Check

You should ask yourself *why* you're having sex with a man you no longer want to live with, says Larry Hof, a certified marriage and family therapist, vice president of relationship consulting at Advanta Corporation, and a United Methodist minister in Spring House, Pennsylvania. "I believe that people should be free to choose what they do and with whom, but it sure helps you and the relationship if you know why you're doing it," he says.

Sex with your ex can be a way of prolonging the inevitable, denying reality, or, on a positive note, re-evaluating the breakup, says Hof, who has authored seven books on marriage and family. Here are a few things to consider before slipping back in the sack after you separate.

Grieve first. "Women who don't want to be divorced or separated may use sex as a way of denying the breakup," Hof says. Even if the woman initiated the divorce, separation is accompanied by grief and pain. Sex soothes the pain, at least temporarily. In these cases, sex can drag out the grieving process. So whether or not the separation was your idea, if you're feeling sad and confused, you should think twice before having a sexual encounter with your ex, Hof says.

Set boundaries. If you and your husband have made the decision to divorce, having sex can really cloud the boundaries of the separation, says Hof. "Before you do it, you should both establish clear boundaries. You have to agree on what the sex means. Does it mean you'll talk on the phone afterward? Does it mean you're open to making other concessions? Or is it just one more passionate fling? Decide first, then proceed or not," he cautions.

Look at both sides. Having sex can really hurt if one of the partners doesn't agree with the separation, says Hof. "If you know that your husband doesn't want to break up and you do, having sex with him after the split isn't an act of kindness. It will only hurt him more. You need to consider the impact of the act on his feelings as well as yours," he says.

Test the waters. It's not impossible to reunite, or even remarry, after a split. Heck, Liz Taylor married Richard Burton twice, and she had plenty of men to pick from. "Sex can be one way for couples who still have strong feelings for each other to test the waters," says Hof. "It lets them see if some of that old flame and chemistry can be revived. That's okay. Just take it slow and communicate. Sometimes good sex means that there can be a good relationship. And sometimes it's just good sex."

Turn-Ons
and Turnoffs

It will come as no surprise that many men find women's breasts a turn-on. But what may surprise you is that Mother Nature planned it that way.

"Take a look around," suggests William F. Fitzgerald, Ph.D., who specializes in marital and sexual therapy at the Silicon Valley Relationship and Sexuality Center in Santa Clara, California. "Human women are the only animals who have permanently swollen mammary glands. Prominent breasts are there not to feed babies—they get even *bigger* then—but to act as a sexual signal to men that the woman is fertile. Men are preprogrammed to be turned on by women who look like they are capable of bearing children."

"Women, in turn, are attracted by attributes that show a man can be a good protector and provider," says Dr. Fitzgerald. "Even though women don't necessarily need those attributes anymore, they're still affected by thousands of years of genetic conditioning. That's why women are often attracted to high-priced cars and designer clothes—they symbolize a man who can provide. But straight white teeth, nice breath, and washboard abdominal muscles also broadcast that he is a good provider—they show that he takes care of himself and has some 'caretaking' left over."

For men and women alike, the conditioning kicks in pretty early in life, explains Dr. Fitzgerald. "Everything we come to associate with sexual pleasure, from music to hair color to fragrances, all becomes part of what is called our love map," he says.

By adulthood, you have developed a pretty clear picture of what works for you, says Dr. Fitzgerald. "The idea is that you'll be able to put all the thousands of men and women you meet through this finely tuned filter of your likes and dislikes and come out with a small pool of acceptable candidates for mating."

If you're interested in resparking your interest in your mate—or decoding what you find sexy in a potential mate—here's where to look.

His Body

Women don't tend to get as turned on by looking at men's genitals as men do by looking at women's, but they do, in fact, enjoy checking out other parts of his anatomy. In a *Men's Health* and *New Woman* magazine survey of more than 2,600 women, almost one-third of the women confessed to eyeing their man's butt. More than one-quarter enjoyed his chest. And an equal number found pleasure in his face.

"A man's more rugged, muscular features are a natural turn-on for women," says Dr. Fitzgerald, "because they show that he's equipped to fight off mastodons, if need be. Nice features and, surprisingly, the most symmetrical face also mean that he'll most likely sire attractive children."

Of course, your bodies will change over the years, but when we love each other, we tend to remain focused on the positive, says Barbara D. Bartlik, M.D., clinical assistant professor in the department of psychiatry at Weill Medical College of Cornell University, and assistant attending psychiatrist at the New York Presbyterian Hospital, both in New York City. "The real problem is that after years of looking at the same person, you sometimes don't notice him like you used to," she says.

Turn-on tip: Take a step back and check your husband out. You may be pleasantly surprised by what you see.

His Clothes

Nothing says "man" like a pair of snug boxer briefs. Or at least that's what the more than 2,600 women surveyed by *Men's Health* and *New Woman* magazines said. About 37 percent reported being turned on by men in these sexy skivvies. Of course, women enjoy outerwear as much as underwear. Blue jeans and white T-shirts are popular turn-ons, as are sunglasses and work boots.

"Men wear plumage for the same reason women do—to attract the opposite sex," says Dr. Fitzgerald. "When he wears clothes that women find particularly masculine, he's saying, 'I can take care of myself . . . and I can take care of you.' Women are naturally turned on by that."

Once men are in committed relationships, they may get slack about keeping their plumage fresh, admits Dr. Fitzgerald.

(continued on page 138)

What Makes Your Motor Run?

An informal poll of men and women asked what turned them on (and off). There were some surprising similarities between the answers of the men and the women—and some interesting contrasts and contradictions. See for yourself, and note well.

Her Body

Turn-ons for men: Well-toned; lots of curves; firm breasts; nice legs; tight butt; friendly smile; cleanliness; long, nicely groomed, or naturally styled hair

Turn-offs for men: Too skinny; underarm or leg hair; tattoos; too much makeup, especially blush; strong perfume; excessively dyed, bleached hair; too much hair spray; a tight, frizzy perm

Her Clothes

Turn-ons for men: Slinky or feminine clothes (especially dresses) with lace and ruffles; short skirts; lingerie from Victoria's Secret; thigh-high stockings; garter belt and thin, lacy bra; jeans and a T-shirt; baseball cap (especially with ponytail hanging from the back); my white dress shirt; waitress uniform; high heels; practical shoes so she can walk anywhere

Turn-offs for men: Tent dresses; nightgowns from a store that also sells garden tools; anything flannel; her ex-boyfriend's sweatshirt; the go-go dancer, barmaid, or hooker look; Birkenstock sandals

Her Behavior and Attitude

Turn-ons for men: Self-confident, optimistic, likes herself and life; smiles at him (often, any time); genuinely likes (or at least tolerates) the Three Stooges, ESPN, war movies, all sports, horror movies, and James Bond; acts feminine; caring, family-focused; classy to guy friends; affectionate; tells me what she likes about me; adventurous, open-minded, fun-loving, willing to try new things; responsive to touch

Turn-offs for men: Demanding, nagging; uses crude language; lives for craft fairs; acts like "one of the guys"; loud, hot-tempered, makes scenes, talks too much; comes on to other men; talks about ex, or men she likes, or men she doesn't like; arrogant; tells everything she doesn't like about me; smokes; drinks too much; gives oral sex grudgingly

Preambles to Sex

Turn-ons for men: Breathing; full-body massage; showering together; romantic dinner together; willing to forgo foreplay

Turn-offs for men: Reading romantic poetry; watching a "chick flick"; never initiates sex; only willing to have sex in the bedroom, on the bed, in the dark

His Body

Turn-ons for women: Good pecs and abs; good shoulders; good grooming; nice teeth; dimples; great haircut; good posture

Turn-offs for women: Dirty or long fingernails; too many tattoos; too much cologne; food in his beard; the big comb-over

His Clothes

Turn-ons for women: Boxer shorts (especially silk); jeans and a sport jacket; white shirts; work boots; leather bomber jacket

Turn-offs for women: Speedo swimsuit; T-shirts with slogans like "Coed Naked Volleyball"; rock concert T-shirts on guys over 30

His Behavior and Attitude

Turn-ons for women: Nice to your parents; nice to children; gives small gifts for no reason at all; nice to animals; tells good jokes; witty banter

Turn-offs for women: Bad table manners; a bad tipper; over machismo; self-centered; drinks too much; tells disgusting jokes; checks himself out when passing a mirror; talking on the phone in the bathroom

Preambles to Sex

Turn-ons for women: Massage; showering together; working out together

Turn-offs for women: Cuts his toenails; flosses his teeth

Turn-on tip: Buy your husband some jeans or boxers you would like to see him in. Don't wait for his birthday or Christmas. Just give them to him for no apparent reason and say, "I just think you'd look so sexy in these," suggests Dr. Fitzgerald. You can be sure he'll wear them.

His Softer Side

Men with babies. Men with puppies. Men who come home bearing flowers. Women seem to love them all. As much as we're turned on by all those masculine attributes, we're often equally aroused by a man's softer side.

"Little acts of kindness and gentle attributes and behaviors turn women on because they show a man who isn't a slam-bam-thank-you-ma'am kind of guy," says Dr. Fitzgerald. "If he has a sweet side, he definitely seems more likely to stick around."

Turn-on tip: Your man hasn't come home with flowers recently? Then bring something home for him, suggests Dr. Bartlik. If you start showing more spontaneous affection toward him, he'll likely respond in kind. You can also get a glimpse of his softer side by watching him play with your children or pets.

The Stuff He Flaunts

Chances are when you and your husband were dating, there was something he had that you thought was pretty cool. Maybe he drove a convertible. Maybe he had a beautiful leather bomber jacket. In every relationship, there's usually a little status symbol that the woman notices and likes.

"Fast cars, big trucks, motorcycles, state-of-the-art stereo systems, and practically anything else that men find impressive are also their way of saying to women, 'I've got the goods,'" says Dr. Fitzgerald. "Of course, he has to have the goods you want."

Once you have the guy and his goods, though, it's easy to take them for granted and stop noticing them, says Dr. Fitzgerald. "Good marriages are like good friendships. You don't stop noticing the things the other person finds special."

Turn-on advice: Pay some renewed attention to what your husband takes pride in. Chances are he'd still like to show off for you, says Dr. Fitzgerald. His excitement may prove infectious.

"Your Song"

Whether it's romantic ballads, tender love songs, or cool, sexy jazz, music is part of almost every woman's love map, according to Dr. Fitzgerald.

"Your first dance obviously makes a big sexual connection with music," says Dr. Fitzgerald. "But it starts way before that. Movies, soap operas, commercials, and TV shows all play music to accompany their sex scenes. It's a natural connection."

Turn-on tip: This one's a breeze, says Dr. Bartlik. "Take the time to light some candles and put some sexy music on the CD player." Some of her suggestions for lifting your libido: Miles Davis's *Kind of Blue* and Sarah McLachlan's *Fumbling towards Ecstasy*.

Your Bedroom

They don't call it a love nest for nothing. Often your surroundings have as much of an effect on how turned on you are as the man you're with, according to Dr. Bartlik. "Women, like men, are turned on by sexy settings. Low lights, a big bed, massage oils on the nightstand—all of these things can be a big turn-on."

There's no mystery here, says Dr. Fitzgerald. "There are certain things, like candlelight and big brass beds with lots of pillows, that we learn to clearly associate with sex," he says. "A big cozy bed also makes us feel safe and comfortable, which is a plus for mating."

Turn-on tip: Re-feather your love nest. If you haven't bought new bedding in ages, you probably don't even notice what you have anymore. Invest in some sexy sheets and comforters. They'll pay off.

When Your Man Turns You Off

So much for what turns you on. What if something about your man turns you off?

"Chances are there's something you can do about it," says Dr. Fitzgerald. "If there was something about your husband that turned you off from the get go, you wouldn't be with him. But if he has just developed a trait or habit that you find a turnoff, you can probably change that."

Topping the list of things that women say squelch their flames are poor hygiene, self-absorption, and overdependence. They aren't terribly fond of poor table manners or guys who don't do their fair share of the housework, either.

"No man is perfect," acknowledges Judy Kuriansky, Ph.D., of the Center for Marital and Family Therapy in New York City, host of the syndicated call-in advice radio show *LovePhones*, and author of *The Complete Idiot's Guide to a Healthy Relationship*. "But there are ways to make those turnoffs less bothersome."

First, try the time-honored technique of making lists, suggests Dr. Kuriansky. "List all the things about your husband (or a prospective mate) that you like, or that turn you on, on one side of a page, and the things that turn you off on the other side. Then review these lists like a balance sheet. If the majority of his traits are favorable, ask yourself how important those few things are that you listed as unfavorable."

What if you really, really hate that he has taken up smoking cigars in the house (or some other objectionable habit)? "Let him know how important it is to you that he hear your request. Let him discuss his feelings," Dr. Kuriansky says. Talk to him about change in a nonaccusatory way. "Offer to alter a behavior of your own that you know drives him nuts if he agrees to alter one of his," she suggests. "Keep a positive spirit about it. Remember that relationships are a give and take."

Virginity

By the time women reach the quarter-century mark, 97 percent have kissed their virginity goodbye . . . at least for the time being. True, we never really get our virginity back. But lots of women *do* go through a kind of "second virginity" later in life, when a broken marriage or loss of a spouse leaves them without a partner, sometimes for years. Surveys show that almost one-third of women over 50 haven't had sex in the past year. The same is true for 15 percent of women over 40. For many of them, the next time really can feel like the first time.

"People used to believe that the hymen (a membrane that partially obstructs the vaginal opening) grew back if you didn't have sex for a few years," says Louanne Cole Weston, Ph.D., a marriage and sex therapist in San Francisco and Sacramento. "It doesn't. But if you haven't had sex in more than a year, the lack of stretching can make your vagina feel tighter than usual. And if you're approaching menopause, your vaginal walls may be thinner, too. So when you try to insert a penis, well, it may feel odd and uncomfortable, very much like the first time you had sex."

And that's only the physical aspect. "Emotionally, some women may have a lot of anxiety about having sex with someone new after a long hiatus," says Dr. Weston. "Some women are concerned because they haven't had many sexual partners, so they're really not sure what to expect. Women also are more likely than men to let bad body image hurt their self-confidence."

Back at the Starting Line

Whether it's your first time ever or your first time in a long time, experts offer the following advice to help make the experience mutually satisfying.

Wait for the right guy — and the right time. As tempting as it may be, resist the urge to leap into bed with the first guy who stirs your loins, says Dr. Weston. "Having sex again after a long dry spell may create all kinds of anxieties. Women often don't know what to expect from a new man. They may have body image worries. It may be quite stressful. Waiting to find someone you really like and then taking the time to really get to know him can ease those fears. It also lessens the likelihood that you'll regret having done it afterward."

Pick your favorite spot. You want to be as comfortable as possible for your first time, says Sari Locker, a certified relationship and sexuality educator, relationship correspondent on CBS television News 2 in New York City, and author of *Mindblowing Sex in the Real World*. "Some women are more comfortable in their own homes or apartments. Others feel more awkward there because it may be the last place they had sex with their husbands. For your first time, pick the location where you can feel the most relaxed and uninhibited, even if it means going away to a bed-and-breakfast for the night."

Calm down while you gear up. Having sex with someone new can be both exciting and nerve-wracking. The former can make the experience great, the latter . . . well, not so great, because too much anxiety can hamper your enjoyment of the event and lessen your chance of having an orgasm, says Nancy Gambescia, Ph.D., a marriage and family therapist in Bryn Mawr, Pennsylvania, who teaches at the Penn Council for Relationships in Philadelphia. Though there's no way you can expect to be cucumber-cool during your first sexual encounter, you can calm your nerves enough to enjoy the experience, she says. "Instead of racing full speed ahead to get to intercourse, take the time during foreplay to really connect. Stroke each other's arms and legs. Rub his back. Take deep, sensuous breaths. By taking your time focusing on foreplay, you will find a rhythm with each other and you'll both begin to relax."

While some people like to take the edge off with a glass of wine or a cocktail before sex, you're best off stopping at one drink, especially the first time with someone new, says Locker. "You're so nervous that it's really easy to overdo it. You want your first time to be memorable, not clouded by alcohol. And you certainly don't want to drink so much that you feel embarrassed afterward."

Do everything but. Take your time and evolve into intercourse gradually, suggests Locker. "Have dates where all you do is kiss. Then have dates where you kiss and touch. Give each other orgasms without having intercourse," she says. "The first time is always better if you've already done 'everything but' at least once or twice, because you're much more comfortable being naked with him and you're readier for that next level of intimacy."

Be prepared. Today, sex with a new partner means taking precautions to protect your sexual health, says Locker. So don't forget to have condoms on hand. "If this is your first time having sex outside a long-term relationship in a long time, introducing the subject of condoms is definitely going to feel awkward," she says. "But don't be shy about it. Have a couple of condoms somewhere close to the bed. And if he doesn't bring his own out first, just say, 'Let me get some protection for us,' and bring out your own. In this age of sexually transmitted diseases, nobody is surprised by condoms. In fact, it's expected that either the man or the woman will have protection for both pregnancy and disease."

Unless both people have been tested for all sexually transmitted diseases and they are both certain that this new relationship is monogamous, a condom should always be used, cautions Dr. Weston. For more details, see Contraception on page 298 and Sexually Transmitted Diseases on page 434.

Enjoy yourself with or without orgasm. When it comes to sheer sexual ecstasy, first times are rarely best times, reminds Dr. Weston. "Great sex takes practice and experience. It's not something you usually achieve the first time with a new partner. New partners may touch you and stimulate you differently than you're accustomed to. It may even take a couple of times until you reach orgasm," she says. "But that's okay. It's more important that you enjoy exploring and learning about each other. Once you do, the orgasms will follow."

PART THREE

Extraordinary Romance

Adventure

A few years ago, at age 49, Susan Agnew and her 55-year-old husband, Hewes, got on their tandem bicycle in Florence, Oregon, and started pedaling.

Before they began their journey—a cross-country ride on the Trans-American Bicycling Trail—the couple, then of Billings, Montana, dipped their front wheel into the Pacific Ocean, a tradition among bicyclists who take the Trail. Biking 70 miles a day, carrying 80 pounds of gear, they pedaled through Oregon, up the Idaho panhandle, and along the Continental Divide through Montana, Wyoming, and Colorado. They pedaled through Kansas, Missouri, the bottom of Illinois, all the way across Kentucky, and into Virginia.

They stopped pedaling some 4,000 miles later, in Yorktown, Virginia, where they dipped their back wheel into the Atlantic Ocean.

For the past 20 years, Susan and her husband, who is director of cardio-vascular surgical services at Pennsylvania Hospital in Philadelphia, have racked up plenty of miles—and adventure—on their bicycle built for two. They've met interesting people and savored breathtaking views. They've also tested themselves and each other. They have waited out thunderstorms in ditches, changed countless flat tires, been filthy and miles from running water, and occasionally squabbled while they pedaled.

With every mile, they've learned problem-solving, communication, and teamwork skills. Just as important, they have had fun. Together. "Our lives together have been enriched because we were able to say, 'Hey, that looks like fun. Let's do it,'" says Hewes.

Such is the essence of adventure.

Break the Boredom Barrier

Every new couple embarks on the ultimate adventure—falling in love. But as the years pass, so do new love's freshness and romance. We know our partners well—at times, too well. Our routines have solidified like concrete. No shake-ups, no surprises. As the song goes, the thrill is gone.

But it doesn't have to be. Couples who search out new experiences, challenges, and interests—in a word, adventure—inject their relationships with new energy. "Pushing past your comfort level as a couple to do something you never thought you'd do can be incredibly stimulating to a relationship," says Michael Perry, Ph.D., a marriage and sex therapist in Encino, California.

And you don't have to travel to the ends of the Earth or blow your individual retirement account to find adventure. Whether you attend the opera in Toledo, Ohio, or learn Italian in Tuscany, go whale-watching off Martha's Vineyard or spelunking in Minnesota, regular doses of adventure do a couple good, says Dr. Perry. Adventure stimulates your brains, tests your muscles, gets you working as a team. As a bonus, you develop a store of memories of your life together.

While local adventures add spice to everyday life, you and your partner might also consider planning and saving for a special trip, the way the Agnews did. You might have it coincide with the year of a milestone anniversary. It's a nice way to show that now, as then, you're on this journey together.

A Primer for New Adventurers

Adventures come in all shapes, sizes, and price tags. The suggestions below can give you an idea of the possibilities and reignite your spirit of adventure. Before the two of you take off for Borneo, however, write for brochures, catalogs, and schedules of events and then pore through them together. These "armchair adventures" will give you a feel for each other's adventure threshold. A smart couple knows whether a week of cave-diving in Malaysia would be a fantasy fulfilled or a nightmare come true—*before* they buy their plane tickets.

Ride the rapids. Ken Streater, president of Destination Wilderness, a venture based in Sisters, Oregon, that puts together rafting, sea kayaking, and other outdoor adventure trips, sees firsthand how a physical challenge can bring out the best in couples. "I've seen people fall in love on river trips and get married, and married people jump out of a raft to save their partners," says the experienced whitewater rafter.

Along with danger and dirt come opportunities for romance. "Sleeping in a tent in the middle of nowhere has a romantic quality to it," says Streater.

Adventure in the Extreme

Not every couple wants to climb mountains, trek through caves, or track tornadoes. But those who do have lots of opportunities for such "extreme" adventures. If you and your partner decide to really shake things up, consider the adventures below. They're expensive, but virtually guaranteed to get your adrenaline pumping.

Australian camel safaris. Travel by camel, cook by campfire, and sleep under the stars deep in the Australian outback. Contact: Australian Tourist Commission, 2049 Century Park East, Suite 1920, Los Angeles, CA 90067-3121.

Storm-chasing tours. Professional storm-chasers (like in the film *Twister*) will move you from storm to storm during tornado season, from Texas to North Dakota, the Rockies to Indiana. Contact: Storm-Chasing Adventure Tours, 7591 Halley's Drive, Littleton, CO 80125.

Field research. Organizations such as Earthwatch and the Smithsonian Institute sponsor a wide variety of programs. Work on scientific research projects in archaeology, endangered species, rain forests, and more. Contact: Earthwatch, 680 Mount Auburn Street, Watertown, MA 02471 or Smithsonian Institute, 1100 Jefferson Drive SW, Washington, DC 20560-0702.

Rock climbing. The Colorado Mountain School (CMS), a climbing school located in Rocky Mountain National Park, offers climbing lessons for beginners as well as rock-climbing vacations. Contact: CMS, P. O. Box 2062, Estes Park, CO 80517.

"Overcoming challenges with your partner can bring you closer together, too. There's an element of feeling successful as a team."

Climb the highest mountain. If you're short on money or time, spend a day hiking in the nearest national or state park. "These days, couples are all so rushed that it seems like we have less and less time to spend together," says Pam Gluck, executive director of American Trails, a national trails advocacy organization in Prescott, Arizona. Hiking is as good for your relationship as it is for your cardiovascular system. "My husband and I hike together almost every day," says Gluck. "That's our time to catch up with each other and to enjoy each other in a nonstressful situation. It's precious to us."

Sail away together. If you'd rather explore water than land, learn to sail. "We've had couples who have gone through our sailing school, gotten their licenses, bought a boat, and taken off," says Jim Schwobel, owner of the Corpus Christi Sailing Center in Corpus Christi, Texas. "Sailing is both romantic and an adventure."

Couples learn more than how to pilot a boat, though. They learn to solve problems and work as a team. "In my view, the best barometer for the strength of a relationship is to face adversity together," says Schwobel.

Adventure also helps a couple grow together, which is a vital part of maintaining a dynamic relationship. "It's important to take yourself out of your comfort zone," says Schwobel. "When you leave the house and go down the road, you get to strip away all the things in your life that constrict not only your time but sometimes also your thoughts. It's fun to go down roads you haven't been down before." And if you can do it with the person you love, says Schwobel, so much the better.

Go back to school. The most intimate couples find and nurture common interests. One way to do this is to take what's called a learning vacation, in which you learn a particular skill. Some travel agencies and many resorts offer learning vacations. If you and your partner enjoy cooking as a team, for example, you might enroll at a weeklong cooking school. "We get a lot of couples who love to cook together and want to develop their skills," says Riki Senn, coordinator of the cooking school at La Varenne at the Greenbrier, a resort in White Sulphur Springs, West Virginia.

Or if you both enjoy working with your hands, consider a vacation at a crafts school, such as the John C. Campbell Folk School in Brasstown, North Carolina. Among the courses offered are jewelry making, quilting, basketry, calligraphy, pottery, blacksmithing, and woodworking. To find other types of learning vacations, check out your local bookstore for ShawGuides, which publishes guides to learning vacations such as recreational cooking, golf camps, writers' conferences, language vacations, and educational travel. For more information, write to ShawGuides, P. O. Box 1295, Ansonia Station, New York, NY 10023.

Allure

B y most accounts, Cleopatra was no raving beauty. But by every account, she was alluring.

She knew the power of a dramatic entrance, wrapping herself in a rug and delivering herself—on the shoulder of a servant—to Julius Caesar, who later became her lover. She had Mark Antony, another powerful man of the day, wound around her bejeweled little finger; he was reportedly so smitten that he rubbed her feet at a banquet.

As Cleo undoubtedly knew, allure is a mysterious quality. It encompasses beauty but isn't defined by it. It can be enhanced by clothing and cosmetics, but it can't be captured by them. Allure is a web spun of charm, mystery, fascination, enticement, magic. An alluring woman glows from within and throws light like a flame.

If you've been with the same man for years, you may think it's impossible to get that magic back. The thought may even make you smile. Me? Alluring to the man I've shared a bathroom with for years? Yes and yes. Because allure isn't just a way to get a partner. It's a way to keep one.

"Making an effort to look attractive to your partner is a sign of respect," says Carol Rinkleib Ellison, Ph.D., a clinical psychologist and sex researcher in Oakland, California. "It says, 'You're important to me.'" That said, allure is most powerful when it's generated from within.

"Wearing lingerie or a low-cut dress isn't enough," says Michael Perry, Ph.D., a marriage and sex therapist in Encino, California.

The key, then, to allure? Spruce up your outside—and cultivate your Inner Cleopatra.

Outward Allure

When you're trying to capture a quality as elusive as allure, the simplest changes are often the most dramatic, says Judith Ann Graham, vice president of the Association of Image Consultants International in Washington, D.C. (Graham's clients include many types of men and women who want to be more attractive, not just executives.) Here's her advice.

Sensational Scents

Perfume has addled men's heads for centuries, and Cleopatra was one of the first women to capitalize on it. The ship upon which she entertained her Roman lover, Mark Antony, was rigged with perfumed sails, her throne ringed with incense burners, her diaphanous gowns drenched with perfume. And her bedroom was knee-deep in fragrant rose petals.

Cleo was going on intuition alone. But modern research into fragrance and pheromones—odorless chemical signals that trigger sexual interest—shows that scent evokes a primal reaction from others. "Perfumes have been used for centuries to elicit sexual arousal," says Alan R. Hirsch, M.D., director of the Smell and Taste Treatment and Research Foundation in Chicago. To select an alluring fragrance and maximize its effect, try these tips.

Reach for lavender or musk. According to a study by Dr. Hirsch, the blood flow to men's penises—an indicator of sexual arousal—increased by 40 percent when they smelled the scent of lavender. (Men also responded to the scent of pumpkin pie, doughnuts, and black licorice, but you're unlikely to find a fragrance that contains these aromas.)

According to Annette Green, president of the Fragrance Foundation in

Apply some lipstick. "Lipstick lights up your face," says Graham. You don't have to go for vixen-red lips (unless you want to). Cool colors, such as cranberry or raspberry, look best on fair or ruddy skin; warm colors, such as brick or coral, on darker skin.

Update your 'do. Many women wear the same hairstyle for decades, says Graham. "Big mistake." But you don't want to entrust just any stylist with your new look. Select a salon with a well-established clientele and a reputation for being trendy, she advises. Once you find the right salon, select the right stylist. "Look for a stylist who's around your age and has an attractive, updated look," says Graham.

Sexier hairstyles are tousled, with lots of volume. But your style should also allow your man to run his fingers through your hair. "It should require a minimum of upkeep, and not too much mousse, spray, or gel," says Kate Weil, a professional image consultant in New York City.

New York City, men also like the smell of musk. But they dislike strong floral fragrances: "Men think they're too sweet and cloying."

Stay inside your circle. Some men hate heavy perfume. If your guy is one of them, use fragrance sparingly. "Your 'scent circle' is approximately an arm's length from your body," says Green. "He shouldn't notice your fragrance unless he steps into your circle."

Start from the ground up. "Fragrance rises," says Green. So spray or smooth scent onto your skin from your feet to your shoulders. If you apply it only behind your ears, it will quickly rise and dissipate.

Gear scent to your skin type. If your skin is dry, reapply fragrance every three to four hours, says Green. If your skin is oily, you only need to apply it every four to six hours because fragrance lasts longer and smells more intense on oily skin.

Perfume your pulse points. You've probably heard that you're supposed to apply perfume to pulse points behind the ears or inner wrists. But don't overlook less obvious pulse points, says Green. These include your inner ankles, the crooks of your elbows, and behind your knees.

Ignore the scale. Just because you might be carrying a few more pounds than you'd like doesn't necessarily mean you're less alluring, says Weil. You just have to flatter your proportions. If you have larger hips, for example, balance your silhouette with shoulder pads. Avoid skirts and pants with pleats, and dress in one color to create a slimming effect. For a casual but attractive everyday look, pair a pretty tunic top with solid-color leggings.

Favor jeans over sweatpants. According to one survey, 19 percent of men surveyed consider a T-shirt and jeans among the sexiest outfits a woman can wear—coming in a solid third just behind lingerie (28 percent) and evening gowns (22 percent). Graham says jeans are most alluring when paired with boots or low-heeled shoes.

If that's not your style, look to the past—your past—for inspiration. "If your partner loved the way you dressed when you first met, recapture the feeling of the style, if not the style itself," says Graham. Whatever you do, skip the sweatpants. "They might be comfortable, but they're definitely not alluring," she says.

Flaunt your assets. The greatest beauty secret of all: Work with what you have—and then work it, says Graham. If you've always been told that you have beautiful hands, treat yourself to a weekly manicure and call attention to your hands with beautiful rings. If he has always loved your breasts, accentuate them with exquisite brassieres and scoop-neck shirts and sweaters. Great calves and tiny ankles? Pull out your pumps and—if you dare—don shimmering or lacy hose.

Perfect your posture. You'll look five pounds thinner and give your bustline an instant boost if you sit and stand straight, says Graham. To find out if you're slumping, take this posture test: Place your fist in the small of your back, at the top of your waistline. If you feel bone, you're slouching, says Graham. "If your fist kind of curves into your spine, you're sitting straight."

Inward Allure

While you're working on your outside, take a look at your inside, says Dr. Perry. Not sure what inner allure is? Neither are men, "but they know it when they sense it," he says. Think subtlety, unpredictability, a dash of mystery. Here's what experts say can enhance your inner allure.

Really notice him. In a man's eyes, the most alluring woman is the one who shows she cares about him, says Dr. Perry. So if you've been less than attentive lately, ask him about the new widget he's developing at work—and listen, really listen, to his answer. Kiss the top of his head on your way to the kitchen. Give him the attention you'd give your mother, your child, your dog. "This kind of allure has less to do with wearing lingerie, although lingerie can be interesting," says Dr. Perry. "It has more to do with giving him your attention—having a look in your eye that says you want him, you love him, you want to be with him."

Surprise him. "Being unpredictable and doing the unexpected is alluring," says Dr. Perry. So speed him off to that new Thai restaurant you've discovered. (Or any cuisine out of the ordinary for the two of you.) On the first day of summer, pack a picnic dinner and celebrate in the park. Instigate a pillow fight before bed—and some impromptu lovemaking afterward.

Cultivate yourself. The most alluring folks cultivate interests outside of those they share with their partners, says Dr. Perry. "I don't care how connected you are to your partner, you occasionally need some time alone," he says. It makes you a more interesting person to your mate and everyone else. As a bonus, taking some time away from your partner to pursue your own interests "can be really exciting because when you get back together—even if you've only been apart a few hours—you're new to each other again," he explains.

Aphrodisiacs

Ask a woman who has been hand-fed plump, perfect, luscious strawberries if she believes in the aphrodisiac powers of food, and you're likely to get an enthusiastic *Yes!* But ask a scientist about aphrodisiacs, and she will probably roll her eyes.

Indeed, there's no scientific proof that aphrodisiacs—substances purported to increase sexual desire—do any such thing. But over the course of history, food has always been linked with love. Casanova had oysters; Mrs. Waters, the wanton woman in the novel *Tom Jones,* had pears; Lady and the Tramp had spaghetti and meatballs. Virtually every culture associates sharing food with intimacy, says George Armelagos, Ph.D., professor of anthropology at Emory University in Atlanta and coauthor of the book *Consuming Passions.* And virtually every food has at one time or another been considered an aphrodisiac. But certain foods, such as oysters, figs, chocolate, asparagus, and peppers, have long been reputed to send the sex drive into high gear.

"Aphrodisiac foods heighten or awaken your senses," says Martha Hopkins, coauthor of *InterCourses: An Aphrodisiac Cookbook.* "Take honey. The way it looks, the way it tastes, the way it feels on your tongue. It's sticky. It's drippy. It's sex."

Cooking with Fire

Want to use food to woo the one you love? Let Hopkins's suggestions, and your own creativity, be your guide.

Give a fig. Figs are a very sensual fruit; in fact, the ancient Greeks ate them at their orgies. "You might just slice open a fresh fig, put it on a pretty plate, and hand-feed it to your partner," suggests Hopkins. The sensual aspects of the food do the seducing for you. It's practically guaranteed to work.

Create the right setting. How you serve food is as important as what you serve. "You can't sit under fluorescent lighting, using paper plates, and

---

What Makes Food Sexy?

When it comes to aphrodisiacs, folklore abounds. Yet some foods that have been used traditionally as aphrodisiacs are rich in substances the body needs to function at its sexual peak, says Cynthia Mervis Watson, M.D., in her book *Love Potions: A Guide to Aphrodisiacs and Sexual Pleasures*. Consider:

Asparagus. According to medieval lore, boiling and eating this light-green, slender stalk three days in a row will stir "bodily luste" in both men and women. Aside from the obvious phallic implications, practitioners of Chinese medicine consider asparagus a tonic for the kidneys. According to Chinese medicine, it is the kidneys that regulate the libido, suggesting that what is good for the kidneys is good for the bedroom.

Chocolate. The Aztec emperor Montezuma drank 50 glasses of honey-sweetened chocolate a day to sustain his virility. Chocolate is rich in the amino acid phenylalanine, which increases the brain's level of the neuropeptide phenylethylamine (PEA), a natural amphetamine-like stimulant that may increase the urge to have sex.

Figs. The ancient Greeks and Romans ate them before every orgy. They contain magnesium, a mineral needed to produce sex hormones.

Honey. The word *honeymoon* was coined in ancient Europe, where newlyweds built up their sexual stamina with mead—honey wine—during the first month of their marriage. Honey provides the body with an easily digested and absorbed source of energy.

Oysters. These shellfish are rich in the mineral zinc, a key ingredient to testosterone production and, hence, sexual performance for both men and women. Zinc is also found in foods not frequently associated with aphrodisiacs such as legumes, pumpkin and sunflower seeds, garlic, and spinach.

expect an aphrodisiac to work," says Hopkins. So dim the lights. Use beautiful linens and your best china and silverware. And eat in bed, if possible. "Also, if you drink, a nice wine helps things along," she adds.

Match the aphrodisiac to the moment. "Love isn't hot and sexy all the time," says Hopkins. "Sometimes love is comforting and sweet." Aphrodisiacs are the same way. "A mug of hot chocolate can be an aphrodisiac; so can a plate of raw oysters. But both are potent, and both have their place."

Double up. Try to see how many aphrodisiacs you can sneak into one meal, says Hopkins. For example, you might serve a generous helping of asparagus at dinner. Add fresh basil (a common, but little-known aphrodisiac) to a garden salad. And then serve fresh figs drizzled with honey for dessert.

Think beyond your stomach. Foods with aphrodisiac powers don't necessarily need to be eaten, says Hopkins. In other words, think of other uses for honey and chocolate sauce.

Cook up something together. Preparing food is itself a seduction, says Hopkins. Meals from the drive-up window, on the other hand, are not. "Taking the time to cook for or with someone says, 'I love you. I care about you. You're worth my time.' And time is so precious, what bigger turn-on could there be?"

Erotic Videos

In magazines, on the streets, out of the corners of our eyes, we admire the breadth of a man's shoulders. The long, lean length of his legs. His dimpled smile. The twinkle in his eye.

And they say that women aren't visually stimulated?

Studies show that, like men, women *are* physically aroused by explicit images, including the sex in erotic videos. But steamy lovemaking alone generally isn't enough to turn us on. "Women also want to see tenderness and emotional connection along with the sex," says Candida Royalle, president of Femme Productions, a company in New York City that makes erotic videos that appeal to women and couples. Such couple-friendly videos—and there are an increasing number of them—don't contain the coarse and often degrading images that women tend to find objectionable, says Royalle. Instead, they serve up romance, tenderness, and—gasp—a plotline.

When done with taste and respect, erotic videos offer couples an opportunity to expand their sexual repertoires and explore their sexual fantasies, says Royalle. "Watching these videos with your partner can open the lines of communication," she says. "It's difficult for some couples to talk about their sexual needs. It's easier when you can point to the TV and say, 'Gee, have you ever thought of doing that? I have.'"

Some couples pop in an erotic video when they feel that they're too tired for sex, says Royalle. "Lots of couples come home from work exhausted," she says. "These videos can really jump-start your desire." They may also inspire some couples to break out of the same stale sexual routines, which can enhance sexual and emotional intimacy, says William F. Fitzgerald, Ph.D., who specializes in marital and sexual therapy at the Silicon Valley Relationship and Sexuality Center in Santa Clara, California.

Losing Your Video Virginity

It's one thing to *want* to rent erotic videos. It can be quite another to enter the friendly neighborhood video store, walk past the romantic comedies, and head for no-woman's-land: the adult's-only section. Once there, you still have to get past the lurid videos you're bound to find and select those you'd be comfortable watching with your partner. These tips can help you get past the jitters.

Do it for science. To reduce your embarrassment, "pretend you're renting erotic videos as part of a research project," suggests Dr. Fitzgerald. "Your assignment is to go into a video store, select some titles, and watch them as part of an experiment. This works for a lot of folks." Or join an out-of-the-way video store so you can rent spicy movies incognito, says Royalle.

Order by mail. If you'd rather not brave the video store, request catalogs from adults-only mail-order businesses such as Adam and Eve (P. O. Box 800, Carrboro, NC 27510), Xandria Collection (P. O. Box 31039, San Francisco, CA 94131), and Good Vibrations (938 Howard Street, Suite

101, San Francisco, CA 94103). To receive information on Femme Productions, contact Adam and Eve and ask for the Femme brochure. These
catalogs really do come in plain brown wrappers, so you can choose your selections and have them mailed to your home with no one the wiser. If you
don't want to be bombarded with sexual junk mail, call the company before
you request a catalog, to make sure it won't sell your name to a competing
company.

Weed out the way-too-explicit. If you're worried about ending up
with a video that goes too far, don't go by the picture and plot synopsis on
the box cover, says Royalle. They're often misleading. A good rule of thumb
is to choose couples' instructional videos or those that say "simulated sex" on
the box cover.

Try a private screening first. Before watching an erotic video with
your sexual partner, watch a few yourself first, says Royalle. "Make sure
you're really comfortable with them," she says. If you like what you see, you
can then decide whether you want to share the experience with your husband or lover.

Remember why you're watching. Some women dislike erotic videos
because they feel that they can't compete with the younger, firmer bodies on-
screen. If this sounds like you, it helps to remember why you're watching
these videos in the first place, says Royalle. "You're not watching to compare
yourself with the women on screen, but to become aroused by the sex," she
says. Also, bear in mind that these women are sexual athletes. "This is the
way they make their living," says Royalle. "So it's not fair to compare your
body to theirs." Besides, your partner may feel just as insecure, says Royalle.
"Remember, he'll be seeing athletic guys with great builds and penises that
look larger than life."

Set the mood. Make video night an event, suggests Royalle. Farm the
kids out to Grandma for the night. Light some scented candles. Enjoy a glass
of wine or champagne. Set out fresh, ripe strawberries to feed one another.
"These special little touches help enhance the sexual mood," she says.

Set boundaries, too. Before you press "play," make an agreement with
your partner: Neither one of you has to do anything you don't want to, no
matter what's happening on the video. "What excites you, or what you fantasize about, is not necessarily what you want to do," says Dr. Fitzgerald.

Fantasies

In the past, only sexually dissatisfied or disturbed people were thought to have sexual fantasies. (Blame Sigmund Freud, who said, "A happy person never fantasizes, only an unsatisfied one.") Today, however, fantasizing is considered a healthy aspect of human sexuality, even if you dream of making love with someone other than your partner.

"Like dreams, sexual fantasies offer insights into our sexuality and relationships and can even fuel our personal growth," says Wendy Maltz, a psychotherapist, certified sex therapist, and licensed marriage and family therapist in Eugene, Oregon, and coauthor of *In the Garden of Desire: Women's Sexual Fantasies as a Gateway to Passion and Pleasure*. That's true whether your sexual fantasy stars Brad Pitt, a co-worker, or a faceless stranger. It's true, whether your role is passive or aggressive, your partner (or partners) male or female, the sex romantic or decidedly pornographic.

"In fact, research shows that sexual fantasies occur most often in people who exhibit the least number of sexual problems and the least sexual dissatisfaction," says Maltz. Fantasies are now considered a universal psychological phenomenon, like dreaming, she adds.

The Function of Fantasy

Why do we fantasize? Because we're human, and humans are creative. Fantasy allows us to escape life's limitations. When we fantasize, anything goes: We're both performer and director, and we control the setting, characters, dialogue, and action.

Fantasies can serve a variety of functions. For both men and women, fantasies stimulate sexual interest and arousal. Fantasies, notes Maltz, have been referred to as a vibrator for the mind.

They also distract us from our sexual fears and anxieties. "By focusing on the steamy images and stories in our minds, we can feel less inhibited and more inspired to be sexually open and expressive," Maltz says.

Fantasy also allows us to "try on" sexual practices we don't necessarily want to act out in real life. "Sexual fantasy offers women a risk-free play-ground where real-life consequences can be ignored or flaunted," says Maltz.

As we grow and change, so do our fantasies, Maltz says. For example, as a woman becomes more sexually experienced, her sexual fantasies may shift from being vague and romantic to being sexually "hot" and graphic.

Enriching Your Fantasy Life

Perhaps you're thinking, "I don't have sexual fantasies." Hooey, says Maltz. "Many women think that they don't have fantasies because they don't have a broad-enough definition of fantasy," she says. "Some women find erotic thrills in roller coasters, saxophones, ocean waves, and mangoes. They can even involve images we don't normally define as being sexual. Fantasies can include any sexual thoughts and images you have while daydreaming or during sex." These tips can help you tap into your erotic imagination and enjoy it more.

Be alert for fantasy fodder. The raw material of fantasy is all around us; you just have to recognize it when you see it. "A new fantasy might start with something as mundane as peeling an orange and sucking the juice from your fingers," says Maltz. You might shape a fantasy around a fleeting glance you once shared with a stranger on a train. A wonderfully romantic passage in a library book. A line from one of your favorite poems or love songs. A steamy love scene in a video. Once you've identified the primary image, fill it in, says Maltz. Make it your own.

Don't save fantasy for the bedroom. Fantasize in nonsexual situations, such as when you're at work, preparing dinner, or just before you go to sleep, suggests Maltz. The more you work your imagination, the easier it will be to slip into fantasy—and the more detailed and rewarding your fantasies will become.

Engage your senses. If your fantasies tend to involve characters and a plot—what Maltz calls scripted fantasies—"try to identify their sensory elements," she suggests. "Does your fantasy contain a certain color, word, phrase, or sound? A sense of movement? Do you taste or smell something in partic-ular?" When you identify the sensory elements, play with them in your head, says Maltz. For example, if your favorite fantasy involves light, play with that.

"What if you added just a little more light? Can you make the light play more intense? Just let your thoughts wander," she suggests.

Try a little romance. Today's romance novels often include explicit yet tasteful love scenes that can fuel a woman's fantasies, says Maltz. For more information on romance novels, see page 181.

"Cheating" in Your Fantasies

Fantasizing about making love with someone other than your partner is normal, for the most part. In fact, it's one of the most common sexual fantasies, both for women and for men.

An occasional fantasy about the guy next door or a colleague at work does not mean that you actually want to make love with the other guy, says Maltz. "It can be an entertaining way to satisfy curiosity and heighten your sexual excitement with your current partner," she says.

Fantasizing about an inappropriate partner over and over—or being unable to reach orgasm unless you do—may signal problems in your present relationship, however. Fantasizing about a past lover, for example, may mean that you have some unfinished emotional business to attend to. Think about what this person represents to you, suggests Maltz, and how you feel when you think of him, whether guilty, angry, or sad.

Some women turn to fantasy because they feel that their present partners are unable to give them the emotional closeness or sexual stimulation they need, Maltz explains. If this is true of you, begin to examine how your relationship is or isn't working for you as well as how you might change it through better communication, sexual enrichment, or help from a therapist.

Should You Share?

Sharing a fantasy with your partner can be a double-edged sword. On the one hand, studies show that men are more likely than women to react to their partners' fantasies with jealousy. Your partner may jump to the conclusion that your fantasy means you are displeased with him as a lover. Or he may conclude that you want to actually *do* all the things you imagine, Maltz explains.

On the other hand, sharing fantasies—especially fantasies about new sexual techniques or circumstances—is one aspect of being open with your

He Fantasizes, She Fantasizes

You've been fantasizing about making love with that hunky telephone repairman—or even a past lover. Should you feel guilty? Are you being "unfaithful"? Do your lusty thoughts mean you don't love your partner?

No, no, and no. According to most research on sexual fantasy, we *all* daydream about having sex with someone other than our mates.

When Karen Nesbitt Shanor, Ph.D., a clinical psychologist in Washington, D.C., and author of *The Fantasy Files: Sexual Fantasies of Contemporary Women*, asked 303 women and 4,062 men what they most often fantasized about while making love, here's what they reported.

Women's most common sexual fantasies

Sex with a new partner

Replay of a past sexual experience

Sex with a celebrity

Seducing a younger man or boy

Sex with an older man

Men's most common sexual fantasies

The image of a nude or seminude woman

Sex with a new partner

Replay of a past sexual experience

Sex with two or more women

Having the power to drive women wild

Most common fantasies for both men and women

Reliving an exciting sexual experience

Imagining having sex with their current partner

Imagining having sex with a different partner

Rest assured, then: Sexual daydreams about other men don't mean you don't love your current partner. They just mean you're human.

partner about sex, says Sharna Striar, Ph.D., a couples therapist in New York City who specializes in sex therapy. The more open you are, the more dynamic your sexual relationship will be. "If you understand what your partner's erotic hot buttons are, you keep the sexual relationship energized," says Dr. Striar. "Sharing fantasies can play into that."

Swapping fantasies with your partner also allows you to pick up on which sense or senses he tends to use during sex and incorporate what you learn into your real-life lovemaking, says Maltz. "If your partner's fantasy includes a lot of sexual words and phrases, then auditory stimulation may be important to him," she says. "So there may be ways for you to use more 'sound effects' during sex—whispering in his ear, perhaps."

Acting out fantasies, however, may be a different story. "Acting out fantasies is probably the least reliable source of sexual satisfaction because there are all sorts of things that can go wrong," says Maltz. What's more, acting out fantasies can be emotionally damaging unless the couple observes certain ground rules. (More about these later.)

Smart Ways to Share

Many women have found that divulging their fantasies with their partners can draw them even closer together, says Maltz—if they share tactfully and in steps. To make sure that you have a safe and enjoyable experience, follow these guidelines on how to share—and enact—a fantasy.

Test the waters. Divulging your sexual fantasies, or asking that he share his, can be tricky business, says Maltz. So approach the topic with tact. Rather than bluntly asking, "What are your sexual fantasies?" try, "What kinds of thoughts and images turn you on?" If your partner reacts with discomfort, back off, says Maltz. But if he responds with interest, proceed slowly. Your next question might be, "Which senses do you tend to use the most? Do you hear sounds?"

Self-edit. Once he divulges his fantasy, he'll want to hear yours. So exercise good judgment in deciding how much detail you want to share, says Maltz. While your partner may be intrigued to hear that you've always wanted to make love in an elevator, he'll likely be less than thrilled if you confess that it's his brother—not him—who's sharing the ride.

Make it meaningful. If you and your partner really want to enact a fantasy, make it a collaborative one based on a shared experience, advises Maltz. For instance, if the best sex you ever had was on your honeymoon on a deserted beach in Hawaii, "weave that experience into your present-day lovemaking," says Maltz. It may not be the wildest fantasy you've ever had, but it will have some personal meaning to the both of you. And that's the whole point.

Think before you enact. Never go along with a fantasy that makes you uncomfortable just to please your partner, cautions Maltz. Going beyond your sexual "comfort zone" can damage your self-esteem. Ditto for acting out a sexual fantasy that would involve risky or illegal behavior.

Set ground rules—and stick to them. It's crucial that a couple discuss what is and is not acceptable sexual behavior *before* acting out a fantasy, especially if the fantasy involves kinky behavior, says Maltz. She advises agreeing on a "safe word" or gesture ahead of time as a signal to stop the fantasy. "One couple I know likes to use the term *red light* as a signal," she says.

When Fantasies Hurt

Sexual fantasies aren't always positive. Some women feel dependent on them, controlled by them, or even disgusted by them, says Maltz. A few even feel compelled to act them out, exposing themselves to physical and emotional harm.

Women who were sexually abused when they were children are especially likely to have harmful fantasies, Maltz says. "These women often have deep emotional conflicts that surface in their sexual fantasies," she says. "When they really analyze their fantasies, they find that they have very little to do with sex and a lot more to do with issues of abandonment and betrayal, or a desire to be loved and respected that was ignored."

Breaking free of destructive sexual fantasies requires the help of a therapist with experience in treating sexual abuse, says Maltz. (And professional help is essential if a woman is involved in any potentially dangerous, compulsive, or high-risk sexual behavior.) "To defuse an unwanted sexual fantasy, you need to explore its dynamics, much like you would a nightmare that bothers you," she says. "An experienced therapist can guide you through it."

Flirting

In the same way that the makers of nature documentaries scrutinize the mating habits of animals in the wild, Monica Moore, Ph.D., has watched men and women flirt for the past 20 years. And to her practiced eye, the mating dance between men and women is just as fascinating—and complex.

"Our courtship dance is extraordinarily beautiful," says Dr. Moore, associate professor of behavioral and social sciences at Webster University in St. Louis. "A woman leans toward a man, tilting her head and presenting her neck. A man leans forward and touches her hand . . . it's gorgeous."

Dr. Moore has identified 52 flirting behaviors women use to attract a potential mate. There's the Type I glance (encompassing the room). The Type II glance (short and darting). Arching her brow. Smoothing her hair. Applying lipstick. And more.

When it comes to attracting men, says Dr. Moore, good flirting skills count as much as good looks.

"In our culture, women get the message that unless we're model-glamorous, we don't stand a chance," says Dr. Moore. "True, research shows that more men than women express interest in looks. But what I see in the field—at bars, parties, skating rinks, and so forth—is that flirting behavior, not attractiveness, more strongly predicts whether a man will approach a woman."

Secrets of Successful Flirting

If you're a natural flirt, this mating behavior may be automatic. But if you're shy, you may need help. Enter Susan Rabin, a relationship therapist who runs workshops on flirting, director of the School of Flirting based in New York City, and author of *How to Attract Anyone, Anytime, Anyplace*; *Cyberflirt: Flirting and Dating on the Internet*; and *101 Ways to Flirt: How to Get More Dates and Meet Your Mate*. To Rabin, flirting is a social skill rather than a sexual one. "Flirting is often viewed as being manipulative and insincere, but it's not," she says. "Flirting is about being playful and charming and making other people feel good."

Mastering "Conversation Lite"

Small talk serves an important purpose, says Susan Rabin, a relationship therapist who runs workshops on flirting, director of the School of Flirting based in New York City, and author of *How to Attract Anyone, Anytime, Anyplace; Cyberflirt: Flirting and Dating on the Internet*; and *101 Ways to Flirt: How to Get More Dates and Meet Your Mate*. First, it weeds out unsuitable prospects. (If you don't like discussing the weather with a man, you're unlikely to enjoy talking to him about anything more meaningful.) It also widens your social network, through which you may someday meet The One. To make small talk easier:

Carry a flirting prop. "They're surefire conversation starters," says Rabin. If you're artistic, carry a sketchbook. Or wear a T-shirt with an interesting slogan or a unique piece of jewelry. Tote the latest bestseller. Carry a bottle of bubbles and break them out at the park. "The successful flirting prop attracts the eye, invites comment, and tells the world how fascinating you are," says Rabin.

Play reporter. The best way to get him talking is to pose interesting questions—questions that require more than a yes or no answer, fit the situation (movie questions at a premiere, favorite comedians at a comedy club), and aren't too personal.

Don't talk about your problems. He has enough of his own.

Don't pretend to be bored or "above it all." A distant attitude may mask your shyness, but it won't make you any new male friends, says Rabin.

What's more, says Rabin, you can learn to flirt the same way you learn to play an instrument or speak Italian: Practice, practice, practice. So get out there and flirt with the best of them. Here's how.

Have fun. This is the first and most important rule of flirting, says Rabin. Don't appear desperate or needy. Men sense when there's an agenda (Might *he* be the one? Does he want kids?) behind the flirtatious glances. "The minute you start being serious, you blow it," says Rabin. "Then flirting isn't charming or fun anymore."

Be blatant. Make sure your signals are coming through loud and clear, says Dr. Moore. "Women sometimes need to be more obvious in their flirting behavior," she says. Research has shown that women tend to make the first move, but women's signals are more subtle than men's, and the "flirtee" may not get the message.

Play peekaboo. When you've settled on your target, employ the Type II glance, suggests Dr. Moore. "Look, then look away. Look, then look away," she says. "The guy needs to know that you're looking at him." Once you've established eye contact, move on to the Type III glance, which Dr. Moore terms the "fixed gaze." "It's a more intimate gaze," she says.

But don't stare. Hold his eye for as long as it takes to say (to yourself), "Hello. I see you"—but no longer, says Rabin. In the animal kingdom, staring is a hostile act.

Smile. Smiling is the most basic and effective flirting behavior, says Dr. Moore. "If you're sitting at your table or at a party looking like your dog just died, a man won't dare to approach you," she says. Smile with your mouth slightly open, advises Rabin.

Check your body language. Don't pair a come-hither gaze with a don't-come-any-closer posture, says Rabin. Slouching or crossing your arms over your chest warns "keep away."

Watch for his signals. Men use some of the same flirting techniques as women, Rabin says. But some signals are uniquely male. For example, if he strokes his tie or smooths his lapels, he's interested and wants to make a good impression. Ditto if he takes your arm at a crowded bar, party, or event. "This is a man who doesn't want to lose you in the crowd," explains Rabin.

Get the story. If the guy is wearing something interesting, approach him, smile, and say, "I'll bet there's a story behind that (ring, watch, tie)," suggests Rabin. "There's a story behind just about everything." Try this line when you have plenty of time to talk, she adds.

Shrug off rejection. Even practiced flirts don't always get their man, says Rabin. So if the guy doesn't pick up on your signals, or the man who took your number doesn't call, move on. "Rejection can be painful, but it is never fatal," she says. "And it's never a reason not to flirt."

Lingerie

A research firm asked 1,000 men and women, "What's the sexiest clothing a woman can wear?"

"An evening gown," said the majority of women. But most men preferred what a woman wears under the gown.

"Lingerie sends a message: 'I'm hot,'" says Norman Scherzer, Ph.D., a member of the Society for the Scientific Study of Sexuality in Mount Vernon, Iowa, and professor of biology and chemistry at Essex County College in Newark, New Jersey. While most men find a nude woman arousing, "a woman who has adorned her body with lingerie is even more of a turn-on," he says.

Fun-to-Wear Underwear

Ready to graduate from "plain vanilla" briefs and bras?

As with blouses or shoes, you may not know what you want until you see it and try it on, says Jerry Robkoff, owner of Naughty and Nice, an adult romance boutique and lingerie shop in New York City. But it always helps to have some idea of what you're looking for. Is it elegant, trashy, or somewhere in between? Which features do you want to accentuate? And what's your psychological comfort level?

Go on a lingerie safari. Wander through department and lingerie stores and see what catches your eye. Bright colors, or dark jewel tones? Silk and satin, or fishnet and feathers? Styles that cover, or reveal? Whatever you choose, "you should feel emotionally comfortable in it," says Barbara Jones Smith, Ph.D., a licensed clinical psychologist in Traverse City, Michigan.

Accentuate the positives. Lingerie should accentuate the body part you're most proud of while it downplays flaws, says Robkoff.

If you're big all over: Robkoff recommends a full-length silk or satin robe or gown (perhaps with strategically placed lace, ties, or cutaways), long poet shirts, or a baby-doll gown that hits your knees.

Garter Belt Sales Soar

Shortly after the release of the film *Bull Durham*, in which actress Susan Sarandon dons a garter belt, sales of garter belts rose 50 percent, according to Frederick's of Hollywood.

If you have heavy hips and thighs: Try a knee-length gown or a baby doll that comes to just above your knees. "And avoid thongs," says Robkoff.

If you have a small bust: Consider a bustier. "Many women think that to wear bustier-type lingerie, you have to be well-endowed," says Robkoff. "Not so. A woman with small breasts can look better in a bustier than a woman who's bigger-busted."

If you're nervous about the whole idea: Go with the classic baby-doll nightie: skimpy panties and a top that looks like a flowing camisole. It can be short-short or skim your knees. "Baby dolls flatter every body type," says Robkoff.

Pick the right color. Color sends a message, too, says Robkoff. "If you want to play the innocent, wear white," he says. "If you want to be the harlot, wear red." If you're not sure, go with classic black.

Add sexy heels. "High-heeled pumps make a woman's legs look longer and thinner," says Robkoff.

Shop together. Order intimate-wear catalogs through the mail and page through them together, suggests Dr. Jones Smith. "It's a sexy, intimate thing to do together, and it's your opportunity to show him what you like."

Wear lingerie as underwear. To feel feminine and sexy at night, start during the day, suggests Dr. Jones Smith.

Locations

Rule one: When you fool around in an elevator, make sure you push the "stop" button first.

"My husband and I love to grab at each other on the sneak in public," says

Stella Resnick, Ph.D., a psychologist in Los Angeles and author of *The Pleasure Zone: Why We Resist Good Feelings and How to Let Go and Be Happy*. "One time, we were in an elevator, and I pawed at him as the door was opening. The woman waiting for the elevator caught me. She didn't say a word; she just walked in and turned her back.

"Then, over her shoulder, she said to me: 'Naughty, naughty.' My husband and I just roared."

What's the appeal of making love (or, in Dr. Resnick's case, pawing playfully) someplace other than the bedroom? "That naughtiness factor," says Dr. Resnick. "And in some cases, the element of risk. Being in a situation where you might be caught really gets the adrenaline going."

Of course, some of us would rather spend our adrenaline on a roller-coaster ride than an elevator encounter. But according to some experts, moving the action to a novel location—be it a deserted stretch of beach or the kitchen table—might be just what the sex doctor ordered. "Having sex in a new place breaks the boredom of always doing it in the bedroom, in bed," says Michael Perry, Ph.D., a marriage and sex therapist in Encino, California.

No Pillows, but More Passion

Of course, no one is advocating public indecency. Says Dr. Resnick, "I wouldn't recommend having sex in a public place. But if you find yourself out in the country somewhere, lying in the tall grass . . . well, there are times when you know you can take the risk." Here are some ideas to inspire you.

Go parking. "Back when you were a teenager, if you wanted to fool around, you got in a car and parked somewhere," says Dr. Perry. At first blush, this idea sounds outrageous. "But rediscovering your sense of spontaneity and adventure can put the spice back into sex," he says. If you're reluctant to park on a public roadway—for good reason—go "parking" in your driveway—if you have a long driveway. Some couples "park" in their garages after an evening out. Maybe that's why sport utility vehicles are so popular. . . .

Venture off-road. "Outside of the bedroom, the great outdoors is probably the most popular place to have sex," says Dr. Perry. You might make love in a meadow along a lonesome stretch of road (wander far, far into the grass),

Novel Places Couples Have Had Sex

According to Michael Perry, Ph.D., a marriage and sex therapist in Encino, California, some of the more unusual places couples he has surveyed have made love include:

- In the gondola of a ski lift

- In an RV driven by a friend

- In the barn of a ghost town

- Under a waterfall

- At a shooting range (not in active use)

- In a kayak in a coastline grotto

- On a swing in a forest

- In the backyard after a food-fight picnic

in a game-hunting blind in the wilds, or on a less-traveled trail while hiking or camping. It's a good idea to keep a soft blanket in the car for such impromptu love-making sessions. (For tips on making love on the beach—a popular spot for intimacy—see Sex on the Beach on page 107.)

Snow yourself in. Dr. Resnick and her husband once made love in the snow. "No blanket, just heavy parkas and lots of spunk," she says. "Fortunately, we stopped at just the right time—before a family came along. It was great fun."

Go to the drive-in. Petting is making love, says Dr. Resnick, and one good place to pet is at the movies. "Start thinking of making love as kissing and holding and flirting and caressing and smooching, not just intercourse," she says. "A little stimulation can go a long way."

Don't risk arrest—or losing your job. Thinking of making love in the restroom of a fancy restaurant or on your boss's desk? Think twice. While many couples crave the adrenaline rush derived from indulging in sex in extremely high-risk locations, don't let your abandon cost you your job or your reputation.

Long-Distance Romance

ఈ

You've met Mr. Right, but he lives in the wrong town. With men and women alike pursuing careers—or moving because of job changes, transfers, or promotions—long-distance relationships are more common now than a generation ago. But they're not altogether new. Jane Proctor Fleming, 49, a business manager in Portsmouth, Rhode Island, recalls the long-distance romance 20 years ago with the man who is now her husband.

"I was living in Washington, D.C., where I had a great job on Capitol Hill as a congressional aide," Proctor Fleming recalls. "Paul was working in advertising in New York, more than 200 miles away. I met him on a blind date on a Friday night and didn't leave until Monday morning."

Three weeks later, Paul visited her in Washington. "It became evident that this was special, and we both wanted it to continue," she says.

The couple "dated" via frequent airline flights and every-day phone calls and married a year after their initial meeting. "When I think about it now, it makes me want to lie down and go to sleep. It was exhausting," Proctor Fleming says. "But, of course, we were in this exciting new relationship, so we just kept going."

"Long-distance relationships have a tremendous potential to work, but not without great effort," says Clifford H. Swensen, Ph.D., psychology professor at Purdue University in West Lafayette, Indiana, who has conducted research on long-distance relationships. (Researchers call them LDRs.) "A certain amount of absence may indeed make the heart grow fonder. We found, however, that after about six months, a long-distance relationship becomes more difficult to maintain."

But sometimes there's no other choice. You care about and maybe even are crazy about each other, but circumstances deem that you live miles and miles apart.

"'Commuter couples' are passionately devoted to each other but also to what they're doing," says Tai Justin Mendenhall, a doctoral student of marriage and family therapy in St. Paul, Minnesota, who has studied long-dis-

Secrets of Long-Lasting Love

Love Letters Bridged the Distance

Karen and Dave Waggoner of Flippin, Arkansas, grew up together in Indiana, but it wasn't until after high school that they became involved romantically. After only a few dates, Karen went to junior college and Dave joined the Navy. Over the next two years, says Karen, they built their relationship through regular love letters and limited time together when Dave had leave from the Navy. They married in the fall of 1958.

Our two-year courtship was a preview of our marriage: Dave and I lived apart for most of the first 17 years we were married. With his position in the Navy, he would be out on ship for eight or nine months at a time. Usually we'd have a couple of months together in between his cruises, but if a political situation arose, that visit would be cut short.

In 1968, my husband was sent to Japan, and the entire family relocated with him. We were thrilled about this because we thought we would all have more time together instead of Dave being overseas while I was back in the States with our two kids. But even in Japan, we were still essentially living apart. My husband was working for military intelligence and was often gone for months on deployments into Vietnam.

But overseas the separation was much more intense. Dave was involved in dangerous work, which worried me and the kids when he was away. We

tance relationships. "They don't want to give up their own dreams and neither do they want their partners to give up their dreams. Living apart is their best option, at least for the time being."

Nurture the Passion

Here's what experts recommend to nurture a relationship with someone who lives at a distance.

Start out strong. The more time you spend together early on, the stronger your relationship will be over the distances, says Dr. Swensen. As

also felt very isolated because we could barely communicate with those around us.

We were relieved to return to the States in 1972, and my husband retired from the Navy in 1975. But oddly enough, after leaving the Navy, he took a job in sales, which also required trips away from home. He finally quit sales when he just couldn't face another trip away from home, and neither could I, for that matter.

We really had no choice but to communicate through the written word. Writing letters to each other every day got us through those years apart. I'd often get five at a time, and I would just stack them up and read them in order.

We also trusted each other completely. We hadn't been married more than three months before he was gone. So it was clear to me early on that if we were going to stay married, with so much time apart, trust would be very important.

It has probably also helped that Dave and I are both very independent people. We've always had our own activities as well as activities we do together. I think that it's important to have your own time in a marriage because that way you can appreciate the time you do have together. I guess Dave and I just had more of our own time than most married couples.

Mendenhall says, "You'll have some kind of history together, and a stronger sense of 'we-ness' as you develop."

Visit at least once a month. A monthly visit helps people approximate the satisfaction of living closer together, according to research on LDR coping strategies conducted by psychologist Gerald L. Stone, Ph.D., director of university counseling services and professor of counseling psychology at the University of Iowa in Iowa City.

Mendenhall concurs. "Try to plan a monthly visit," he says. "It comes up again and again in the published research. Fewer visits than that and the relationship gets a lot harder."

Balance romance with reality. One problem with the high-energy, sparks-flying courtship style of LDRs is that you may expect everything to be exciting and wonderful forever, which sets you up for disillusionment, says Mendenhall. How to avoid this?

"It's a good idea to normalize your visits a little," Dr. Stone says. "Go off and do the laundry together or something else people who live together do."

Share your relationship with others. As tempted as you may be to spend every precious moment holed up together, you would do better to expand your universe to include friends and family. "You'll have more fun plus a greater sense of connectedness if you spend part of your time socializing together with others," says Mendenhall. "Go out and meet the people in your partner's world and vice versa. Get to know them and, in the process, get to know your partner's experience of life when you're apart."

Connect the dates. As your visit winds down, set a date for the next one. Don't say things like, "Maybe we can get together next weekend, but maybe not for a couple of weeks," because this will leave you hanging in painful limbo, says Mendenhall. "Commuter couples find it easier to say, 'Goodbye, I'll see you on such-and-such a date,' even if it's a month away, rather than deal with not knowing when the next time will be," he says.

Modern Love Letters

If you're in love, you probably don't need a book to tell you to call, write, or e-mail your sweetheart frequently. It comes naturally—and pays off. In fact, successful commuter couples tend to develop stronger communication skills than couples who live close by, says Mendenhall, "because they have to."

"Paul and I talked to each other on the phone almost every night," recalls Proctor Fleming. "It was the next best thing to coming home to each other."

Electronic mail via the Internet runs a close second to phone calls for everyday intimacy, says Dr. Stone. While no replacement for hearing your partner's voice, e-mail can contribute a lot to sustained communication, he says. Just don't e-mail each other at work, where you leave a permanent trail accessible by others.

Writing letters—the old-fashioned kind that you put in a stamped envelope—allows you to express yourself in ways you might not otherwise in the spoken word. And letters have a long-lasting impact compared to phone calls, says Dr. Swensen, "because you can carry a letter around in your pocket and pull it out anytime to reread it."

Equalize the effort. If one or the other of you is always doing the commuting, making all the phone calls, or paying for all the dinners, your relationship is going to feel lopsided and insecure, says Mendenhall. "Couples in long-distance relationships whom I interviewed said they feel best when they feel like they're doing about half the work, working as a team for the relationship." The point isn't to keep score but to figure out a fair balance. "If one partner is better able to pay for the phone bill, she or he should be the one who calls more often or sends the other partner money so that the bills are equally spread out."

Live your life. "Recognizing that you don't need someone else in your life for you to be happy is good whether you live with someone or not," says Mendenhall. "Men and women in successful long-distance relationships keep themselves busy with friends and activities. They don't sit around the house making themselves more miserable about how sad and lonely they are."

"I don't remember sitting around pining for Paul," recalls Proctor Fleming. "I wanted to be with him, but by the same token, I certainly wasn't going to stop having fun until I saw him again."

Happily Ever After?

Long-distance relationships cannot go on for long without a commitment because they're too much of a strain, says Dr. Swensen. "At a certain point, you finally have to face it: Either commit or end it."

And don't even bother getting involved in an LDR in the first place if you think you want to continue dating other people, says Mendenhall. "It just won't work. Ultimately, somebody across the distance is not going to be as attractive as somebody across the street."

Set a deadline. One of the key characteristics of happy LDRs is setting a date by which you will finally be together, says Mendenhall. "Long-term ambiguity is too painful," he says. As soon as you can, engage in discussions along the lines of, "We can move in together as soon as you're transferred back to headquarters next June." While the dates and details may change along the way, start negotiating anyway. "A deadline will vary from couple to couple, but everybody needs one," says Mendenhall. "Because sooner or later, even if you love each other, living long-distance gets old."

Movies

In solid relationships, women and men motor along like well-oiled machines. But let them try to pick out a video or decide what movie to see at the cinema, and the machine chokes, sputters, and grinds to a halt. He wants an action movie, with plenty of explosions, car chases, and hot sex. She's in the mood for clever dialogue, intricate plot, loving sex, and resolution of emotional problems.

While the stereotypes don't always hold, "there's certainly a lot of truth to them," says Jami Bernard, film critic for the *New York Daily News*, member and past chairperson of the New York Film Critics Circle, and author of *Chick Flicks: A Movie Lover's Guide to the Movies Women Love*. "Many movies are targeted to the genders," says Bernard. "Men like gadgets, power plays, and archetypal displays of good versus evil. Women like human-scale scenarios and character development."

Granted, there are plenty of women who love high-tech action films. And an equal number of guys who like thoughtful relationship flicks. If your tastes jibe, no problem. But what if they clash?

"Being forced by a significant other to watch a movie you really didn't want to watch can leave either you or your guy restless, if not downright resentful," says Bernard.

But there's hope: Both men and women want characters they can relate to, says Bernard. Use that common ground to decide which video to rent or movie to see.

The Critics Pick Flicks

Here, two film critics—one male, one female—pick their top films in specific categories. Their mission: to choose films that men *and* women can enjoy together. "He" is Anthony P. Montesano, film critic for *Cinefantastique* magazine and former associate editor of *American Film* magazine. "She" is Vicki Woods, director of the Film Series at Webster University in St. Louis, Missouri.

Movies You Can Enjoy Together

Casablanca is the ultimate couple-friendly flick, says Jami Bernard, film critic for the *New York Daily News*, member and past chairperson of the New York Film Critics Circle, and author of *Chick Flicks: A Movie Lover's Guide to the Movies Women Love.*

"Bogart is the all-controlling anti-hero men want to be, while married Bergman gets to justify cheating on her husband."

Here are four more.

- *Jerry Maguire.* "Men get football and office politics. Women get to watch the cutest guy in the world make a commitment."

- *The English Patient.* "Espionage, Nazis, torture, and adventure for men. For women, a love so powerful that Ralph Fiennes sacrifices himself to keep Kristin Scott Thomas's deathbed promise."

- *The Silence of the Lambs.* "Men get lurid serial killing. Women get to watch Jodie Foster use her superior intellect to solve the case."

- *Laura.* "A whodunit with a mysterious beauty for men. For the women, a macho cop who is so entranced with her that he doesn't even mind that she's dead."

Best First-Date Movies

He says: *When Harry Met Sally.* "This film illustrates that there are many paths to true love. Harry and Sally progress through different stages for over a decade before they actually become a couple."

She says: *Four Weddings and a Funeral.* "This film shows the main characters gradually falling in love, but not a whole lot of sex. Watching sex scenes on a huge movie screen can be really uncomfortable on a first date."

Worst First-Date Movies

He says: *Basic Instinct* or *Fatal Attraction.* "These films push too many hot buttons and magnify everything dysfunctional about a relationship—infidelity, distrust, tension, the inability to communicate, using one another on a surface level. You don't want to sit through these on a first date."

She says: "Virtually anything directed by Woody Allen, especially his later films. Most are very anti-relationship."

Chick Flicks Men Like

He says: *Field of Dreams.* "This was supposed to be a chick flick when it was released, but it was the men who left the theater crying. A true phenomenon in terms of appealing to both sexes."

She says: *Henry and June.* "It's a period piece, which most men hate, but a very titillating period piece. This wouldn't be a good first-date movie, though."

Adventure Movies Women Like

He says: *Raiders of the Lost Ark* or *Romancing the Stone.* "In both films, a strong female plays an integral part in the action. Also, *Romancing the Stone* starts off as a romance novel being written by a woman. So, in that regard, the story is coming from a woman's point of view."

She says: *Speed, The Terminator,* or *Die Hard.* "Lots of women love adventure movies, especially ones with a strong female lead like Sandra Bullock or Linda Hamilton. It's the vigilante films—like *Death Wish* or *Rambo: First Blood Part II*—and westerns that they have a hard time with."

Movies That Stimulate Erotic Desire

He says: *Indecent Proposal.* "Here's a beautiful married woman being propositioned for one night of sex for $1 million by Robert Redford, and both she and her husband agree to let it happen. There's sort of a visceral erotic thrill about that."

She says: *Body Heat* or *The Postman Always Rings Twice.* "The sex scenes are passionate and convincing. You also feel that the women are fully in control of their sexuality, which most men like."

Movies to Make Up To

He says: *Tootsie* and *Groundhog Day.* "At their core, these films are about making mistakes and being forgiven. In *Tootsie,* there's a tremendous deception going on, but not one that the main character intends to perpetrate on the woman he falls in love with. Ultimately, his mistake is forgiven.

"There's a moment at the end of the film when he admits that he learned more about being a man when he was a woman than he ever did as a man.

He convinces Jessica Lange that their relationship can work because they have already become good friends. The film illustrates what the true foundation of a loving relationship is—friendship.

"In *Groundhog Day*, the main character begins as a self-centered, disgruntled person. But in the end, after repeatedly being given the opportunity to redeem himself, he has a spiritual awakening about himself and about relationships in general."

She says: *Forget Paris.* "They fight, and yet things work out."

Best Classic Love Stories

He says: *Sleepless in Seattle.* "What I like about this movie is that the Meg Ryan character doesn't know who the guy she hears on the radio on Christmas Eve is. But she falls in love with something intangible—his soul. That's a classic element of love."

She says: *Casablanca.* "It's clear that they're going to love each other forever. But he gives her up for something bigger than their love—the war. This film shows how much people are willing to do for each other."

Romance Novels

We all know what's between the covers of romance novels. The heaving bosoms of virginal heroines. The sweet, savage love of dark-eyed strangers.

And plenty of other clichés.

Myths, all myths, say romance writers, who have grown used to defending their work.

"People think romance novels are stupid and shallow and badly written. They're not," says Linda Lael Miller, author of more than 40 best-selling romance novels, including *Two Brothers* and *The Vow.* "Some of the best writers in the world are writing romances."

Nor are romance novels pornography for women, as a lone study has suggested. "Pornography is directed toward, shall we say, solitary satisfaction," says

More Romance
for Novel Fans

In a landmark study conducted a few years ago, women who read romance novels made love with their partners twice as often per week as women who didn't.

Jennifer Blake, another best-selling romance novelist whose works include *Kane* and *Shameless*. "Romance novels are about mutual pleasure between a man and a woman and the emotional bond that makes a sexual encounter special."

It's this fusion of emotional connection and sexual desire that makes romance novels attractive to women, says Wendy Maltz, a psychotherapist, certified sex therapist, and licensed marriage and family therapist in Eugene, Oregon, and coauthor of *In the Garden of Desire: Women's Sexual Fantasies as a Gateway to Passion and Pleasure*. Maltz, herself a fan of romance novels, recommends these books to women struggling with low sexual desire, sexual inhibitions, and sexual fears. "I'd say 8 times out of 10, these women find the books very helpful."

While romance novels aren't a substitute for a real relationship, the best ones can teach a woman about herself and her intimate relationships, says Maltz. The passion between the hero and heroine can stoke your sexual fantasies. The modern heroines, who are strong and courageous, teach the value of taking risks for love. And the commitment and mutual respect that's at the core of the best romance-novel relationships can inspire you to work toward your own happy ending.

Living the Fantasy

The following expert tips can help romance-novel neophytes and long-time fans alike.

Choose carefully. So what's a "good" romance novel? "One in which the sexual relationship emerges from an emotional relationship that has been built over time, and that involves genuine caring and respect," says Maltz. "And the heroine is not just the receiver of sexual attention. She also has a sense of her own sexual drive."

If the main characters' sexual relationship seems emotionally degrading, or if it involves rape or physical abuse, stop reading. "These aren't healthy relationships," says Maltz. (Fortunately, such "bodice-rippers" have long been out of favor.)

Suggest a story hour. If you like what you read, consider reading your partner passages that move you and tell him why, suggests Maltz.

"I hear of couples reading together all the time," says Miller. "Most men would be willing to be more romantic; they just don't know how. Men who sincerely wonder what it is that women want should read these books because they would make it very clear."

Be your own hero. No self-respecting romance heroine would dream of living through her man, says Miller. The fuller your own life, the more you bring to your relationship. "Romantic heroines are strong and independent," she says. "They have their own lives and their own goals. And while this might not seem romantic in the conventional sense of the word, it is."

Some Steamy Reads

If romance novels are a new genre for you, or you'd like to expand your repertoire, try these authors and titles, suggests Wendy Maltz, a psychotherapist, certified sex therapist, and licensed marriage and family therapist in Eugene, Oregon, and coauthor of *In the Garden of Desire: Women's Sexual Fantasies as a Gateway to Passion and Pleasure*. "These represent romance novels that deal with women's own passion and desire for sex and model healthy sexual relationships," she says.

- Susan Johnson: *Blaze, Pure Sin, Golden Paradise*
- Jayne Anne Krentz: *Trust Me, Grand Passion*
- Elizabeth Lowell: *Enchanted, Where the Heart Is*, and her *Only* series—*Only His, Only You*, and *Only Mine*
- Susan Elizabeth Phillips: *Nobody's Baby but Mine, Dream a Little Dream*
- Nora Roberts: *The Dream Trilogy (Daring to Dream, Holding the Dream, Finding the Dream)*

Valentine's Day

 ❧

Call it the St. Valentine's Day Panic: Man rushes to drugstore, stands elbow to elbow with other like-minded fellows, pores over the few remaining romantic cards, and picks up a box of candy . . . if any are left.

Or maybe he blows off the whole thing.

To be fair, men aren't the only ones who put off dealing with Valentine's Day. In one survey, 78 percent of men said they dreaded Valentine's Day. But so did 22 percent of the women surveyed. So odds are, some men end up disappointed with their ladies' approach to Valentine's Day.

If Valentine's Day has always been important to you, you're bound to feel hurt if he comes home empty-handed, says Michael Perry, Ph.D., a marriage and sex therapist in Encino, California, and producer for Access Instructional Media, which makes instructional erotic videos. And that hurt can lead to resentment, an emotion that can poison a relationship.

While it can be crushing if your partner forgets this most romantic of holidays, it isn't necessarily a sign of a bad relationship, says Dr. Perry. Still, what do you do if you always want a pull-out-all-the-stops Valentine's Day celebration and he always wants to forget the whole thing?

Pull out the stops yourself, advises Dr. Perry.

When you become the Valentine's Day master (or is that mistress?) of ceremonies, the holiday instantly becomes more fun and less frustrating, says Dr. Perry. You get to feel the pleasure of doing something nice for your partner while getting what you want: a romantic February 14th. Not a bad deal.

Sweet and Spicy Strategies

A Valentine's Day surprise can be traditional or quirky, a gift or a gesture. But it should always be personal. To inspire you, romance experts offer these suggestions.

Buy *him* flowers. A dozen red roses is the most traditional of Valentine's Day gifts. As you might expect, 84 percent of men who purchase flowers on February 14th buy them for their wives or significant others. But so do 21 percent of women.

"So surprise him with flowers," suggests Norman Scherzer, Ph.D., a member of the Society for the Scientific Study of Sexuality in Mount Vernon, Iowa, and professor of biology and chemistry at Essex County College in Newark, New Jersey. "He'll love it."

Give him the keys. Here's a truly romantic idea: Hunt down an old-fashioned key at an antiques store or thrift shop. Wrap it in beautiful paper. When he opens it, tell him it's the key to your heart, suggests Paul Inman, manager of interactive marketing at Hallmark Cards in Kansas City, Missouri. "I did this for my wife on our wedding day," he says.

Give him a "Valentine's Kiss." Even a simple kiss can be creative, says Tomima Edmark, author of *The Kissing Book: Everything You Need to Know*. To make your kiss special, copy the Morse code for "V": three short, closed-mouth pecks, followed by a long, deep kiss. Of course, men like all kisses, says Edmark. Give him an extra supply.

Do the unexpected. Instead of going the flowers-and-chocolate route, "do something different—maybe something radical or goofy," suggests Dr. Perry. For example, toilet-paper his car, then fill the front seat with flowers.

Be his private dancer. Do a little bump-and-grind for him, suggests Gio, a legendary stripper and star of the video *How to Strip for Your Man*. Her advice: Pick slow, sultry music. (Rhino Records offers a whole CD of stripping music, called *Take It Off! Striptease Classics*, including the classic "The Stripper" by David Rose and His Orchestra.) Never take anything off over your head. "If it gets stuck, the effect is ruined." And forget the candles. "Fling a garment the wrong way, and you've started the wrong kind of fire." Above all, relax. "If your body isn't perfect, it doesn't matter. He loves you; he's not going to be looking for cellulite."

Dress up for him. Wear a peekaboo nightie. "If you've been married for a while, you've probably made love in every room in the house, or done it in every position," notes Dr. Scherzer. "So if the sex act itself isn't going to vary that much, then change the view." You're the view.

Set a calendar countdown. Build the anticipation—and jog his memory—by performing small romantic gestures the week before Valentine's Day, suggests Gregory J.P. Godek, author of the best-selling *1001 Ways to Be Romantic*. "You don't have to spend a fortune, or any money at all, if you don't want to," he says. The first day, you might leave a romantic song on your Valentine's home answering machine (or send him a romantic e-mail at home). On day two, leave him a token (a small toy, perhaps, or a small bottle of cologne) on his pillow. The third day, leave him a lipstick kiss on the bathroom mirror before he goes in to shave. On day four, tuck a love poem where he'll be sure to find it (such as his coat pocket). And the day before Valentine's Day, wake him up 15 minutes early with fresh-baked muffins and gourmet coffee on a tray.

Resolve to strengthen your love. "Look at Valentine's Day like New Year's Eve," says Godek. "But instead of resolving to lose weight or quit smoking, you resolve to make your relationship even better." You might resolve that, for the coming year, you'll be more adventurous, sexually or otherwise. Or learn to fight constructively, instead of hurtfully. Or schedule a "date night" once a month. The biggest bonus, says Godek: "If you're working on your relationship in little ways all year long, there's no pressure come next Valentine's Day."

Weekend Getaways

Ask any longtime couple what their relationship lacks, and the inevitable answer is passion. Well, sure. But passion is a heck of a lot easier to come by when there's time to pursue it. Time for the long talks and tender gestures they once shared (she says). Time for the gourmet lovemaking they used to feast on, instead of the McSex they have now (he says). Time out from the kids, the bills, the day-to-day drudgeries of life that sap their energy and spirit ("amen," they both say).

But there *is* no time. So you have to steal it. You have to become time bandits, thieves of love. In short, you have to plan the perfect getaway. Kind of romantic, isn't it . . . two desperate people going on the lam for love?

A weekend getaway can add spice to a great relationship, deepen a good one, or rejuvenate a relationship that has been operating on autopilot. It's 48 hours to loaf, laugh, be solicitous of one another's every whim, and rediscover what it is about each other that made you connect in the first place.

Any couple can benefit from a weekend getaway, says Pepper Schwartz, Ph.D., professor of sociology at the University of Washington in Seattle and coauthor of *The Great Sex Weekend*. "But longtime lovers who've lost their longing and passion for each other stand to gain the most," she says. "Couples need to continue to surprise each other, to make sure that they're not taking each other for granted. A weekend getaway gives you the opportunity to seduce each other." Ideally, couples should take off for a just-for-the-two-of-us weekend every three months, says Dr. Schwartz.

Emotional Foreplay, Pyrotechnic Sex

The occasional just-for-the-two-of-us weekend brings a longtime couple's gently simmering relationship to a full boil again in several ways. First, it's a return ticket to the early days of courtship, says Richard Kogan, M.D., acting director of the Human Sexuality Program at New York Hospital-Cornell Medical Center in New York City.

"Established couples often don't make as much time for each other as they did when the relationship was new," Dr. Kogan says. When he advises a couple in the relationship doldrums to take off together, "it's amazing how powerful their response can be," Dr. Kogan says. "Couples say, 'We felt like newlyweds again.' That's because they put energy into creating a situation in which their romantic and erotic feelings could flourish."

Physically distancing yourselves from your everyday routine can also free your sense of spontaneity and adventure. You become a romantic couple again. You can sit in the hot tub in your hotel for as long as you want, emerging only to eat and make love. You can get tipsy, dance the night away, and wake up late in each other's arms. You can remember the good times and dream about the future.

And let's not forget about the sex. The connection between emotional intimacy and spellbinding sex is especially strong for women. The lovers' ges-

Fantasy Getaways for Real People

So your credit cards are maxed out and your to-do list looks as long as a Russian novel. That doesn't mean you and your partner can't make a Great Escape. Whether you're watching your budget or the clock, there's a getaway just for you. Use our list for inspiration.

If you're short on money

Fantasy vacation: Climbing the Himalayas

Weekend getaway: Hiking and camping in a state park

Fantasy vacation: A wine-tasting tour of Italy

Weekend getaway: A tour of a local vineyard or winery, and accommodations at a nearby cozy inn

Fantasy vacation: A safari in Kenya

Weekend getaway: A trip to a game preserve

---

tures once lavished on one another—the long talks, the neck-nuzzles, the murmured endearments—are a sweet prelude to the physical act of love. Having a weekend to yourselves gives you time to engage in this kind of emotional foreplay.

The Great Escape

A truly memorable getaway starts with planning, attention to detail—and each partner's willingness to please the other, says Dr. Schwartz. These tips can make your weekend getaway an affair to remember.

Sell the sizzle. Promote the idea of a getaway as an adventure rather than as a pick-me-up for an ailing love life, says Dr. Schwartz. "Treat the idea in a lighthearted manner," she says. "You don't want to say, 'We have to do something about our sex life!'"

Plot your escape together. Planning is a prime opportunity to ease into intimacy—to talk, reminisce, anticipate. So unless you're orchestrating the getaway as a surprise for your partner, let him in on the logistics—where you'll go, what you'll do, how you'll get there, recommends Dr. Schwartz.

If you're short on time

Fantasy getaway: A weekend of skiing in the Rockies

Day trip: Tobogganing in a local or state park, followed by a tailgate party for two

Fantasy getaway: A weekend in the country

Day trip: Horseback riding at a local stable, followed by lunch at a nearby inn

Fantasy getaway: A romantic weekend out of town at one of the best hotels in a big city

Day trip: A romantic weekend at one of the best hotels in *your* city

Fantasy getaway: A relaxing weekend at a mountain retreat

Day trip: A tour of a nearby monastery or abbey

Break out the maps. Pore over the travel section of the newspaper together. Decide what you want to eat, what you should bring, whether to book a room with a hot tub or a fireplace.

Pick a doable destination. There's nothing romantic about driving five hours to a mountain hideaway and arriving too wiped out to enjoy yourselves. So make sure your getaway is a comfortable distance from home. You should be able to make the trip in two hours or less.

Don't overschedule. Skip destinations that offer too many activities or attractions. "The point of this particular weekend is not about golf or shopping," says Dr. Schwartz. "It's about focusing on each other and being together."

Keep it private. While bed-and-breakfasts can be charming, they're not very private, says Dr. Schwartz. "Most have shared walls, shared bathrooms, shared hallways . . . you don't need that," she says. If you love B and Bs, consider only those that provide detached cottages or rooms with thick walls and private bathrooms, she advises.

Pack a goody bag. When children attend birthday parties, they often get a "goody bag" filled with candy and small toys. Treat yourselves to an adults-only version, suggests Dr. Schwartz. "Fill it with massage oil, bubble bath, scented candles, a new silk or satin nightgown, a good bottle of wine, and perhaps a romantic comedy or erotic video."

Practice a hands-off policy. Don't make love the whole week before your getaway, says Dr. Schwartz. It will whet your appetite for the sensuous weekend ahead.

Let the Games Begin

Once your weekend getaway begins, says Dr. Schwartz, give your guy your undivided attention—and throw in a few surprises. These strategies can help heat things up.

Enjoy the ride. Make getting to your getaway part of the fun, recommends Bonnie Jacobson, Ph.D., director of the New York Institute of Psychological Change in New York City. Pack a picnic lunch and stop at a particularly beautiful spot, or take back roads to your destination.

Go with the sexual flow. The first night of your getaway, "don't feel obligated to have intercourse," suggests Dr. Schwartz. "You don't have to do positions A through Z right away. Build up some anticipation." You might treat each other to a full-body massage (using the oils you've packed in your goody bag) or kiss one another from head to toe. "Activities like this might sound hokey, but they're not," says Dr. Schwartz. "They're intimate and should arouse a kind of playfulness."

Go AWOL

Here are five signs that you and your partner need a getaway, says Pepper Schwartz, Ph.D., professor of sociology at the University of Washington in Seattle and coauthor of *The Great Sex Weekend*.

1. If you put sex on the back burner—and you're both secretly relieved
2. If you're not openly affectionate with each other
3. If you take each other for granted
4. If you think longtime couples are *supposed* to be bored
5. If you think you don't need a getaway

Eat light. "Passion can get thwarted by a full stomach," says Dr. Schwartz. So nibble on sensuous finger foods such as smoked oysters on crackers, cold shrimp cocktail, and fresh strawberries or grapes. If you go out for a romantic dinner, order high-protein fare (such as fish) and a salad, rather than carbohydrates (such as pasta), which can make you sleepy or sluggish.

Slip into something comfortable. At some point during the weekend, go shopping—together—for sexy loungewear, suggests Dr. Schwartz. (Silk boxers for him, a short kimono-type robe, teddy, or satin gown for you.) You'll enjoy modeling your purchases later that night.

Ravish him. The number one complaint most men have about their sex lives is that they have to do the wooing—and the work, says Dr. Schwartz. So if your guy normally initiates lovemaking, pounce on *him* for a change. Let him know that he's still got it, and you want it. "You get to be the sexual aggressor and he gets to feel desired, a wish men often express," she says.

Shelve the guilt. If you're leaving children behind, try not to fret: You and your partner deserve this time alone, says Dr. Schwartz. "Kids take so much out of you. Every so often, parents need to get away to remember that they still love each other as lovers."

Don't raise your expectations too high. "Some getaways are spectacular, others merely restful," Dr. Schwartz says. "Just delight in each other's company, especially if this is your first getaway. Everything else is optional."

Plan the next trip. On Sunday afternoon or evening, before you return home, choose a date for the next getaway. Then write it in your calendar at home and work—in ink. Your anticipation will spill over into your everyday life.

PART FOUR

Extraordinary Dating

Cyber-Dating

⟨✷⟩

Welcome to dating's new frontier—the world's biggest singles' party, a seven-days-a-week, 24-hours-a-day chatfest that just might replace blind dates, singles' bars, and the gym as the prime place to flirt, date, and, sometimes, even discover love.

Power up your computer, log on to the Internet, and suddenly, you'll find yourself in a world where the men outnumber the women by more than two to one. Enter a chat room or place an online personal ad, and you may encounter dozens of men eager to make your acquaintance. Problem is, they're all total strangers—and possibly dangerous. As in the real world, the world of cyber-dating has its share of geeks, Don Juans, jerks, and nerds—and even the occasional stalker!

In addition, online romance has its own puzzles: You can't easily tell, for example, whether the person typing those torrid love notes is the single, well-built, curly-haired professional guy he says he is.

So, if you're considering this route, proceed very cautiously, if at all. "Statistically, the odds of really connecting with a suitable person online are only slightly better than if you're just out meeting people in public," says Esther Gwinnell, M.D., a psychiatrist in Portland, Oregon, and author of *Online Seductions: Falling in Love with Strangers on the Internet.* "You have a slight edge because you can meet a lot of men online, find those you like, and then become friends before you meet in person."

At the Electronic "Masked Ball"

You can meet men three ways on the Internet: through chat rooms, online personal ads, and forums. Chat rooms allow you to send messages to groups of people (with similar interests) online at the same time, or pair off for private conversation with one other person. They offer more spontaneity than forums or newsgroups (also called bulletin boards), where someone may not respond to your posted message about the topic at hand for hours or even days. Personals on the Internet are much the same as magazine and newspaper personals, except that responses will come to you via e-mail.

What's the world of cyber-dating like? Dr. Gwinnell compares it to a masked ball, where we can hide our true identities, take on new personalities, and act in new ways because conventional social rules are suspended. The result? A freewheeling, anything-goes atmosphere that can be liberating, yet confusing. It's a place that can help us make new connections, yet could hide dangers. Thanks to online anonymity, a woman can:

Develop intense relationships. "Women who've had positive experiences with Internet relationships say that it's great getting to know someone from the inside-out, through a true soul-to-soul meeting," Dr. Gwinnell says. "But if both people haven't been completely honest, or if you discover that there's more to this person that you really don't like, it can be wrenching or even dangerous."

Emotional relationships can form quickly via e-mail because real-world clues can't intrude. (Does he have spinach in his teeth? Is he lazy? Ambitious? Rude? Sensitive? A genuinely nice guy? A con artist? You may never find out for certain until you meet in person.) "As a result, you're free to form a fantasy and then have an emotional connection to that fantasy person," Dr. Gwinnell says. "This freedom is one of the best aspects of, and the biggest problems with, Internet relationships."

Explore—and develop—your own personality. Online, you can create and re-create yourself—no one has preconceived notions based on your voice, your appearance, your age, or your gender. A woman can use this anonymity to begin expanding aspects of her personality. Shy? Try flirting. Wish you were a better conversationalist? Find a serious chat room and test your opinions on politics, the economy, or the latest movie. "Change does begin with baby steps, which a woman can start taking online," says Marlene M. Maheu, Ph.D., a psychologist in San Diego and editor of the online publication *Self-Help* and of *Psychology* magazine, where she conducted a reader poll on cybersex. "She should realize, though, that moving those skills into the real world will still take more effort."

Many women even experiment with online sexual relationships, either in chat rooms or via private e-mail, exchanging explicit descriptions of an imagined, in-the-moment sexual encounter with a partner (or, sometimes, with multiple partners) they quite often have never met in real life. Be prepared: The Internet is crawling with chat rooms devoted to every conceivable variety of sexuality. Cybersex experts also say that sex often becomes a topic of conversation very early in the game when women and men meet through singles' chat rooms and online personal ads.

Remember, you are perfectly within your rights to end any e-mail conversation that gets too steamy, too fast—or to tell your cyber-acquaintance that he better slow down. "Don't move into a sexual relationship if you don't feel ready," Dr. Maheu advises. "And don't do anything that you won't feel good about later on."

Tips for Cyber-Virgins

Ready to surf the 'net for love? This expert advice can help you meet men confidently and safely online.

Keep your name out of it. Never give out your real name, your phone number, or your address when you're online, cautions Dr. Gwinnell. (After all, you wouldn't give that information to strangers on the street, would you?) Instead, use a "screen name" as your alias. (For more on screen names, see below.) If an online relationship progresses to the point where the two of you want to talk by phone, get *his* phone number.

For even greater privacy, you can also keep your e-mail address confidential by choosing chat rooms and online personals that not only allow you to post under an alias but also provide "anonymous remailing," meaning e-mail messages are sent to a common address and then forwarded to individuals, says Joe Bargmann, former senior editor of the Web site Swoon, which features personal ads. That way, no one gets your e-mail address until you give it out.

Select an appropriate "screen name"—or two. Your chosen alias speaks volumes about your online personality. Choose one that accurately reflects your interests and intentions online—and provides a "hook" to attract the kind of man you're interested in meeting. ("Sex Kitten" will work if you're hungry for raw cybersex; "Tennis Star" might be better if you want to find like-minded guys.) One New York writer who has chronicled the cybersex phenomenon adopted five different screen names so that she could assume slightly different personalities depending upon her mood.

Look for love in all the right places. Don't expect romance to blossom in one of the many explicitly sexual chat rooms, Dr. Gwinnell says. "That's like looking for a marriage partner in a singles' bar," she notes. "It's not why the men are there. Sure, they'll respond to you, but you won't get a long-term relationship out of it."

Instead, follow the specific directions provided by your particular service provider (such as America OnLine, Microsoft Network, or CompuServe) to access chat rooms, and then check out the wide variety available to find one that matches your interests. The same goes for newsgroups. Or you can let potential dating partners know exactly what you want by using online personal ads instead.

First, be a tourist. Get comfortable with the etiquette, the cast of characters, and the flow of conversation in your chosen chat room by "lurking"— Internet parlance for simply hanging out and reading what others have to say. If the chat room isn't right for you, move on, suggests Patti Britton, Ph.D., a sex therapist in San Francisco who runs an online practice. But don't be surprised if someone sends you a private message—your screen name will be posted whether you participate or not.

Put cyber-guys through a screening process. Before agreeing to talk by phone, meet in person, or even launch a long-term cyber-relationship, learn all you can about the man behind the computer messages, Dr. Maheu suggests. "Have a standard set of questions and ask them all, every time you become interested in a new man," she suggests. Among the issues to raise: Are you single? What are your hobbies? Occupation? Religious beliefs? Have you ever been married? Why did your last serious relationship end? How do you like to spend a weekend? How do you spend your money? What do you look like? Do you have any health conditions? Have you ever been arrested or spent time in prison?

"Ask the serious questions after you feel comfortable with someone," Dr. Gwinnell suggests. "If you do it too soon, you're apt to scare your e-mail partner away. Wait too long, and you may get a shock if reality isn't what you expected."

Trust your instincts. If a cyber-guy seems weird, unstable, violent, or condescending, move on. "Pay attention to what they talk about and how they talk about it," Dr. Gwinnell says. You can't always pick out the creeps, bores, and liars, but you can help yourself by paying attention to your gut instincts. Stay alert, and you'll be more likely to pick out the nice guys when they come along.

Face-to-face? Play it smart and safe. If you've progressed from chat room to private e-mails to phone conversations, both of you may be ready for a "virtual" experience: meeting face-to-face, in the real world. Even if you've developed a high degree of intimacy online and on the telephone, it's crucial to set up a safe meeting, just as you would if you were meeting someone for the first time through a newspaper personals column, Dr. Maheu says.

Meet in a public place such as a coffee shop or restaurant. Use your own transportation. Tell someone where you're going, who you're meeting, and when you expect to be back. For extra safety, also give that person his phone number or e-mail address.

Dating

T alk about first-night jitters. When Gloria Jeckert dated again for the first time in 36 years, she says, "I was a nervous wreck. I ran downstairs to ask my daughter, 'What am I going to do? Does this outfit look okay?' She laughed and told me everything would be fine. And it was."

Jeckert, an outgoing retired bookkeeper from Lyndhurst, New Jersey, hadn't gone out with a guy since her early twenties, when she met and married her late husband, Al. "We were married for 34 years," she says. "We were best friends. Dating again was hard at first. I compared everyone to my husband. And the first time a man put his arm around me—that really felt weird!"

Jeckert found what many newly single and ever-single women have discovered: The dating game is different today than it was back when they first said "yes" to a nervous young man's invitation to the homecoming dance at age 16.

"The dating world has changed radically in the past 20 to 30 years," says Lila Gruzen, Ph.D., a psychotherapist and marriage, family, and couple counselor in Sherman Oaks, California, and author of *10 Foolish Dating Mistakes That Men and Women Make and How to Avoid Them.* "If you're still playing by the rules you learned in your teens, it's time for an update."

A Change for the Better

The new rules? Today it's perfectly acceptable for a woman to do the asking and the paying—something that would have scandalized folks 20 or 30 years ago.

The players—women *and* men—have changed, too. Today's eligible guys may be divorced or widowed, younger than you or somewhat older. They're also a bit harder to find than single men were back when you were in high school or in your early twenties.

At the same time, you may have higher expectations, and you may have less time for a social life if you're juggling a job, a household, child-rearing, and maybe the care of elderly parents. You may also wonder sometimes if you still have what it takes to date successfully. "Women feel that they must be

Ladies and Gentlemen, Adjust Your Speed

According to a survey of 2,315 single men and women conducted by the Chicago-based dating service It's Just Lunch, men and women approach dating at different speeds. Consider:

Average length of time it takes a woman to decide if a man is worth dating a second time: 1 hour

Average length of time it takes a man to decide if a woman is worth dating a second time: 15 minutes

The vast majority of men will call for a second date within 24 hours.

Percentage of women who say that a man's income is an important dating criterion: 90

Percentage of men who say that a woman's income is an important dating criterion: 51

Percentage of women who date for more than six months before having sex: 17

Percentage of men who date for more than six months before having sex: 7.5

young, tall, and attractive to find eligible men and get dates, but that's just not true," says Dr. Gruzen. "The best preparation for dating is to feel good about yourself—without getting a face peel, plastic surgery, or trying the latest crash diet. Most men—the ones worth dating—want a woman who is honest and emotionally available, not a fashion model."

Ready, Set, Go

If you haven't dated in a while or feel that you could use some brushing up, use this expert advice to help prepare yourself for the dating world.

Draw strength from your experience. Remind yourself that you have a lot of strengths—including a degree of maturity and emotional security that many younger women lack, says Dr. Gruzen. As a result, it will be easier to flirt (you have a whole life to talk about!) and easier to weather the possibility of rejection (you have, or can create, a full life to satisfy your physical, emotional, and intellectual needs).

Shop for a dating wardrobe. Re-entering the dating scene? "Go shopping!" suggests Maureen Callahan, 38, a single mother of two from the Indianapolis area. "There's nothing more uplifting for a woman than getting some new clothes, perhaps makeup, and a new hairdo as well. Buy clothing that accentuates your positive qualities. It should be eye-catching and even perhaps a bit sexy, but classy."

Experts agree. "You need a dating wardrobe, usually something casual that you can dress up or down, like silk pants and a silk blazer," says Nina Atwood, a licensed counselor and dating coach in Dallas and author of *Date Lines* and *Be Your Own Dating Service.* "Business suits on dates are a little out of place, and jeans are often a little too casual. Look for something good-looking that's in between."

Build your own singles' network. Divorced, widowed, or simply not getting out enough? "Build a community of single friends, male and female," Atwood suggests. "You'll have like-minded people to socialize with, and you never know who will know a single man who's perfect for you."

Practice, practice, practice. The singles' network serves a second function: It gives you experience at going out and being social without the added pressure of potential romance, the experts say. "I know women who haven't had a date in 10 years," Atwood says. "The best way to ease in is to

Dating, with Children

Call it the world's toughest balancing act: You're single-handedly raising your children, and now you have a date for Saturday night. "This is a big challenge in terms of time and physical and emotional energy," notes Wendy Kyman, Ph.D., a certified sex therapist and assistant professor of health education at Baruch College in New York City.

Her advice?

Build a babysitting network. "Make your date night a fun night for the kids, too," Dr. Kyman suggests. "Have friends, family, and babysitters ready to look after your kids. Arrange a special sleep-over night. Or date on a night when their father is with them."

Realize your kids want to see you happy. "Children don't want to have the burden of being the mom's sole source of connection and intimacy. If mom is happy, children are happy," Dr. Kyman says.

Keep the details to yourself. Don't use your children as confidants on relationship matters.

Limit contact between your children and the men you are dating. Until a relationship is serious, keep your kids and your guy separate. "Never let a man you're dating sleep over if your children are in the house," says Dr. Kyman.

do safe things in groups—the bowling league, softball after work, a 'girls' night' with a woman friend."

You can also learn to feel comfortable with intimacy this way. "For women who find they've been so busy that they don't have very close, intimate relationships with anyone, I usually recommend letting go of the idea of meeting a man for a little while and concentrating on developing friendships with women," says Lita D. Mustacchi, a clinical social work psychotherapist who practices in New York City and in Rockland County, New York. "You'll learn about yourself, feel good about yourself, and also develop a wonderful support network."

Acknowledge guilty feelings. If you're a single working mother, taking time away from your children to date may make you feel extremely guilty. "I encourage these women to go ahead and have a social life," says

Wendy Kyman, Ph.D., a certified sex therapist and assistant professor of health education at Baruch College in New York City. "Children need to see that their mother has picked herself up after a divorce or widowhood and is building a life that includes taking care of herself. It's a healthy lesson."

Pack away bitterness. "The real reason men date younger women? It's not because they're cuter or more energetic," maintains Connie Merritt, a dating coach based in Laguna Beach, California, and author of *Finding Love (Again!): The Dating Survival Manual for Women over 30*. "Time and time again, men tell me it's because these women aren't bitter. They don't tell stories about the ex-husband or former boyfriend who did them wrong. For older women, this is an important lesson—these war stories have no place in your new relationships."

Don't bury these feelings—just don't get stuck in a one-woman pity party. Talk with your women friends, keep a journal, or join a divorce-recovery group so you can talk your feelings out and find ways to nurture yourself, Merritt suggests.

Playing the New Dating Game

Ready to go? Let our dating experts guide you through the rules of the new dating game.

Set your standards in advance. Too choosy, and you won't have many dates. Not selective enough, and you'll find yourself wasting your time with too many Mr. Wrongs. The answer? "Women should have three or four immutable 'can't stands' about the guys they meet, unchangeable things that they won't tolerate," Merritt suggests. "Perhaps yours are no smoking, no men over 50, no men who don't read books." Any guy who meets your criteria then becomes worth talking to. Sure, you'll meet many who aren't your dream date, but you'll also increase the odds that you will find a good dating partner and possibly begin a relationship, she adds.

Circulate. True, single men are a bit harder to find now than when you were a teen or twenty-something. Stack the odds in your favor by getting out often, suggests Sandra Reishus, a clinical sexologist and relationship consultant in Sacramento, California, who formerly ran a match-making service. "The more open a woman is to having new experiences, going out, and meeting people, the more likely she is to find a mate. If a woman is hypercritical and turns down most invitations, her chances drop. You never know who will introduce you to the perfect man."

Make dating your project. When you're ready to date, use all possible means to find eligible men, Dr. Gruzen suggests. That includes dating services, matchmakers, personal ads, the Internet, and your friends. "Finding eligible men doesn't 'just happen' anymore. You can't expect the same level of success with your love goals that you do with your career goals if you only spend a few minutes a week trying to meet new men," she says. "So make it a project. Don't be shy about telling your friends what you're looking for."

Know when to pull out the credit card. These days, there's no simple answer to the question of who should pay, says Atwood. "The best advice? Be willing to negotiate—politely, and with a sense of humor," she says. "Generally, on the first date, whoever did the asking-out should be prepared to pay. But even then, and on later dates, a woman can certainly offer to pay for her share." Paying her own way makes many women feel more comfortable because it lifts the feeling of unspoken obligation that may be present if the guy always foots the bill.

Of course, there are other ways to reciprocate: Offer to cook a meal, or bring takeout for your next get-together, for example.

Ask him out. Dating experts say that men enjoy having the tables turned, if the asking-out is done with finesse. "It's very difficult for a woman to ask a man out for a first date," Atwood notes. "But if the man is doing all the asking, it's good to readjust the balance of power. You might initiate once in a while, in part to show that you're truly interested."

One easy way to do this: Ask a man to a specific event, one you'd like to attend anyway, Merritt suggests. "Say, for example, 'I have two tickets to *Phantom of the Opera* for the third Saturday in March. Would you like to go with me?'" she suggests. "If he says no, he's turning down the event, not you." Don't ask too far in advance, however. "Three weeks is good," she notes. "Two to three months ahead isn't. Then there's an unspoken expectation that the two of you will be an item until then."

Your First Date: An Insider's Guide

Ah, the art of the first date. A time to learn all you can about a new man—without interrogating him. To reveal who you are—without spilling too much of your soul. To listen, and at the same time manage not to dribble your coffee, trip over a table, or get tangled up as you take off your coat. With

Best—And Worst—First Dates

Surprising news from the dating world: Your first meeting with a new man isn't the right time for romance, thrills, or catching the latest movie, notes Nina Atwood, a licensed counselor and dating coach in Dallas and author of *Date Lines* and *Be Your Own Dating Service*. "First dates should be mutual interviews and nothing more," she says.

The best first-date strategy? Arrange a short meeting, in a public place, where the two of you can talk (as opposed to a movie or play, where you sit beside each other in silence for two hours or more). And save the candlelit dinners, dancing, and spectator events for future get-togethers, after you've established some kind of groundwork.

Here are the best and worst spots for a first date, according to dating coaches.

Best

A coffee shop—for cappuccino and conversation

A walk—on the beach, in a park, through a historic or interesting part of town

Brunch

A quick get-together for ice cream or frozen yogurt

The zoo

A museum or gallery

Worst

Bars

Movies

Sports (spectator or participatory)

Romantic (and expensive) dinners

Dancing

Concerts

Plays

Your place

His place

the following expert advice, you can manage—and even enjoy—that all-important first meeting.

Befriend the clock and avoid bad dates. "Pick out a coffee shop where you can get together over latte or a soda and talk for a half-hour or 45 minutes," Merritt says. "On the first date, you simply want to spend a little time with him, ask some important questions, and decide whether or not you'd like to get to know him better."

Set a time limit ahead of time—graciously, of course, Atwood suggests. This not only protects a good first date from becoming too long and too intense but also gives you a graceful way out if the date isn't a good experience. For example, if you realize immediately that this isn't the man of your dreams—or worse, if the encounter is awkward, painfully boring, or mildly unpleasant—you won't be committed to an entire evening together.

Keep it public. Your home—and his abode—should be off-limits until the two of you have had several dates, says Atwood. Public places, such as restaurants, are a better choice for first (and second and third) dates because they offer safety (after all, you're meeting a near-stranger) and control (if need be, you can make your excuses and end the date early—which can be difficult if he's at your place), and they lack the overtones of familiarity and sexuality that can color the atmosphere at home.

Skip the drinks. Productive first dates are more like interviews than romantic encounters, Dr. Gruzen says. "I think alcohol clouds your judgment," she says. After a glass of wine or an after-dinner cognac, you might miss warning signals that this guy isn't right for you.

Reveal the real you. Don't try to impress your date, win him over, or in some way act "better" than the other women you may imagine he's also dating, Atwood says. Your job on Date Number One is to be yourself. So talk about your hobbies and interests, your hopes and dreams, your family background, your view of current events, people who've inspired you, and the kind of relationship you'd like to have, she suggests.

It's fine to talk briefly, and in a positive way, about past relationships, but don't criticize past partners or complain across-the-board about the opposite sex, Atwood notes. And avoid these conversational pitfalls: name-dropping; gossiping; calling attention to your own wealth or success; complaining about your health, your kids, your boss, or your life; or giving intimate details of your ongoing therapy or self-help efforts.

Then turn the tables. Use your first date together to learn more about who he is, Merritt and Atwood suggest. In a conversational way, ask a few questions such as "What do you do when you're not working?" "Do you see your family often?" "Where did you grow up and go to school?"

How can you get him to open up without turning a date into an interrogation? One good strategy is to talk briefly about some aspect of your own life, then ask, "How about you?" This can be a good way to bring up sensitive topics, such as past relationships. "You might say, 'I've been married once and have been divorced for five years. How about you?'" Atwood says. "Don't go into why you were divorced or ask him to give you intimate details—that will emerge if the two of you develop some kind of connection and trust over future dates."

Rein in the eager overachiever. If the guy across the table comes on too strong—if, for example, he tries too hard to impress you by bestowing endless compliments, bringing flowers or a gift, or ordering expensive food or drink—remember that he's probably nervous, and not necessarily a geek. If his behavior bothers you or makes you feel uncomfortable, try to defuse the situation. Thank him for his generosity, then deliver a compliment of your own. Tell him—gently—that such gestures make you feel a little uncomfortable when you're just getting to know someone, and (if necessary) that you don't feel comfortable accepting a gift right now. Then tell him that what you'd really like is to learn more about him, Merritt suggests.

If he's already talking plenty about himself—if he boasts too much about his income, his career, his friends, his car, or his computer, for example—don't be afraid to change the subject. Ask him some of the basic questions suggested above, but weave in information about yourself. If he doesn't get the hint that your date should be a conversation and a mutual exploration, then perhaps he's not Mr. Right.

Be prepared for the truly intolerable date. Perhaps he's inconsiderate, or even disrespectful. Maybe he bores you to tears, or complains incessantly. Suddenly, a hot prospect has become the date from hell.

Your escape hatch? If you've arranged a short date, it's a simple matter to thank the guy, say you've enjoyed chatting, and then be on your way. "If he asks you for another date, suggest talking on the phone sometime in the future," Atwood suggests. "If he calls, tell him you've thought about it and don't think it will work for you."

If you're stuck in the early stages of a longer date together (such as dinner or a day trip), you can still cut things short. "You can always say, 'You know what, I've changed my mind about this. It's time for me to go home,'" Atwood suggests. "If he asks what's wrong, simply say you've decided this won't work out. Women should know they don't have to be nice and pretend to enjoy an experience that's actually unpleasant." Of course, this works best if you have your own transportation—or at least extra cash for a taxi.

Say goodbye with a handshake. Even if it goes well, save kisses, hugs, and affectionate parting words for future dates together, Merritt says. End a first date with a smile, a handshake, and a brief, gracious parting line, such as "I'm really happy we've had the chance to meet," she suggests.

If he attempts to plant a kiss anyway, simply step back and explain that it's really too soon—you've enjoyed the date and feel flattered, but that's not where you are right now. "An aware, tuned-in guy will respect your feelings," Atwood notes. "If, on the other hand, he gets offended, it may be an indication that he's insensitive."

Sounds prudish? You may feel comfortable giving, and receiving, a quick kiss on the cheek. But Atwood advises women to put off physical intimacy for a few dates so that the two of you can develop a relationship with a strong emotional connection before your libidos take center stage. "If you share a passionate kiss on the second date, where do you think you'll be by the fifth date? For many couples, the answer is in bed," she says. "Physical intimacy can make the two of you feel like a couple even before your hearts and minds are ready. I think it's important to wait, even before you kiss, so you can build a bridge to the heart first."

Be second-date savvy. If you both seem sure you'd like to meet again, plan a second date when the first one ends, Atwood suggests. But be aware: Ending a first date often feels awkward, and first-daters often discuss getting together again simply as a way to ease that tension, she notes.

If he suggests a second date but you feel uncertain (or sense that he's unsure), suggest instead that the two of you talk about it by phone on a specific night later that week. This gives you time to think it over, Atwood says.

If you're sure you don't want to meet him again but he presses for a second date, simply say, "Thank you, but that won't work for me," Merritt suggests. But if waiting a few days has only confirmed to you that you'd like to see him again, make that second date with confidence: This could be the start of a beautiful relationship.

Dating Services

Turned off by singles' bars, personal ads, and blind dates set up by well-meaning friends? Looking to expand your network of dateable men? Busy?

You may be the perfect candidate for a dating service, experts say. "Pick the right service, and you can meet some great men," notes Patricia Moore, president of the International Society of Introduction Services in West Hills, California. "The truth is, dating services aren't for geeks and desperate people. They're used by assertive, successful people who want help finding the right man or woman."

There are three basic kinds of services, says Moore.

Video and computer dating. This is the most affordable dating service. You either put together a personal video profile, or your biography and a digitized photo are entered into a computer database. In return, you get to watch videos or scan computer biographies of potential male matches. Video services can cost a few hundred to a few thousand dollars. Computerized services are usually less than $400.

"I think video dating is a great idea. When you can see a man talking, hear his voice and the rhythm of his speech, and see how he presents himself, it's much more revealing than words on a page or a snapshot," says Lila Gruzen, Ph.D., a psychotherapist and marriage, family, and couple counselor in Sherman Oaks, California, and author of *10 Foolish Dating Mistakes That Men and Women Make and How to Avoid Them.*

Introduction services. This is the most expensive option, with search costs starting at about $500 per match. (In fact, Moore knows of very selective searches that have cost customers as much as $50,000!) Why the steep price tag? Personal service. A professional matchmaker interviews her clients extensively about their values, interests, and life goals, then suggests matches accordingly. "A reputable service will stick to your guidelines," Moore notes. "They won't introduce you to a plumber if you have a Ph.D. in philosophy unless you want them to. And you get preapproval. The service calls each person and gives them basic background information before setting up a first meeting. You have a lot of control."

"Matchmakers who work with you one-on-one are the greatest invention," says Dr. Gruzen. "You know any potential mates are serious about meeting somebody. And the one-to-one contact with the matchmaker means that a match will be based on more than statistics."

Before You Sign Up

No matter which method you choose, the following advice will help you get the most from your dating-service experience.

Specialize. Look for a service that meets your specific needs, Moore suggests. Are you just looking for casual dates, or are you ready for marriage? Would you prefer a service that specializes in matching singles of a particular religious faith?

Investigate. Before signing a contract, be sure the dating service is reputable and has a good pool of available men, says Moore. Find out how long they have been in business, what the membership fee will be, how many matches you'll receive for your money, and what their success rate is—how many long-term relationships, engagements, and marriages do they have to their credit?

Include a background check. Call your local Better Business Bureau before you sign up, Moore suggests. Find out if anyone has lodged a complaint against the service.

Ask about the men. Go for a service with a large number of available men in your desired age range, suggests Nina Atwood, a licensed counselor and dating coach in Dallas and author of *Date Lines* and *Be Your Own Dating Service*.

Give older guys a chance. Over 40? Consider dating men 5 to 10 years older than you, and you'll give your matchmaker or dating service a better chance of finding suitable matches, Moore says. "Even if you feel like you're 25 and your friends say you still look 25, the truth is that younger men are often not interested in dating older women," she says. "Forty-plus women who think they should be dating younger men can be the hardest clients to match. They're missing out on interesting, exciting men who have just a few more years on them."

Friends Who Date Friends

ྀ༘

He's always there when you need him—to laugh or commiserate, move furniture or offer tips on fixing a leaky kitchen faucet. Perhaps he has even interpreted the erratic and inscrutable behavior of the men you've dated.

But suddenly, this old friend is looking . . . well, darned appealing. You notice the endearing crinkles at the corners of his eyes. His smile. His thoughtfulness. His dependability. His wit. (And how could you have overlooked how gorgeous he looks in that blue denim shirt!) Should you ask him out? Ask him over? Add a little kiss to the friendly hug you always share when you say goodbye? And if you don't act, won't some other woman snap him up?

Hold on a minute, say experts. While an enduring, intimate love relationship can grow from a friendship between a man and a woman, dating your buddies for the wrong reasons can jeopardize precious friendships, says Nina Atwood, a licensed counselor and dating coach in Dallas and author of *Date Lines* and *Be Your Own Dating Service*. "Dating someone you're friends with can be risky. It only works if both of you have a strong feeling that you are soul mates who have been kept apart and now can be together. If it looks like the two of you could really sail into a wonderful future, go for it. But casual dating among your friends is not a good idea."

No Turning Back

Cross the line between "friend" and "potential boyfriend" and you may not be able to go back, ever. "It can be hard to get back on the friendship

track once you've blurred those lines," says Elizabeth Wolfson, Ph.D., an adjunct faculty member at the Columbia University School of Social Work in New York City and a therapist in Ridgewood, New Jersey. "It's hard to get back to that feeling of safety you have with a friend, that sense that you can discuss practically anything more or less neutrally. Suddenly, much more is at stake."

It can take months or even years to develop a good friendship. And for busy women, building new friendships is a time-consuming task that often goes by the wayside when we're trying to shoehorn a job, perhaps a family, a social life, and some personal time into a day that's only 24 hours long.

Then again, slowly growing to love a friend can be the best basis for a long-term relationship, notes Bonnie Jacobson, Ph.D., director of the New York Institute for Psychological Change in New York City and author of *Love Triangles* and *If Only You Would Listen*. "When you don't have the pressure of dating and you're just hanging out together, you can see where your feelings take you as you get to know a man better," she says. "It can be the best way to start a romantic relationship."

To sort it all out, follow this advice.

Ask the tough questions. Before turning a friendship into a possible romance, be clear within yourself about why you want to take this step, Dr. Wolfson suggests. Ask yourself:

• What do I want down the road? Can I see myself in a long-term relationship with this man? If you can't, resist the temptation and preserve your friendship.

• Am I acting out of loneliness, or is this a guy with whom I want to move into an intimate relationship? If you're feeling a general sense of loneliness, it's time to try to meet other eligible men. Place a personal ad, ask your friends to recommend eligible single men they know, or join a special-interest organization. Circulate!

Take it slowly. Some of the best intimate relationships begin as friendships, Dr. Jacobson notes. If you're beginning to feel that spark, don't rush, she suggests. "If you feel sexually attracted, you can act on it very slowly by opening up little by little. As you feel comfortable, show more caring and attention. Start to talk about how you feel." By giving yourselves and the relationship time to evolve, neither of you will find yourself in over your head, or regretting a too-quick plunge. You'll stand a better chance of preserving a valuable friendship, no matter what happens.

Infatuation

Infatuation—that giddy, swept-off-your-feet, I'm-in-love-even-though-we-just-met feeling—isn't reserved for ingenues. So says Nancy Burns.

"I see it all the time," says Burns, who until recently ran an upscale nail-care salon in Sacramento, California. "My single girlfriends get very infatuated and become very free with their emotions and affections. Not that they're necessarily sleeping with the guy. But they're doing extra-nice things, getting extra-involved. It has happened to me, too. We're *too* nice. And then, reality hits. You discover that the guy isn't really right for you, or he breaks up with you."

Infatuation may feel like extraordinary togetherness—but it's the farthest thing from lasting love, says Kathleen Mojas, Ph.D., a psychologist in Beverly Hills, California. "It's only human to idealize another person and fantasize that he's exactly what you want," she notes. "In fact, that's a normal, early stage in many relationships—followed by the stage where we see the person as he really is and learn to adjust." It's also normal for one person in a couple to feel somewhat more infatuated than the other.

But when that love-at-first-sight feeling clouds your judgment, you stop connecting with the real person across the restaurant table, Dr. Mojas says. You may miss—or refuse to notice—red-flag signals that scream, "Wake up,

Taboos: Guys Never to Have a Crush On

Your lawyer is looking awfully cute lately? Ready to ask your auto mechanic out for a cappuccino? Resist. Familiarity can breed a dangerous allure, notes Linda Barbanel, a psychotherapist in New York City. And dating more or less "taboo" men can have serious, or at least potentially inconvenient, consequences. Here's a list of some men you should leave alone.

Real Taboos—Just Say No

- Married men. (Obviously.)

- Your boss. (It can only lead to trouble.)

- Your doctor. (It's better to keep your family doc, gynecologist, or other physician impartial and professionally compassionate.)

- Your therapist. (This is against all the rules of a healthy therapist-client relationship. It destroys trust.)

- Your lawyer. (You want this guy on your side—at all times.)

Lazy Dating—Stay Away

- Your girlfriends' old boyfriends. (Why antagonize a valuable woman friend?)

- Your former boyfriend's roommate, best friend, or brothers. ("That's just lazy dating," Barbanel says. "Instead, get out of the house, take a risk, and meet some new people.")

- Your ex-husband's best friend or brothers. (Same as above.)

Sticky Business If You Squabble or Break Up

- Your landlord. (Do you really want to make *this* phone call: "Hello, Bill? I know we're not on speaking terms, but my hot water is on the fritz. Could you fix it?")

- Your car mechanic. (Avoid this relationship unless you can find another mechanic who's equally adept at tuning up your chariot.)

- Your hairdresser. (If you two call it quits, will your hair ever look the same?)

this guy's not for you," such as serious character flaws, important areas of incompatibility, and a lack of shared interests, values, or goals. You may tolerate unhealthy or dangerous behaviors, such as alcoholism, disrespect, or even abuse. Or you simply may prolong a dating relationship with a guy who's perfectly nice, but just not Mr. Right.

The end of the story? Reality wins, fantasy loses. "Often, as normal conflicts arise and we see who the other person really is, with all his human weaknesses and flaws, disillusionment takes the place of infatuation," Dr. Mojas says. "If a woman has been extremely infatuated, there can be bitter disappointment because the relationship and the partner are not perfect."

Waking from the Dream

What's behind the cycle of infatuation and disappointment? "Low self-esteem, fear of loneliness, and a lack of trust that a woman will be able to find a good relationship," says Linda Barbanel, a psychotherapist in New York City. "Any or all of these could lead a woman to put on her rose-colored glasses and believe that a guy or a relationship is much better than he or it really is—and make her work hard to convince herself that it's true."

These are hard truths to accept. The good news is that you can learn to overcome the infatuation habit and date with greater success and confidence, relationship experts say.

The first step is to recognize the following warning signs of infatuation.

- Thinking that a romantic relationship—*any* romantic relationship—will solve all your problems or fill a void in your life. This kind of thinking is a setup for infatuation, not honest, down-to-earth love, says Ann L. Weber, Ph.D., professor of psychology at the University of North Carolina at Asheville.

- Being unusually impulsive. Uncharacteristically risky or overly generous actions—like loaning your car or a large sum of money to a guy you've just started dating, taking in his laundry, agreeing to pet-sit for his five dogs and six cats for a week, letting him move into your place, or sleeping with him very early in the relationship—are all hallmarks of infatuation, Dr. Weber notes. "You may even catch yourself rationalizing your actions, saying something like, 'Oh, I just know I can trust him' or 'I wouldn't normally do that, but this time it's different,'" she says.

- Doing all the work. Are you doing all the calling, all the asking-out, creating all the special moments, and giving all the endearing little presents? Then you're certainly making more of the relationship than your guy is, Dr. Mojas says.

Do Less, Listen More

You'll be able to break free of infatuation with these expert guidelines.

Slow down. The next time around, get acquainted at a relaxed pace, Dr. Mojas suggests. "Find out who this guy really is before you sleep with him or start seeing him exclusively. Try dating him just once a week, not every night. Don't talk on the phone every day."

Resist the urge to buy him presents, take care of him, or appear extraperky, peppy, or pleasing, Barbanel cautions. "You don't owe him anything, except to let him know you've had a nice time," she notes. "If need be, explain that you'd like to take your time getting to know him because you're old-fashioned. It's a sign of self-esteem."

Look and listen. When you're with him, pay attention to clues that reveal his true nature, Barbanel suggests. Ask yourself: Is this a good person? Does he share? Does he cooperate? What are his friendships like? How does he handle money? Does he have habits that make me uncomfortable, such as smoking or excessive use of alcohol? What's his relationship with his family like? Does he seem to have a balance in his life between work, interests, and a social life?

Call on your support system. If you tend to become very involved very quickly, then this s-l-o-w approach might make you feel anxious or nervous at first, Dr. Mojas notes. You may feel insecure, for example, because the two of you don't talk on the phone often. Now is the time to confide in your best friends, your sisters, or whoever gives you good emotional support. "When you soothe your anxious feelings, you're better able to resist the urge to merge—and you'll be more successful at deciding whether or not this relationship has potential," says Dr. Mojas.

Cultivate a full life of your own. Develop your talents, pursue your interests, nurture your friendships—and keep it up even when you're dating a new man, Dr. Mojas suggests. "Having a nice balance in your life, a feeling that there's meaning and friendship and fun in your life even without a man, will help you maintain self-esteem and a sense of satisfaction," she says. "That way, you can feel freer to walk away from a new relationship if it's not right for you. You won't be depending on another person to give you things you can actually give yourself."

Old Flames

Twenty-five years after they said goodbye, Kaye Strayer and her first love met again in the small Pennsylvania town where they had dated as teenagers. "It was amazing," she says. "We went back to the same restaurant where we used to hang out, and we were waited on by the same waitress. Then we drove to the same place where we used to 'park' and we necked. The feeling was as strong as it was back then."

Strayer, 51, who leads singles' groups in Charlotte, North Carolina, didn't pursue a relationship with this oldest of old flames. But she learned a lesson that researcher Nancy Kalish, Ph.D., psychology professor at California State University, Sacramento, and author of *Lost and Found Lovers*, has documented in her Lost Love Project, an academic search for people who reconnected with significant others from the past: The loves of our youth can have surprising intensity.

Dr. Kalish sent anonymous questionnaires to 1001 men and women who had originally broken up their relationships for situational reasons (such as parental disapproval, being too young, or moving away)—circumstances that were no longer a factor when the couple was reunited. Reunited old flames who married reported a low divorce rate—less than 2 percent. And many of those who had been together for 22 years or more said that they still felt like newlyweds.

"Old flames are your most important romances," Dr. Kalish says. "You're going back to puppy love. These are people you met at school. You're from the same community. You share a common history. You know his family, he knows yours. You met before life made you cynical. It's a wonderfully grounded reason to have a romance."

Revisiting Your Past

Even if meeting an old flame doesn't lead to rekindled romance, the experience can allow you to relive happy memories—and resolve unfinished business.

"We all carry these emotional pictures from the past. Sometimes women dwell on these pictures and fantasies—*What if I had married John instead of Bill? Maybe I made the wrong choice*—to help them get through bad relationships and hard times," notes Nina Atwood, a licensed counselor and dating coach in Dallas and author of *Date Lines* and *Be Your Own Dating Service*. "Then you almost have to pursue the old flame, to see what's really still there. Reconnecting with an old flame can be a good transition back into the world of dating."

It can also be an emotionally safe way to experience dating again, adds Atwood. "It's a safe date with someone you already know. You can explore, see if it will go somewhere or not. If not, it's certainly a great preparation for dating. Old boyfriends can be so complimentary and validating—it's great for your ego."

Before you dial that old, smudged phone number in your address book, follow this expert advice to ensure a fail-proof second meeting.

Remember why you broke up. Successful reunions between old flames share a theme: Something outside the couple broke them up the first time around, Dr. Kalish says. Maybe your parents kept you apart for religious reasons. Or you went to college in California and he signed on with an Alaskan salmon-fishing boat. In other words, maybe it had nothing to do with not getting along.

If you initially broke up over infidelity, incompatibility, or abuse, however, then chances are your old flame won't suit you any better now than he did in high school or college, Dr. Kalish says.

Find out if he's married or not. According to Dr. Kalish, the single most common reason why relationships with old lovers don't work out: One or the other was married or deeply involved with someone else and could not leave his or her significant other. If you're getting interested, but he's hitched, just say no to a get-together—even if his wife would be present. "You may not be prepared for the huge emotions that will follow," Dr. Kalish explains. "You'll get hurt."

Say, "*Que será, será.*" "Whatever will be, will be" is the perfect attitude for a woman looking up a lost love, Dr. Kalish says. You'll need optimism and self-confidence, and you'll need to feel comfortable taking risks. After all, calling or writing a man you haven't seen in decades requires sticking your neck out just a little.

One-Night Stands

It seems to happen with amazing speed: One moment the two of you are out on a date, the next you're at his place (or yours), tangoing between the sheets. By morning, you've gone your separate ways and may never meet again.

End of story? Hardly. For many women, the emotional fallout from a one-night stand—casual, one-time-only sex with someone you often barely know—can be devastating, says Elizabeth Wolfson, Ph.D., an adjunct faculty member at the Columbia University School of Social Work in New York City and a therapist in Ridgewood, New Jersey. So can the physical consequences, thanks to HIV (the virus that causes AIDS) and other sexually transmitted diseases.

"If a woman has never been married, or if she's at the point where she really wants to be married or in a committed relationship again, there can be many regrets, many questions afterward," says Dr. Wolfson. "She may wonder, 'Did this guy really like me?' and 'Will he ask me out again?'"

Participating in a one-night stand because you feel you must prove your worth, your beauty, or your willingness to do what your date wants can be unhealthy, emotionally and physically. "If the two of you sleep together but can't discuss HIV and safer sex, you're putting yourself and your whole future at risk," says Lila Gruzen, Ph.D., a psychotherapist and marriage, family, and couple counselor in Sherman Oaks, California, and author of *10 Foolish Dating Mistakes That Men and Women Make and How to Avoid Them*. Even the best spur-of-the-moment protection, such as latex condoms and safer-sex practices, can't completely eliminate the risk of infection.

And yet, for a few women, casual sex can be a simple, no-strings-attached experiment, Dr. Wolfson notes. "A woman just coming out of a marriage may go through a kind of second adolescence. She wonders, 'Am I still sexual? Do I want this?' She may only have ever had sex with her former husband, and she may be ready for new experiences."

Thinking It Through

Thinking you might cross that line from date to one-night affair? Or have you crossed it already? Follow this expert advice for avoiding, or dealing with, the fallout.

Consider HIV. The best way to be certain that your partner doesn't have HIV is to insist that he be tested before you two have sex, says Karen Martin, a certified sex therapist and program coordinator at the sexuality center at Hillside Hospital at Long Island Jewish Medical Center in Glen Oaks, New York. (Of course, both of you should be tested and not have unprotected sex with others in the meantime.)

But if you find yourself about to yield to temptation, follow safer-sex guidelines to the letter. (For more information on safer sex, turn to Sexually Transmitted Diseases on page 434.)

Sex-proof your date. You can help yourself resist the siren call of casual sex. Some experts' suggestions: Avoid alcoholic beverages during your date—we all know what they do to otherwise good judgment. Go out with a group of people, not just the two of you. Don't invite him up to your place, and don't accept an invitation to his. And leave something at home that you would absolutely need if you were going to stay over (such as your contact lens case or medication you must take in the evening or morning).

Have a heart-to-heart—with yourself. Suspect you might sleep with him tonight, but aren't sure it's a good idea? Early in the date, ask yourself:

- "Why do I want to have sex with this guy?" If you answer, "Because he may never ask me out again if I don't," then you're better off without him, Martin notes.

- "Do I just want to have a good time, or do I want more from this relationship?" If you're interested in getting to know this man better, stay out of the bedroom for a while, Dr. Gruzen says. The truth is that a man truly worth getting to know will be willing to wait until the time is right for sex.

Forgive yourself. Feeling regretful or self-critical after the fact? Acknowledge that everyone makes mistakes and move on, Dr. Wolfson suggests. "Think about why it happened, so you'll be ready to do what's best next time around," she says.

Reset your boundaries. If you and your date want to keep seeing each other, but you don't want to have sex again until you know each other better, discuss it briefly, Dr. Wolfson says. "Frame it in a positive way," she notes. "Say, 'Look, this relationship is so compelling that I moved too quickly. Let's relax and get to know each other.'"

Personal Ads

B lue-eyed professional lady, nifty 50, seeks honest friendship with business or professional man. Seek health-consciousness, positive attitude, sense of humor. Let's explore new places, concerts, enjoy each other. See what happens.

Tucked into the personals column of a small California newspaper, those 31 words brought author Peggi Ridgway the man who would become her long-time companion—"a sensitive, caring engineer with a passion for fishin' and the game of handball, a love of jazz and classical music, an endless sense of humor, and great friends, kids, and grandkids, too!" is how she gleefully describes him.

A fluke, you say? Aren't personals the last resort for dazed and desperate dweebs, Barney Rubble types who claim to resemble Robert Redford, and rich tycoons ISO (that's "in search of," in personals parlance) nubile, blonde 25-year-olds?

Think again. Healthier than a smoke-shrouded singles' bar, more convenient than primping for yet another blind date, personal ads can deliver a multitude of dating opportunities the easy way—via the mail, the phone, the

back pages of your local newspaper, and by computer. Call it catalog shopping—not for curtains or lingerie, but for men. And whether you place your own ad or respond to his, experts on personal ads say that the savvier you are, the better the odds that you'll meet someone who will, at least, be amusing for a half-hour of coffee and conversation.

"You have so much control," says Ridgway, of Buena Park, California, whose own positive experience led her to write *Romancing in the Personal Ads: How to Find Your Partner in the Classifieds.* "And you encounter so many more possibilities—it's not like going to a bar or a big party with your friends, where you just have to take potluck."

Shop-at-Home Convenience

Whether you place your own ad or plan to cruise the "Men Seeking Women" column for interesting prospects, these tips can help you make the most of your personal-ad experience.

Target the right market. Focus on publications most likely read by the type of man you hope to meet, Ridgway suggests. Looking for a local guy? Then advertise in the local newspaper. Hoping for an up-market date? Pick a glossy, upscale regional magazine. Want a man with special interests or characteristics? Consider a special-interest magazine or newspaper. "You're more likely to meet people you have something in common with," she notes.

And don't forget about the Internet—many publications also post personals online.

Ask about *all* the costs. Some publications offer free ads, but then charge a per-minute telephone rate when you retrieve phone-message responses. At $1.95 a minute, for example, a five-minute check-in would cost nearly $10! Others charge callers who want to respond to ads. Still others charge a per-line fee for placing an ad, and may tack on extra charges if you want phone-message response service or special placement for your ad, such as on the first page of the personals section.

Crack the code. Like real estate ads, personals are usually loaded with abbreviations. Most are fairly obvious: for example, S = single, D = divorced, F = female, M = male, W = White, B = Black. Others may be a bit puzzling at first. See if the publication includes a glossary, suggests Joe Bargmann, former senior editor of the Web site Swoon, which features personal ads. For example, did you know that A = Asian, C = Christian, J = Jewish, VGL = very good looking, and LTR = long-term relationship?

Play it safe. Don't give out your last name, your home phone number, or your address when contacting a man through the personals, advises Connie Merritt, a dating coach based in Laguna Beach, California, and author of *Finding Love (Again!): The Dating Survival Manual for Women over 30.*

When getting together for the first time, plan a short meeting with a definite ending time (have lunch or meet over coffee for a half-hour), drive your own car, tell a friend or relative where you're going, and don't call it a "date," Ridgway cautions. That carries too many romantic connotations for a first-time get-together.

Responding to His Ad

If you decide to answer a guy's personal ad, the following tips can help you make an informed choice.

Filter out the clichés. He likes long walks on the beach, or a cold night's cuddle by the fire. Well, who *doesn't*? Ignore the romantic mush and focus on the sentences that really describe him, says Bargmann. Do you share the same hobbies, musical tastes, social habits? Do you both love hiking? Books? Motorcycles? Backgammon? Those are the kinds of questions you want answered in his ad, Bargmann says.

Don't miss the forest for the trees. It's all too easy to see only the positive attributes in a personal ad, Bargmann notes. Perhaps you notice that you and Joe both like to ski, but you ignore the fact that he smokes—and you detest the smell of cigarettes. "Take in all the details, not just the ones you like," he says.

In Search of SM . . .

Placing your own ad takes a little more work and opens you to a little more emotional risk, yet it can have greater rewards, Ridgway says. You get to specify the type of man you're looking for, and you can sort through the replies for suitable prospects. Here's how to compose a winning ad.

Paint a quick self-portrait. Start with your marital status (single, divorced, or widowed), ethnic background and religion (if this is important to you), and age. Move on to a brief description of your personality, profession, and interests. "Have a 'hook'—something short and very interesting that says who you are," Ridgway says. "I once saw an ad that said, 'I like baking chocolate chip cookies at 2:00 A.M.' That told me this was a fun-loving, spontaneous person."

Get (a little) physical. Be honest, yet brief, about your physical appearance, suggests Ridgway. The truth is that men want to know how you look. In one study of personal ads, researchers at the University of California, San Francisco, and the University of Rhode Island found that men sought "general attractiveness" when answering women's personal ads.

If you don't look like Sharon Stone, take heart. Choose your best feature, or describe yourself in a positive—yet realistic—light, Ridgway suggests. Are you curvy? Polished? Willowy? Voluptuous? Dainty? Rubenesque? Elegant? Then say so. "Above all, if you expect to gain someone's trust and friendship, be up-front about your weight, age, and appearance," she says.

Say what you want. Be specific about the kind of man you'd like to meet, suggests Bargmann. Must he be a nonsmoker? Want a man who loves concerts? Need a nondrinker? Then say so.

Keep it light. Even if your personal goal is a long-term relationship and/or marriage, keep the pressure off by leaving this information out of your ad, Ridgway suggests. Right now, you're simply trying to meet men—not sign one up for a tuxedo and a honeymoon. Set the stage for that spontaneous, fun, getting-acquainted stage of a relationship.

Phone Tactics

N ever call a guy before he calls you. If and when he calls, wait a few days before returning his call.

Your mom probably issued those edicts back when you were in junior high school. The premise: You don't want him to think you're too readily available. Or you must play hard-to-get to lure a man into a lasting relationship.

Mom meant well. And back then, her phone rules may have made sense. Today, however, psychologists say the advice is passé. In fact, playing hard-to-get can hurt your chances of finding lasting love—or even a date.

"I asked one of my psychology classes whether it was okay for a woman to call a man. The students all laughed and thought the question was so funny. They said, 'We'd never have a date if we waited for the guy to make the first move,'" says Glenn E. Good, Ph.D., president of the Society for the Psychological Study of Men and Masculinity and associate professor in the department of educational and counseling psychology at the University of Missouri-Columbia.

Practical, Not Desperate

If you rely on luck alone, a guy might be able to track down your unlisted phone number or intuitively know you're interested. Then again, maybe he won't. So if you want a date with a man, you may have to make the first move.

Making the first move allows you to gather some important information. Does he get flustered? Maybe he's not comfortable with self-assured women. Or maybe he's just old-fashioned. If so, do you still want to date him? On the other hand, if he says, "Wow, I'm so happy you called," you know you have a potential catch, says Dr. Good.

Here's how to call an interested prospect without seeming too forward.

Learn from his mistakes. Remember the men you didn't want to date because of their phone styles? The ones who annoyed you by calling and hanging up? By not taking no for an answer? By ringing you at midnight? Or

---

The Mysteries of Sex

Question: Why do men say they'll call even if they have absolutely no intention of phoning you?

Answer: He thinks that's what you want to hear. So he says it.

"In a sense, he ends up hurting your feelings to avoid hurting your feelings," says Martin Malone, Ph.D., a sociologist at Mount Saint Mary's College and Seminary in Emmitsburg, Maryland, and author of *Worlds of Talk: The Presentation of Self in Everyday Conversation*.

Or maybe you misunderstood him. To men, "I'll call you" can also mean "good night" or "see you later." It's a man's way of ending a date or a conversation, says Dr. Malone. So the next time a guy says he'll call you, don't take him literally.

If you want to see him again, make plans for another date in person, before he gets out the door. And then call him to confirm.

---

by talking until your answering machine ran out of tape? Don't take after them, says Karen Martin, a certified sex therapist and program coordinator at the sexuality center at Hillside Hospital at Long Island Jewish Medical Center in Glen Oaks, New York.

The phone traits that make a man seem desperate to you will make you seem desperate to him. Follow the Golden Rule: Treat him the way you'd like him to treat you, says Martin.

Pretend he's a she. The next time you find yourself staring at the phone and wishing it would ring, ask yourself if you would agonize over calling a female friend. Would you wait for a woman you just met to call you? For how long?

"If you want to go to the movies with a girlfriend, you pick up the phone and you say, 'I want to see such and such. Do you want to go see that?' She says, 'No, I already saw that film.' You say, 'Okay, what else do you want to see?' You have this conversation. You don't throw yourself down in traffic over it," says Martin.

Silent Types

&

D ating a man of few words can be refreshing. Even gratifying. At first. His silence is attractive. You talk, he listens. He seems strong and assured. You feel appreciated.

But as time progresses, listening may not be enough. You want to know him better. You want him to respond to you. Talk to you. Entertain you. Tell you how you've turned his world upside down. But he does none of the above.

What's going on? Psychologists say that a silent man may simply be shy. He may be a sensitive type who's trying not to dominate the conversation. He may be a regular guy who simply doesn't divulge the intimate details of his life as readily as you would—a common difference between men and women. Or, he could be the classic "silent type"—a rugged, emotionally remote individualist à la John Wayne or the Marlboro Man.

"As little boys, men learn to harden themselves to emotions that make them feel vulnerable," says Glenn E. Good, Ph.D., president of the Society for the Psychological Study of Men and Masculinity and associate professor in the department of educational and counseling psychology at the University of Missouri-Columbia. "They're given messages such as 'Boys don't cry.' 'Be a man—not a sissy.' And 'Compete, compete, compete.'" As a result, while a silent type may look strong, in fact he often has great difficulty expressing or discussing emotions—something that can hinder or harm an intimate relationship, Dr. Good says.

Shy, Macho, or Sensitive?

How can you discern what's really behind his silence? Follow this expert advice.

Draw him out—gently. Ask open-ended questions about his interests. For example, instead of, "So you play basketball three nights a week?" try, "Tell me why you get such a big kick out of basketball." "Shy people actually love to talk—but only when they feel comfortable," says Bonnie Jacobson, Ph.D., director of the New York Institute for Psychological Change in New York City and author of *Love Triangles* and *If Only You Would Listen.* "If he gives you one-word answers, ask him to expand on it." You may discover he isn't a silent guy at all!

Don't judge. Shy guys and strong, silent types alike don't like to be grilled about their economical vocal styles, says Dr. Jacobson. "Don't make a reticent man feel self-conscious," she cautions. "Don't call attention to his lack of words. It will just make a shy man clam up."

Further, pointing out his vocal style could annoy or even enrage an entrenched silent type, Dr. Good notes.

Set your own tolerance level. If he doesn't become chatty after a few dates, you need to decide whether or not you feel comfortable with a man of few words, Dr. Jacobson says. "Remember, emotional support comes in more ways than one," she notes. "If he's there for you and lets you know he cares, that may be enough. Some women don't like talkative men."

On the other hand, if he seems uncomfortable when you discuss emotional issues, the two of you may have difficulties in the future dealing with conflict and with the inevitable emotional ups and downs of life, Dr. Good says.

Singles' Bars

In a world where intimacy seems to be harder and harder to achieve, singles' bars may look enticing, but they're the wrong route to extraordinary togetherness, dating experts say emphatically.

"Imagine the scene: The music's very loud, the lights are so dim that it's hard to really see anyone, and there's alcohol involved," says Lila Gruzen, Ph.D., a psychotherapist and marriage, family, and couple counselor in Sherman Oaks, California, and author of *10 Foolish Dating Mistakes That Men and Women Make and How to Avoid Them.* "Those are all factors that end conversations, not nurture them. Imagine trying to yell questions to a guy over the blare of the music. 'WHAT? YOU WERE MARRIED FOR HOW LONG?' Not very intimate, is it?"

What are the odds of finding a long-term relationship in a bar? It's hard to tell. Of the married people in the *Sex in America* survey conducted by University of Chicago researchers, just 10 percent met in a bar, through a personal ad, or on vacation (a combined category). Meanwhile, 8 percent met at church, 15 percent at work, 23 percent at school, and 14 percent at a party, social club, or the gym.

Connie Merritt, a dating coach based in Laguna Beach, California, and author of *Finding Love (Again!): The Dating Survival Manual for Women over 30*, even asks her clients to promise not to look for love, or even for a date, in the meat-market atmosphere of the singles' bar.

"Yes, there's always the fluke—the woman who just happened to be in the bar and met the guy who became her husband," Merritt acknowledges. "But once you get beyond college students, a lot of people who hang out in bars and clubs don't have much else going on in their lives."

What it comes down to, says Merritt, is that guys who hang out in bars a lot are good at the bar scene, and nice guys aren't. "Do you really want someone who hangs out in bars all the time?" she asks. "If there's a truly nice, sensitive, well-rounded guy hanging out somewhere in the bar on the night you're there, chances are you'll never meet him—he probably won't be good at approaching someone in such a high-stress atmosphere."

Her prime reason to look elsewhere? "If you meet someone in a bar or club, you've missed a real key issue: How do you trace him? How do you check him out? It's better to use your own network of friends, join organizations, or do volunteer work to meet worthwhile men of quality and substance." (For more ideas on places to meet men, see "More Than 40 Great Places to Meet Guys—Other Than Bars" on page 230.)

Where to Meet Men

W hat do *Star Trek* conventions, target ranges, blind dates, and bars have in common? They're all ways to meet men. But are they the best ways to meet guys? Maybe. Maybe not.

"The settings that we find ourselves in that are designed purposely just to meet people—like blind dates and bars—are the most difficult places in

More Than 40 Great Places to Meet Guys —
Other Than Bars

To meet men who share your interests, values, and attitudes, think beyond classes in auto mechanics. (That's not a bad place to start. But it's so obvious.) To jump-start your thinking, consult this master list of potential mating events and places.

Art shows and gallery openings

Auctions

Auto shows

Bait and tackle shops

Bartending school

Beer and wine tastings

Boat shows

Bookstores and book club gatherings

Bowling leagues

Car races

Churches, synagogues, or other places of worship

Civic service organizations (the Rotary, Kiwanis, etc.)

Coaching kids' teams (soccer, swimming, Little League)

Collectible shows (baseball cards, etc.)

College alumni association get-togethers

Community cleanup days

Computer classes

Conventions for your trade or profession

Cooking classes

which to do so," says Martin Malone, Ph.D., a sociologist at Mount Saint Mary's College and Seminary in Emmitsburg, Maryland, and author of *Worlds of Talk: The Presentation of Self in Everyday Conversation.*

They're difficult because they don't provide conversation material. Or introductions. At a bar or night club, you scan the room for an attractive man. When you find one, you only know one thing about him: He's attractive. And maybe he wears nice clothes. And maybe he smokes. Maybe he doesn't. It's no wonder that walking up to him and starting a conversation out of the blue makes you nervous.

Approaching a guy would be a whole lot easier if you could somehow hide your romantic interest and make it seem like you need to talk to him for a totally different reason. And you can do that. But you can't do it in a bar.

Country clubs

Cultural events (ballet, theater, symphonies)

Dance classes

Fishing clubs and tournaments

Fund-raising events (charities, hospitals, etc.)

Golf courses

Health food stores

Hiking clubs

Home and garden centers

Horse or hunt clubs

Horse races

Humane society shelter

Language classes and clubs

Microbreweries and winery tours

Movie matinees

Package tours for singles

Parent Teacher Association (P.T.A.) meetings

Political campaigns

Pool or billiard game rooms

Professional associations (managers, nurses, business owners, etc.)

Public radio membership meetings

Public speaking clubs (such as Toastmasters International)

Record stores

Ski clubs

Stockholders' meetings

Theater tryouts

Town council meetings

Wrestling matches

Yoga classes

The best places to meet men have little to do with romance and a lot to do with your (or his) interests: art, sports, religion, literature, you name it. "You're better off with a situation designed for other purposes, such as a hobby, recreational activities, or church. Then you don't have to focus on each other," says Dr. Malone.

Here are some worthy strategies.

Join a club. For just about any interest, indoors or out, you can find a club that will satisfy your needs while putting you in touch with interesting men, says Karen Martin, a certified sex therapist and program coordinator at the sexuality center at Hillside Hospital at Long Island Jewish Medical Center in Glen Oaks, New York. Interested in conservation? Write to the Sierra Club at 730 Polk Street, San Francisco, CA 94109, to locate your local chapter. Birdwatching? Contact the National Audubon Society at 700 Broadway, New York, NY 10003.

Go back to school. Continuing education courses provide a perfect setting for meeting men. Choose a subject in which you're sincerely interested: The man you meet at meteorology school will assume you like talking about the weather.

Rekindle religion. Having shared values is among the most important ingredients in a lasting relationship, says Martin. And statistics suggest that married couples who met at church tend to stay married longer. Don't just show up for worship and split, though. Attend a Bible study class. Help out with church socials. Join a committee.

In other words, to get involved, get involved.

Workplace Romance

He's good-looking, well-spoken, and has a solid career—you know, because you work with him. Does that make him perfect, or a guy you should avoid at all costs, unless you're willing to risk your job?

You've heard all the warnings: An office romance can fuel the company gossip mill and make your life miserable if your relationship is discovered—or the two of you break up. It can also leave your boss worried, for while few companies have rules prohibiting love between co-workers, many employers still fear that smitten, spurned, or sexually involved employees won't give their all between 9:00 and 5:00.

Yet more and more women throw caution to the wind and say "yes" when Dave from marketing or Tom from payroll calls. (Or *they* say "yes" when a woman calls.) In a fax poll conducted by the New York–based American Management Association, more than one woman in five confessed that she had gone out with an office colleague at least once. (Fifteen percent had done

A New Benefit:
Corporate Dating Services?

In Japan, the Hitachi corporation runs a dating service called Tie the Knot for unmarried employees who work such long hours that finding a mate on their own is out of the question. The service is headed by a director known as the Wedding Commander.

so more often.) Of those who had, 41 percent said an office romance led to a long-term relationship or marriage.

"In today's workplace, it's easier than ever to cross over from a business acquaintanceship to a romantic interest," notes Joni Johnston, Psy.D., a clinical psychologist in Del Mar, California, who holds workshops for companies in the United States, Canada, and Mexico on workplace behavior issues, including dating. "More women are in the workforce than ever before, and in more equal positions with men at many job levels. We spend more hours at work than ever before—and we meet people there who are smart, people who are like us because we share common interests. And there's always that natural attraction that can happen between men and women."

Dangerous Liaisons?

Diana Gunion, 43, a single mother from Carmel, Indiana, has been dating a colleague at the mortgage-lending company where they both work for several months—much to her own surprise. "I have never dated a co-worker before," she says. "But this happened so naturally. We knew each other for about a year first. It was a great opportunity to find out what kind of person he was, without any romantic pressures."

Gunion and her friend, who also play on the company softball team together, are discreet, keeping their relationship completely out of the office. "I've caught myself a few times almost saying something like, 'That restaurant was really great,'" she says. "But I haven't slipped up. We both feel better keeping work and our private lives very separate."

Should You Tell Your Boss?

The truth is that most bosses don't want to know if you're dating a co-worker. According to a *Fortune* magazine poll of the nation's top chief executive officers, three out of four CEOs believe office romance is "none of the company's business." Still, psychologists say there are benefits to divulging your secret in two specific circumstances.

- "If you're going to get married, tell your supervisor about it when you set the date, and tell him or her that you don't want your marriage to adversely affect your careers or the company," says Neil Lewis, Ph.D., a management psychologist in Atlanta. "In fact, it would probably be polite to invite your boss to the wedding."

- If you break up with a co-worker and worry that your job performance may suffer temporarily, consider telling your boss, Dr. Lewis says. "Simply explain and ask if he or she can cut you a little slack," he suggests. "A good supervisor will be glad you were honest." Try this one only if your boss is a reasonably flexible person and the two of you already have a good relationship, he adds.

Psychologists say that Gunion's experience illustrates the four forces that account for the irresistible allure of the office romance.

Proximity. "When men and women work in close proximity, it's inevitable that 'boy-and-girl' stuff happens," says Neil Lewis, Ph.D., a management psychologist in Atlanta. "But unlike the 'old days,' when office romance was seen as fooling around between bosses and secretaries, today's relationships are more often between peers—and so are seen as having more potential to have a future."

Familiarity. We used to search for potential mates at church, at social or civic clubs, or through networks of family and friends, Dr. Johnston notes. And many people still do. "But these days, work has replaced many traditional institutions as the most stable community for many people," she notes. "So it makes sense that we would meet dating partners there as well."

Intensity. Close collaboration to meet a deadline, finish a report, craft a sales campaign, or solve any business challenge creates its own excitement—a kind of mental and physical arousal that easily transfers from the work to the co-worker, Dr. Lewis says.

"Stress and excitement lower our inhibitions, so it's easier to feel close," explains Dr. Johnston. "If my co-worker is a woman, we may begin to feel more like sisters. If my co-worker is a man, he may begin to feel like my brother—or I may begin to take a more romantic interest in him."

Safety. Unlike personal ads, blind dates, Internet connections, or simply bumping into someone in the supermarket, work gives you the unique opportunity to observe someone for a long time before deciding whether or not you'd like to date, Dr. Johnston says. Among the important information you might glean: Does he have a temper? Does he treat people well? Does he seem to have any unhealthy habits? Is he truly single?

Where's the danger lurking in all this? "The relationship might end—as most dating relationships do," Dr. Lewis notes. "And typically, relationships don't end gently. That can get messy in a work situation—especially if you're in the same work group, or if one of you is the subordinate and the other is the boss."

Eight Rules for "Safe" Office Dating

It is possible to date the guy in the next cubicle without getting burned—provided you follow a few simple, commonsense guidelines.

Steer clear of boss-subordinate liaisons. "It is incredibly risky to date someone you supervise, or who supervises you," Dr. Johnston says. "It's questionable whether it can truly be a relationship between equals, when one person has power over the other's paycheck." Further, it may open the door to sexual harassment charges.

Other potential sticking points include conflicts of interest (Can you really give a fair performance evaluation to a subordinate whom you're dating?) and the appearance of favoritism (What's the real reason for all those perks, promotions, or plum assignments you've gotten, others wonder?).

Put your career first. If your career matters deeply to you, think carefully before crossing the love line at work, Dr. Lewis advises. "It's hard to control the outcome of a relationship," he says. "If things go badly, your professional life could be harmed or undermined."

Think ahead. Early on, consider how you will get along if the two of you break up, Dr. Johnston says. "Ask yourself, 'If this ends, can I still work next to this person?' If the answer is no, this may be a relationship to avoid."

Start slowly. If you go ahead, take your time getting to know your co-worker as a dating partner. "You may be the kind of person who can keep dating and work separate, but you want to make sure you can trust the other person, too," Dr. Johnston says. "Have a discussion to make sure you both agree on how to handle things at work." Then see how the two of you actually deal with your double life.

Don't kiss in the cafeteria. Keep all demonstrations of affection out of the workplace, Dr. Lewis advises. "Be appropriate," he says. "That means no holding hands walking down the hall, ducking behind a pillar for a quick kiss, or terms of endearment." Be 100 percent professional on the job.

"Not only will you avoid embarrassment, but you will also be nurturing your own professional reputation," Dr. Johnston says. "You want your manager and co-workers to focus on you and your work, not on the fact that you're the girlfriend of the guy over in accounting."

Never use company e-mail or voice mail to send love messages or make personal arrangements. It's all recorded, retrievable, and easily accessed by others. Even if you delete your messages, your company may keep old e-mails in computer back-up files. And phone or computer messages sometimes get misdirected. So share your deepest sentiments—and plans for your next date—on your home phone or computer, suggests Dr. Lewis.

Keep cool if you're found out. What if a co-worker spots the two of you walking across the parking lot of the local bistro, holding hands, laughing, generally looking like a couple? "If the co-worker asks you about it, simply tell the truth and leave it at that," Dr. Lewis suggests. "There's no reason to deny or downplay it, no reason to explain or justify. Say something like, 'Yes, we're going out. As a matter of fact, we'd just come from a great Italian restaurant.' And then move on to something else."

After a breakup, date elsewhere. If the two of you stop seeing each other, take a break: Don't date anyone else from your company for a few months, Dr. Johnston advises. "Otherwise, it can get really, really tense," she says. "Your breakup will cause some disruption for the two of you. Bringing in a third person could make things worse for all three of you. If you're sensitive to this possibility, you can successfully avoid it."

PART FIVE

Extraordinary
Marriage

Children

$\mathcal{S}^{Q}$

G irl meets boy, girl falls head over heels for boy, girl marries boy. In due time, girl and boy start having girls and boys of their own . . . and then things get tough, the delights and the demands of parenthood threatening to turn their partnership into a distant second thought.

"We observe this with so many of the hundreds of couples we've worked with," says Claudia Arp, who with her husband, David Arp, is a marriage and family educator based in Knoxville, Tennessee, who conducts Marriage Alive workshops all over the world and has coauthored numerous books on marriage. "People love their kids, but they tend to run out of time and energy before they get to work on their marriage."

Yet it's important to sustain a great relationship with your spouse even when responsibilities toward your children, from dirty diapers to adolescent angst, seem to loom larger, say experts. In fact, it's crucial.

"Your marriage is the anchor relationship, the foundation of your family," says Arp, who is the mother of three now-grown boys. "Mom can love the child and Dad can love the child, but unless Mom and Dad love each other, their child can still end up feeling insecure."

Kids Benefit from a Well-Nourished Marriage

"Never feel guilty about working on your marriage, because when you're working on your marriage, you're also working on your family," says Arp.

Maintaining a strong partnership also helps sustain your identities as two adults who are attracted to and intrigued by one another, says Paula Leonhauser, a licensed marriage and family therapist in Los Angeles. "You have to nourish what brought you together in the first place."

Not that it's easy. "Raising children is traditionally a low-intimacy time of marriage," says Wayne Sotile, Ph.D., a psychologist in Winston-Salem, North Carolina, and coauthor of the book *Supercouple Syndrome: How Overworked Couples Can Beat Stress Together*. "Expect challenges and don't let yourself get disillusioned. Couples who make it through this passage later

Secrets of *Long-Lasting Love*

Raising Kids Was
Their Biggest Challenge

Rhonda, a hospice nurse, and Victor Lipinski, a social worker, from Eden, New York, were married more than 30 years ago, in November 1968. They met in college during a summer internship at the same hospital. Rhonda cites several factors as key to the success of their marriage.

At the end of our summer romance, I knew that Vic was my future and that we were going to marry. Everything was perfect—he was the right guy for me, and it was the right time for both of us. We finished our degrees, were engaged the summer after graduation, and married that fall.

Marriage has been fun, but it *is* hard work. But Vic and I married each other forever, and we work hard to honor that vow.

The toughest part of our marriage has probably been raising our three children. Vic and I come from different family backgrounds with different family dynamics. He was raised in a strict Polish Catholic family that talked openly about their feelings, and I was raised in a strict Methodist family where we didn't talk about our feelings. To raise our kids the way we wanted them to be raised, we had to find a balance between our backgrounds early on. We also had to find a balance between our careers and our kids. After our first child was born, I stayed home with the kids

come to enjoy higher and deeper levels of passion than couples who haven't worked at it."

Here's what experts suggest to assure that your marriage survives your kids.

Don't pit parenting against partnership. "Life may seem to force you to choose between either being child-centered or marriage-centered, but in fact you can and must do both," says psychologist Leslie Parrott, Ed.D., who is the mother of an infant and who with her psychologist husband codirects the Center for Relationship Development at Seattle Pacific University. "Not that you can focus on both at the exact same time," she says, "but you have to give them each equal creative importance and trust that you really can do both."

while they were young, while Vic worked two or three jobs to cover expenses.

With three kids and Vic working several jobs, life got pretty hectic. Right from the start, we made open communication a priority. We always phone each other during the day to touch base. In the evenings, we'll go for a walk or sit down to talk.

We've also made each other a priority. Vic is the most important person in my life, and I'm the most important person in his life. I feel very strongly that making your partner number one is the only way to maintain the closeness that a marriage needs to survive.

Vic and I also have rituals that confirm how important we are to each other and how much we appreciate each other. Every Friday we do something fun together, whether it's getting ice cream or going to a movie. It's a way to kick-start the weekend and recognize that we have a few days off together. And almost every night, we take a bath together. This is our time to relax, acknowledge each other, and confirm how beautiful our bodies are in each other's eyes.

Vic and I have learned a lot throughout our 30 years together. Most important, marriage has taught us that by appreciating our differences, we have made our relationship even stronger.

Accept the hard work. Raising kids is one of the most demanding jobs there is. "You're working harder than ever before," says Leonhauser. "Your life is filled with taking care of your child, making sure enough money is coming in, and managing every other aspect of your life. Problems arise when each of you starts feeling like you're doing all the work, operating at 110 percent and totally unappreciated. Meanwhile, you don't notice that your spouse is working just as hard. On top of this, there's tremendous pressure as parents to 'do the right thing.'"

Face it: This is hard work for both of you, "especially during the first year of a child's life when you're totally in the trenches," Leonhauser says.

Team up. Having kids fosters teamwork—and requires it, says Arp. And teamwork enhances your marriage. "Anything you do with your husband, you do for your marriage," she says. "Rather than having the attitude of 'I'll do my 50 percent and he can do 50 percent,' each of you should be giving 100 percent."

Consider, for example, what you can do to lessen stressful situations such as "morning madness." One of you might assume the responsibility for breakfast while the other makes sure the kids get up, get dressed, and stay on schedule, Arp suggests.

Secrets of Long-Lasting Love

Compromise Eased Tension of a Major Move

Bonnie Yazel first married in 1952 and had a daughter, but that relationship was short-lived, and she divorced 2 years later. After 9 years on her own, she met Fred Yazel at a church softball game. He jogged slowly so he'd just make it to first—the base that Bonnie was playing. They dated off and on for 5 years before they married on June 15, 1963. Today, the couple lives in Des Moines, Iowa. After more than 35 years of marriage, Bonnie says that an overseas move (coupled with tension between her daughter from her first marriage and her husband) was a major test of their relationship. But they passed.

My eldest daughter, Gwen, who was nine when Fred and I met, had a difficult time adjusting to him. They cared for each other, but they butted heads for a long time. They have such different personalities that it was difficult for them to understand each other.

Two years into our marriage, we moved to American Samoa, which didn't help ease the tension between my daughter and my husband. Fred had an opportunity to teach for four years in Samoa, and he wanted to go. Gwen, understandably, didn't want to leave her friends in Iowa. I was also quite apprehensive about going. American Samoa was far away for a woman who'd

See the positives. Parenting brings rewards to relationships. For one, having a child can connect you even more deeply to your partner. "In that moment when a child is born, a couple feels extremely close," says Leonhauser, who is the mother of two young children. "It's an incredible bonding experience."

"Even though my husband and I have been together for 14 years, I've never felt so permanently established in my commitment to my marriage," says Dr. Parrott. "Having a child forces us to grow together and have a shared purpose from now on."

What's more, parenting brings out a lovable new dimension in your

spent her entire life in Iowa. It created conflict between Fred and me as well. But we discussed it and came up with a compromise—we'd go to American Samoa as long as we kept the house we owned in Iowa. Having a home to return to meant a lot, and once that was settled, I got excited about our trip.

All of us enjoyed our four years in American Samoa, but we were ready to come back. Fred and I wanted to settle down in a permanent location for the children. Not only did we have Gwen to worry about, but now we also had our son David, and soon after we would have our daughter Leslie. So we returned to our home in Des Moines, Fred returned to his teaching position, and I stayed home to raise the children.

Once the kids completed college, I returned to my teaching career. Since my husband and I now share a similar schedule, we have lots of time together. Taking a lot of trips keeps the romantic side of our relationship on track. And if there isn't time for a trip, we enjoy sports together, like watching baseball or playing tennis.

Fred and I have a successful marriage because we both wanted to get married, and we wanted to get married to each other. When we committed to each other, we committed to love each other even when one of us did something that wasn't so loving. For us, it's what works.

partner, Dr. Parrott notes. "There's this mysterious new aspect to him that I'm now getting to know, and it's so fun. I always imagined that he'd be a good dad, but I didn't have a picture of just how great he'd really be. It's just so sweet to see this whole new tender part of him."

Change places. If you don't feel that your husband is helping out, switch roles once in a while, Dr. Parrott suggests. She cites a personal example of how her husband took the "night shift" during their son's early infancy. "When he had to work out of town for a few days, I got a taste of what it was like at three o'clock in the morning with the baby . . . and I found new appreciation for him," she says.

Keep it simple. "In this age of soccer moms and dads, you might do well to lead a less frantically active life," suggests Dr. Sotile. "Kids are better off with fewer activities and calmer parents," he says. Think before you sign up your children for one more sport, music lesson, or other activity. And resist the temptation to engage in nonstop activity while you're at home. "Remember that you deserve a recess," Dr. Sotile says. "Take time today to simply enjoy your family."

Negotiate your parenting conflicts. "It's definitely normal and okay to have some differences in parenting styles," Leonhauser says. "In my practice, for example, I see the stereotype over and over again: The father is more demanding and sets firmer limits, while the mother is more nurturing. People start arguing, 'You're too soft,' or 'You're not being understanding enough of the kid.'" Instead of arguing, she says, you need to sit down together and find compromises that you both can accept. "Discuss these things calmly between the two of you, and not in front of your kids," she says. "Then present your rules to your children as a united front. Otherwise, the kids get confused and problems never get resolved."

Take time for each other every day. You and your husband need to find time to give each other undivided attention. Even the smallest of efforts helps keep you emotionally connected, says Dr. Sotile.

Turn off the radio in the car and talk instead. If tonight's your child's softball practice, drop your child off and enjoy a walk around the field with your husband, suggests Arp. Or after your kids are in bed, watch a video or read books together—the kinds of things you used to enjoy as a couple before you had children, suggests Leonhauser.

Go on dates. "A healthy, growing marriage relationship requires friendship, fun, and romance—the things that dates are all about," says Arp, who with her husband coauthored *10 Great Dates to Revitalize Your Marriage.*

"Great dates are more than going to see a movie and tuning out the world for a while," she says. "They involve communicating with one another, reviving the spark that initially ignited your fire, and developing mutual interests and goals that are not focused on your careers or your children."

"Until we had kids, we never understood parents having a date night," says Dr. Parrott. "Now we do it once a week. It feels sort of artificial, but we now realize that it's really our only choice. You have to strategically plan for time to yourselves, or you end up emotionally distant, without a shared, private, adult life."

Aim for a date at least every couple of weeks, and be sure to put your dates on your calendar the same way you schedule other important activities.

Take a break from kid talk. Talking about your children nonstop, even when you're on a date with your husband, is an occupational hazard, says Arp. But give yourself a break. "Try making the agreement, 'Okay, for the next two hours we'll talk about us.' Not, 'Don't talk about the kids,' but, 'Let's talk about us.'"

Nurture your sex life. "Having a creative, passionate sex life during your parenting years is the elusive glue that holds you together," say the Arps in their book *Love Life for Parents: How to Have a Sex Life, Too.* "My husband and I have been married for 35 years, and to be really blunt, our love life is the best it has ever been. The key is that we didn't ignore sex when we had our kids. We schemed and overcame obstacles and found time for each other," she says.

Go ahead and plan for romance, contrived though that may seem. "People tell us all the time that it wouldn't be fun if it wasn't spontaneous," Arp says, "but if you wait for spontaneity when you have children, you could be waiting a very long time. And romance thrives on overcoming obstacles. Taking on the challenge should promote your creativity and make it even more fun."

If your kids are still small, put them to bed early and hit the sack yourselves for romance, Arp suggests. If your kids are older, sneak time for sex while they're at choir practice or sleeping in on a Saturday morning. If your kids are at home and you feel self-conscious about making love, "soundproof" your bedroom with a stereo system to provide a noise buffer, and be sure to lock your door. For more information on having sex while raising children, see Privacy on page 93 and Weekend Getaways on page 186.

Attend to your individual needs, too. For women especially, conflicts about taking care of others versus taking care of oneself are all too common. "There's a myth that says, 'What I want is not as important as what others need,'" says Dr. Sotile. "This myth leads us to not assert and nurture ourselves, leaving us feeling lonely, taken advantage of, and unloved. But you can't be effective in relationships until you learn to nurture yourself."

"When you have children, you wonder if you've lost your place of importance," Dr. Parrott says. "It's not that you don't want your children to have what they need. You just feel that your own needs are now not as important as they used to be." Doing things for yourself takes extra effort, she says. "You have to consciously tell yourself, 'I'm going to do something for myself,' and you have to do strategic planning. I have to call a babysitter to come to my house so I can go for a run in the morning."

"By nurturing yourself," says Dr. Sotile, "you come back to your marriage refreshed instead of viewing it as just another demand."

Cultural Differences

In many communities a generation or two ago, marriage between men and women from two different European cultural backgrounds—say, English and Italian—was irregular. (Not to mention marriage between people of different races or religions.) But the salad bowl of cultures and faiths that America is today, coupled with the globalization of jobs and academics—people who either travel abroad or come here to work or study—has changed all that.

"We live in an increasingly multicultural world, and the ethnic diversity of our country reflects this," says Michele Harway, Ph.D., an expert on multiculturalism, member of the core faculty and director of research at Phillips Graduate Institute in Encino, California, and consulting faculty member at Fielding Institute in Santa Barbara, California. "People are dating and marrying across cultural lines in greater numbers than ever before, partly because of the sheer magnitude of the numbers and partly because of the increasing acceptance of intercultural marriages."

Yet when marriages are multicultural, the potential for misunderstandings increases. "Every culture has basic underlying values that shape the way we look at and act in the world, from our view of human nature to what we consider appropriate ways to express emotion," says Dr. Harway. Multicultural herself (her mother is French and her father is of Russian Jewish heritage), she says, "I grew up learning French and English and knowing that the world was different depending on what language and what culture you looked at it from."

Marriage between people with two different skin colors can be especially tough because our society sends disapproving signals. Yet even subtle cultural differences can bring conflict, Dr. Harway says. "Take regional differences," she says. "People raised in the Pacific Northwest have very different notions about life and relationships than people who were raised in the South."

Interfaith marriage brings its own form of cultural clashes—even for those who don't consider themselves to be particularly religious.

"So many people go into marriage naively thinking that religious differences are a nonissue, especially if they've distanced themselves from the church they were brought up in," says the Reverend Anne Kimball, an Episcopal priest and associate dean of the Berkeley Divinity School at Yale University. "They think, 'We're in love and the fact that he was raised Catholic and I'm Jewish, or I'm an evangelical Baptist and religion is really everything in my life, and he's an Episcopalian who goes to church once a month, won't make any difference at all.'"

But it does, especially during a crisis or upon the birth of a child, Rev. Kimball notes. "Couples find themselves suddenly arguing over which church they're going to have their child baptized in, and it's a big deal because they think that one way or the other is going to doom the child to hell," she says.

Cultural conflicts about child-rearing come up, too, says Dr. Harway. "An American wife might want to raise her children to be independent and to achieve and get ahead the American way, while her Asian husband might want his children to put individual needs second to helping everyone in their extended family."

Different but Equal

Navigating your way across different cultural maps isn't easy, but these signposts can help.

Accept your differences. "One of the most important aspects of any successful marriage is learning to value the ways in which you're different instead of trying to change the other person," says Dr. Harway. "One culture isn't better than another, just different."

Seek guidance. A therapist experienced in multicultural issues can help you clarify yours. Dr. Harway's clients fill out questionnaires on their backgrounds, then discuss them together with her. "It's a real eye-opener," she

Secrets of Long-Lasting Love

Unified by Cultural Separation

Kay and Manucher Ranjbar of Indianapolis met during the summer of 1957. Manucher had financed his way from Persia (known today as Iran) to study in the United States at a Kansas junior college where Kay was a student teacher. It was love at first sight, and they were married four months later. Their biggest challenge, says Kay, was dealing with cultural differences that threatened to separate the couple and their children forever.

After we married, we started planning a family right away. I was pregnant with our first of five children just a few months into our marriage.

With a child on the way, we were forced to confront the differences in our Eastern and Western upbringings, specifically our religious upbringings. While we are both very spiritual, I practiced Christianity, and Manucher practiced Baha'i—a progressive religion that developed in the spirit of the Muslim religion and teaches us that we are here on Earth to develop for the next world. We studied each other's religion and decided together to raise our children in the Baha'i faith.

After deciding on one faith, we thought all our cultural differences were resolved. Little did we know that a trip we would take to Iran to meet Manucher's family would again bring our cultural differences into the limelight. Upon arrival at the border, Iranian government officials took my husband's passport because he had not served his mandatory stint in the military.

says. "There's a lot of, 'Aha! When we were having that discussion the other day about such-and-such, we were coming from such different places because of the different ways we were raised.'"

Reverend Kimball sees many couples in premarital counseling, when she addresses interfaith issues head-on. "If, for example, somebody Jewish is marrying somebody Episcopalian, we have to look at how involved they are in these religions. There are also practical aspects like which day of the week is

We had high hopes while in Iran that Manucher would be allowed to return to the United States. After our third year there, we were so certain that I packed up the children and returned to Kansas to wait for my husband. I waited an entire year for him to come home—a year in which our communication was essentially limited to letters. Eventually, I returned to him in Iran. My children needed their father, and I needed my husband. We lived in Iran for nine years before he was granted immunity from his military requirements.

For some couples, an episode like our years in Iran would have destroyed their marriage. But for my husband and me, the experience solidified it. Living in Iran gave me a rare opportunity to experience and understand the culture my husband grew up in. Afterward, we spent a number of years in Africa, India, and Pakistan, with time back in the United States between each relocation.

All this travel and meshing of Eastern and Western cultures has taught us that life is not a selfish thing. When we married, we became a unit, and both of us honor and respect that. We share everything, and we put each other first because if the two of us fail, nothing else is important. We're very open with each other. We've had to be with so many cultural influences on our relationship. But we've managed to work together to better understand and embrace these differences.

the holy day. Otherwise, they get married and suddenly they're face-to-face on a Sunday and the Episcopalian is saying, 'This is great, a day of not doing anything,' but the Jewish partner is saying, 'No, let's get busy, Saturday is the day when you don't do anything.'"

Sort out society's hang-ups. "Our society really has a problem with cultural differences, especially if different skin colors are involved," says Dr. Harway. "This adds an additional level of stress from the outside world, reminding you at every juncture that not only are you different but we're not sure that's okay."

The best way to cope with prejudice is to "keep the lines of communication with your spouse open and try to separate out those negative messages you're being bombarded with," Dr. Harway says. If someone in your family or at work makes a snide remark about your spouse's skin color or culture, for example, share this with your spouse, telling him how you feel about it. If you can, talk to the person who made the remark, too. "This doesn't solve the problem," says Dr. Harway, "but it makes things a little more bearable."

Take the case of Ann Stark, a 40-year-old public relations manager in Chicago. "When I first started dating Bijan (now her husband), who was born in Iran, I heard that one of my friends made a joke to another friend about my going out with a cab driver, this stemming from the fact that Middle-Eastern men are often behind the wheels of cabs in Chicago. I talked to Bijan, and we agreed that the remark was ridiculous and offensive. If I hadn't told him, the remark might have festered inside of me and unconsciously colored my view of him. After all, I counted on my friends for letting me know if they thought the men I dated were total jerks or idiots or cheating on me or whatever. I concluded that the cab driver remark was not a useful critique."

Learn about each other's culture. Immerse yourself in your spouse's world. "Read books on his culture, including novels that portray what people and life in that culture are really like," Dr. Harway advises. "Eat the food so you can at least tell the difference between a good version of a classic dish and a bad one. Attend cultural events so they don't seem so strange."

Learn the language. If your spouse and his family speak a foreign language among themselves, you don't have to become fluent in that language, says Dr. Harway. "But you have to be able to understand what your spouse's conversations are about so that you understand everything that's transpiring. Otherwise, things start becoming secretive, which can be very destructive."

Learn about each other's religion. Attend a service at your spouse's religious institution, study books, and otherwise educate yourself about this different tradition, advises Rev. Kimball. "If you're a Christian marrying a Jew, spend a couple of hours with a rabbi. Conversely, if you're Jewish, spend some time with a pastor or priest."

Think twice, by the way, about switching to a "compromise religion," Rev. Kimball says. "That doesn't really work. It's like homogenizing the whole thing. What's more important is understanding and accepting each other's beliefs, and coming to a place of conciliation that you can both live with."

Practice each other's rituals. If you're Jewish and your husband is Protestant, celebrate both Hanukkah and Christmas, Rev. Kimball says. "Don't choose one over the other. Celebrating both is particularly important if a holiday or ritual meant a lot to you when you were a child."

Coming up with variations on traditional rituals works, too. Ann Stark says that she and her husband and his family celebrate Thanksgiving every year, but instead of turkey and stuffing, they feast on classic Middle-Eastern stews and rice dishes. "You can also create rituals all your own, like a special holiday to celebrate winter," Dr. Harway suggests. "Rituals offer a way to celebrate your unique cultural blend and make your partnership even more special."

Dual Careers

I t was horrible," says Maya Jackson, 42, of that tough period in her marriage a few years ago. She was teaching literature while completing her graduate degree at a local university. Her husband was becoming a media star in a major city on the East Coast. And they were raising their then-three-year-old son.

"It was a huge, huge strain on our marriage," Maya says. "Here he was with his skyrocketing career, doing a newspaper column and TV commentaries and lectures all over the country, swamped with work all the time. I felt terribly guilty about being so busy, too, but my career is really important to me. We ended up being very angry at each other. Absolutely furious."

Secrets of a Long-Lasting Love

The Dual-Career "Breakfast Club"

Lisa, a librarian, and Scott Hummel, a professor of engineering, from Albany, New York, got together during their junior year of high school. They met at band practice and thought it would be fun to go out on a date. That date turned into several dates, and a few high school proms and college parties later, they married. As part of a dual-career couple, Lisa says making time for each other is one of their biggest challenges.

After we graduated from high school, Scott and I were apart for the first time. He went to school in Connecticut, while I went to school in New Jersey. After that year, we knew we wanted to be closer to each other, so I transferred to a school in Connecticut. It was a risk because we might not work out as a couple, but it was a risk we wanted to take because we wanted to be a part of each other's daily life.

About halfway through college, we started talking about marriage. We married three weeks after graduation on June 11, 1988.

Marriage has been a lot of fun for Scott and me. We have a shared history we can look back on and laugh about. But that shared history doesn't mean that we know each other completely; we still learn from each other every day. Scott and I are not only spouses and lovers but also very good friends. We respect each other a great deal, and we treat each other with kindness, extending the same courtesies to one another that we extend to any friend.

Whether you're at the top of the corporate ladder or hovering down near the bottom, most modern-day couples grapple with the pressures brought on by dual careers. Fewer than 15 percent of American households have a spouse who doesn't work.

"We have a whole generation of men and women facing lofty expectations for fulfillment in their family, work, and self," says Wayne Sotile, Ph.D., a psychologist in Winston-Salem, North Carolina, and coauthor of the book *Supercouple Syndrome: How Overworked Couples Can Beat Stress Together*. "To cope, we try to become superpeople, but in the process we develop abnormal

As fun as it has been, we have both always had hectic schedules, and the biggest challenge in our relationship has been finding time just for us. The most difficult period was when Scott and I were both in graduate school. I studied for my masters in library science; Scott pursued his masters in engineering at night. He also worked full-time during the day to support us and did his homework on the weekends. Scott's constant shuffle between work and school left us with very little time for each other.

We realized that if we wanted to have time together, we had to make time for each other. Since the only time we were both in the house was in the early morning, we started having breakfast together. Breakfast became our time to share and connect with each other, and it still is. Our standing date in the morning gives our relationship some normalcy when things get crazy. Recently, we've added a nightly walk with our dog to our "connect time." We've also taken up biking and hiking together on the weekends.

Scott and I have changed a lot since we started dating at 16. But we've managed to roll with the punches and grow together. We give each other our best, and we support each other completely. With that support, the rest just falls into place.

levels of stress, fatigue, and tension. The crunch of our lifestyles is hurting us at home and at work."

A major contributor to the problem, Dr. Sotile says, is that people with demanding jobs tend to apply the same aggressive traits that make them successful in the business world—traits like being in control and moving at a fast pace—to their relationships. "This tactic makes a relationship yet another burden rather than the pleasure it ought to be," he says.

"We need to take charge of our work lives to the fullest extent that we can," says Ellen Bravo, director of 9 to 5, the National Association of

Working Women in Milwaukee. This may entail everything from taking a closer look at your priorities to trying to make "family-friendly" changes to company policies, she says.

Taking Control

Here's what experts recommend to help you manage your career and your marriage.

Put your marriage first. Many of us put work first, convinced that our job security, income, status, and success depend on it. Not true, says Dr. Sotile. "The number one cause of burnout on the job is discord in one's personal relationship," he says. "A caring connection with your mate is the most important factor determining success in your work, because that connection improves your resilience in the face of stress."

Aim to spend 15 hours a week together. "A couple needs to try to spend about 15 hours a week together no matter how much their jobs and the rest of their lives demand them to not be together," says Willard Harley, Ph.D., president of the Marriage Builders Corporation in Minneapolis and director of the Marriage Builders Internet Web site. You and your partner probably gave each other this much attention when you were dating, but now work, kids, and other commitments may seem to always come first. "Many people try to meet each other's needs with time 'left over.' Then, when there isn't much time left over, they become emotionally disconnected," he says.

Schedule time together during which you aim to meet these four emotional needs for each other: conversation, affection, recreational companionship, and sexual fulfillment. Go on a weekly date. Have breakfast together before the kids are up or watch a favorite movie together before bed. If 15 hours is unrealistic, just do your best. Give each other attention when you get home, while you prepare dinner, as you eat and clean up, and after the kids go to bed. The point is to put time together at the top of your "to do" list. Otherwise, it gets pushed to the bottom.

Beat stress together, not solo. It's important to come up with ways to cope with work stress—but be careful. "If your work is already disconnecting you from your partner, don't add stress-management activities that further separate you," Dr. Sotile says. He cites the example of a client who "makes it a religion to eat right, to exercise regularly, to meditate frequently—all those

Are You (or Is Your Husband) a Workaholic?

Do you or your husband put off making love so you can get more work done?

"Stretched-to-the-limit couples maintain that they never have enough time for their partnerships because of the constant demands of their jobs," says Jaine Carter, Ph.D., a relationship coach in Naples, Florida, and author of *He Works/She Works: Successful Strategies for Working Couples*. But upon closer examination, it turns out that some people actually prefer working to the hard work of relationships.

If you (or your mate) recognize yourself in six or more of the following statements, you're working because you want to, not because you have to, says Dr. Carter. Discipline yourself to work less and play more.

1. I get so caught up in my work that I forget the time.
2. I would rather be working than interacting.
3. I enjoy the challenge of my work.
4. I prefer vacations that can be combined with work.
5. I find it difficult to envision a life without work.
6. I feel most alive when I'm working.
7. It is difficult for me to concentrate on making love when I am involved in a project.
8. I do things myself because I like to stay involved.
9. I would rather work than go to a social event.
10. I am too involved in work to have time to disagree with someone.

sorts of stress-relief techniques. The problem is that this formula completely alienates him from his spouse because either he's doing all these things or he's working."

Try teaming up with your partner to soothe stress. Take yoga or meditation classes together, but keep it fun, Dr. Sotile says. Don't let it become another hard-driving activity. "My wife and I walk together a couple of times a week, in addition to exercising individually at other times," he says. "This is a time for a kind of healthy meandering in our relationship, a communication-generating ritual." And it counts toward your 15-hour-a-week quota.

Keep him primary. Comradery at work is great, but make sure that your spouse is the primary person you turn to to share information about yourself. Otherwise, intimacy in your marriage shrinks while intimacy with your co-workers expands. "What too often happens," says Dr. Sotile, "is that as our involvement at work increases, we start sharing more of the intimate details of our lives with our colleagues than with our spouses. Our co-workers know our opinions and the stuff that makes us laugh. They also know everything that's going on at work and how you're feeling about it. Pretty soon, you start dreading going home because you don't feel you have a friend there.

"Spend part of every day finding out what each of you thinks, feels, needs, and wants," Dr. Sotile says. Even if your work or the work of your spouse is highly technical and the details are complicated, "share what it's like to deal with that stuff and with the people on the job."

Don't jump at every opportunity. You've been offered a promotion? Congratulations, but try to pause before you say yes, advises Dr. Sotile. "Even if the opportunity is positive and exciting, ask yourself whether the price you will pay adjusting to the change makes the stress worthwhile—for you and for your loved ones," he advises. And be sure to ask your loved ones how they feel about it.

If your husband is offered a promotion or job transfer, encourage him to think through the demands on your marriage before he accepts. Maya Jackson and her husband saw a counselor about the strains her husband's ambitions were putting on their marriage and, after years of striving, her husband decided to quit pushing so hard. "He realized that he had achieved some important goals and then discovered that it didn't mean that much to him. It meant more to him to be with us, his wife and his son. He sort of came to his senses."

Refigure your finances. While your bankbook may require that you work, keep a close accounting of the energy and hours you're investing toward your earnings. Recalls Dr. Harley, "Early in my career, I got to a dangerous point where I was making a tremendous amount of money counseling people 14 hours a day, 7 days a week. But my wife and I never got to see each other. It got to the point where I was asking whether it was worth 'losing' a certain amount in income to take my wife out for an evening. Eventually we realized that the answer was yes, but for a while we couldn't see past the money." Calculate how much money you really need for the life you desire. "Money creates quality of life, but if the cost of your money is to reduce your quality of life, then what good is it?" Dr. Harley asks.

Share the housework. A survey of 3,000 men and women showed that even when women are contributing half or more of the family income, they are 5 times more likely than men to cook for the family, 5 times more likely to do the family shopping, and 11 times more likely to do the household cleaning.

"Repeat to yourself, 'Housework is work to be done by those who live in the house,'" says Bravo. And share the concept with your family. "Then don't ask for help. Expect it." Make a housework plan detailing who does what and when for the whole family and follow it, she says. Most important, come up with objective evaluations that everyone can agree upon, from dinner plates free of grease after washing to a bathroom that doesn't look like the last re- maining rain forest. "This enables you to avoid being the cop who has to po- lice the whole process," she says.

Negotiate on your job. Some workplace expectations, such as over- time, put overwhelming demands on a working woman with a family. Start negotiating now for a better deal, urges Bravo. "Don't wait until you're asked to stay late. Bring it up with your supervisor on your own initiative at a time when it isn't a crisis," she advises. "Present it something like, 'It would be very difficult for me to stay past 5:15 because the child care center closes at 5:30. If there will be times when there's an extra workload, let's think about who can handle it. Somebody here might like the extra hours. I'd be happy to organize a meeting where we can all talk about this.'" This strategy, Bravo says, can simultaneously get you off the hook and present you as a problem- solver.

Rigid starting times that conflict with getting the kids off to school are another common problem for working women, Bravo says. "You end up get- ting to work late, feeling stressed and guilty," she says. If your workplace al- lows for flextime, negotiate for more flexible work hours. "Talk to your supervisor about moving your starting and ending times back a half-hour," she says. "Present it positively, saying something like, 'This would be really helpful for me and I imagine for other people, too.'"

Reconnect—with yourself and your mate. If your job is hectic and everything there is urgent, chances are you carry this frame of mind home with you, Dr. Sotile points out. "Do you finish other people's sentences for them? Are you always in a hurry? Do you get mad at your spouse when he turns right on the way to the restaurant, making you arrive 30 seconds later than you would have if you'd gone left?"

Relationships grow from connections, not from performance or management, Dr. Sotile says. To connect, you must slow down, pay attention, disclose yourself, and nurture yourself and your partner.

For starters, connect with yourself, even if only during small chunks of time. Read something purely for pleasure. Watch a favorite TV show that you usually deny yourself. Take an extra-long, hot bath. And engage in fun, playful activities with your partner. "You may have to force yourself to re-learn what pleasure is," Dr. Sotile says. "Start by doing more frequently the things that used to bring you pleasure, the stuff that makes you squirm with anticipation."

Getting Married

For some couples, deciding to get married is easy. In addition to being physically attracted to each other, they may share common goals, interests, and dreams. For other couples, though, the decision may be a little more difficult.

"Being 'in love' is certainly necessary, but it's not sufficient to get us through the lifelong challenges of marriage," says Karen Blaisure, Ph.D., a marriage and family therapist and associate professor in the department of counselor education and counseling psychology at Western Michigan University in Kalamazoo. "You simply can't count on those warm and bubbly feelings to get you through it all."

A Grown-Up Guide to Marriage

In effect, getting married is a decision to grow up, says Dr. Blaisure.

"If you're convinced that the relationship is working well, that you can communicate and handle conflict, you're probably ready to marry a particular person," says Dr. Blaisure. If you want to get married but aren't sure you're ready, she suggests the following "marriage readiness" checklist. (If you answer "no" to any or all of these questions, your relationship may need further work.)

1. Are you equals? The best relationships are between two people who consider themselves equals, says Dr. Blaisure. That means having an equal say on issues and decisions.

2. Emotionally, do you give as much as you get? "You should have a sense that over the long haul you're not giving more than you're receiving, or vice versa," Dr. Blaisure says. "It is this kind of egalitarian friendship that can blossom into a good marriage."

Love at First Sight
Does Last

According to a survey of 605 people ages 18 to 82, 88 percent of whom were in stable partnerships, one-fourth of the respondents reported falling in love "at first sight" or "on the first day." Another 45 percent said they fell in love "within the first eight weeks." The remaining 30 percent took longer to fall in love.

These results show that love at first sight leads to a stable relationship just as often as falling in love during the course of a year or longer does, reports Willi Jurg, M.D., a Swiss psychiatrist who conducted the study. What's more, those who fell in love with their partners "at first sight" or "on the first day" were just as happy with their partnerships as those who took longer to fall in love.

3. Can you accept your differences? Forget the fantasy that the perfect marriage is one in which you and your prospective husband will see eye-to-eye on every issue. This is immature and unrealistic, says Marty Gilbert, who leads workshops with her husband, Roger, in Norwalk, Connecticut, teaching engaged couples communication and conflict resolution skills.

"People get tripped up because they think they have to be the same,"

Secrets of Long-Lasting Love

How I Knew He Was "The One"

When women who had been married for 40 years or more were asked how they knew their husbands were "the one," their answers varied widely. Here's what three women had to say.

Ann Parrinello, Leesburg, Florida, married 42 years

"I had not one doubt about getting married to Nick," says Ann. "I knew he would be a loving and faithful husband. And he is."

The Parrinellos met at a church dance in Brooklyn when they were both 24. They married 14 months later.

"We gave marriage a lot of thought," Ann says. "Back then, when you got married, you got married for life. We had four beautiful daughters and have 11 grandchildren. I've had no doubts. I knew I made a good choice from the very beginning."

Karen Waggoner, Flippin, Arkansas, married 45 years

Their first encounters as teens gave Karen and her husband Dave little indication that they would end up married for 40-plus years.

"Our dates were disastrous," recalls Karen. "He tripped over things and embarrassed me in public. He did things that made me think I'd never, ever want to be seen with him again."

But Karen intuitively felt that they belonged together, and the couple kept dating and got married in their early twenties.

says Marty. "Recognizing that you're two different people, that differences are always going to crop up, relieves so much stress and tension in a relationship."

Of course, for this to work, your fiancé also has to accept differences of opinion. "I can focus on our differences and let them drive me crazy if I want," says Roger. "Or I can decide to accept them. I've found that accepting them works a whole lot better."

"To be honest, I wasn't at all sure that I'd done the right thing until we'd been married for about 10 years," says Karen. "It was a slow process, but I discovered that there was a whole lot more to Dave than I'd thought. It was a revelation, and it took a long time, but I reached a point where I could say, 'This is a good thing.' "

Marty Gilbert, Norwalk, Connecticut, married 43 years

"I can't tell you how I knew. I just knew at a gut level that Roger was right for me," says Marty Gilbert.

The couple had known each other for several years and had had an intense romantic relationship—much of it long-distance—for about a year. Yet when Roger first proposed to her, Marty's response was, "Not yet." She had just graduated from college and had moved out of her parents' house to New York City. "I was enjoying the freedom of this new life," she says.

Roger was disappointed when she declined his proposal, but a year later he asked again and she assented.

"During that period, I did go on dating," Marty says. "That's when I re-alized above all that I felt so comfortable with this man. I just knew very clearly inside of me that this was right."

4. Do you both put your love into action? "Love is a set of actions, the intent of which is to promote and support the well-being of the person you love," according to David Sanford, Ph.D., a licensed couples therapist and newspaper columnist in Portland, Maine, and founder of Couples Place, an Internet Web site. "To love is to strive—against your own native self-cen-

---

Cures for Commitment Phobia

Symptoms: Until now, the two of you have been inseparable, but suddenly, something is feeling a little off. You have noticed that he's withdrawing, or becoming critical. You're pulling away, finding fault, fearing that you'll become lost in your relationship, or feeling reluctant about getting too close.

Diagnosis: You've caught a case of commitment phobia—a kind of relationship flu.

"Commitment requires us to enter into the give-and-take of adult relationships," says Lila Gruzen, Ph.D., a psychotherapist and marriage, family, and couple counselor in Sherman Oaks, California, and author of *10 Foolish Dating Mistakes That Men and Women Make and How to Avoid Them.* "Committed couples need to compromise, negotiate, and be more unselfish than most single people." The realization that you won't always get your own way can leave you with cold feet—or in a cold sweat.

Why are we so scared? What makes us pull away from serious relationships when talk of living together, marriage, or even just becoming a committed couple comes up? A number of things. You—or your man—may feel:

- Intimidated about being sexually faithful

- Wary about having to account to someone else for how you spend your time and money

- Reluctant to make sacrifices, large or small

teredness—to embrace the beloved, in your understanding, your empathy, and your behavior."

Again, reciprocity is the key. "In our workshops, I use this example," says Roger Gilbert. "Suppose Marty asks me to help her with something, and I'm feeling very uptight or into my own work at the moment. I really don't feel

- Nervous about giving your partner the level of attention you give yourself, or of giving him so much attention that you no longer attend to your own needs sufficiently

- Afraid of being known intimately by your partner (Will he see me in the bathroom? Will he find out what I'm really like?)

You (or your prospective mate) may also have been hurt by a romantic partner in the past and may feel scared about trusting again.

The following tips can help you (or your significant other) move out of commitment limbo, one way or another.

If you've caught commitment phobia: Practice assertive behavior. Say "no" when you mean "no," ask for what you need, and discuss your feelings. Promise yourself that you won't lose yourself in the relationship, but will still work on meeting your own needs. And discuss your fears with your partner. "Remember," Dr. Gruzen notes, "commitment is a chance to build love and intimacy. It shouldn't be a trap."

If your partner is commitment-phobic: Try talking to him about his feelings—and back off just a little. "Reassure him that you like him as a friend," suggests Glenn E. Good, Ph.D., president of the Society for the Psychological Study of Men and Masculinity and associate professor in the department of educational and counseling psychology at the University of Missouri-Columbia. "By giving him a little space, he may feel that you really want to get to know him and aren't simply intent on becoming engaged, married, or committed for the sake of settling down."

like helping her right then, but in spite of that feeling, I can make a decision to love her by helping her anyway." Would your guy do that?

5. Do you listen to each other? You and your partner probably listened to each other for hours on end when you were first dating. But as time goes on, listening can get harder, especially if what you need to listen to is something you don't want to hear. Barriers like being distracted or just itching to issue your own opinion block genuine listening.

"It's hard to listen, but if you don't, you'll never resolve conflict," says Dr. Blaisure. In classes she teaches to help couples prepare for marriage, she borrows a metaphor from a colleague and likens the process of listening to prairie dogs popping in and out of their holes. "In relationships, we want to share who we are, all of ourselves, but it takes time. We'll pop up and give a little information, then pop back down and pay attention to how the information is taken. If we haven't been listened to, we're not going to pop back up. If we have been listened to, we'll pop up again, offering a little more information. It usually takes three or four tries in an interaction for a person to really start disclosing."

"Listening well is a complex skill," says Dr. Sanford. He recommends these steps: Look and act attentive. Don't do anything else at the same time. Face your partner and make eye contact. Nod, smile, make friendly or sympathetic noises, offer encouragement, and otherwise act in a manner that communicates, "I am listening; I am following; I am with you; I care about what you're saying."

"Even if you're not really listening deeply, you're listening with attention, which is a very good beginning," says Dr. Sanford. "And by the way, don't be surprised if, in acting as if you're listening, you soon find that you really are listening."

6. Have you considered premarital classes? "You put the odds for a successful marriage in your favor by getting certain skills under your belt," says Dr. Blaisure. "Most people want to succeed in marriage, but unless we learn healthy new skills, we revert to the old ways of doing things—the ways that we saw our parents handling conflict, for instance." Look for a class that requires that you actually practice skills like listening and resolving conflict. "Workshops where you write love letters to each other are fine, but research shows that the classes that make the difference are skills-based," she says. For help in finding skills-based relationship counseling, contact the Coalition for Marriage, Family, and Couples Education at 5310 Belt Road NW, Washington, DC 20015-1961.

Honeymoons

Instead of a heart-shaped bed, newlyweds Jane and Roger Bennett slept in a tent when they honeymooned.

"Our idea of perfection is cuddling up in front of a campfire with a bottle of champagne," says Jane, 36, who is from Los Angeles. During the day, the couple hiked through the wilderness in nearby Joshua Tree National Park. "It was great," she recalls. "Being in nature, away from everyone and everything, we could really focus on enjoying each other."

Creative Honeymooning

A treasured honeymoon doesn't just happen. You have to create it. Here's how.

Plan ahead. When you start to plan your wedding, start to plan your honeymoon. This widens your options instead of leaving you with the left-over travel packages and hotel rooms that nobody else wants, says travel consultant and honeymoon specialist Sandy Hollander, of Carlson Wagonlit Travel in Woodland Hills, California. Planning also saves you money on things like airfare. And getting your honeymoon plans squared away early means there's that much less to worry about as your wedding day approaches.

Decide what *you* really want. You might find yourselves arguing over your honeymoon plans—maybe you're hot to hit the beach in St. Thomas, but your partner is roaring to mountain bike in Montana. "Hear each other out," advises Paula Leonhauser, a licensed marriage and family therapist in Los Angeles. "Take turns saying, 'This is what I want to do, and this is why I want to do it.'" Once both your itineraries are on the table, aim for a compromise. It helps, Leonhauser says, to remind yourselves that your honeymoon isn't the first and last vacation you'll ever take together but, hopefully, one of many.

Keep it simple. Too much fun can be no fun at all, says Leonhauser. "One couple I was working with was planning a car-driving honeymoon through California, but they kept tacking on place after place to visit, and they also wanted to fly to Hawaii afterward. It sounded to me like a real or-deal. Why put yourself through such a grind?"

Denise and Barry Atkinson, another couple from Los Angeles, both have very high pressure jobs. So they plopped themselves in a bed-and-breakfast inn with plans for exploring the local Northern California wine country. "We

What's Your Honeymoon Personality?

Make no mistake about it: It's *your* honeymoon. So be sure you and your husband do what you really want to do, not what the guidebooks and ads tout as the perfect honeymoon.

Your choices? Camping. A cruise. A weekend at Disneyland. Skiing in the Rockies. Gambling in Las Vegas. Vegging out on a beach in Hawaii. Bicycling through the French countryside. Snorkeling in Jamaica. Tracking wild animals on a safari. Trekking in Nepal. How do you know what's right for you? Start by asking yourself a few of the questions travel consultant and honeymoon specialist Sandy Hollander, of Carlson Wagonlit Travel in Woodland Hills, California, asks her clients.

What are your interests? Are you and your spouse antique collectors? Motorcycle enthusiasts? Lovers of fine wine? Consider a honeymoon where your greatest interests come into play.

What special thing have you always wanted to do? Ride the world's fastest roller coasters? Cruise among glaciers in Alaska? Visit a rain forest? Your honeymoon presents an opportunity to finally do it.

Where have you visited in the past, and what did you think? Say you've been to Palm Springs and discovered that you love the desert, or you went to New Orleans and loved the food. Or you visited New York City and hated the crowds. Keep your previous experiences in mind while you make your plans.

Do you enjoy organized activities or would you rather go off on your own? If you like group activities or scheduled events, a group tour or an all-inclusive resort will probably keep you hopping. But if you like to explore on your own or do things on the spur of the moment, they're not for you.

didn't want to have to follow a strict schedule or be anywhere at any particular time," Denise says. "It was perfect, extremely relaxing."

Stick to a budget. Don't bankrupt your marriage before you even get home. Set a honeymoon budget and stick to it. "You can have a great time without going overboard," says Hollander. For example, skip the honeymoon suite and choose a regular hotel room with a nice view instead. Rather than having room service deliver overpriced dinners and champagne to your room, go out to an interesting restaurant.

You can also arrange for a honeymoon gift registry, a clever way to boost your honeymoon bankroll. Plan your trip with a travel agency. Then, on your wedding gift registry, describe the trip along with the name and phone number of the agency. Gift-givers may contribute any dollar amount toward your honeymoon, and you may find your honeymoon paid for before you even get to "I do."

Set realistic expectations. "We tend to think that a honeymoon has to be the greatest, most carefree vacation of our lifetimes—romantic, memorable, and more," says Leonhauser. "I don't think any vacation can meet all those expectations, including a honeymoon. You can't expect it to be romantic 24 hours a day. Expect a very nice vacation and leave it at that."

Expect to be exhausted. Chances are you'll arrive at your honeymoon site emotionally and physically drained, says Leonhauser. "You've been working on your wedding for months and now it's all a blur, you rushed out of town, you get to your honeymoon, and guess what? You're exhausted." Relax. Get some sleep. Give yourself a break.

Make love, but only when you feel like it. "People think they're going to be having sex for hours a day," says Leonhauser. "When they don't live up to this expectation, or if every sexual encounter isn't the greatest, they end up disappointed." The fact is, you and your husband may not really feel like sex bunnies, and that's fine. Enjoy each other's company, whether or not nonstop passionate lovemaking is part of it.

Take turns on fun stuff. You're not going to see eye-to-eye on every day's activities. Don't get locked into a power struggle over things like swimming versus shopping, advises Leonhauser. Instead, take turns. "One day do what you want, the next day do what he wants."

Spend some time apart. You were surrounded by hordes of people at your wedding, and now you and your spouse are left to yourselves on your honeymoon. "Admit it," says Leonhauser. "You could probably both use some time apart."

"You hear about couples who think they have to do absolutely everything together on their honeymoons, and they drive each other bananas," says Maura Talio (not her real name), who with her husband, Tim, decided that at least part of the time, she'd stay in their hotel room reading while he sunned by the pool.

"Go off on your own or allow your husband to go off on his own and don't take it personally," advises Leonhauser. "There's nothing wrong with some time alone. In fact, it's healthy."

Expect glitches. Your plane is delayed. Your luggage is lost. Your hotel room has two twin beds. "Expect some glitches," says Leonhauser. "Anything could happen." The Talios both got sick from the water on their honeymoon and spent their first night together in the bathroom vomiting, something they laugh about today. Just relax and go with the hand you've been dealt, says Leonhauser.

In-Laws

Get married, and most likely, you also get a second set of parents and siblings. It's a package deal—for better or worse.

The mere act of merging two families through marriage can feel very threatening to everyone involved, and to mothers in particular, says Charles Kogon, a licensed marriage, family, and child therapist in Los Angeles. These feelings can lead to discord.

"People feel like they're losing a family member," says Kogon. "And the new person marrying into the family isn't really one of them. You're from another family, another place."

Building Alliances

Most of us learn to get along just fine with our in-laws. But there are always going to be moments when you wish you could banish the lot of them to Siberia. And sometimes, in-law problems can be a real teeth-gritting test of the strength of your marriage. Here's how to foster extended-family harmony.

Get to know them. Instead of taking your in-laws' behavior as a personal affront, "try to understand who they are, what their expectations are, and their place in the family," Kogon suggests. Maybe your father-in-law's running commentary on your spending habits stems from his paternal attempt to save you from financial insecurities he has experienced. The better you know your in-laws as individuals, the easier you'll find it to deal with them.

Make yourself familiar. Regular phone calls, letters, get-togethers, and other friendly gestures help break through the wall of unfamiliarity, Kogon says. "Ultimately, you want to reach a kind of joining of families. You want your in-laws to see you not as someone who is stealing their child but as someone who wants to share a new experience."

Make a special effort. It's the small stuff that can make the biggest difference. Recalls Kogon, who is Jewish but whose wife isn't: "When we were first married, she learned how to make Jewish cookies and would send them to my mom. She got major points for that."

Meet control with compromise. Parents can feel displaced when their children leave home and start families of their own. "This is when struggles over control come up," Kogon says. "The parent who tries to get his offspring to do things the old, familiar way is trying to assure himself that they haven't really switched allegiances."

When your husband's mother still expects him to show up every Sunday for dinner but you two have other ideas, resist trying to prove you're a grown-up by blowing her off completely. Instead, consider a compromise such as one Sunday dinner a month with an occasional Sunday phone call thrown in.

Put your marriage first. "If you want a decent marriage, you must learn to put your mutual interests before all others, including in-laws," says Willard Harley, Ph.D., president of the Marriage Builders Corporation in Minneapolis and director of the Marriage Builders Internet Web site. "No responsibility to in-laws should supersede your responsibilities to your spouse."

A woman once complained to Dr. Harley that her lonely mother-in-law was turning to her husband almost daily for advice on everything from programming the VCR to complex legal transactions. "Whatever a man does for his mother must be with his wife's enthusiastic agreement, or he should not

Secrets of Long-Lasting Love

Making Room for Mom

When Dorothea Rodda applied for a job with the recreation department in Teaneck, New Jersey, at the age of 19, she knew she wanted to get to know the superintendent who hired her much better. Richard Rodda and Dottie started dating that summer. Their love affair continued for two years, before they married on February 23, 1946. Today, they are retired and live in South Hamilton, Massachusetts.

Dorothea's mom, Ester, lived with her and Richard until Ester died in 1989. The living arrangement was a situation that Dorothea views as a plus.

The first year of our marriage was a particularly difficult time of adjustment for me. Up until then, I didn't know what it was like to have a man in the house. My father died when I was 10 years old, and my mom never remarried. It had always been just Mom and me, and when I married Dick, I had to adjust to having an energetic, masculine personality around.

It helped that my mom and I were very close—more like sisters—and I could share anything with her. All of us, including our two children, enjoyed having Mom around. She was a part of our family, yet quite independent.

I used to tease Dick that he married two women when he married me; that's how close Mom and I were. If there were disagreements in the house,

do it," Dr. Harley says. The wife, for her part, must realize that her husband can't turn his back to genuine need.

Stand up for each other. Situations may arise when you must defend your mate against your parent, says Kogon. "Sometimes a guy has to say, 'Look, Mom, I know that you're used to having the kitchen a certain way, but when you come over to our house, it's not okay for you to go in and rearrange my wife's kitchen.'" The key, Kogon says, is to be empathetic yet firm.

Stand up for your kids. Conflicting views with in-laws on child-rearing are a common problem. "Set boundaries and explain how *you* want to do it," Kogon advises. "You might need to tell them, 'We know the kids

it wasn't unusual for Mom and me to have the same view on the subject. Not that we ganged up on him, but with two of us having the same opinion, well, it's probably a good thing Dick and I don't really fight. We have always been good about getting things out in the open before they escalate into a fight.

Having Mom, children, ourselves, and our careers to balance made life pretty hectic at times. When the kids were at home, we had a standing date as a family every night at the supper table. Supper seemed to be the one time of the day that everyone in the family was around, so it became the time that we shared our daily activities with each other. Dick and I also have a standing date with each other on Thursday nights. Even at the most active points in our lives, we reserved our Thursday nights for each other. It's our time to go to dinner, the movies, or whatever, just to be with one another.

I think Dick and I have been successful in our marriage because we appreciate and make time for each other. We've learned the importance of listening to one another, even if we hold different opinions. Listening is often the only thing that can keep us in tune with each other. We've also learned that change is the only constant in our lives, and you have to work with it, help it, and support it if you expect your relationship to last.

get out of control sometimes, but we don't spank them and we don't want you to spank them.'"

Listen to their advice. Parents—yours and his—will always be on the ready with advice whether you want it or not, says Kogon. Instead of trying to prove that you're a grown-up by arguing, hear them out. "Some of the advice might actually be quite sound," he says. "Even if you don't like it, you can always reflect it back, saying something like, 'What I'm hearing you say is that you think I should do this.' Then ignore it and go ahead and do things your way."

Give them credit. It's not all a battle. Give your in-laws credit where credit is due. And be sure to recognize your in-laws along with your own parents on those parent-only holidays. "It's a little tougher now that I'm married," says Kogon. "Before, I had just one person to remember on Mother's Day, but now I have two. But that's okay. I just make sure I call my own mother first."

Living Together

The number of people opting to live together has increased dramatically since the 1950s. For some couples, "living together is a stage, a part of their evolution as they move toward marriage," says Dr. Sills. Some couples will continue living together unmarried, while others will break up.

Just because you're sweet on each other, though, doesn't mean that living together is going to be a piece of cake.

"Living together increases intimacy, and intimacy increases conflict," says Judith Sills, Ph.D., a psychologist in Philadelphia who works with many cohabiting couples. "Conflict, in turn, offers a chance to practice conflict resolution—or not." And on this rides the success or failure of a living-together lifestyle.

Learning to Share

"As happy as you are to be with this person, once you start sharing space, resources, body fluids, and everything else, you have to start dealing with things that you used to take for granted," says Judith Coche, Ph.D., a clinical psychologist and director of The Couples School in Philadelphia. For example, "when you were single, you could handle money as you wished and you could go to sleep whenever you felt like it. Now you have to start working things out together." Here's how.

Make joint decisions. You talked excitedly for hours about moving in together. Once you move in, you have to talk about the tough stuff, says Dr. Coche, from paying the rent to cleaning the litter box. So one at a time, calmly present your positions. While your partner talks, you keep silent and listen. "You

Exit Signs

You've been living with someone for a while in the hopes of someday getting married. But something's wrong. To save yourself grief in the long run, certain tough issues are better faced now, experts say.

He says he doesn't want to get married. "If a man says he just wants to live with you but doesn't want to get married, that's exactly what he means," says Judith Sills, Ph.D., a psychologist in Philadelphia who works with many cohabiting couples. "And you're not going to change him."

He wants to go out with other women. "Your relationship has to be primary," says Karen Blaisure, Ph.D., a marriage and family therapist and associate professor in the department of counselor education and counseling psychology at Western Michigan University in Kalamazoo. "If he's having a sexual or even an emotional relationship with someone else, that's a triangle that's not going to work."

You want kids, he doesn't. His stance is perfectly acceptable, and you have to accept it at face value, says Judith Hurvitz, a licensed social worker who focuses on relationship issues, and a certified PAIRS (Practical Application of Intimate Relations Skills) instructor in Arlington, Virginia. "Don't think, 'Oh, this is such a wonderful relationship that certainly one day he'll want kids.' That's asking for trouble."

He's dishonest. When he tells you something, do you suspect that he's lying? "Character issues like this are tough," says Hurvitz. "I think that most people understand what they want in terms of character, but in the chemical insanity of courtship, they get confused." Reframing the situation as this question might help: Is this man a person I'd want to be in business with?

He's abusive. Physical, emotional, or sexual abuse or abuse of drugs or alcohol is unacceptable, says Dr. Blaisure. He needs help or you need to move on.

For information on alcohol abuse, see page 463. For more information on physical or sexual abuse, see page 466.

Secrets of Long-Lasting Love

They Passed the "Living Together" Test

When Jan Bulla-Baker, the owner of a small business, and her husband Jack Baker, an engineer, from Bloomington, Indiana, were first introduced by mutual friends in 1971, they were instantly interested in one another. Unfortunately, they were already involved in separate relationships. Fate reunited them a year later when they were both unattached, and sparks flew. They knew immediately that it was love, and they became inseparable. They lived together for five years before getting married on December 27, 1977. Jan says that living together before marriage enabled them to test the waters and be sure their relationship would work—and it did. She says their marriage has been successful for all these years because they appreciate and respect each other.

Because I was still in school working on my master's degree, living together seemed more appropriate than marriage at that time in our lives.

For the most part, Jack and I agree on all of the big issues in our relationship. But we've learned that agreeing on how to handle things doesn't necessarily make them any easier to handle. This especially rang true when we made the decision not to have children. After a series of fertility tests, we realized that having kids would be a very clinical process for us. Therefore, if it wasn't going to happen naturally, neither Jack nor I wanted to go through all the emotional and physical ups and downs of that process.

must try your best to acknowledge that even though his position is different from yours, it may be equally valid and deserves respectful consideration," she says. It helps to try to find a compromise. The goal is for each of you to "get your way" about half of the time. "Research shows that this 50-50 balance makes the relationship satisfying enough to stay in it," Dr. Coche says. "You start making decisions for the good of the relationship, not just for yourself."

Manage money equitably. No matter how much or how little of it you have, money takes on new meaning when the bills have both of your names

Extraordinary Marriage   275

Deciding not to have children was easier for Jack than it was for me. He was an only child and had lost both of his parents at an early age, so he grew up on his own, for the most part. I, on the other hand, grew up surrounded by family, parents, and siblings. Since Jack hadn't experienced this family closeness, he never felt attached to the idea of a family like I did.

This difference in our family backgrounds probably also accounts for our difference in social needs. Jack needs a lot more solitude, and I need a lot more time with people. But we've managed to find a balance between our time with friends, our time together, and our time alone.

I think what has worked for Jack and me is that we respect each other and the differences we have to offer to our relationship. We've learned that often it's the small differences in perspective that add to our relationship. If you value the differences, you will keep learning from one another. And if you're still learning, that keeps things fresh and exciting.

We also don't forget the details of making our relationship work. When you've been with someone for a number of years, you have to remember to compliment that person and to take time to focus on each other like you did when you first started dating. We've learned to savor the simple things, like a good meal together or an evening relaxing in our garden. The best gift we can give each other isn't something we can buy—it's giving each other some of our time and our energy.

on them. "If you're going to be a solid couple, you have to figure out how to share money," says Dr. Sills. Maybe one of you pays the rent while the other takes on groceries and household expenses. Or you divide everything half-and-half. Figure out what works for you.

Share space fairly. "When you're in love, you don't care about someone's space," says Dr. Sills. "When you move in, this changes." Where once you felt you were welcome to everything at his place, now he expects you to fit all of your belongings into two dresser drawers. Compromise to each get your fair share.

Sort out your stuff. His pool table, your piano. Unless you're living in a place the size of Long Island, you have to discuss your possessions. Do you really need two stereo systems? Are you particularly attached to certain possessions? Talk it out together. Buying furnishings together can also cause conflict. "Maybe she wants to spend $2000 to buy the couch of her dreams, while he'd be perfectly satisfied with an old sofa from a consignment shop for $200," says Dr. Coche. Instead of arguing about the couch, talk about your thoughts and feelings about the couch, she advises. "You may say, 'I think a pretty couch is really important,' while he says, 'But we have a dog and a pretty couch makes no sense at all.' Then work your way from there and try to come to an agreement. It's hard, but the bitterness is harder."

Split the chores. Living together seems to allow more flexibility than marriage when it comes to issues like who does the dishes and laundry, says Dr. Sills. "It's a bit freer psychologically. You're more apt to tell him, 'Wash your own dirty sweatpants.'" Assign yourselves chores and stick with them.

Honor each other's use of time. He's an early bird exerciser but you love to sleep in? Just because you're living together doesn't mean that he's allowed to rouse you out of bed or that you can demand he stays under the covers. When you are living with someone, your differences can work in sync, says Dr. Coche. "For example, he gets up at 5:00, finishes his morning run by 6:30, comes back, and makes coffee or tea. Then you get up, and the two of you have breakfast together."

Balance time together, time apart. "Our culture expects couples to enjoy spending too much time together," says Dr. Coche. In reality, we all need time to ourselves as well as time together. You might try spending time "apart" in the same room. One of you can read a book while the other listens to music. And, at times, it helps for each of you to have your own activities.

Keep being yourself. Just because you've moved in together doesn't mean that he can't have the guys over for Sunday afternoon football anymore and you can't go out to dinner with your friends. "If problems start emerging over these sorts of issues, you have to ask yourselves why," says Dr. Sills.

Nurture your relationship. Defy the temptation to start taking the person you live with for granted. "You have to make an ongoing effort to nurture your relationship, or it starts going downhill," says Dr. Coche. Keep treating your partner as special and appreciated. "Say supportive things like,

'Gee, you look great today,' or 'Thanks for calling, it was nice to hear from you.'" The couple who builds these good habits from the start of their life together has a much higher likelihood of staying together, she says.

Marriage Proposals

Proposing marriage is exciting. "Let's do it!" it says. "Let's tie the knot." But on the flip side is a certain anxiety. What's important is to clearly communicate your feelings for each other and your desire for marriage. Here's what experts say can make it a little easier.

Start talking long before proposing. The prospect of marriage shouldn't come as a surprise to either person, says Glenn E. Good, Ph.D., president of the Society for the Psychological Study of Men and Masculinity and associate professor in the department of educational and counseling psychology at the University of Missouri-Columbia. "I would hope that most contemporary, well-communicating couples would be discussing important aspects of their relationship all along," he says. "The prospect of marriage shouldn't come up as a sudden 'popping the question.'"

Don't wait for him to ask. Traditionally, the man is the one who is supposed to do the proposing. "For many women, popping the question doesn't feel good. They want to feel chosen, pursued, and special," says Judith Hurvitz, a licensed social worker who focuses on relationship issues, and a certified PAIRS (Practical Application of Intimate Relations Skills) instructor in Arlington, Virginia.

But if the question begs to be asked, just do it, advises Dr. Good. "Many women in my classes at the University of Missouri took this initiative with their subsequent husbands," he says. "Whether it's the man or the woman officially asking the other person doesn't matter." What matters is getting the issue on the table.

Reword it. Talking about your goals and needs instead of asking point-blank, "Will you marry me?" takes some of the angst out of the process.

"You might say to your partner, 'I want to be married and have a family. And you are the person I would most wish to do this with,'" suggests Hurvitz. "Instead of asking for something, you're telling him, 'You're the most important person in my life; you're the person I want to spend my life with.' And then you shut up."

If he doesn't respond immediately, don't bug him. "If he backs off, don't call him or show up on his doorstep," Hurvitz advises. "If he's still with you, great. Now start talking about what you're going to do together to make it work."

Accept less than yes. You or he may need more time. "Having to give someone time can feel agonizing and horrible," says Hurvitz. "But sometimes you really have no choice. If there's a chance that it will work later, and you're willing to wait, then wait."

Don't pressure him. "One of the things men fear most is being trapped and controlled," says Hurvitz. "The worst-case scenario is a marry-me-or-else ultimatum. Being given an ultimatum is probably not going to be well-received by either a man or a woman."

Money

Of all the things couples fight about, money tops the list, marriage experts say. She complains that he doesn't update the checkbook. He says she has expensive taste in clothes. She thinks the car is on its last miles. He thinks they can squeeze another year out of it.

Money is an inflammatory issue among couples because it isn't just about dollars and cents. It's a powerful emotional issue rife with hidden meanings. "Money issues with our partners start way back when we're dating," says Daniel L. Kegan, Ph.D., a licensed organizational psychologist with Elan and Associates, a company that provides corporate counseling, and an attorney in Chicago. "Did the man pay for dinner, and if so, why? So he could feel important? Or did she make a point of dividing the tab in half to assert her equality? These sorts of things are going on all the time, but they're usually unconscious. Even if you're aware of them, it's hard to talk about them."

Further muddying the waters are dark feelings like shame that can emerge with money problems. "Having a debt problem was humiliating," says Carla Goldman (not her real name), a Los Angeles musician who had racked up $60,000 in credit card debt even before she got married four years ago. Meanwhile, her husband-to-be owed $30,000. "We were pretty much in denial for years," she says.

Fight Less (and Stay Solvent)

Money problems can be resolved, and couples who make the effort to do so can find their way to richer relationships.

"Getting responsible about money changed us personally and spiritually," says Goldman. "We fell deeper in love because we were watching each other blossom and change."

Here's what experts advise for keeping your marital budget balanced.

Quit the blame game. "It's always the other guy's fault," says Richard Pittman, director of counseling and housing for the Consumer Credit Counseling Service of Los Angeles. "But one person isn't right and the other wrong. There's a lot more going on."

Get familiar with your feelings. Money conflicts often aren't about money at all, says Dr. Kegan. "There are lots of issues people have in life, but if they aren't readily able to identify what's bothering them, often the issues pop up in a different format—such as a problem with money." For example, do you like to be in control of situations? Recognizing this feeling may help you manage a tendency to try to control others through money.

Examine what money means to you. Conflicting perspectives on what money means are the source of many misunderstandings, says David Sanford, Ph.D., a licensed couples therapist and newspaper columnist in Portland, Maine, and founder of Couples Place, an Internet Web site.

"Money for one person is abundance and enjoyment, an expression of life's bounty, while for another, it's scarcity, the feeling that there's never enough," Dr. Sanford says. "Money for some people is security. For others, it's power or independence or superiority."

Try this exercise suggested by Dr. Sanford to explore what money means to you and your partner: On separate pieces of paper, write as many sentences as you can beginning with the words "Money is." For example, "Money is a headache. Money is a way to make money. Money is freedom." When you're finished, circle those that have particular significance for you.

Now compare notes with your spouse and consider any relationship prob-

Do You Need a Prenuptial Agreement?

Celebrities have them. Business tycoons have them. Your friend's sister who married a man who inherited money has one. Should you be thinking about a prenuptial agreement, too?

It depends.

A prenuptial agreement is primarily a means of protecting any financial assets you bring into a marriage, says Thomas D. Colin, a matrimonial attorney in Greenwich, Connecticut. The more substantial your assets, the more sense a prenuptial agreement makes.

"Two scenarios are most common for a prenup," Colin says. "First, if it's a second marriage for someone with children from a previous marriage, he or she may want to ensure that those children will receive their money in the event of a death. And second, if a person has inherited a lot of money, he or she may want to ensure that the money stays in the family."

To determine if you would benefit from a prenuptial agreement, see an experienced matrimonial attorney before broaching the issue with your fiancé, Colin advises. "You may find out that your situation is not suitable for a premarital agreement, in which case you've saved yourself what could be a difficult discussion with your fiancé."

Don't wait until the last minute to check into a prenuptial agreement. Get the ball rolling at least four to six months prior to your wedding date. "Signing a premarital agreement in the limousine on the way to the church is just asking for trouble," Colin says.

lems that result from your conflicting views. Finally, try to find areas of compromise and compatibility between your different views.

Talk about what money meant to you as a kid. Childhood experiences with money color our present-day perspectives, says Dr. Sanford. "Consider the role that money played in your childhood," he suggests. "Was there enough money in your home or not enough? What was communicated to you about having or spending money? Did your parents fight or cooperate about money? Who earned the money, and who decided how it would be spent? Did your parents pool their money or keep it separate?"

Becoming aware of your childhood lessons about money provides another tool for taking charge of your money today.

Talk to yourself. "A money dialogue helps you further define your lifelong personal relationship with money," says Olivia Mellan, a psychotherapist in Washington, D.C., who specializes in money issues and conflict resolution and is author of *Money Harmony: Resolving Money Conflicts in Your Life and Relationships*. On a piece of paper, pen a conversation between yourself and money about how your relationship is going. "An overspender might say to money, 'I love throwing you around,' while money responds, 'You don't treat me with respect,'" Mellan says. "Or a hoarder might say, 'Holding on to you makes me feel so secure,' while money responds, 'You're holding me so tight I can hardly breathe.'"

When the conversation winds down, Mellan says, have four voices in your head comment on the dialogue: your mother, your father, any other strong influence in your life, from your spouse to your great-aunt who hid money in her mattress, and finally, a higher power or your inner wisdom.

"My clients find this to be a very powerful exercise," Mellan says. "Do it once a week and you'll find yourself evolving in awareness."

Depolarize. Very often, husbands and wives "polarize" at opposite ends of the spectrum in regard to money, says Mellan. A classic example, she says, is the marriage between a hoarder, who likes to save, budget, prioritize, and plan, and a spender, who loves to spend money and hates to budget. There's also the money worrier and the money avoider combination—one who pays a lot of attention to money and one who pays none.

Mellan puts her clients who are polarized over money on this four-point program.

Secrets of Long-Lasting Love

They Balanced Their Checkbook— And Their Relationship

Pat and Al Brandstetter, who live in Sarasota, Florida, met over four decades ago while they were both working in a clothing factory. Pat's co-worker, who dated a buddy of Al's, thought it would be fun for all of them to go on a double date. That date to the drive-in turned into several dates, and they married on December 1, 1956. The couple's biggest challenge, says Pat, has been a combination of working through money matters and raising their children.

Al and I have always lived the simple life. We've never had enough money to live extravagantly, and that's fine by us. Money was particularly tight when we first got married—we had no savings, and we basically lived from paycheck to paycheck.

When we started having children, Al and I decided that one of us should be at home with the kids while they were young. So I gave up work and stayed home to raise our three children. It was difficult at times with only one income to support five people, and sometimes we couldn't even rely on Al's income. He worked for a major truck manufacturer, and it wasn't unusual for the workers to be on strike or laid off. But when that happened, I'd go back to work part-time so we had some cash.

1. Acknowledge your secret envy and appreciation of your partner's style. For instance, a hoarder may appreciate a spender's ability to enjoy life, while a spender may secretly admire a hoarder's ability to set priorities and maintain some control.

2. Practice being more like your mate at least once a week. If you hoard money, practice spending. If you're a spender, practice putting money in the bank.

3. Reward yourself with something that doesn't undermine your new behavior.

Every penny Al and I had went to raise our family. We never took big vacations, just a couple of days at the beach every year. But all in all, both Al and I think it was worth it to have less money and more time with our kids.

Because money was tight, it was often the reason for our disagreements. But we also disagreed early on about how we should discipline our children. Al and I were raised very differently. I grew up in a strict household and he didn't. So it took us some time to get in sync with how our children should be disciplined. It helped that we had open communication and were willing to compromise to reach a decision. Usually we'd have our big outburst, and then we would sit and talk things out, but we never let things go without discussing them. Al and I have gotten in the habit of using the time before bed to catch up. We'll get into bed, lie next to each other, and talk about what's on our minds before we drift off to sleep. Sometimes if we both wake up in the middle of the night, we'll talk then as well. Bedtime is our time.

What's worked for Al and me is open communication and love—unconditional love. He and I have never thought about leaving each other. You can't think like that in a loving marriage, or it would be too easy to walk away during the tough times. And most important, we've learned that we can't let money determine our happiness.

4. Monitor your progress by keeping a written record of how it feels to be dealing with money differently, and talk with your partner about your feelings.

Plan life goals together. Put your plans, desires, and expectations on the table with your partner. "It's amazing how many people don't even think to do this," says Pittman. "That's how situations arise where a couple is struggling along with four kids but the husband doesn't want to give up his Porsche. You have to start communicating and compromising."

Figure out your budget. Life without a budget invites confusion and crisis, says Pittman. "A budget incorporates monthly expenses with occasional expenses like auto license renewals and anticipates emergencies such as the roof blowing off," he says. If you're new to the concept, start by keeping tabs on what you're already spending for a month or two. Then work your way back from there.

Give yourself an allowance. Include in your budget equal amounts of "mad money" that you and your spouse each independently control, says Pittman. "Everyone should have a few bucks in their jeans that they have complete control over."

Divide expenses equitably. Given that many working women earn less than men, it's only fair that expenses be divided fairly along these lines, says Pittman. "If I earn 60 percent of our income and my spouse earns 40 percent, we can figure our expenses on a percentage basis," he says. "My 60 percent could represent the mortgage and utilities, while her 40 percent could take care of the rest." After a few years of marriage, though, a lot of couples simply throw everything into the pot, regardless of who makes what, and pay expenses out of their joint accounts.

Share money management. "Fifteen years ago I fell off our roof and shattered my leg," Pittman recalls. "One of the first things I remember in the hospital was my wife sitting on the corner of my bed with our bills, saying, 'You always pay the bills, which ones do I pay?'"

Split money management duties so no one is left in the dark, he urges.

Hold money meetings. Carla Goldman and her husband sit down together once a week to review their budget (they prefer to call it a spending plan). "I'm not saying this is our favorite thing to do, but it's really helpful to keep close track of where our money is going. Recently, for example, we discovered that we've been spending a ton of money on junk food. We had our meeting and decided we'd rather spend that money on CDs."

Educate yourself. "Everyone should learn how the money world works," says Dr. Kegan. "Learn the vocabulary and mechanics of money. Learn to read the financial page of the newspaper and know how that stuff works." Read books. Take classes. Attend investment seminars.

"Nobody understands everything about money, but the more you understand about finances, the better your decisions about marriage and your life can be," Dr. Kegan says. "Otherwise, you're not going to be in control."

Monogamy

⁓

The retreat of romance for reality, be it day-to-day boredom or downright disillusionment, is a perfectly normal experience for many longtime couples, experts say.

"At first we believe we have found in each other the fulfillment of all our dreams," says Wayne Sotile, Ph.D., a psychologist in Winston-Salem, North Carolina, and coauthor of the book *Supercouple Syndrome: How Overworked Couples Can Beat Stress Together*. "But as time goes on and infatuation dwindles, we discover that many of the traits we attributed to our mates simply aren't there. The landslide soon begins. Typically between years four and eight of a relationship, we lose each other. Many couples simply quit. Even if they stay married, many aren't intimate."

Become Passionate Friends — For Life

Here's how to help your marriage thrive over the long haul.

Never stop working at it. "Marriage is a journey, not a destination," says Claudia Arp, who with her husband, David Arp, is a marriage and family educator based in Knoxville, Tennessee, who conducts Marriage Alive workshops all over the world and has coauthored numerous books on marriage. "Marriage is not the end of the story, the prince and princess riding off together into the sunset. Instead, it's like riding up the rapids. If you stop paddling, you don't stay in the same place but start sliding backward."

Troubled times can offer the very opportunities we require to forge stronger, truer bonds based on real rather than romantic love, says Hedy Schleifer, a certified marriage therapist and clinical psychologist in Winter Park, Florida, who conducts "Getting the Love You Want" workshops internationally with her husband, Yumi.

"You begin to learn that your marriage has a higher purpose: to help each other become mature adults by being passionate friends," says Schleifer.

Secrets of Long-Lasting Love

Time-Out Tactics Settle Spats

Constance and William Kelly of Andover, Massachusetts, met in 1945. Bill had just returned from World War II to a civilian job at the company where Connie was employed. They dated for three years and eventually married on March 20, 1948. Connie says that the success of their 50-year relationship boils down to their commitment to each other and their marriage.

Bill and I have always had an open and loving relationship. And the relaxed nature of our marriage made things that others might view as difficult not so difficult.

Take raising children, for example. I know lots of people who thought raising children was a challenge. Bill and I had four children together, but aside from occasionally trying our patience, they weren't difficult. They were just kids. Bill and I used the time-out tactic when either of us got frustrated with them: We would walk away and calm down before disciplining. It made dealing with our kids much easier, and it kept tensions in the house low.

Bill and I also apply that time-out tactic to the disagreements between the two of us. If we are having a little sparring match over something, we walk away for a while and then come back to discuss it. That is, if there is something to discuss; very often after a time-out, we won't remember what we were so angry about in the first place. Sometimes all you need is a little

Embrace conflict. "Conflict is your best friend, an opportunity for growth," explains Schleifer. Conflict dissolution begins with getting to know your partner as he really is rather than who you think he should be. "Think of intimacy as 'into-me-see,'" she says.

Keep talking. Conversation is one of our most important emotional needs, according to Willard Harley, Ph.D., president of the Marriage Builders Corporation in Minneapolis and director of the Marriage Builders Internet

distance from the issue so that small disagreements don't evolve into something larger than they should, and you don't say something that you shouldn't.

Our easy-going dynamics and the comfort we feel when we're together keep everything in our relationship on track, especially the romance. Sometimes all it takes is for us to glance at each other and there are sparks. You can really tell a lot about what a person is feeling just from eye contact.

In recent years, the romance has intensified for Bill and me. Over the Christmas holiday in 1997, we had quite a scare that made us realize just how important we are to each other. Until that Christmas, we had always been healthy. But Bill woke up one morning complaining that he couldn't breathe. He's not usually a complainer, so I immediately drove him to the hospital. It turned out that he had blockages in his coronary arteries, and the doctors performed quintuple bypass surgery. During those three weeks that Bill was in the hospital, all I could think about was how much I wanted him to get healthy again. And now that he is healthy, we treasure the time we have together.

I also know that what has really held our marriage together over the years is the unconditional love we have for each other and the commitment we have to our marriage. It may sound old-fashioned, but we took those vows for better and for worse, and we're in it until the end.

Web site. "A husband who meets your need for conversation will make you feel in love with him," he says.

Sadly, many couples come to a conversational standstill during marriage. This is much different from the nonstop talk that goes on during courtship, when we're highly motivated to gather information about each other.

Stimulating conversation may take some, well, stimulation, says David Sanford, Ph.D., a licensed couples therapist and newspaper columnist in Portland, Maine, and founder of Couples Place, an Internet Web site. He suggests applying a conversational formula such as "What was it like when. . . ?" For instance, ask your husband, "What was it like for you when you were in the first grade? Or when you and your parents argued? Or when you moved to another state in the middle of your sophomore year?" Since the flipside of talking is listening, be open to really hearing your husband's answers, too, reminds Dr. Sanford.

Show your appreciation. "Most of us have a deep desire to be respected, valued, and appreciated by our spouses," says Dr. Harley. "We need to be affirmed clearly and often." Remember to tell your partner thanks—for helping you sort out a problem, for doing the dishes, for laughing at your jokes.

Keep dating. Just because you're committed doesn't mean you should stop courting. Aim to go out on a date at least every couple of weeks, says Arp, who coauthored *52 Dates for You and Your Mate* and *10 Great Dates to Revitalize Your Marriage*. Take your dates seriously enough that you put them on your calendar.

In addition, developing what Arp calls a dating mentality can turn even the most mundane of activities into a date. "Since we're in our fifties now, my husband and I have to really watch our health," she says. "So now every summer we have two 'dates,' one to go get our eyes checked together, and the other to get our physicals. We have a great time together."

Have fun together. "We fall in love with people who make us laugh," says Dr. Sotile. "We stay in love with those who make us feel safe enough to come out to play."

If your laughter pump needs priming, buy a joke book and read jokes to each other, suggests Arp. For cheap laughs, go to a greeting card shop, pick out silly cards, read them to each other, and put them back on the shelf. Hanging around with funny friends helps, too.

Work at being affectionate. "For many people, affection is the essential cement of a relationship," says Dr. Harley. "Without affection, they feel totally alienated. With it, they become emotionally bonded."

Upping your affection quotient "re-romanticizes" your relationship, says Schleifer, who encourages "100 caring behaviors a day." For starters, she suggests that you and your partner make individual lists of all the things that make you feel thoroughly loved. Then trade lists and start producing. "A little wink, a little 'honey, I'm proud of you,' a note here, a squeeze of the butt there . . . you will not believe how these behaviors can change the whole climate of a relationship."

Flood your partner with positives. In her workshops, Schleifer asks couples to do the following re-romanticizing exercise: While one of you quietly sits in a chair, the other circles for 15 minutes, describing all the things that he loves about you, from the way you look to the things you do. Finally, he stands in front of you, jumps up and down, and yells, "I love you! I love you! You are the most incredible, extraordinary person in the entire universe!" Then the roles are reversed. This exercise infuses both partners with warm, wonderful feelings that renew their commitment to each other, Schleifer says.

PART SIX

Extraordinary Sexual Health

WOMEN'S
SEXUAL HEALTH

The Female Body Map

༝

If you don't know how your genitals work, you can't maximize your sexual pleasure or expect your partner to do so. And you can't understand all your treatment options when it comes to managing menstrual discomforts, pelvic pain, infertility, or vaginal or urinary tract infections. So learning the ins and outs of your feminine plumbing not only demystifies "down there," but it can also embolden you to reap certain benefits, sexual and otherwise.

Never fear: You don't have to examine your genitals with a hand mirror. Just take this crash course in female anatomy—a part-by-part guide to your private and not-so-private parts. You'll learn what they do, how they work, and how they contribute to your sexual pleasure, your reproductive functioning, or both.

Lips and Breasts: Erogenous Zones North

Kissing is one of the most sensuous experiences humans can undertake. For good reason. The lips are packed with sensory receptors, making them exquisitely sensitive to touch, pressure, warmth, and cold. This means that there are an infinite number of ways to explore their erotic potential. For example, you can nibble, suck, or lick your lover's lips; alternate feather-light kisses with hot and heavy smooches; or alternate kisses with sips of an icy-cold or hot drink.

Breasts aren't quite as sensitive to stimulation as lips, but they run a close second. They're made up of two types of tissue. Fatty tissue determines the size of the breast. Glandular tissue contains mammary glands, which secrete milk after childbirth. Some women enjoy having their breasts stroked and fondled; others don't find it as arousing.

The nipple, which lies in the center of the areola, or dark surrounding area, is perhaps the most sensitive part of the breast. Nipples are richly endowed with nerve endings, and many women find that stimulation of their nipples increases their sexual arousal.

The Vulva and Vagina: Erogenous Zones South

The outer sex organs are known as the vulva. This area includes:

The labia majora. The hair-bearing outer lips of the vagina, the labia majora are packed with nerve endings, making them sensitive to sexual stimulation.

The labia minora. The thinner, softer inner lips, the labia minora cover the vagina and the urethral opening, which leads to the bladder. The labia minora come in all shapes and sizes, and like the labia majora, they're highly responsive to touch.

The urethra. A woman's urethra is about 1 to 1½ inches long; a man's is 6 to 8 inches long. Because our urethras are so close to our external genitals, it's easier for bacteria from the vagina or rectum to travel from the vagina, up the urethra, and into the bladder, causing a bladder infection. During intercourse, infection-causing bacteria from the man's sex organs can also travel this same route.

The average vagina is only three to five inches long. But during childbirth, the vagina stretches and elongates to accommodate a full-term baby. The opening of the vagina is behind the urethra and in front of the anus. The outer third of the vaginal walls consists of ridges and folds of tissue and is packed with nerve endings, making it the most sensitive part of the vagina, responsive to light touch or friction. The remaining two-thirds is smoother and has few nerve endings, making it more sensitive to pressure. Located on each side of the vaginal opening are the Bartholin's glands, which lubricate the vagina during sexual excitement.

A Fancy Name
for a Simple Tube

The fallopian tubes, which lead from the ovaries to the uterus, were named after Italian anatomist Gabriel Fallopius. (Until recently, medical tradition held that the first person to find an organ got to name it.)

Located under the labia minora, the clitoris is often compared to a man's penis. But unlike the penis, this exquisitely sensitive organ has only one mission: to give a woman sexual pleasure.

The clitoris ranges in size from three-quarters of an inch to two inches long. In many women, most of the head, or glans, is hidden by a fold of skin called the clitoral hood. The rest extends inside the body into the pubic region. Like the penis, the clitoris becomes erect when stimulated. It's the head that swells during arousal.

Though less than one-third of women can climax without clitoral stimulation, men often say that they have a hard time finding the clitoris or don't know how to stimulate it. You and your partner should experiment with different strokes and touches.

The Female G-Spot

The cushion of tissue, nerve endings, and blood vessels wrapped around the urethra is sometimes called the G-spot (after physician Ernst Grafenburg, who first identified it). It's located on the upper wall of the vagina, an inch or two behind the back of the pubic bone. While some women report that stimulating this spot culminates in orgasm, others report feeling nothing. Some women say that it helps to be somewhat aroused before attempting to stimulate the G-spot.

If you'd like to try to find your G-spot, try this exercise, suggests Joel Block, Ph.D., a clinical psychologist and sex therapist at the Human Sexuality Center of Long Island Jewish Medical Center in Glen Oaks, New York, and author of *Secrets of Better Sex*. Lie face-to-face with your partner. Have him insert his lubricated index finger and middle finger into your vagina. He should push gently in the outer third of the vagina's top region until you feel a sensitive place that feels rougher than the surrounding area. Your partner should then stroke the spot, using the "come here" gesture. If you feel the urge to urinate, stop and try later with an empty bladder.

Your Hormones, Your Self

A woman's body may be like a map. But it's her sex hormones—estrogen, progesterone, and testosterone—that provide the fuel for the trip. Here's how each of these hormones affects our sexual behavior.

Estrogen, the "she" hormone. Estrogen, the main female sex hormone, is responsible for our feminine characteristics such as our breasts, rounded bodies, and body hair distribution. Estrogen also makes us receptive to sex, says Theresa Crenshaw, M.D., a certified sex therapist in San Diego and author of *The Alchemy of Love and Lust.* "Estrogen is the Marilyn Monroe in you," she says.

As we approach menopause, our ovaries produce less and less estrogen. This waning supply can cause vaginal dryness and thinning of the vaginal walls as well as a reduced appetite for sex, says Dr. Crenshaw. Hormone-replacement therapy can reduce these symptoms.

Progesterone, the baby-making hormone. The hormone progesterone stimulates the development of the lining of the uterus, the endometrium, in preparation for pregnancy. Ironically, while progesterone is vital for reproduction, it reduces sexual desire, according to Dr. Crenshaw.

Testosterone, the pursuit hormone. This is the aggressive sex drive hormone. While estrogen makes us receptive to sex, testosterone makes us actively pursue it, explains Dr. Crenshaw. You might say that testosterone plays Arnold Schwarzenegger to estrogen's Marilyn.

In many women, levels of testosterone wane during menopause, and this can reduce their desire for sex. Research suggests that testosterone-replacement therapy can help restore it.

The Egg Factory

The ovaries—two almond-shaped organs located in the lower abdomen, one on each side of the uterus—produce the female sex hormone estrogen as well as progesterone and a small amount of testosterone. These hormones are essential to our ability to reproduce, and they also contribute to our sexual drive and functioning.

The ovaries also house and nourish a woman's eggs, or ova. During ovulation, an ovary releases an egg, which then travels toward the uterus through one of the two fallopian tubes. If the egg is fertilized, pregnancy results. If not, the egg is shed during menstruation.

About the size and shape of a pear, the uterus is a child's first home. The opening to the uterus, the cervix, opens into the vagina. The lining of the uterus, called the endometrium, thickens with blood and tissue each month in anticipation of pregnancy. If a fertilized egg doesn't implant in the uterus, we menstruate. That is, the endometrium breaks down, and the lost blood and tissue flows out of the cervix and vagina.

The uterus usually slants forward. But 10 percent of women have a so-called retroverted uterus, which tips backward. These women can find certain sexual positions painful.

Hysterectomy, or the removal of the uterus (and sometimes the ovaries and fallopian tubes), can affect a woman's sexuality because she no longer produces estrogen. Some women find that sex after a hysterectomy improves greatly; others report a drop in their sexual desire. Hormone-replacement therapy can help treat low libido and other symptoms associated with hysterectomy, such as vaginal dryness and thinning.

Working Your PC Muscles

The pubococcygeal (PC) muscles are tiny muscles that run from the pubic bone to the tailbone. Some women find that regularly exercising the PC muscles by doing what are called Kegels can lead to better sex and even stronger, more intense orgasms. (Kegels are also a first-line treatment for certain kinds of urinary incontinence problems.)

To locate your PC muscles, stop and start your flow of urine. Contract the

PC muscles hard for one second, then release. Once you've learned how to isolate these muscles, you can work them when you're not urinating. Repeat the contraction 15 to 20 times. Do two sessions twice a day. Gradually work up to two sets of 75 per day.

When you can do 150 short "squeezes" a day, add a series of long Kegel squeezes. To do them, perform the regular Kegel, but hold the contraction for a count of three. Relax between contractions. Start with two sets of 20 and work up to two sets of 75. (You'll now be doing 300 a day—150 short "squeezes," 150 long.)

Contraction

From condoms to the Pill, vasectomies to hormone injections, couples have more than a dozen ways to avoid or delay pregnancy. With so many options, you'd think that virtually no unplanned pregnancies would occur. But they do. Why?

Because short of complete abstinence, birth control methods aren't always 100 percent effective. Much of the difference, it seems, is between "perfect use" and "typical use," explains Herbert B. Peterson, M.D., chief of the Centers for Disease Control and Prevention Women's Health and Fertility Branch. Perfect use means what you'd expect—using birth control each and every time you have sex, with no slipups. In real life, though, things go wrong. A condom tears, a pill is forgotten, and—voilà!—you're parents.

Convenience also plays a role. If using a contraceptive ruins the moment, interrupts lovemaking, or is messy, you're less apt to use it consistently. If you use a diaphragm, for example, you must insert the device and then wait a few minutes before having intercourse, which can affect spontaneity, tempting you to skip the diaphragm "just this once," possibly leading to pregnancy.

Conversely, if you choose a method, such as the Pill or IUD, that's invisible—or even enhances intimacy—you're more likely to use it more often, use it right, and avoid unwanted pregnancy. The key is to choose a form of birth control that makes sense for you and your mate. The right choice depends on various factors, including where you are in your relationship; your family planning goals; whether you also need protection against sexually transmitted diseases; your health and medical history, or your partner's; and what you can afford, or what your health insurance plan covers. Even what kind of person you are (organized or not, spontaneous or regimented) is a factor.

"I urge couples to look at contraception not as a barrier or burden to a relationship but as an opportunity to explore the relationship and their communication at new, intimate levels," says Joel S. Feigin, M.D., associate clinical professor of family medicine at Robert Wood Johnson Medical School in New Brunswick, New Jersey, and director of the Coventry No-Scalpel Vasectomy Center in Phillipsburg, New Jersey. "When a couple first becomes intimate, they're very cautious—they have to be concerned about sexually transmitted diseases like AIDS. As the relationship progresses, they're more comfortable talking about the technical details of the intimate part of their relationship. Either way, it's very important to be open and frank."

But once a method is chosen, having protection can be liberating. "For women of childbearing age, having to think or worry about birth control and pregnancy can decrease sexual desire, especially if the woman already has young children," says Ann Langley, Ph.D., a marriage and family counselor with the San Jose Marital and Sexuality Center in Santa Clara, California. People who use reliable methods of birth control often indulge in more frequent and spontaneous lovemaking (provided that those mothers with young children aren't exhausted by bedtime).

"The most important things about a method of birth control are that it's used, that it's effective, and that it's safe," Dr. Feigin emphasizes.

"You don't have to make a big issue out of choosing a single 'ideal' method of birth control," says Katherine A. Forrest, M.D., a medical consultant with Forrest Associates in Portola Valley, California. "Explore all your options, try more than one, and decide what best suits you and your mate. You may find that you're in different moods at different times, so trying different methods gives you other options if you can't use your old favorite. Everyone benefits if they have more than one way of getting and giving pleasure—and protecting themselves in the process."

It is important that both people in the relationship choose the method together. "It takes two to have a pregnancy, so there are two partners who need to be involved in selecting the birth control method," says Allan Rosenfield, M.D., professor of public health and obstetrics and the dean of the Joseph L. Mailman School of Public Health at Columbia University in New York City.

Even if you're in a long-standing relationship and have been using birth control for years, you may want to periodically discuss the method or methods you are using and make sure you and your mate are happy with your choice. Consider the pros and cons of each method. As long as you've chosen a reversible birth control method, you can always try something new.

Male Condom

The traditional male condom takes a lot of ribbing (no pun intended), but next to the female condom, it's the best defense against sexually transmitted diseases, and it helps protect against pregnancy. That makes it an important birth control method, especially for couples in a new relationship.

Male condoms are made of latex, polyurethane, or natural membrane (lamb's intestine) and are placed over an erect penis. Male condoms come in many colors, sizes, and styles, but all have the same purpose—to catch sperm and prevent it from entering a woman's body.

Male Condom

Effectiveness with typical use: 86%

Protects against STDs: Yes

Prescription needed: No

Cost: Ranges from 60 cents to $2.50 per condom

How well does it work? Some condoms are more effective than others, depending on the material used. "If used correctly and consistently, male latex condoms do the best job of preventing the transmission of HIV (the virus that causes AIDS)," says Dr. Peterson. "After abstinence, it's clearly the number one choice for couples at risk for HIV transmission."

Don't use petroleum jelly (Vaseline) or other oil-based lubricants or mineral oils with a latex condom, because they can make the rubber disintegrate. Instead, opt for a water-soluble jelly, such as the K-Y brand. Using a spermicidal jelly, foam, or cream (discussed separately) increases protection against pregnancy and decreases friction.

What you can expect: Since you can't put on a condom until his penis is erect, you have to stop lovemaking to use it. But you can speed up that process.

"Before lovemaking, open the packet and know which way the condom is sitting, so you can put it on quickly," Dr. Forrest advises. "And before you even start using condoms for the first time, you may want to unroll a few, to get used to putting them on quickly and smoothly."

After ejaculation, your partner should remove his penis from your vagina before his erection subsides, holding on to the rim of the condom so the ejaculate doesn't enter your vagina.

Is it right for you and your mate? Most couples who use condoms are at the beginning stages of their relationship, where they are just learning about each other's sexual history and exploring all the physical feelings of being close to another person. It is also a time when they are trying to make good impressions. A cautious approach may temper the "rush" of a new relationship, but protection against pregnancy and sexually transmitted diseases is serious business. So you may need to be assertive, Dr. Feigin says.

"If it's a new relationship," says Dr. Feigin, "it's okay to discuss the issue and say, 'This is important, and we need to use a condom or we're not going to do anything at all.' But there's almost an expectation today that early in an adult relationship, condoms will be used."

Impress Your Date
with Condom Trivia

Legend has it that condoms are named after the Earl of Condom, an English knight and personal physician to King Charles II in the 1600s. Charles, who had several mistresses, asked Dr. Condom to produce a foolproof method of protecting the king against syphilis.

How to Get Him to Use a Condom

Early in a relationship, a man may wonder, "Will she or won't she have sex?" while the woman is likely to be thinking, "Will he or won't he wear a condom?"

It's not that men don't understand the need for a condom. Most do. They just don't like to use them. Men who object to slipping on a sheath complain about loss of sensation or disruption in lovemaking. Here are some useful hints for persuading your guy to use protection, without ruining the moment.

Be prepared. Half the condoms sold these days are purchased by women. So don't be afraid he'll think you're a floozy, says Ann Langley, Ph.D., a marriage and family counselor with the San Jose Marital and Sexuality Center in Santa Clara, California. "It's the new sexual etiquette to approach a sexual encounter prepared with birth control," she says. "A woman should carry fresh condoms in her purse, just like a man carries them in his wallet."

Point out that you both benefit. When men think of condoms, many think of AIDS only, not other sexually transmitted diseases like chlamydia or genital herpes, says Dr. Langley. "Your man may assume that if he hasn't had any homosexual partners, he's not at risk and you're both safe. But he could contract HIV from sex with a woman who has been with a bisexual man."

Depersonalize the issue—ahead of time. "Don't make using a condom a matter of trust," says Katherine A. Forrest, M.D., a medical consultant with Forrest Associates in Portola Valley, California. "Just tell him, 'This is

If couples have been dating for a while before becoming intimate, they usually have developed a closeness that allows them to discuss the need for condoms prior to initiating lovemaking, notes Dr. Feigin.

Tips for first-time users: You must use a new condom for each sex act. Always carefully check the condom for tears and holes before and after intercourse.

my rule, and it has nothing to do with who you are, it's just how I do things. A lot of people are infected with disease and don't know it. Using a condom is a way to protect myself.' Say this well before you get involved in love-making, so it won't ruin the moment."

Give some thought to fit and comfort. Make your man comfortable, and he's more likely to use a condom. "If your man likes the feeling of move-ment, get a condom with a 'relaxed-fit' tip, which has more room for the penis head to move," Dr. Forrest advises.

Take your time. "Putting on a condom can be part of the exploring and getting-to-know-each-other part of foreplay," says Joel S. Feigin, M.D., as-sociate clinical professor of family medicine at Robert Wood Johnson Med-ical School in New Brunswick, New Jersey, and director of the Coventry No-Scalpel Vasectomy Center in Phillipsburg, New Jersey. "There's nothing wrong with slowing down the sexual act."

Lubricate from the inside out. Wetness helps lovemaking. "Before putting on a condom, put a little extra dab of lubricant inside the condom to increase sensation for him," Dr. Forrest suggests.

Get in on the act. Offer to help your man get "prepped" for using the condom; then make a game out of rolling it on. "You can say or do sug-gestive things while putting on the condom," says Dr. Forrest.

Spice it up with variety. Just as trying different positions can enhance lovemaking, so can trying different condoms. Fun colors or ribbed varieties can tickle your fancy.

Female Condom

If your guy is adamant about not using a male condom, you might want to consider the female condom, a relatively new form of birth control. It looks like a male condom, with an open end and a closed end. The polyurethane sheath has a flexible ring at each end; one ring is placed against the cervix and the other outside the vagina. The condom retains ejaculate, preventing sperm from entering the vagina. It is available without a prescription in drugstores.

How well does it work? Used properly and consistently, the female condom is almost as effective as the male condom. The female condom has one big advantage over the male condom: It is inserted before love-making begins, so there is no disruption in your passion.

Female Condom

Effectiveness with typical use: 79%

Protects against STDs: Yes

Prescription needed: No

Cost: Approximately $3 per condom

What you can expect: The female condom is more expensive than the male version, and it may require lubricant on the outside to help with insertion into the vagina, and on the inside to reduce friction on the penis. To avoid tears or punctures, women must also be careful of their sharp nails or jewelry when inserting the condom. After intercourse, twist and squeeze the outer ring as the condom is removed, so the ejaculate doesn't leak into the vagina. Discard the condom, making sure to use a new one each time you make love.

Is it right for you and your mate? Condoms are often used at the beginning of a relationship, when protection against sexually transmitted diseases is especially important. The female condom actually provides more protection than the male condom against sexually transmitted diseases that infect the external genital area, such as genital herpes and genital warts.

Women who anticipate a man's reluctance to using a condom can discuss the advantages of the female version. "There's a pretty good chance that a guy hasn't seen one, so perhaps a woman can show her guy one and say, 'I've tried this and it seems to work really well for me,'" Dr. Forrest recommends. "Also, tell him that men find they have more stimulation when they use the female condom rather than the male condom, because they can feel movement against the skin of the penis and get more rubbing action than with a male condom."

Because one inch of the open end remains outside the vagina when the female condom is inserted, make sure you discuss using this method before you get passionate, so your lover is less likely to be surprised or turned off. "With something that's going to be a somewhat intrusive form of contraception, where the other partner will know it's there, I think it's best to discuss it before you're in bed and in a heated love-making session," Dr. Forrest says. "That's particularly true for the female condom, which is novel and is not used by many people."

Tips for first-time users: Use your hand to guide your man's penis into the condom. Because this condom is not wrapped around a penis, you and your partner must make sure that during intercourse the penis head enters inside the condom, not to the side, where sperm can be ejaculated into the vagina.

Diaphragm

The diaphragm is a rubber dome wrapped around a pliable metal rim that is filled with spermicidal jelly or cream and inserted into the vagina before intercourse to cover the cervix. This action blocks the entrance to the cervix and also kills any sperm that get past the diaphragm before they enter the uterus. Spermicide must be reapplied before every sex act, with the diaphragm still in the vagina, and the diaphragm must stay in place for at least six hours after the last intercourse, which can make this method inconvenient.

Diaphragms are available only through a doctor. Your doctor will fit you for size during a pelvic examination, plus instruct you on how to insert and remove the diaphragm to make sure you understand how to use it.

How well does it work? The diaphragm is an inexpensive and fairly reliable option, but you have to learn how to insert it. Once you get the hang of it, you and your husband can insert it together during foreplay, if you wish. But this barrier method does require couples to plan ahead for lovemaking. And it can be messy, so it doesn't hide the fact that birth control is being used.

In addition to protecting against pregnancy, the diaphragm can also

> **Diaphragm with Spermicidal Cream or Jelly**
>
> **Effectiveness with typical use:** 80%
>
> **Protects against STDs:** No
>
> **Prescription needed:** Yes
>
> **Cost:** The examination and fitting cost from $50 to $120. Diaphragms average from $13 to $25 each; a kit of spermicidal cream or jelly costs from $8 to $17.

be used to temporarily stop the flow of menstrual blood from the vagina when a woman has her period, so couples can enjoy intercourse without that distraction.

What you can expect: A diaphragm is fairly low-maintenance. Before lovemaking, hold the diaphragm up to the light to look for holes and tears.

Some men may actually like to help insert the diaphragm as a part of foreplay, though Dr. Langley says "those are pretty progressive couples." Even many women say diaphragms feel uncomfortable and strange to insert, especially because slippery spermicidal jelly is used.

After insertion, the diaphragm should go unnoticed. "Usually, men cannot feel the diaphragm. But those who do say it feels kind of nice, and it acts as another firm area he can rub up against," Dr. Forrest says.

A diaphragm can be dislodged in the woman-astride love-making position, and it can feel uncomfortable if the penis pushes the rim of the diaphragm against the cervix, Dr. Langley notes. You need to leave the diaphragm in place for a minimum of six hours after intercourse in order for the spermicide to do its job. After removing the diaphragm, wash it with water and mild, unscented soap; then dry it away from heat and cold. Check it again for holes or tears. If you find a hole or tear, call your doctor and ask if you need emergency contraception (birth control pills or an IUD can prevent pregnancy after sexual intercourse).

Having to leave a diaphragm in for a minimum of six hours after intercourse means that you may feel messy for a while. And another negative, Dr. Langley says, is that some women have difficulty urinating when a diaphragm is in place.

Because the diaphragm puts pressure on the urethra, which may block the flow of urine and allow bacteria to grow, using one may contribute to urinary tract infections. And either partner may be allergic to the spermicide or rubber.

On a positive note, long-term use may reduce a woman's risk of developing cervical dysplasia, abnormal changes in the cells of the cervix that can lead to cancer.

Is it right for you and your mate? "Because the diaphragm must be inserted in advance and because it doesn't protect against sexually transmitted diseases, the diaphragm is for couples who know each other and plan where and when to have sexual activity," Dr. Feigin says.

It is not recommended for couples who are allergic to either rubber or spermicide, or for women whose pelvic muscles or tissues were stretched during childbirth and may not be strong enough to hold the diaphragm securely in place.

Even with perfect use, the diaphragm is less effective than oral contraceptives and the male condom. But Dr. Forrest says that it's a good option for women who are concerned about health issues and don't want to take the hormones found in oral contraceptives, discussed later.

Tips for first-time users: You can have intercourse more than once while the diaphragm is in place. But you need to apply more spermicide before each act of intercourse. And you'll need to be refitted for and purchase a new diaphragm each year. The size of the diaphragm should also be checked if you lose or gain 20 pounds or more, or if you have surgery on your cervix (cervical conization, for example) or on your vagina and urethra (for urinary incontinence).

Cervical Cap

Similar to a diaphragm, the cervical cap is a rubber or latex dome about the size of a thimble that has a pliable, metal rim. Before intercourse, the cap is filled with spermicide and inserted into the vagina to cover the cervix and prevent sperm from entering the uterus. The cap is held in place through suction (a water-based lubricant will help make a seal) and the support of the vaginal wall. This method is an alternative to the diaphragm, though it is smaller, a bit trickier to use, and less effective for women who have already had children. It does, however, have some advantages over the diaphragm.

The cap is smaller than a diaphragm, so it should fit more securely. But its smaller size can make the cap difficult to fit, insert, and remove. It also may move during intercourse, which would affect its role as a contraceptive.

On the positive side, the cap can be kept in place for up to two days.

> **Cervical Cap with Spermicidal Cream or Jelly**
>
> **Effectiveness with typical use:** 80% for women who've never had children; 60% for women who've had children
>
> **Protects against STDs:** No
>
> **Prescription needed:** Yes
>
> **Cost:** The examination and fitting cost from $50 to $120. Cervical caps average from $13 to $25 each; a kit of spermicidal cream or jelly costs from $8 to $17.

And it requires less spermicide than a diaphragm, so that may help couples enjoy oral sex more since the taste and smell of spermicide are sometimes unpleasant.

How well does it work? Not very. "Failure rates are pretty high for typical users, and even the perfect-user failure rate is still relatively high," Dr. Peterson says.

What you can expect: Using the cervical cap means that you must plan your lovemaking, because the cap must be in place for 20 to 30 minutes before intercourse. It must stay in the vagina for at least 8 hours after intercourse, and it must be removed within 48 hours. After 48 hours, the risk of infection increases and the spermicide may begin to smell unpleasant.

After intercourse, check to make sure the cap didn't move. If it did, quickly push it back into position and insert an application of spermicide into your vagina. After it is removed, check the cap for holes and tears.

Occasionally, use of a cervical cap will increase the bacterial count in the vagina, predisposing you to a urinary tract infection.

Is it right for you and your mate? Given the high failure rate, this method is not a good idea for women or couples who are adamant about not getting pregnant just yet. And the need for prior insertion precludes any spontaneity in lovemaking.

Tips for first-time users: Once the cap is in place, you can make love as often as you wish. But before each act, you need to apply more spermicide. Also, you'll need to see your doctor every year, or after pregnancy, to make sure the fit is still correct.

Spermicides

Spermicides are foams, suppositories, films, creams, or jellies that a woman places in her vagina, close to the cervix, before intercourse to kill sperm. They are primarily used in conjunction with barrier birth control, such as the diaphragm and cervical cap, to increase the effectiveness of those contraceptives.

- Foams come in aerosol containers and require a special applicator that women fill with the foam and then insert into the vagina, similar to using a tampon. The chemical is effective for one hour.

- Suppositories are bullet-shaped tablets of spermicide. They're inserted by hand into the vagina 10 to 15 minutes before intercourse so they will melt. They are effective for one hour.

- Films are thin, two-inch square pieces of spermicide that are inserted by hand into the vagina 5 to 10 minutes before intercourse so they will melt. They are effective for about two hours.

- Creams and jellies are usually used with a diaphragm or cervical cap.

How well does it work? "Spermicides alone are not highly effective methods of contraception and don't protect against sexually transmitted diseases, so they're usually used in conjunction with a diaphragm or condom," Dr. Feigin explains.

If you're using a spermicide alone, however, Dr. Forrest suggests using foam, because it spreads throughout a larger area in the vagina.

> **Spermicides**
>
> **Effectiveness with typical use:** 74%
> **Protects against STDs:** No
> **Prescription needed:** No
> **Cost:** A kit costs from $8 to $17.

What you can expect: Some people experience a mild burning or rash in the vagina or a watery discharge after using a spermicide. Others complain of the messiness, leakage, smell, and taste. While women may be tempted to douche to feel "clean" after intercourse with a spermicide, this should be avoided, says Dr. Feigin.

Some couples may even find the noise distracting. "You can get a funny sucking sound with the foam when the penis goes in and out, which can be embarrassing and detract from intimacy," Dr. Langley says.

Is it right for you and your mate? If you and your partner are using a diaphragm or cervical cap, you will need to use a spermicide together with that barrier method. You may also choose to use spermicides as extra protection in conjunction with condoms.

Whatever your reason for choosing spermicides, you can make them a fun part of your lovemaking.

"I think there's a lot to be said for sexual lubricants in general," Dr. Forrest shares. "If you think of creams, gels, and foams as being lubricants for sex, you can think of them as something that makes intercourse more slippery."

Try using foam as an erotic part of lovemaking, suggests Dr. Forrest. "Let him use the foam applicator, tease her on the outside of her genitals, and say things like, 'Imagine me squirting you like this' or 'How about we try something bigger?' If you make the contraception playful and an anticipatory form of sex, then it's less burdensome."

Dr. Feigin agrees that spermicides can enhance intercourse. "It can be more pleasurable having a liquid, cream, or jelly to reduce friction. And because some women need more lubrication, spermicides can make lovemaking more enjoyable that way, too."

Tips for first-time users: Be prepared for a little messiness. And reapply for each act of intercourse.

Oral Contraceptives

Birth control pills are one of the most popular, and reliable, methods of contraception used in America. And they offer more health benefits than risks, a fact that surprises many women and men.

There are two basic types of oral contraceptives: the combination pill and the mini-pill.

Combination pills contain synthetic estrogen and progestin, which are hormones similar to those already produced by a woman's ovaries. These pills prevent ovulation from taking place. Combination pills are available as monophasic pills that provide estrogen and progestin at the same doses throughout the pill pack, and as biphasic and triphasic pills that vary the amount of hormones in the pill pack.

Mini-pills contain progestin only. They do not consistently stop ovulation. They do, however, thicken the mucus over the cervix to prevent sperm from entering the uterus for the women who do ovulate. They also stop the uterine lining, or endometrium, from growing, which makes it more difficult for a fertilized egg to implant itself in the uterine wall.

Oral Contraceptives

Effectiveness with typical use: 95%

Protects against STDs: No

Prescription needed: Yes

Cost: Combination pills are $20 to $35 per pack; progestin (or "mini") pills are approximately $25 per pack. A visit with a health care provider is $35 to $150.

How well does it work? The effectiveness of birth control pills is highly dependent on the user. "Women who use oral contraceptives and don't miss pills will very rarely have failures," says Andrew M. Kaunitz, M.D., of the department of obstetrics/gynecology at the University of Florida Health Science Center in Jacksonville, Florida. The most common reasons for failures are forgetting to take a pill or forgetting to start a new cycle of pills on the right day.

The best way to remember to take birth control pills is to keep them in the open so you'll see them. If you are likely to forget a pill, keep the pack in your purse so they're always with you and you can take a pill when you remember. You might also write yourself a note and post it where you'll see it. Keeping an extra pill pack available also makes sense in case you lose one pack.

A man can help his partner remember to take a pill, too. "Whoever is the more regular in his or her habits is a great one to remember things that have to be done daily," says Dr. Forrest. "If it's the guy, he can remind his partner to take the Pill or help her make it part of her daily ritual."

What you can expect: Questions about the Pill's safety (such as its potential link to cancer or increased risk of heart disease) concern some women, but studies confirm that there are more health benefits than risks for most women.

"Oral contraceptives are very safe," Dr. Rosenfield states. "The variety of noncontraceptive health benefits far outweighs the small amount of risk. They protect against endometrial cancer and ovarian cancer, the latter being the most deadly of the gynecological cancers. And cardiovascular risks are minimized with effective screening by physicians before women take them."

In fact, women who take oral contraceptives can reduce their risk of developing endometrial or ovarian cancer for up to two decades after stopping the Pill. And the longer women remain on oral contraceptives, the lower their risk; staying on the Pill for 10 years or more reduces their risk for these cancers by 80 percent, according to Dr. Peterson.

Many women are also concerned about a possible link between oral contraceptives and breast cancer, but research shows that 10 years after discontinuing the Pill, the risk of breast cancer in former users of the Pill is identical to that of women who never used the Pill. This holds for short-term and long-term users and for those with a family history of breast cancer.

"Past use of the Pill will not increase breast cancer risk, regardless of how long you used it, your age at first use, or a family history of breast cancer," Dr. Peterson states.

Also on the positive side, the Pill may:

- Make periods more predictable, lighter, shorter, and occur with fewer cramps
- Be used for years without affecting a woman's fertility; in fact, fertility returns quickly after a woman stops taking the Pill

- Reduce risk of endometriosis and perimenopausal bone loss
- Decrease risk of ovarian cysts (if the higher-dose pills are used)
- Reduce risk of ectopic pregnancy, pelvic inflammatory disease, iron deficiency anemia, fibrocystic breasts, and symptoms of early menopause such as painful, heavy, or irregular periods
- Improve acne
- Increase a couple's frequency of lovemaking, because the risk of pregnancy is greatly reduced

Some women should not use oral contraceptives. These include smokers over the age of 35 and women with a history of blood clots, because using the Pill may increase a woman's risk of heart attack, stroke, or blood clots. Women who just had a baby and are breastfeeding should not use the combination pill because the synthetic hormones may decrease the quality and quantity of breast milk. (The mini-pill, however, may actually increase milk production and is often prescribed for nursing mothers.)

On the negative side, the Pill may also:

- Decrease sex drive
- Increase weight
- Decrease vaginal lubrication
- Cause nausea, breast tenderness, spotting between periods when first taking the Pill, depression, headaches, swelling or pain in the legs, yellowing of the eyes or skin, or excessive hair loss or hair growth

If you experience sudden abdominal, chest, or arm pain, shortness of breath, blurred or double vision, or loss of vision in one eye, contact your doctor immediately.

Is it right for you and your mate? Oral contraceptives are a good option for women who are consistent in their habits and will remember to take pills.

The Pill does not offer protection from sexually transmitted disease. Couples who chose this method are usually in a committed, monogamous relationship and want long-term contraceptive protection.

"With this method, the woman is taking medication that has potential side effects and risks, so it's an important decision about your body and health," Dr. Feigin emphasizes. "If you're in a strong relationship, the man should have concerns about the woman's health. In that case, it's a decision both partners should make together."

"A lot of men are ill-informed about contraceptive methods, and they don't want their women on the Pill," Dr. Forrest adds. "But if a man gets the facts from a health care provider, he can clear up his misconceptions about the Pill and its health effects on women."

Tips for first-time users: Discuss the risks and benefits with your doctor, since oral contraceptives are hormones. And use some kind of reminder to take your pill at the same time every day.

Intrauterine Device (IUD)

A small T-shaped device that is inserted in the uterus, an intrauterine device (IUD) acts as a foreign object in the body, causing an inflammatory response in the uterus and preventing a fertilized egg from implanting. Of the two models available in the United States, the most widely used is the ParaGard (Copper T 380A), which contains a small amount of copper that has a spermicidal effect. The Progestasert model contains the synthetic hormone progesterone. The progesterone thickens cervical mucus, providing a barrier that prevents sperm from entering the uterus. It also affects the lining of the uterus in ways that would prevent implantation if an egg were fertilized, which is very unlikely.

How well does it work? IUDs work about as well as sterilization, says Dr. Rosenfield.

"The current copper IUD is an underused, misunderstood, but outstanding method of birth control," Dr. Rosenfield states. "It has a very low failure rate (less than 1 percent), and it has relatively few side effects. Women who use it express greater satisfaction than with any other reversible method. It doesn't

---

Intrauterine Device (IUD)

Effectiveness with typical use: 98% for progesterone type and 99.2% for Copper T 380A type

Protects against STDs: No

Prescription needed: Yes

Cost: The exam, insertion, and follow-up visit range from $250 to $450 for the progesterone type; the one-time complete cost for a Copper T 380A is $400 and up.

---

require women to do something every day, like the Pill. And it provides protection for up to 10 years." He adds that the rate of women continuing to use the IUD is higher than the rates of other reversible methods.

That said, many women—and even many gynecologists—are reluctant to consider the IUD based on bad publicity surrounding the Dalkon Shield, which was taken off the market in 1975. The Shield was implicated in 20 deaths and many cases of pelvic inflammatory disease (PID). According to experts, however, today's IUDs are a safe and effective option for couples looking for long-term contraception. The problem with the Dalkon Shield, say researchers, was the braided cord—it acted as a conduit for bacteria. New IUDs have a nonbraided cord.

"I know of no deaths from IUD use," Dr. Rosenfield states. "And women should understand that the IUD does not markedly increase risk of infection or infertility." The risk of infection with the ParaGard (Copper T 380A) is low—less than 1 per 1,000 among women at low risk for STDs.

What you can expect: Possible side effects include longer periods, spotting, and cramping, though these symptoms usually lessen over time. The Progestasert version minimizes cramping and bleeding, but it must be replaced annually, while the ParaGard can be left in place for up to 10 years.

On a rare occasion, an IUD may be expelled during the first few months of use, especially from contractions during a woman's period. If this happens, you need to visit your doctor and have the device reinserted.

Is it right for you and your mate? A woman who has gone through childbirth is a good candidate for an IUD, because her uterus has expanded and it is less likely to expel the device. As women get older, however, they are more likely to have uterine abnormalities such as fibroids (benign muscle growths), which may limit their ability to use an IUD.

The IUD is also a good method for a woman who has just had a baby and doesn't want hormones to interfere with breast milk production, and for a woman who doesn't want to change her natural hormonal balance or fertility.

A couple in a long-term, monogamous relationship should consider an IUD if they want spontaneous lovemaking but still want to feel comfortable that their birth control is covered.

"People considering an IUD are not ready for permanent contraception, but they are usually sexually active and don't want to use oral contraceptives or a barrier method," Dr. Feigin says. "It gives a couple a sense of comfort that it's an effective method and they don't need to plan in advance to use it."

"The best candidates are women who are at low risk of contracting sexually transmitted diseases and those who have had children but don't want an irreversible method. They still want to be fertile, but they don't want more children," Dr. Kaunitz says.

Tips for first-time users: Find a doctor who is trained and experienced in inserting IUDs. To make sure the IUD hasn't become dislodged or expelled, a woman is encouraged to feel for the IUD's string (which hangs in the vagina) every month after her period. If you don't feel the string, try bathing. "This sometimes brings the string back," says Dr. Feigin. If that doesn't work, see your doctor.

Emergency Contraception

When your regular method of contraception fails, or if you have spontaneous intercourse at any time without protection, you may be able to avoid pregnancy if you act quickly. Several forms of emergency contraception are available, though many couples are not aware of them. The two main methods are emergency doses of either combined oral contraceptives (progestin and estrogen pills) or the progestin-only mini-pill. The ParaGard (Copper T 380A) intrauterine device (IUD) can also be effective. These methods prevent pregnancy by interfering with fertilization or implantation. So even though sperm have entered the system and encountered an egg, the system will not sustain their growth.

Treatment with combined oral contraceptive pills must be started within 72 hours of unprotected intercourse. The dosage is either two or four pills (depending on the dosage of the pill) immediately and then again 12 hours later. Progestin-only mini-pills must be taken within 48 hours of unprotected intercourse to be effective. The IUD must be inserted within seven days after unprotected intercourse, says Dr. Rosenfield.

> **Emergency Contraception**
>
> **Effectiveness with typical use:** 75%
>
> **Protects against STDs:** No
>
> **Prescription needed:** Yes
>
> **Cost:** An emergency contraception pill pack is $8 to $25; one pack of combination pills is $20 to $35; one pack of progestin-only pills is approximately $25. A visit with a health care provider is $35 to $150; a pregnancy test is about $10 or more; the ParaGard (Copper T 380A) IUD costs about $400 for the exam, IUD, and insertion.

How well does it work? "Emergency contraception is a very important new advent in birth control," says Dr. Rosenfield. "Women who had unexpected mid-cycle intercourse can decrease their chances of becoming pregnant by about 75 percent by taking these oral contraceptives."

What you can expect: Possible side effects from the oral contraceptives can include nausea, headaches, breast tenderness, light vaginal bleeding, or spotting. Antinausea medication may help in some cases.

The IUD may increase a woman's risk of developing pelvic inflammatory disease, while the hormones in the oral contraceptives may affect a fetus if a woman is already pregnant from previous intercourse.

Is it right for you and your mate? While not a method couples should plan on, emergency contraception is something they should know exists.

"I think most men don't even know it's available and wouldn't understand how it works, so the decision to use this method rests with women," Dr. Feigin says. "But if, for example, a condom broke, it may provide an opportunity to talk about how the couple can be more careful in the future."

Tip for first-time users: If you need emergency contraception, quickly call your doctor for an immediate appointment.

Tubal Ligation

With tubal ligation, a woman's fallopian tubes (located between the ovaries and the uterus) are either looped and banded closed with rubber rings, pinched closed with a metal clip, cauterized (burned) with an electric current and cut, or cut and tied off with stitches. This prevents the sperm and egg from ever meeting. Techniques used include laparoscopy (where a small incision is made in a woman's abdomen), laparotomy (a larger incision), mini-laparotomy, and culdoscopy or colpotomy (where the incision is made in the vagina). Scarring is minimal or invisible.

If the couple decides on the surgery ahead of time, tubal ligation can be done immediately after childbirth, when the uterus and fallopian tubes are still high in the abdomen and easy to reach. It can also be done by an obstetrician gynecologist or general surgeon during a 10- to 45-minute procedure under general or local anesthesia, usually in a hospital.

How well does it work? Cutting off the opportunity for an egg and sperm to unite makes tubal ligation a highly effective method, Dr. Peterson says.

What you can expect: Aside from lowering pregnancy risk to almost zero, tubal ligation may also reduce the risk of developing ovarian cancer.

Some women experience some discomfort for several days following the procedure.

While the chance of an egg or sperm sneaking through the barricade is remote, the chance of ectopic pregnancy (in the fallopian tubes) is increased, and it can happen even 10 years later.

Is it right for you and your mate? Tubal ligation is a form of permanent contraception that should be seriously considered before being chosen. Although the procedure may be reversible, reversal surgery is complicated and expensive, and it's often unsuccessful.

If you're sure you do not want to become pregnant, however, tubal ligation is a convenient and lifelong method that involves only a one-time inconvenience.

> **Tubal Ligation**
>
> **Effectiveness with typical use:** 99.5%
>
> **Protects against STDs:** No
>
> **Prescription needed:** No, but it's a surgical procedure.
>
> **Cost:** $1,000 to $2,500 for the most common procedures

"The younger people are when they have it done, the more likely they are to regret it," Dr. Rosenfield explains. "If people are under the age of 35, they should very seriously consider other birth control methods that are just as good as sterilization."

If you're over 35 and already have a family, sterilization might be the right method for you. "There comes a point with couples, especially married couples, when they are comfortable with their current family size and are ready for a permanent contraception method," Dr. Feigin says. "It's a wonderful enhancement to a relationship not to worry about unwanted pregnancy." And without having to worry about birth control, you can be more spontaneous in your lovemaking.

But don't choose tubal ligation because you think it's the only method available to you. "I often notice women choosing sterilization thinking it's appropriate for them or their partners not because they don't necessarily want more children but because they think it's the only highly reliable method of birth control," Dr. Kaunitz says. "That's not true. If they use hormonal or intrauterine methods appropriately, they can achieve rates of effectiveness that are equal to sterilization."

Vasectomy

You might say that vasectomy is the male counterpart to tubal ligation—only simpler and more convenient. The surgery takes up to 20 minutes, and it's performed in a doctor's office using local anesthesia. Part of the vas deferens—the ductwork from the testicles to the urethra, through which sperm travel—is removed, then tied off. This prevents sperm from passing through. A man is still able to get and maintain an erection, and he is still able to ejaculate. His sex drive and hormone levels are unchanged.

How to Coax Your Husband into Considering a Vasectomy

You may think a vasectomy pales compared to childbirth or a tubal ligation, but to a man, it's a major event.

While women are accustomed to doctors probing the depths of their reproductive systems, men fear any procedure conducted "down there," especially surgery. Particularly surgery performed while they're awake.

So before you broach the subject, consider his emotions. "A man's fear is that he's losing his potency when he loses his ability to procreate," says Marc Goldstein, M.D., professor of urology and director of the Center for Male Reproductive Medicine and Microsurgery at New York Hospital-Cornell Medical Center.

Pick the right time to discuss the subject, which may be when you're pregnant. "If couples decide that this will be their last child, they often talk about whether or not the wife should have a tubal ligation at the time of delivery," says Charles S. Carignan, M.D., president of Stanwood Associates, a reproductive health consulting firm in Baltimore. So it's only natural to bring up the subject of vasectomy at this time, as an alternative. You might suggest that your man have a vasectomy soon after the baby comes "because there isn't much sexual contact in the first few weeks after delivery," says Paul D. Blumenthal, M.D., medical director of Planned Parenthood of Maryland and an obstetrician gynecologist in Baltimore.

It may take less persuading than you think. "Many men are present in the delivery room and see the pain their wives go through, so when it comes time to think about permanent contraception, they see a vasectomy as their obligation," Dr. Carignan explains.

Understand that he has to make the decision. "A mistake women make is to say, 'I don't want any more children, and I want you to have a vasec-

How well does it work? Vasectomy is even more foolproof than tubal ligation.

What you can expect: Except for a small—less than 2 percent—risk of infection, vasectomy is safe and uncomplicated, say doctors. Some men may

tomy.' Then it becomes an order," says Dr. Carignan. If he feels coerced, he may regret it later.

You can also offer him the following facts and reassurances.

- Modern no-scalpel vasectomy can be performed in as little as five minutes in a simple office procedure, with minimal pain and without a scalpel or stitches.

- He can still get an erection and ejaculate.

- His semen will not look, smell, or taste noticeably different.

- Vasectomy is generally less expensive than a sterilization procedure for women.

- With pregnancy no longer a risk, you could have more spontaneous sex.

If your man still isn't convinced, offer to make an appointment for him with his doctor. "In some relationships, a man may find it hard to accept getting important information from a woman," Dr. Blumenthal says.

Other guys can help, too. "If one of his friends had a vasectomy and says that his sex life hasn't suffered (or that it has improved), a man is more likely to have one," says Dr. Carignan.

Finally, don't give up. Couples usually take 1½ to 2 years to decide about vasectomy.

"With any idea that's threatening, you need to approach it gently and give it time," says Shirley Glass, Ph.D., a psychologist in Owings Mills, Maryland. "Maybe wait six months and then discuss it again.

"In the meantime, use condoms," Dr. Glass adds. "That might be more persuasive than anything a woman could say."

experience minor swelling or pain in the scrotum for one to two weeks, but a few days of rest, ice packs, and nonprescription pain relievers makes them comfortable.

"The most significant advance over the traditional vasectomy is the no-scalpel vasectomy, or NSV," says Dr. Feigin. As the name implies, there's no scalpel involved in the procedure, which can be done in 5 to 10 minutes in a doctor's office. "The risk of complications, such as bleeding and infection, is reduced 10 times, and so they are rare. Furthermore, there is little or no pain during or after the procedure." Even for the traditional vasectomy, there are no serious complications, Dr. Feigin emphasizes. "No one has ever died from having a vasectomy." And despite what you may have heard, men who have a vasectomy are not at increased risk for developing cardiovascular disease or prostate cancer.

> **Vasectomy**
>
> **Effectiveness with typical use:** 99.85%
>
> **Protects against STDs:** No
>
> **Prescription needed:** No, but it's a surgical procedure.
>
> **Cost:** $240 to $1,000

Is it right for you and your mate? Some men are reluctant to give up what they consider to be a sign of their "manhood"—their fertility, especially since they are theoretically able to father children throughout their adulthood.

Men in secure, long-term relationships often welcome the opportunity to play an important role in the couple's family-planning efforts. "It's very important in terms of demonstration from the man about the love he has and is willing to express for his partner," Dr. Feigin says. "It's usually with a sense of love and pride that a man feels he can now take on some responsibility for ongoing contraception." Adds Dr. Peterson, "It is safer and more effective than tubal ligation."

While the effects of a vasectomy may be reversible, that type of corrective surgery is complicated, expensive, and not always successful. So as with tubal ligation, neither you nor your husband should approach vasectomy as something that can be undone later.

Norplant

Looking for a long-term, reversible method of contraception that does not involve taking daily pills, applying a barrier, or interrupting sex in any way? Consider Norplant. A set of six matchstick-size capsules that contain the hormone progestin (the same hormone found in oral contraceptives) is inserted just below the skin inside a woman's upper arm. They are visible but not unsightly, and one visit to the doctor is all it takes to arrange for years of protection.

Twenty-four hours after insertion, the capsules begin to slowly release the hormones. For up to five years, the hormones block ovulation and thicken the mucus that covers the cervix, which helps prevent sperm from entering the uterus.

How well does it work? When it comes to preventing pregnancy, Norplant is similar to both tubal ligation and vasectomy, making it just about the most effective birth control method going. All you have to do is remember to have the capsules reinserted every five years or so.

"It's a long-acting method that is highly effective and does not rely on user compliance very much," Dr. Peterson says.

What you can expect: Norplant requires a minor surgical procedure to insert the implants. Women should expect tenderness and bruising at the insertion site for

> **Norplant**
>
> **Effectiveness with typical use:** 99.95%
> **Protects against STDs:** No
> **Prescription needed:** Yes
> **Cost:** $500 to $600 for the exam, implants, and insertion; an additional $100 to $200 to remove Norplant

a few days. But there are other possible side effects—common enough to prompt women to have the capsules removed.

A fair number of women stop using Norplant because of side effects like irregular bleeding, missed periods, spotting, and weight gain. "They're major disadvantages, and ones that are so common they ought to be understood up front as side effects," Dr. Peterson emphasizes.

Once Norplant is removed, women can become fertile again within three weeks. This is an advantage for couples planning to have children sometime in the future, but not immediately.

Is it right for you and your mate? Your age and family-planning needs will affect your decision to use this method. "Norplant is a really nice option for somebody who doesn't want to get pregnant now but doesn't want to preclude it as a long-term option," Dr. Forrest says. "It's great for teenagers or older women who've had their kids but don't want to give up the option of having more."

Tips for first-time users: Be prepared to deal with irregular bleeding and spotting, particularly during the first year. Men who do not like to have intercourse while there's any bleeding can use a condom at these times, Dr. Forrest suggests.

Depo-Provera

Given by injection, Depo-Provera is a shot of medroxyprogesteroneacetate, and it contains progestin, a synthetic form of the female hormone progesterone. The injection prevents pregnancy by preventing ovulation. The shot is administered by a doctor or nurse to a woman's shoulder or hip every 90 days and provides contraceptive protection within 24 hours.

How well does it work? "Women who use injectable methods of birth control like Depo-Provera and don't miss a shot very rarely have failures," Dr. Kaunitz states.

"You have to pay attention when it comes to the end of the three-month cycle and you need another shot," Dr. Forrest emphasizes.

Depo-Provera

Effectiveness with typical use: 99.7%

Protects against STDs: No

Prescription needed: Yes

Cost: Anywhere from $35 to $125 for the exam; further visits cost from about $20 to $40. Each shot is approximately $30 to $75.

What you can expect: "The most significant side effect is that women may have irregular bleeding or spotting at first, but then have no bleeding at all after long-term use," Dr. Kaunitz says. Eighty percent of women who use Depo-Provera for at least five years cease having their periods. "Many women are happy not to have to deal with their periods," he says. An additional side effect, however, is that long-term users of Depo-Provera may experience thinning of the bones.

Is it right for you and your mate? Long-term birth control with minimal inconvenience makes Depo-Provera an ideal choice for many women, especially those who are likely to forget to take a pill every day. If needles make you queasy, however, it may not be right for you.

If a woman decides to discontinue injections, it takes up to 18 months for her fertility to return. Because Depo-Provera has long-range effects on fertility, it's best used by couples who want ongoing contraceptive protection. "It's not suitable for couples who might want to get pregnant soon," Dr. Kaunitz says.

Tips for first-time users: "To keep track of the date when you need subsequent injections, write it in your pocket calendar," says Dr. Forrest. "Men can also make a note in their calendars and remind their partners to get a shot."

Natural Birth Control

Couples who don't want to rely on barriers, surgery, or hormonal methods of contraception but still want to have sex have five choices: Using the calendar (often called the rhythm method), basal body temperature, cervical mucus, the postovulation method, or withdrawal. The first four track a woman's monthly cycle to predict ovulation; couples then have intercourse only when conception is unlikely. The other involves withdrawing the penis before ejaculation. (Total abstinence is 100 percent effective, but not a desirable option for most married couples.)

The calendar method designates the first day of a woman's period as Day One, and considers the four days on either side of Day 14 as the fertile period. Intercourse is avoided for Days 10 through 18. Because the number of days between periods can vary, women should track their periods for several months and use an alternative birth control method before relying on the calendar method.

For the temperature method, women record their body temperatures (orally, rectally, or vaginally) daily on a chart. They usually take their temperatures using special oral thermometers before they get out of bed, and always at the same time of day. For most women, 96° to 98°F taken orally is considered normal before ovulation. The temperature rise that signals that an egg has been released is about $\frac{5}{10}$ of one degree. The rise may be sudden or a gradual climb over several days. This temperature shift cannot predict when the release will occur. The fertile period is the first three full days or so after temperature is elevated.

For the third method, the couple determines ovulation by changes in a woman's cervical mucus, which can be checked visually on the woman's underwear or on a pantiliner (provided she secretes enough that it shows up externally). The mucus is usually cloudy and sticky. Seven to eight days before ovulation, it becomes clear and slippery, appearing almost like a stretchy raw egg white at ovulation. To avoid conception, couples abstain from intercourse while the mucus is clear and slippery. The mucus disappears or becomes cloudy and sticky again after ovulation.

The postovulation method involves abstaining from intercourse from the first day of a woman's period through the morning of the fourth day after ovulation should have occurred—Days 1 through 18.

How well does it work? With natural birth control, there's a wide, wide range of effectiveness between "perfect use" and "typical use." In reality, the pregnancy rate runs as high as 25 percent—pretty high if you're trying to avoid conception.

> **Natural Birth Control**
>
> **Effectiveness with typical use:** 80% for all, except withdrawal (82%)
>
> **Protects against STDs:** No
>
> **Prescription needed:** No
>
> **Cost:** None

"The way most people use the rhythm method is not terribly effective," Dr. Forrest says. "If you do it conscientiously and the woman's cycle is consistent, then it can be okay. But you have to have biology on your side." For example, the calendar method may not work well for women who are in their midforties or older because they are more likely to have irregular menstrual cycles.

A woman's body temperature can be affected by fever, stress, and other disruptions, making temperature readings inaccurate. And the cervical mucus method can be difficult because some women don't secrete enough mucus to evaluate it.

"I don't recommend the rhythm method or temperature and mucus methods. There are too many variables with ovulation," Dr. Langley says. "They're like a shot in the dark."

Withdrawal relies on a man's self-control and the couple's trust with one another. "Withdrawal has gotten a bad rap," Dr. Forrest says. "There are rumors of millions of sperm in pre-ejaculate. But if the man has urinated since his last ejaculation, there are no live sperm there. So, with experience, withdrawal is at least as effective as the diaphragm, and it's free. But guys have to pay attention to their feelings of when they're going to ejaculate, and they must pull out before that happens."

What you can expect: Birth control that depends on the couple abstaining from intercourse for several days each month can be difficult—something you should know up front.

But natural methods can enhance intimacy. "If you're in an established relationship and want to try something different, this is a good way of sharing the responsibility for birth control," Dr. Forrest says. She adds that men can participate in the birth control process by taking the woman's temperature and helping keep track of dates for the different methods on a chart or calendar.

Is it right for you and your mate? Couples usually choose natural birth control methods for religious reasons, or because the woman cannot take or is not comfortable with taking hormones. With a pregnancy rate of up to 25 percent, however, these methods leave the largest room for error.

"Unless a pregnancy outcome would not be a problem, I don't recommend the rhythm method. It's a potential disaster waiting to happen," says Dr. Feigin. "If you heighten your enjoyment of life by walking to the brink, this is the way to do it."

Some couples do, however, have good reasons for considering natural birth control, acknowledges Dr. Feigin. "It allows the woman and her partner to be much more in tune with her reproductive cycling and fertility, and that can be enhancing and exciting to a relationship because you can use the method to plan or prevent pregnancy," he points out.

It's important to work as a team when using natural birth control, stresses Dr. Rosenfield. "These methods are for those couples who are highly motivated and willing to follow the guidelines, abstaining when they have to abstain. They are also for couples who won't use anything else."

Tips for first-time users: Whichever natural method a couple chooses, they may want to consider some alternatives for certain times of the month. "Couples can lower the risk of pregnancy by using a barrier method in conjunction with natural birth control during ovulation," Dr. Feigin says.

Hysterectomy

ॐ

Simply put, hysterectomy is the surgical removal of the uterus. Sometimes the ovaries and fallopian tubes will be removed at the same time. It's the second most commonly performed operation on women in this country. (Cesarean sections are the first.)

But as common as hysterectomy is, the decision-making process (and criteria for surgery) is different for every woman. Some choose to have the procedure, some feel they have no choice. Emotions range from relief to regret.

Hysterectomy affects our sexuality, too. Sometimes, sex gets better than it was before. Sometimes, it's trickier to get the libido revving again. But in the midst of all these changes, one thing stays constant: Having a hysterectomy is not the end of your femininity—or your sexuality.

How Hysterectomy Affects Sex

Most women undergo hysterectomies to end severe pain or uterine bleeding caused by fibroid tumors (noncancerous but abnormal growths) or endometriosis (where tissue similar to the lining of the uterus is located outside the uterus). Just 10 percent of hysterectomies are performed because of cancer.

There are two main types of hysterectomy. In what's often called a partial hysterectomy, the uterus is removed, but the ovaries, fallopian tubes, and the cervix (the opening of the uterus) are left intact. In the second type of hysterectomy, a complete hysterectomy, the uterus, cervix, fallopian tubes, and ovaries are removed. This procedure is typically reserved for cancer of the uterus, vagina, fallopian tubes, or ovaries, or it may be performed after menopause with the hope of reducing the risk of ovarian cancer.

A hysterectomy where the ovaries are preserved has little or no effect on most women's desire for sex, says Donald Swartz, M.D., chief of the section of complex pelvic surgery and urogynecology at Albany Medical College in New York. In fact, it can bring welcome relief from pain and bleeding, making sex far more enjoyable and spontaneous. "In most cases, a woman who has had a partial hysterectomy can resume making love in four to six weeks, depending on the type of procedure performed," he says. "If the cervix has been removed, vaginal intercourse should be postponed for six weeks to allow for complete vaginal healing."

For some women, a partial hysterectomy can result in less intense orgasms, says Linda Kames, Psy.D., a certified sex therapist at Tufts University Medical School in Boston. Some women's uteruses contract when they climax, she explains. So removing the uterus removes this pleasurable sensation, even if you still have your ovaries.

Of the two, a complete hysterectomy is most likely to cause loss of sexual desire, says Dr. Swartz. Without her ovaries to produce testosterone and estrogen, the sex hormones that fuel sexual desire, a woman is thrown into instant menopause and her libido may diminish. And as with a partial hysterectomy, without her uterus, she misses out on uterine contractions sometimes associated with orgasm.

If Desire Fades

"There's no doubt about it—a woman's loss of sexual desire following a complete hysterectomy can affect her relationship with her husband," says Dr. Kames. "She may feel that she's less feminine, or that it's no longer appropriate to be sexual. Or she may feel guilty, ashamed, or angry that her sexual feelings seem to have evaporated."

What about her partner? Making love is the way many men express emotional closeness, says Dr. Kames. "So when you reject his sexual overtures, he may think you're rejecting him," she says. And even if he understands that your lack of desire has a physical cause, repeated refusals can hurt.

Dubious Rite of Passage

One woman out of three in the United States has had a hysterectomy by the time she's 60. Most women who undergo hysterectomies are between 35 and 45.

As difficult as it may be, "try to maintain some level of sexual contact with your partner," advises Dr. Kames. "You don't necessarily have to have intercourse." Engage in mutual masturbation or oral sex. You might also watch erotic videos together, hold or caress him while he masturbates, or stimulate him manually. Or give each other full-body massages with the works—scented oil, candlelight, and champagne (if you drink). "These are all ways to get comfortable with the idea of making love again," she says.

Frequently, the solution to a lack of sexual desire is hormone-replacement therapy (HRT), a combination of the female hormones estrogen and progesterone that makes up for the hormones produced by your ovaries before they were removed. Make sure your doctor explains the pros and cons of HRT before you choose to undergo or reject it, says Dr. Swartz.

Ask about androgen-replacement therapy, too, Dr. Swartz advises. Besides estrogen and progesterone, the ovaries produce androgens, or male hormones. Women whose ovaries have been removed are low on androgens as well as estrogen.

The primary androgen, testosterone, fuels libido in both men and women. Some research suggests that women with low testosterone levels have a lower sex drive, and that supplementary testosterone can help restore it.

Mastectomy

In 1989, seven months after marrying her second husband, Andrea Martin learned she had breast cancer. The tumor was larger than a golf ball. Martin, then 42, underwent a mastectomy.

In 1991, breast cancer struck again. She underwent a second mastectomy—and returned to work two weeks later.

Martin, an attorney and restaurateur at the time of her first diagnosis, founded and is now executive director of the Breast Cancer Fund in San Francisco. She speaks to breast cancer support groups across the country. Her husband, Richard, comes with her.

Her double mastectomy didn't end her marriage. Quite the opposite. "I've found a level of intimacy with my husband that I never dreamed possible," she says.

The sex is pretty great, too. "Before I got cancer, nothing in my experience led me to believe that this time of my life would be my most lusty, my most juicy, my most satisfying," she says. "I've learned things about my body and about my ability to have orgasms. And I learned them because I was thrown into menopause at age 42 because of the chemotherapy."

A Matter of Body and Soul

Each year, approximately 178,700 women are diagnosed with breast cancer and begin their own journey of healing. And approximately 76,000 get a total mastectomy—the surgical removal of the entire breast.

There are several variations to the total mastectomy. In a partial mastectomy, the lump and a small section of the surrounding breast are removed. In a modified radical mastectomy, the breast, a small portion of chest muscle, and the surrounding lymph nodes are removed. A lumpectomy is the removal of just the lump, which spares the breast but can leave a scar. Research shows that for early-stage cancers, lumpectomy—followed by radiation treatment— has a survival rate equal to that of total mastectomy.

Whatever the procedure, a mastectomy or lumpectomy turns a woman's world upside down, forcing her to see her body, her relationship with her partner, and her sexuality in new, and sometimes terrifying, ways. She must grieve the loss of one or both breasts and come to terms with an imperfect body. She must struggle to share her painful and frightening feelings with her partner and listen to his. And, often, she must fight to feel like the sexual woman she was before her surgery.

In the process, however, a woman and her partner can tap into strength, courage, and resiliency they didn't know they had, survivors say. Discovering these qualities in yourselves, they say, can heighten your capacity for intimacy as a couple. "I'm here to tell you that if Richard and I made it, anyone can," says Martin.

Every woman who loses a breast to cancer finds her own way back, in her own time, says Ronnie Kaye, a licensed marriage and family therapist in Marina Del Rey, California, and author of *Spinning Straw into Gold: Your Emo-*

Secrets of Long-Lasting Love

New Intimacy after Breast Surgery

In 1993, a routine mammogram revealed that Myrna Riesz, a sales manager in San Francisco, had a lump in her breast. It was cancer. The tumor was stage 2A, which has a five-year survival rate of 80 percent.

Two days after diagnosis, the then 46-year-old underwent a lumpectomy, a procedure that removes the tumor but leaves the breast intact. Her husband of 20 years, Darrell, was by her side when her surgeon removed the bandages.

I couldn't look. I looked in Darrell's eyes because I knew they would tell me everything I needed to know.

What he saw was a four-inch-long incision—a pretty invasive one. But his eyes never wavered. He told me that I was beautiful, and that I was still me.

The scar is pink now rather than an angry red. But it's a constant reminder of what my husband and I have learned about ourselves—and our marriage—on my trip through the vortex, as I call my experience with cancer.

We learned that it's possible for intimacy to deepen. When cancer hits

tional Recovery from Breast Cancer. Still, unresolved issues around body image, intimacy, and sexuality can stall recovery, making it more painful than it has to be, she says.

What follows is a discussion of the issues most women who face breast cancer and mastectomy must wrestle with, whether their surgery was days, months, or years ago.

Growing beyond Fear

What women with breast cancer fear most isn't losing a breast. It's dying.

"During my radiation treatment, I bought a beautiful navy blue linen dress," says Myrna Riesz, who underwent a lumpectomy in 1993. "After a while, I returned it because I didn't think I would live to wear it."

you, either your relationship shatters or it becomes stronger. Ours got stronger. We're gentler with each other. We're more honest. Our relationship is more playful.

We also learned that sex would be good again. Eventually. We didn't make love for nine months after my surgery.

For women, sex starts in the brain. And when your brain is cluttered with life-threatening issues, it's hard to turn on sexually. But Darrell was patient. The message was that he loved me and that he could wait until I was ready. When it was right, it was right.

We learned that intercourse isn't the only way to express physical love. There were days when I didn't want to get out of bed. I'd put my head on his shoulder, and he'd read to me. We caressed one another, we held one another. It was the only time I felt safe.

Most important, we learned not to sweat the small stuff, which I think is a tendency that can hamper a couple's ability to draw closer. We both realized the fragility of life and how important we are to each other. I appreciate Darrell and the other people I love more than anything in this world.

Men, too, fear losing the women they love to cancer. A man may not be able to touch or look at his partner's scarred chest because it's a reminder of her mortality, says Judi Johnson, Ph.D., a health educator in Minneapolis and founder of I Can Cope, the American Cancer Society's education program for people with all types of cancer.

Men may also fear saying or doing the wrong thing. Here's what might run through a man's mind after his wife's mastectomy, says Kaye: "I don't know where to touch her anymore. If I touch her scar, it might hurt her physically or remind her of her cancer. So maybe I'd better not. But if I don't look at it or touch it, she'll think I'm uncomfortable, and I need to make her feel that I am comfortable—even though I'm not."

When a couple avoids talking about the fears and changes cancer and mastectomy bring into their lives, they miss an opportunity to connect in a deeper way and to comfort each other, says Kaye. "A woman with breast cancer needs her partner's love, support, and strength more than ever," she says. "People gather strength and courage from facing their worst fears—and facing them means talking about them."

What if you and your husband aren't entirely comfortable discussing your deepest feelings? If you want to give each other strength and comfort, says Kaye, you must find a way—together.

"At some point, you need to say, 'If I'm handling my cancer the way I've handled everything else in my marriage, and it's not working, am I willing to learn a new way?'" says Kaye. "In the midst of this challenge, there's an opportunity for growth."

That doesn't mean that your husband is able to see this same opportunity, Kaye adds. "But you can hope that he's willing to try. In a good marriage, you can find that willingness."

As much as you need your husband, however, you also need the emotional support of women who have shared your experience.

"I highly recommend finding a breast cancer support group and attending on a regular basis," says Martin. This "home group" can listen as you explore your changing feelings about your body and relationships, and it can serve as your anchor when the going gets tough, she says.

If you're not a "group" type, consider individual counseling with a therapist who specializes in counseling women with breast cancer, suggests Martin. "They're out there."

Loving Your Body Again

When a woman loses a breast or breasts to cancer, her image of her body is often shattered. She may feel mutilated, even unacceptable. She may refuse to undress in front of her husband, or take pains to be covered at all times.

"It can be hard to love yourself when you look in the mirror," says Dr. Johnson. "I remember a woman in one of my groups who couldn't believe that her husband still loved her. She first had to learn to love herself again."

Your husband may mourn the loss of a breast or breasts as much as you do, says Kaye. "In a good relationship, a woman's breasts may be considered community property. So when a part of that community property disappears, the loss is experienced by two people."

Allow the man in your life to mourn, Kaye says. "And don't see his grief as proof that you're no longer desirable." In fact, it's only in giving yourselves time to mourn that the two of you can eventually come to accept this loss, she explains.

Reconstructive surgery can be done immediately after a mastectomy, or soon after. Women who undergo breast reconstruction and are pleased with the results say that it helps improve their body image and emotional well-being as well as their feelings about their femininity and desirability.

Reclaiming Your Sexuality

Making love is often a familiar and comforting part of a long-time relationship. But mastectomy and treatment for breast cancer can severely strain this aspect of intimacy, says Dr. Johnson. "Most of us feel that our breasts are an important aspect of our femininity, and to lose one—or both—can make us wonder whether we'll ever feel sexual again," she says.

"Along with accepting their 'new' bodies, many women must undergo additional procedures such as radiation, chemotherapy, or drug treatment," says Adelaide Nardone, M.D., an obstetrician and gynecologist at the Women's Medical Associates of Westchester in Mount Kisco, New York. The side effects of these procedures—nausea, fatigue, hair loss, and hormonal changes, among others—can negate a woman's desire for sex, she says.

For example, chemotherapy shuts down the ovaries of 40 percent of women under the age of 40 and 90 percent of women over 40. The drugs destroy the ovaries, so they can no longer produce the female sex hormones estrogen and progesterone, explains Dr. Nardone. For women who have not yet reached menopause, this will trigger premature menopause. Side effects may include hot flashes and vaginal dryness (which can make sex painful and dampen sexual desire).

This is what happened to Martin. "It was a rude process," she says. "I say that I underwent a libido-otomy. I had absolutely no desire for sex."

And yet, "even during that terrible year, Richard and I made love," she continues. Her husband's gentle encouragement helped. While he never forced the issue, "he wouldn't let me totally disconnect from sex, either," she says. "I'm so grateful because as I know now, a woman's sexuality, sensuality, and intimacy with her mate are vital to life and need not wane after menopause or breast cancer."

It took work, says Martin, "but my interest in sex gradually returned. It helped that I had already forgiven my body for betraying me. I understood that hating my body was not in my best interest."

For Riesz and her husband, it was "talk therapy" that helped them find their way back to physical intimacy. "We talked a lot about sex," she says. "I understood why he was missing it. First, because it was always wonderful with us. Second, because making love would have reassured him that I was okay and that we were going to be okay."

For her part, "I was able to say, 'I want this part of my life back, but I'm not ready. It frightens me.' My husband knew that I was very fearful and so unsure about the future."

How long does it take to get comfortable with sex again? Every woman is different, says Dr. Johnson. But she encourages women who have undergone a mastectomy and their partners to explore different ways of expressing intimacy that don't include intercourse, such as touching, kissing, and massage. "You can also take off the pressure of intercourse by contracting with your partner for a specific period of abstinence," she says. "Then use this time to discover who you are—a person to love and be loved."

The following statements might help you express to your partner how you might be feeling about sex, says Dr. Johnson.

"My body has changed so much that I don't feel very lovable. But that doesn't mean I don't need and want your love."

"I need to be caressed and held, but I don't think I'm ready to make love tonight."

"My sexual appetite just isn't as strong anymore. But I need your closeness and support more than ever before."

Moving Forward — Together

It can't be stressed enough: The most important thing you and your partner can do, both before and after mastectomy, is talk, says Kaye. The tips below can help keep the dialogue flowing.

Find mentors and role models. Actively seek out other women who have had mastectomies, says Kaye. You can find them at breast cancer support groups or through your surgeon.

"Some doctors keep lists of women who are willing to talk to other women about their experiences and display their scars," Kaye adds. That's right: They'll show you what a real, healed mastectomy looks like. Ask your doctor if you can see a real mastectomy rather than viewing before-and-after photographs. "To my mind, seeing the real thing is better than looking at photographs, which are often taken immediately after surgery and can be frightening and impersonal," she says.

Don't hide. Right from the start, allow your partner to look at the scar—preferably, at the same time you do, says Dr. Johnson. "The longer you wait, the harder it is."

Depressurize the bedroom. Designate a room other than your bedroom as a place you can both look at and touch the scar and talk about how you're feeling, suggests Kaye. Having these talk-touch sessions outside of the bedroom allows you to adapt to the changes in your body without raising the possibility of sex, which can reassure both of you.

Explore your skin. If your breasts have been an important part of your pre-mastectomy lovemaking, try sensate focus, suggests Kaye. In this technique, partners take turns touching each other's entire bodies except for the breasts and genitals. This "no-touch" rule releases both of you from the pressure to have sex, she explains.

The rules are simple: As your husband touches you, focus on what you're feeling. Close your eyes. Have him use his fingertips to trace the softness of your skin, the curve from your back to your hip, the sensitive area behind your knees. Your husband should also focus on the sensations he's receiving—the feel of his palm on your belly, or the softness and fullness of your lips as he touches them with his index finger. "Sensate focus is a valuable technique, especially for women who are struggling with a negative body image," says Kaye. "It teaches you that your entire body—not just your breasts—experiences sexual pleasure."

Never go it alone. Every woman who undergoes a mastectomy makes an emotional recovery in her own time, says Kaye. "Six months is very fast; two years is on the slower side," she says. But no matter how long it has been, if you're struggling to cope, seek counseling. It's especially crucial to reach out if you're feeling stuck and unable to move forward, she says.

Menopause

Way back in the 1960s, one leading hormone researcher pronounced a woman in menopause "the equivalent of a eunuch." No wonder a generation of women—and their daughters—thinks of menopause as the formal end of lusty, juicy, rewarding sex.

Nothing could be farther from the truth. "Most menopausal women enjoy their sexuality and adjust quite well to the biological changes associated with menopause," says Carol Landau, Ph.D., clinical professor of psychiatry and human behavior at Brown University School of Medicine in Providence, Rhode Island, and coauthor of *The Complete Book of Menopause*. Hard evidence backs up her claim. One large survey found that 95 percent of married women in their fifties, most of them postmenopausal, were still making love.

Apparently, they've never heard the phrase "finished at 50."

Of Hot Flashes and Hormones

Think of menopause as a change in the hormonal climate of your reproductive organs, which now produce less of your female hormones, estrogen and progesterone, and the "male" hormone testosterone. Strictly speaking, you have officially reached menopause when you've gone 12 consecutive months without a menstrual period, either because your ovaries have naturally stopped producing enough estrogen to trigger menstruation, or because they have been removed for some reason. In the United States and other Western countries, most women reach menopause anywhere between the ages of 45 and 55, with the average being age 51.

Women begin to experience physical changes associated with the change in their hormonal "weather patterns" in their late thirties or early forties, during the six years or so before menopause known as perimenopause. Even for women who enjoy lusty sex lives, some of these changes can affect sexuality. Additional changes may disrupt life in other ways. Here's how.

Hot flashes. Estrogen helps regulate body temperature. So declining estrogen production disrupts your internal thermostat, triggering a hot flash (or, sometimes, chills). A woman having a hot flash becomes extremely warm and may perspire profusely.

As many as two-thirds of all perimenopausal women experience hot flashes. Anything that raises body temperature—hot weather, wine, or sexual activity—can tend to trigger a hormonally related hot flash. Fortunately, only 10 to 15 percent of women experience hot flashes that are intense or frequent. More typically, hot flashes are quite manageable: Many women never even bother telling their doctors about them.

Night sweats and insomnia. Nothing more than hot flashes that occur at night, night sweats (or nocturnal hot flashes) often awaken women, who then have a difficult time getting back to sleep, says Dr. Landau. Night sweats are no gift to a woman's love life, either. If you wake up drenched every night—then stay awake—you're likely to become too exhausted and grumpy for sex.

Vaginal changes. Estrogen keeps vaginal tissue moist, thick, and flexible. So when estrogen wanes during menopause, the vagina shows it. For example, you may not lubricate as much as you used to, or you may lubricate much more slowly. The tissue lining the vagina may also become thinner and less elastic. These changes can make sex painful—sometimes too painful to deal with.

Ironically, lots of sex may actually help matters. Middle-aged women with active sex lives report fewer problems lubricating and fewer vaginal changes than those who make love infrequently. (For information on other quick fixes, see Painful Intercourse on page 350 and Vaginal Dryness on page 365.)

Waning sexual desire. Some menopausal women may feel less interested in sex than they used to, says Susan R. Johnson, M.D., professor of obstetrics and gynecology at the University of Iowa College of Medicine in Iowa City.

Sometimes, psychological or relationship issues are at play in this loss of interest in sex, says Dr. Landau. But for some women, declining levels of the

Having the Time
of Their Lives

According to a Gallup survey of 750 women between the ages of 50 and 65 who had reached menopause, 51 percent said they felt happier and more fulfilled than ever.

male hormone testosterone, which fuels sex drive in women as well as men, may be a contributing factor.

Still, testosterone levels don't drop as much as estrogen levels. So while your fire down below may be banked, it's definitely not out. Besides, any sex therapist will tell you that the brain is still the primary sex organ.

Putting Out the "Flash Fires"

You want hot sex. Instead, you have hot flashes. Hormone-replacement therapy (HRT)—often prescribed to help preserve bone strength and protect heart health in women past menopause—can relieve bothersome changes associated with menopause. But HRT isn't the perfect solution. Many doctors advise against HRT for women who have had breast cancer or are at increased risk for it due to their family histories. Other women are reluctant to take hormone-replacement therapy because they object to taking what they consider "medication" for a condition that isn't a disease. And among women who try HRT, 38 percent (about one out of three) stop by the end of the first year because of side effects like menstrual bleeding, bloating, premenstrual-type irritability, cramps and breast tenderness, headaches, weight gain, depression, and changes in their skin and hair.

If HRT works for you, fine. If it doesn't, or if you've just begun to experience the first signs of menopause and it's too soon to start HRT, these tips can help ease your heat so you and your partner can create some of your own.

Make love between flashes. Hot flashes seem to be most frequent from 6:00 A.M. to 8:00 A.M. and from 6:00 P.M. to 10:00 P.M., says Dr. Landau. So if hot flashes are a big impediment to your sex life, you might try scheduling "sex dates" outside of these times. If you and your partner both work close to home, consider meeting for a lunchtime rendezvous.

Sweat out flashes. Exercise for at least 30 minutes five times a week, recommends Dr. Johnson. Women who work out on a regular basis report fewer hot flashes than women who don't. (Exercise can also increase sexual desire, studies show.) The theory is that exercise improves circulation, making the body better able to tolerate temperature extremes and more proficient at cooling down fast.

Consider working out with your mate. Afterward, the two of you can work up a sweat in bed.

Just say "soy." Eat more soybeans and foods made from soybeans, such as tofu, soy milk, and soy flour, recommends Christopher Gardner, Ph.D., nutrition researcher at the Stanford University Center for Research in Disease Prevention. Soy is a rich source of phytoestrogens, natural compounds that act as a weak form of estrogen, replacing the estrogen lost during menopause. In one Italian study of 104 postmenopausal women, those who consumed about two ounces of isolated soy protein (a powdered form of soy) each day for 12 weeks reported that their hot flashes became much less severe.

Specialty soy products, such as isolated soy protein, are available at health food stores. But other products, such as tofu, soy milk, and soy cappuccino, are popping up in the produce and dairy sections of more and more neighborhood supermarkets.

Mix up a hot-flash cocktail. At a health food store, purchase tinctures of motherwort and black cohosh. Blend two parts motherwort tincture with one part black cohosh tincture, suggests Patricia Howell, a professional member of the American Herbalists Guild who practices in Atlanta. Start with one-quarter teaspoon of the formula, mixed into a cup of water or tea, three times a day. Some herbalists recommend increasing the dosage to one-half teaspoon three times a day.

Some women experience queasiness at higher doses. If that happens, cut back. And don't use black cohosh for more than six months.

Research has shown that motherwort helps lower blood pressure, which may be why it's thought to relieve hot flashes. This herb also has sedative qualities that ease insomnia. As for black cohosh, studies show that this herb can be as effective as hormone-replacement therapy for relieving hot flashes and other menopausal difficulties.

Use an herbal triple-punch. A combination of the herbs dong quai, chaste tree (chasteberry), and damiana can help relieve hot flashes, says Andrew Weil, M.D., director of the program in integrative medicine at the University of Arizona College of Medicine in Tucson, and author of *Spontaneous Healing*. He suggests taking two capsules of each herb (or one dropperful of liquid extract of each herb, mixed into a cup of warm water) once a day at midday.

If you have high blood pressure, read labels carefully: Some chasteberry supplements may contain licorice and/or Siberian ginseng, which can elevate blood pressure.

Cool Tips for Hot Nights

The fatigue and irritability that often accompany night sweats can cool the lustiest woman's ardor. You already may have tried to turn down the heat—which makes sense. Keeping your bedroom at 72°F or less can help, says Suzanne Woodward, Ph.D., a psychologist and assistant professor of psychiatry at Wayne State University of Medicine in Detroit. So can sleeping with a fan by your bed, even in the winter. If night sweats are still a problem, here's what else to try.

Change your bedding. Switch to all-cotton bedding and sleep in all-cotton nightwear, suggests Susun S. Weed, an herbalist and herbal educator from Woodstock, New York, and author of the Wise Woman series of women's herbal health books, including *Menopausal Years*. The usual polyester blend used in sheets and nighties encourages night sweats and leaves you feeling damp and clammy.

Buy really cool undies. Wiggle out of nylon or polyester sleepwear, which traps rather than releases heat, and into lingerie made of a highly breathable fabric that wicks away moisture. For a catalog offering sleepwear designed especially for women bothered by night sweats, write to As We Change, 6335 Ferris Square, Suite A, San Diego, CA 92121-3249.

Try yoga. Poses called inversions, in which the entire body or just the lower half is upside down, seem to reduce the frequency and intensity of night sweats, says Judith Lasater, a physical therapist and author of *Relax and Renew: Restful Yoga for Stressful Times*.

Here's a good beginner's pose, called legs-against-the-wall: Lie on your back with your bottom about 6 to 10 inches from a wall and your legs elevated and resting on the wall. (If this is uncomfortable, move your bottom a few more inches from the wall.) Place a folded towel or small pillow under your head and neck if you find your chin jutting up higher than your forehead. Close your eyes and breathe slowly and deeply. Hold the pose for 5 to 10 minutes.

Get Some Sleep—And More Sex

You may not be sleeping. But your sex life sure is a snoozefest. If insomnia is draining your sexual energy, try these herbal remedies. A few nights of uninterrupted sleep could make all the difference.

Let lavender bid you good night. Sniffing some lavender can help promote deeper, more restful sleep, according to Harold H. Bloomfield, M.D., author of *Healing Anxiety with Herbs*. Essential oil of lavender is widely used to relax patients at Churchill Hospital in Oxford, England. Nurses there use lavender oil, vaporized or applied by massage, to help reduce anxiety and induce sleep.

Before applying any new, undiluted essential oil, try a small amount on the back of your wrist first. If it irritates your skin, bathe the area with cold water and try diluting the oil with an equal amount of plain vegetable oil. And don't get essential oil in your eyes.

Drift off with chamomile. The herb chamomile has been used to treat insomnia since antiquity, says Ellen Hopman, a professional member of the American Herbalists Guild who practices in Amherst, Massachusetts. Most folks use chamomile as a tea. Pour one cup of boiling water over one tablespoon of dried chamomile (available at health food stores), steep for 10 minutes, and strain. Drink one cup before bed.

Avoid chamomile if you're allergic to closely related plants such as ragweed, asters, and chrysanthemums.

Sleep soundly with valerian. Valerian is one of the most widely used natural sleep aids in the world, says Christopher Hobbs, a professional member of the American Herbalists Guild who resides in Santa Cruz, California, and author of *Valerian: The Relaxing and Sleep Herb*.

The herb's active ingredients include a group of compounds called valepotriates. Research indicates that these components in valerian attach to the same brain receptors as tranquilizers like Valium, but without causing dependency.

Health food stores and natural food stores sell valerian in several forms, including tinctures, tablets, and teas. But most people prefer taking the tinctures or tablets instead of the tea, which smells like stinky feet. Hobbs recommends one to two dropperfuls (one-half to one teaspoon) of the tincture in a little water or one or two 500-milligram capsules 30 minutes before bed.

Don't use valerian if you're taking any sleep-enhancing or mood-regulating medications. If you experience nervousness, agitation, or heart palpitations, discontinue using the herb.

Libido-Revving Remedies

For women who find themselves less interested in sex at menopause, experts suggest the following aphrodisiacs.

Down some damiana. Damiana has a long reputation in folk medicine as an aphrodisiac. It seems to lower anxiety and may be slightly stimulating, says Margi Flint, a professional member of the American Herbalists Guild from Marblehead, Massachusetts, who teaches herbal approaches to health at Tufts Medical School in Boston.

To make damiana tea, steep one teaspoon of dried leaves in a cup of boiling water for 10 minutes. Strain and drink. If you want to take damiana on a regular basis as a tonic, use 15 to 20 drops of tincture three times a day, says Aviva Romm, a professional member of the American Herbalists Guild in Bloomfield Hills, Michigan. For a quick passion boost, take 20 to 30 drops in one-quarter cup of warm water about an hour before lovemaking, she suggests.

Get your blood flowing. Stimulating herbs that get blood circulation flowing enhance sexual feelings in women, Romm notes. "With more blood flow to the pelvis, you'll feel more aroused," she says.

Simmer the following herbs in two cups of water for 20 minutes: one tablespoon grated fresh ginger, 7 to 10 cloves, two to three cinnamon sticks, four or five black peppercorns, and 7 to 10 cardamom pods. Strain and add small amounts of milk and honey to taste. If you wish, add one-quarter teaspoon of vanilla. "Vanilla comes from the orchid family, and orchids are incredibly sensual flowers," says Romm. "It's an aphrodisiac."

Consider hormonal help. If the strategies above don't help, you may want to consider testosterone therapy, suggests Dr. Johnson. Several studies have shown that supplementary testosterone (in pill or shot form) can increase sexual arousal in some postmenopausal women, especially in women whose ovaries have been removed. Your doctor can explain the benefits and drawbacks of testosterone therapy.

Menstruation and PMS

B iology is loaded with ironies. For example, dips in the female hormones estrogen and progesterone just before the start of menstruation make some women a little weepy and irritable just before their periods. But those same changes—and the fact that a tiny bit of testosterone is the dominant hormone by default—make her more eager to pursue sex.

The reason? The complex, day-to-day interplay among the sex hormones estrogen, testosterone, and progesterone. Awash in estrogen, as we are in the beginning and middle of our cycles, we feel soft, womanly, especially receptive to a man's advances. When, just before our periods, we're low on estrogen and progesterone but fueled by testosterone, we can be weepy and confused—the classic signs of premenstrual syndrome, or PMS. At menstruation (beginning on the first day of your period), the whole sex-hormone dance begins again.

Of course, some of us experience these hormonal fluctuations more intensely than others, says Theresa Crenshaw, M.D., a certified sex therapist in San Diego and author of *The Alchemy of Love and Lust*. And many women don't notice them at all. But that doesn't mean that none occur, she says. "Every hormone involved in the menstrual cycle has the power to affect our minds, our moods, and our interest in sex—including whether we're feeling sexually receptive or sexually aggressive."

Even if we do occasionally feel like bubbling cauldrons of sex-hormone soup, that doesn't mean we're at the mercy of our hormones. "The more we understand the role hormones play in our day-to-day moods, the better equipped we are to deal with our own feelings and those of our partners," says Dr. Crenshaw.

Meet Your Sex Hormones

Each phase of the menstrual cycle, including the premenstrual phase, is ruled by a specific hormone or hormones. The hormone that dominates each

When to See the Gynecologist

Even if nothing is amiss, you should see your doctor once a year for an abdominal exam, a pelvic exam, and a Pap test, advises Theresa Crenshaw, M.D., a certified sex therapist in San Diego and author of *The Alchemy of Love and Lust.* But make an appointment sooner should you experience any of the following symptoms.

- Your period comes less than 21 days or more than 35 days after the onset of your last period (21 to 35 days is the normal range).

- Your period is frequently irregular.

- Your period lasts more than a week.

- Your flow is heavier than normal.

- You experience more menstrual pain than normal.

phase, or the interplay among hormones, can influence our behavior, which in turn affects the way we relate to our partners, says Dr. Crenshaw.

Estrogen is the sex hormone that gives us our female characteristics—such as our breasts and our soft voices—and regulates our menstrual cycles. Estrogen also regulates what Dr. Crenshaw calls our receptive sex drive—that is, our willingness to engage in sex. According to some studies, estrogen can also improve psychological well-being in menopausal women.

Testosterone is a predominantly male sex hormone. Women produce it, too, but in much smaller amounts—20 to 40 times less than men. It governs our "active" sex drive, which makes us actively pursue sex, and promotes aggression. "Thanks to testosterone, a woman will go after a man," says Dr. Crenshaw. But in some women, the interaction between testosterone and progesterone causes irritability and aggression.

Dr. Crenshaw describes progesterone, a primarily male hormone, as having "a schizoid personality." One persona of progesterone makes women irritable and aggressive, while the other makes them nurturing, especially toward their children. When it interacts with testosterone, it cancels out testosterone's effects, reducing sex drive. In effect, says Dr. Crenshaw, "progesterone just says no to sex." In fact, a synthetic version of this hormone is used to chemically castrate sex offenders. Progesterone also aggravates PMS, or pre-menstrual syndrome, a diverse cluster of physical and emotional symptoms (such as bloating and irritability) that affect some women.

Here's a blow-by-blow account of your hormonal activity during each phase of your menstrual cycle, along with Dr. Crenshaw's advice on how to work with your hormones. (Or, in the case of PMS, how to work against them.)

The First Two Weeks

At a glance: The first phase of the menstrual cycle, called the proliferative phase, begins with the end of menstruation (the last day of your period) and lasts 14 days in an average 28-day cycle. During this phase, the ovaries prepare for ovulation, and the lining of the uterus, the endometrium, develops in preparation for fertilization.

Dominant hormone: Estrogen.

How you feel: Estrogen gives a woman a sense of well-being, says Dr. Crenshaw. "She feels great, confident, social."

Influence on sex drive: Estrogen makes a woman receptive to a man's sexual advances, says Dr. Crenshaw. "With estrogen flowing, a woman opens her arms and wants to be penetrated. She's flirting and flexing her sexual muscle."

Influence on your relationship: With estrogen pumping, a woman is most likely to be easygoing, according to Dr. Crenshaw. "She has good will toward her man, if not all men."

Game plan: Since your "estrogen high" is making you feel emotionally tranquil and sexually responsive, this is a great time to take a weekend getaway with your partner or plan activities that you both enjoy, says Dr. Crenshaw. It's also a good time to talk about your relationship, if need be, says Dr. Crenshaw. "You're not as likely to get irritable or defensive, as you might later in your cycle."

Ovulation

At a glance: During this second stage of the menstrual cycle—at around day 14 of a 28-day cycle—estrogens in the blood reach their peak, causing an ovary to release an egg, or ovum. If the ovum is fertilized by male sperm, pregnancy results. If not, it's shed later, during menstruation.

Dominant hormones: Estrogen is high and testosterone peaks.

How you feel: Some women have discomfort or cramping when they ovulate. This pain is called *mittelschmerz* (German for "middle pain") because the pain occurs halfway between menstrual periods.

Influence on sex drive: During ovulation, sexual receptiveness peaks. Yet some women become sexually aggressive. Dr. Crenshaw isn't sure why. She speculates that it's because we're also pumping out lots of testosterone.

What's more, during ovulation, our bodies produce inordinately high levels of phenylethylamine (PEA), a hormonelike substance that makes us feel good. (Sometimes known as the molecule of love, PEA is also abundant in chocolate.) This rush of PEA may influence our urge to mate and procreate during our most fertile time.

Influence on your relationship: Although your hormones are fluctuating dramatically, "ovulation is a pretty peaceful time in a woman's cycle," says Dr. Crenshaw. That's because you're still producing a lot of estrogen, which promotes feelings of emotional well-being.

Game plan: Whether you're feeling receptive to your mate's advances or you're pestering *him* for sex, take advantage of a higher-than-average capacity for arousal, suggests Dr. Crenshaw. And remember that this is your most fertile time.

After Ovulation

At a glance: In the third part of the menstrual cycle, the secretory phase—from about day 15 to day 28—the endometrium thickens, and the ovaries produce large amounts of estrogen and progesterone. These hormones cause glands in the endometrium to secrete nutrients to nourish an implanted egg. If the egg is not fertilized, the levels of these hormones plummet.

Dominant hormones: Progesterone rises; estrogen peaks, then quickly falls; testosterone wanes.

How you feel: Progesterone is a two-faced hormone, says Dr. Crenshaw. It can make a woman feel nurturing and yearn to be cuddled—or irritable and snappish. "We can't explain this," she says.

Influence on sex drive: During the second half of a woman's cycle, progesterone can sharply curtail a woman's interest in sex.

Influence on your relationship: This can be a good time for couples to be physically close in a nonsexual way, such as massages, back rubs, and cuddling, says Dr. Crenshaw. But it's not the best time to broach a serious discussion with your mate. "As a woman approaches PMS and her progesterone rises, talking can become more emotionally charged, and she's more likely to misinterpret in the negative," she says.

Game plan: Keep things loving, but be aware that you're entering PMS territory, with its ebb and flow of sex hormones. "Don't get into heavy issues unless you have a lot of problem solving to do," says Dr. Crenshaw.

PMS

At a glance: PMS isn't an official part of the menstrual cycle, yet for four to six days before the start of menstruation, three out of four women experience some kind of discomfort, such as anxiety, anger, irritability, difficulty concentrating, lack of energy, insomnia, or feeling overwhelmed or out of control. Or they may experience physical problems such as headaches, breast tenderness, or weight gain or feeling bloated.

Experts still aren't sure what causes it, but one thing's for sure: Your hormone levels are going haywire. "A complex combination of molecules is terrorizing the bloodstream, with each hormone offering its special brand of torment," says Dr. Crenshaw.

Dominant hormone: Estrogen and progesterone drop; testosterone rises.

How you feel: "Women who suffer from PMS would like to run away from home, and sometimes their husbands and kids wish they would, too," says Dr. Crenshaw. The irritable, snappish feelings are caused by the relative rise in testosterone, compared to the low levels of feel-good estrogen. "And yet, this irritability and aggression mask the fact that women are really sensitive and tender during this time," she says.

Influence on sex drive: Despite their intense and unpredictable emotions, many women crave sex during PMS. Dr. Crenshaw speculates that even though testosterone is lower than the levels in males, estrogen is at its

fascinating
FACTS

Men Say They Feel the Effects of PMS

According to one survey, 79 percent of women reported experiencing emotional symptoms associated with PMS. But so did the men around them.

- 84 percent of men say they know women who experience PMS.

- 48 percent of men say that their relationship with a female co-worker is negatively affected by the co-worker's PMS symptoms.

- 49 percent of men say that their relationships with their wives or partners are negatively affected by PMS symptoms.

lowest level and progesterone is almost nil. So testosterone wins by default. Some women also masturbate more frequently during this time.

Influence on your relationship: If you can tell your mate how you're feeling, your monthly battle with PMS doesn't have to strain your relationship, says Dr. Crenshaw. In fact, it may actually strengthen it.

"If you can say, 'I feel terrible; the world is black; I'm angry with everyone, including myself. Would you hold me and take care of me for a while?' you may be pleasantly surprised by your partner's response," says Dr. Crenshaw. "The majority of men would love to do something to help. Women are so sensitive and vulnerable during PMS that if a man can be unusually tender or sweet, the warmth and love and appreciation that a woman can express can be greater than at any other time of the month."

Game plan: Acknowledge PMS blues without letting them take over your life. If you can, postpone critical meetings at work and big decisions at home. "While it's not always possible, it's possible much more than most women will admit," says Dr. Crenshaw. Also, indulge yourself. Get a manicure, or hand over the kids to your spouse or a sitter so that you can browse in a bookstore.

Never act in haste. "Women may be prone to making major life decisions during this time, such as, 'I think I want a divorce,'" says Dr. Crenshaw. "To go against your hormones and keep your life in balance, tell yourself, 'I'll reevaluate this decision in a week, when I'm feeling better.'"

If you can, make love or masturbate to orgasm, suggests Dr. Crenshaw. "A woman with PMS is accumulating blood in her pelvis, which can cause discomfort," she explains. "The contractions of the pelvis and uterus during an orgasm force all those fluids to recirculate, and she gets some physical relief."

Better yet, exercise. "Exercise is really important because a component of PMS is sometimes depression or feeling down," says Mary Lake Polan, M.D., Ph.D., professor and chairman of the department of gynecology and obstetrics at Stanford University School of Medicine. "Exercise releases endorphins, brain chemicals that make you feel better, so it's a natural way to lighten your mood." Experts recommend doing aerobic exercise for 20 to 30 minutes at least three days a week.

Nutritional strategies also may help. Vitamin B_6 seems to help in the production of serotonin, a brain chemical that may be linked with PMS. A 100-milligram daily dose may ease your PMS symptoms. Don't take more than that; larger amounts can cause nerve damage.

Even though you may be craving sweet treats like Death by Chocolate, pass them up and choose instead snacks that are high in complex carbohydrates, such as bagels and fresh vegetables. Unlike sugar, which sends your blood sugar on a roller-coaster ride, complex carbohydrates keep your blood sugar and energy on the level.

If you're particularly bothered by headaches and insomnia, two herbs may help—feverfew, touted as herbal headache help for 200 years, and valerian, which may calm you down and help you sleep. Both herbs are available at health food stores. Pour one cup of boiling water over one teaspoon fresh or dried feverfew leaves or one teaspoon dried valerian root powder. Cover to prevent the oils from evaporating, steep for 10 minutes, strain, and then drink.

Menstruation

At a glance: Menstruation occurs when estrogen and progesterone levels decline so dramatically that they can't sustain the endometrium. If a woman doesn't become pregnant, she sheds this uterine lining in her menstrual flow.

Dominant hormones: Progesterone and estrogen are at their lowest levels of your entire cycle. They're so low, in fact, that your ovaries are signaled to secrete estrogen, triggering the onset of another proliferative phase. A tiny bit of testosterone is the dominant hormone by default.

How you feel: For many women, menstruation brings an overwhelming sense of physical and emotional relief, especially if they are plagued with moderate to severe PMS, says Dr. Crenshaw.

Influence on sex drive: Many women experience a surge in sexual desire during menstruation. It could be because the uterus is engorged with blood, making it more sensitive than usual. "Or maybe it is just the refreshing aspect of the absence of progesterone, and the relative absence of estrogen allowing the little bit of testosterone to exercise more power," says Dr. Crenshaw.

Influence on your relationship: If you experience PMS, you're likely to become "yourself" again, says Dr. Crenshaw. Your husband and kids no longer have to walk on eggshells around you.

Game plan: Make love, if possible, suggests Dr. Crenshaw. The contractions of the uterus that occur during orgasm may help relieve cramping by dispelling blood that's congested in the pelvic region. (Orgasms achieved through masturbation can relieve cramping just as well, she adds.)

If your guy is squeamish about having intercourse while you have your period, he could use a condom for sanitary reasons, even if you are on the Pill and don't have to worry about birth control.

Painful Intercourse

Not so long ago, if a woman complained of pain during sex, her doctor was likely to think the problem was all in her head. Now, doctors know better. In most cases, painful intercourse has a physical cause, says Ingrid Nygaard, M.D., associate professor of obstetrics and gynecology at the University of Iowa College of Medicine in Iowa City.

To identify what's causing the pain, it's important to distinguish "external" pain from "internal" pain, says Dr. Nygaard.

Pain that occurs on the vulva, or external genitals, or upon penetration is often caused by vaginal dryness, which is itself caused by insufficient arousal

When Pain Is in the Brain

While most cases of painful intercourse have physical causes, it can be related to psychological factors as well.

Emotional stress, past sexual abuse, guilt about sex, or unresolved conflict with a partner can hinder the physical process of sexual arousal. These negative feelings can keep a woman's vagina from lubricating, causing discomfort during sex.

Fear of penetration and other anxiety can also cause the muscles in the vagina to contract involuntarily, making penetration difficult or impossible. While rare, this condition, known as vaginismus, can be a cause of painful intercourse. But because a woman's anticipatory fear of the pain can cause her vaginal muscles to contract, vaginismus can also be a *result* of painful intercourse.

With the help of a sex therapist, it's possible to learn how to relax the vaginal muscles. To help with the relaxation, some therapists use behavioral exercises in which plastic dilators of increasing size are inserted into the vagina (often in combination with relaxation strategies, with or without the partner).

or lubrication, says Dr. Nygaard. External pain can also be caused by an allergic reaction to spermicides or condoms or by yeast or bacterial infections. Vulvodynia, or chronic inflammation of the vulva, can also cause painful sex, as can vulvar vestibulitis, a type of vulvodynia that affects only the area surrounding the vaginal opening.

Pain that occurs with deep penetration may be caused by anything from a pulled muscle in the abdomen to constipation, says Dr. Nygaard. It can also be caused by fibroid tumors or endometriosis, in which the lining of the uterus invades the ovaries, fallopian tubes, or abdominal cavity. (If you're experiencing any kind of pain, consult your doctor to find out why.)

Whatever the cause, chronically painful sex can affect a woman's mood and self-esteem, says Amy Stockman, Ph.D., a health psychologist in the department of obstetrics and gynecology at the University of Iowa Women's Health Center in Iowa City.

"Many women with this problem feel guilty, depressed, or anxious," Dr. Stockman says. These negative feelings can strain intimacy between a couple, she says, especially if a woman doesn't tell her husband why she has stopped wanting to make love.

Because of this, it's important to look for solutions to the pain, rather than avoid sex or suffer in silence, says Dr. Stockman. Women who take charge of the problem and seek active solutions tend to do better emotionally, and have a more intimate relationship with their partners, than women who passively endure the problem, she says.

From Pain to Pleasure

If the pain lingers or has become chronic, or if you suddenly experience pain in the lower abdominal area, see your gynecologist promptly, says Dr. Nygaard. Sudden, severe pain could be caused by a ruptured cyst or ectopic pregnancy. But if painful sex is a once-in-a-while problem, the cause is usually obvious (irritation caused by a new type of spermicide or feminine hygiene product, for example). These tips can help identify the culprit and offer relief.

Take a look. Get a hand mirror and examine your inner and outer vaginal lips for cuts, sores, rashes, unusual discharge, or redness or irritation. A small cut or irritation will likely heal on its own, says Dr. Nygaard. A crop of sores or a rash warrants an immediate visit to your gynecologist. So does unusual discharge, even if you think it might be a yeast infection. "What appears to be a yeast infection may not be," she says.

Hit the drugstore. If the pain is at the entrance to your vagina or upon penetration and your vagina feels dry, try an over-the-counter vaginal lubricant such as Astroglide, says Dr. Nygaard. You'll find these products in the feminine hygiene aisle. (If you don't have any Astroglide on hand and can't get to a drugstore, regular cooking oil will do.)

Vary your positions. Women with endometriosis often find that making love in the female superior position (woman on top) or side-by-side is less painful than the missionary position or vaginal entry from behind, says Dr. Stockman. "These positions allow a woman to control the depth and speed of thrusting, so she'll experience less pain and feel more in control."

Fiber up. If intercourse hurts when your partner thrusts deep inside you, take fiber supplements for a week, says Dr. Nygaard. (Follow the directions on the label.) Severe constipation is a common, yet little-known cause of painful intercourse, she says. Increasing the soluble and insoluble fiber in your diet will help to prevent dry, hard stools and add bulk to the stools respectively.

Ask about anesthetic gel. Some women with vulvodynia or vulvar vestibulitis apply an over-the-counter cream that contains the topical anesthetic lidocaine before they have intercourse, says Dr. Nygaard. But don't try this on your own; consult your doctor first. Additionally, Dr. Nygaard cautions not to apply lidocaine on skin ulcers or broken skin.

Find a specialist. If the pain is caused by a chronic condition, find a therapist who specializes in pain-management techniques, says Dr. Stockman. She can teach you pain-control strategies that will help make sex more comfortable, such as visualization and progressive muscle relaxation.

Pregnancy

Nothing bonds a man and a woman more than waiting for a child—their child—to be born.

There's also nothing more challenging to their relationship.

When a baby is on the way, virtually everything in a couple's orderly world is affected, from what they eat for breakfast to what they think about before they fall asleep at night.

The changes are more than external, however. Expectant parents will also experience inner changes—changes that can affect their partnership, says Joel Block, Ph.D., a clinical psychologist and sex therapist at the Human Sexuality Center of Long Island Jewish Medical Center in Glen Oaks, New York, and author of *Secrets of Better Sex*. While many couples draw closer during pregnancy, others are pulled apart by the stresses and strains of impending parenthood.

If you're expecting your first baby, you may be shaking in your low-heeled and very comfortable shoes. But take heart. If you and your husband nurture your relationship and prepare for the inevitable changes, your post-baby relationship can emerge stronger than ever, experts say.

If you're waiting on Baby Number Two (or more), you already know what's ahead. Your mission: to make time in your schedule—and your heart—for your partner in the face of 3:00 A.M. feedings, endless diapers, and the demands of your other child or children.

Fortunately, nature gives us nine months to prepare for one of life's most unsettling and exhilarating events. Here's how expectant couples commonly

Post-Baby Couplehood

Too often, new parents concentrate on their child's needs and ignore their own, says Joel Block, Ph.D., a clinical psychologist and sex therapist at the Human Sexuality Center of Long Island Jewish Medical Center in Glen Oaks, New York, and author of *Secrets of Better Sex.* "But the health of your relationship demands that you make time for each other," he says.

So before too long, hire a sitter, get out of your sweatpants and into some real clothes, and get out of the house together. Alone. Take in a movie. Dine with friends. Treat yourselves to massages at a day spa. These dates give you a temporary respite from the demands of parenthood and remind you that you're lovers as well as parents.

Your child or children benefit from your "couple time" as much as you do. "A loving relationship is one of the most important things you can give a child," says Dr. Block. "Don't neglect it."

One sign of neglect: Your partner becomes withdrawn or even jealous of the baby because he no longer has your undivided attention, says Adelaide Nardone, M.D., an obstetrician and gynecologist at the Women's Medical Associates of Westchester in Mount Kisco, New York.

As much as you may yearn to, don't tell him to grow up. Instead, compare your all-consuming passion for motherhood to starting a new job and being nervous about your performance, suggests Dr. Block. "Then tell him that you miss him, too." More than likely, he'll be more understanding of your new-mother jitters.

feel about sex, love, and their relationships, along with expert advice on how to roll with the changes.

Pregnant Sex: Fact and Fiction

Among all the myths that surround pregnancy, one of the most enduring is that pregnant women want more sex. Or less.

The truth is, every woman is different. "I call it the rule of one-thirds," says Adelaide Nardone, M.D., an obstetrician and gynecologist at the Women's Medical Associates of Westchester in Mount Kisco, New York. "One-third of women become lustier, one-third lose interest in sex, and one-third don't change at all."

In the first three months of pregnancy, nausea and fatigue, which are associated with elevated levels of the hormones estrogen and progesterone, may leave a woman feeling too, well, sick and tired to have sex. "If getting pregnant was difficult, or if she has had miscarriages in the past, she may feel that intercourse may hurt the baby," says Dr. Block.

The second three months, however, "can be a sexy time," Dr. Block adds. Some women are more interested in sex or enjoy it more at this time. Their breasts are sensitive and may be easily stimulated. What's more, increased blood flow to the vagina and uterus can make orgasm more intense. (That said, some women still can't even *think* about sex.)

In the last trimester, a woman's sheer bulk, and the fatigue it causes, may dampen her desire again. If she does have intercourse, her orgasms may be either harder to achieve or more explosive—again, because of the large amount of blood and fluid in the pelvic area.

How a woman feels about her ever-expanding body affects her interest in sex as well. While many women feel voluptuously sexy, some women feel unattractive or think that their partners find them so. Either way, feeling bad about her body can make a pregnant woman shy away from sex, says Kenneth J. Reamy, M.D., professor of obstetrics and gynecology and behavioral medicine at the West Virginia School of Medicine in Morgantown and a certified sex therapist.

Expectant fathers can become less interested in sex, too, says Dr. Block. They may fear hurting their wives or their unborn children. Or they may be too preoccupied with their own anxieties about becoming a father.

Obviously, it's ideal when a pregnant woman and her husband are in sexual sync, says Dr. Block. But regardless of whether he's raring to go and you're not or vice versa, you won't be the first couple to hit a sexual lull while waiting for a baby to arrive, points out Dr. Reamy. As you'll see, it's both possible and important to express physical affection without having intercourse. But first, it's important to understand how and why your relationship outside the bedroom may change in the upcoming months.

When Two Become Three (or More)

Even before it's born, a baby can influence a couple's relationship.

In a few short months, or less, the energy that you and your husband have put into your relationship will be diverted to a tiny new party. You'll both need to shelve your own plans and desires, at least temporarily.

All parents-to-be have "some conscious and unconscious anxiety," says Dr. Reamy. "They think, 'I have to be more than a spouse and lover. Now I have to be a parent, too.'" And men and women deal with the emotions of impending parenthood in different ways.

During pregnancy, women can undergo dramatic emotional changes, Dr. Reamy says. Many women are thrilled to be pregnant, and their joy spills over into their relationships. Others have mixed feelings. They may have trouble adjusting to their ever-expanding bodies or fear that the baby will jeopardize their careers or independence.

Men may feel frightened, says Dr. Block. They worry about their job security, the size of their 401(k), their fitness to be a father. This fear can cause some men to feel trapped, he says. To deal with their fears, they may withdraw their emotional support at a time when their partners need extra snuggling and reassurance. A few may even pretend they're single again, carousing with the boys in an attempt to deny their impending fatherhood.

Like many expectant couples, you and your husband are likely to feel a whole range of emotions, both positive and negative. The best advice: Accept negative feelings and talk about them openly. Fear and anxiety are normal responses to a stressful event like pregnancy, says Dr. Block, and admitting these feelings can make them less threatening.

"Join a childbirth preparation class and talk to friends with children to help you both sort out your feelings and ease your fears," suggests Dr. Reamy.

Keeping Intimacy Alive

While pregnancy can strain your relationship, it doesn't have to break it—as long as you reach out to each other, physically and emotionally. These tips can help you close ranks with your partner before the baby comes.

Keep in touch. If you're not making love as often, find other ways to express physical affection. "Give each other massages or back rubs, or take baths or showers together," suggests Dr. Reamy.

Most pregnant women crave nonsexual physical contact, says Dr. Block, so ask your partner for extra cuddling if you need it. Explain that even touching that doesn't lead to intercourse can make you feel secure, loved, and connected.

Don't sweat your sex life. Some couples enjoy sex right up to the ninth month. (See Intercourse and Positions on page 70.) But if you and your husband aren't one of these couples, that's okay. Really. While you don't have to be ecstatic about it, "remember that this, too, shall pass," says Dr. Reamy.

Say "no" with love. It's difficult, of course, when you want to make love and he doesn't. Or vice versa. But lopsided desire doesn't have to come between you. When you don't feel like making love, "refuse rather than reject," says Dr. Reamy. Refusal is done tactfully and with love, he says; rejection is done with little regard for how your partner may be feeling. Say, "I'm feeling so tired; can we try for tomorrow or the next day?" rather than, "I said no! Leave me alone!"

And once in a while, consider making love just to please your husband. Think of it as a gift. "I think the average husband would be very pleased with a quickie," says Dr. Reamy.

Build your nest together. When a man shares pregnancy milestones with his partner, such as picking out a crib and attending birthing classes, he becomes more involved with the pregnancy—and feels closer to his partner, says Dr. Reamy. If your man hasn't yet joined in this "nest building," give him some gentle encouragement. "For example, he might want to come to one of your obstetrical exams to listen to the baby's heartbeat," he suggests.

Confront baby shock now. As your belly grows, so should your thoughts about how your lives are about to change. "It's smart to talk ahead of time about what life will be like, so you can head off at least some problems," says Dr. Block.

Some potential topics of discussion: How you and your partner will find time for each other once the baby is born. How you'll divvy up housework and caring for the baby. Above all, how you feel about the fact that your lives are about to change. Such ongoing discussions will strengthen your commitment to work as a team, says Dr. Block.

Sex after Pregnancy

Having a child puts a woman's mind and body through momentous changes. Sadly, so does losing a child before it's born. It's not surprising, then, that both childbirth and miscarriage affect our sexuality.

While a woman's body is ready to resume intercourse a few weeks after childbirth, her mind often needs time to adjust, says Jennifer Niebyl, M.D., head of the department of obstetrics and gynecology at the University of Iowa Hospitals and Clinics in Iowa City. Remember that it's as important to take stock of your feelings as it is to monitor your healing body. Here's what to expect.

Post-Baby Sex

According to most obstetricians, a new mom should wait six weeks after the birth of her child to resume intercourse. That's enough time for an episiotomy (a surgical incision that widens the birth opening) to heal and for the uterus and other organs to return to the nonpregnant state.

That said, a six-week wait isn't mandatory. "Some women have intercourse three to four weeks after delivery with no problem," says

When You Lose a Pregnancy

One in six pregnancies ends in miscarriage, the spontaneous loss of a pregnancy before the fifth month. Most miscarriages occur because of abnormalities in the fetus, placenta, or uterus, not because of anything a woman did or didn't do.

Understandably, many women who experience miscarriage (and their husbands) go through a difficult period of grief, doubt, and regret in its aftermath. Normally, a woman who has had a miscarriage can resume intercourse after two weeks, when the risk of infection has passed. But many women won't be emotionally ready to make love again for longer than that, says Jennifer Niebyl, M.D., head of the department of obstetrics and gynecology at the University of Iowa Hospitals and Clinics in Iowa City. A woman's interest in and willingness to resume sex will depend on a variety of factors, including whether or not this was a wanted pregnancy, how long she had been trying to conceive, and whether she had lost other pregnancies.

Men suffer, too, says Dr. Niebyl. Some men worry about their partners' physical and emotional well-being; others feel somehow responsible for the miscarriage. Men may also have a harder time grieving, she says. This inability to express their sadness can strain a relationship at a time when both partners need it the most.

After a miscarriage, it's important that you and your husband both talk *and* listen, says Dr. Niebyl. Revealing your feelings will help you grieve together instead of pulling away from each other.

While grieving your loss is natural, some women may need short-term counseling to help them come to terms with a miscarriage, says Dr. Niebyl. One study of 229 women who had had a miscarriage found that they were 2½ times more likely to become depressed in the six months following the miscarriage than 230 pregnant women who had not had a miscarriage. Consult a therapist if mild depression lasts more than a month or if severe depression lasts more than two weeks.

Dr. Niebyl. If you're raring to go before the six-week moratorium, have your obstetrician examine you to make sure you're ready to resume sex, she says.

Realistically, however, most new moms are too busy dealing with the emotional and physical changes of childbirth to even think about sex. They're exhausted from the birth. They bleed for three to six weeks after childbirth—a form of vaginal bleeding called lochia. Their episiotomies can be tender for months after childbirth. There's just not much incentive to get romantic.

Breastfeeding may further reduce a woman's desire to have sex, says Dr. Niebyl. Nursing a child causes levels of the female sex hormone estrogen to decline, she explains. Low estrogen levels are associated with a reduction in sex drive.

While all of these changes are normal, it's still important to talk with your partner about how they're affecting your sex life, says Joel Block, Ph.D., a clinical psychologist and sex therapist at the Human Sexuality Center of Long Island Jewish Medical Center in Glen Oaks, New York, and author of *Secrets of Better Sex*. Reassure him that these changes are temporary.

Also, find ways to stay physically close, suggests Dr. Block. Touches, kisses, and caresses can keep the sexual spark alive during this chaotic and exhausting time, even if you're not quite up to making love. You can also try creative sexual techniques other than intercourse. (For ideas, see Oral Sex on page 79 and Sensual Massage on page 99.)

Some women find that, once they weather these changes, there's another fringe benefit. "Women who experienced discomfort during sex before they had a child may say they enjoy sex more after giving birth," says Dr. Niebyl.

An important note: If you don't want to become pregnant again immediately, use birth control as soon as you resume making love. (If you've used a diaphragm in the past, you should be refitted.) Also, don't count on breastfeeding to protect you from pregnancy. It's rare, but not unheard of, to become pregnant while nursing a child.

Urinary Incontinence

ॐ

L eak when you laugh? Dribble when you cough? Gush when you lift a basket of laundry? You're not alone. Women account for 85 percent of all Americans with urinary incontinence, the accidental loss of urine from the bladder.

Why? For starters, a woman's urethra (the tube through which urine leaves the body) is 1 to 1½ inches long. A man's is 6 to 8 inches long, making him five times more leak-resistant.

Then there are pregnancy and childbirth. Both stretch and weaken muscles in the pelvic area that keep the bladder closed, impairing your ability to hold urine in. In addition, declining estrogen levels in the years after menopause can cause the tissues lining the urinary tract to lose their hormone-fueled plumpness and flexibility. This thin, brittle tissue leaks.

For some women with incontinence, sex is a source of anxiety rather than pleasure. "It's hard to make love when you're worried about leaking on your partner," says Kristene E. Whitmore, M.D., chief of the division of urology at Graduate Hospital in Philadelphia.

How much you leak varies. Women with mild stress incontinence (the involuntary loss of urine when you cough, sneeze, or laugh) may lose less than a teaspoon of urine during sex. Those with severe stress incontinence may leak the entire time. Urge incontinence, the inability to get to the toilet on time (sometimes called an overactive bladder), can lead to accidents during sex.

Don't let embarrassment keep you from getting help. While less than half of the women with incontinence seek treatment, up to 80 percent with the condition can reduce leakage or eliminate it entirely. "Getting help can significantly improve your quality of life—and your sex life," says Dr. Whitmore.

It's important to see a doctor for any kind of incontinence, to rule out an underlying condition that could make the problem worse, Dr. Whitmore cautions.

Keep-Dry Advice

There is a lot you can do to reduce leakage on your own. Here's what to try.

Go before you leak. Use the toilet before you make love, says Dr. Whitmore—even if you don't think you need to. This simple act can reduce leakage during sex or eliminate it completely.

Sneeze with your knees. Before you sneeze, cough, or laugh, cross your legs. Women who do lose nearly one-tenth less urine than women who don't, research shows.

Don't smoke. The nicotine in cigarettes irritates the bladder and increases the chance of leakage, says Frederick R. Jelovsek, M.D., professor of gynecology and obstetrics at James H. Quillen College of Medicine in Johnson City, Tennessee. And smoker's cough can trigger an accident.

Disarm your bladder. Avoid coffee, tea, and carbonated drinks (even decaffeinated), alcoholic beverages, and acidic foods such as tomatoes and citrus fruits or juices. They can all aggravate an already touchy bladder.

Drink up. Many women with incontinence think that the less they drink, the less they'll leak. But drastically reducing your intake of fluids makes urine acidic—which is yet another bladder irritant.

Strengthen pelvic floor muscles. Start doing Kegel exercises, says Dr. Whitmore. They strengthen the pubococcygeal (PC) muscles, which run from the pubic bone to the tailbone, and can improve and even prevent incontinence. To perform Kegel exercises, pretend to stop and start your flow of urine. (You should feel a clenching sensation.) Contract hard for one second, then release. Repeat 15 to 20 times. Do two sets of regular, short squeezes twice a day. Gradually work up to two sets of 50 per day, holding the contraction for up to 10 seconds and totally relaxing for 10 seconds.

Fifteen to 25 percent of women with mild incontinence will stay completely dry if they perform Kegels correctly. Another 50 percent will reduce the frequency and severity of leakage by half. There's even a bonus: As a woman's PC muscles get stronger, her orgasms may become more intense, says Dr. Whitmore.

Ask about vaginal cones. Can't get the hang of Kegel exercises? Vaginal cones are an excellent way for premenopausal women with stress incontinence to build up the pelvic floor muscles, says Dr. Jelovsek. Available through your doctor and through some specialty mail order catalogs, these

Hidden Causes of Leaky Plumbing

If you accidentally lose urine at times, this handy guide can help you figure out why. A combination of do-it-yourself and medical treatments can help solve the problem and give you peace of mind during love-making.

If you . . .	You may have . . .
Leak when you cough, sneeze, or exercise	Stress incontinence, caused by weakened pelvic muscles supporting the bladder. The damage can be caused during pregnancy and childbirth or surgery (such as hysterectomy).
Often can't get to the bathroom on time	Urge incontinence, caused by urinary tract infections, a bladder stone, severe constipation, drinking a lot of caffeine, changes in pelvic muscles associated with menopause, or stroke.
Experience a frequent or constant dribble	Overflow incontinence, caused by diabetes or nerve damage. Improvement depends on treatment of the underlying health condition.

devices are about the size and shape of a tampon but vary in weight. Typically, the lightest cone is inserted into the vagina for 15 minutes twice a day. As the pelvic floor muscles become stronger, you "graduate" to the next cone until you can successfully hold in the heaviest one, which weighs about an ounce. In three studies of 103 women using vaginal cones, 68 to 79 percent said their leakage lessened within four to six weeks.

What Your Doctor Can Do

If do-it-yourself remedies don't help, a doctor's probably will. Here's what he or she might recommend.

Bladder training. This is the most effective way to treat both stress and urge incontinence, says Dr. Jelovsek. "The idea is to urinate before you get the urge, thereby 'retraining' the bladder to respond to your control," he says.

The technique takes five weeks. For the first week, urinate every waking hour, on the hour. (Buy a watch with a beeper; it will remind you to go, says Dr. Jelovsek.) The second week, urinate every 90 minutes. The third week, go every 2 hours. The fourth week, urinate every 2½ hours. By the fifth week, you should be able to urinate every 3 hours.

Topical estrogen. In women going through menopausal changes, estrogen applied or inserted into the vagina can plump up the tissues of the vagina and urinary tract. Normally, doctors prescribe an estrogen cream or ring (a small, flexible ring that can remain in the vagina even during sex). Be patient: It takes three months to see results, says Dr. Jelovsek.

Medication. If you have urge incontinence and dread accidents during sex, ask your doctor about tolterodine tartrate (Detrol), suggests Dr. Whitmore. Taken 30 minutes before lovemaking, this medication quiets the bladder. "It's often possible to get through an entire love-making session without an accident," she says. Other drugs such as oxybutynin (Ditropan) and hyoscyamine (Levsin) can help, too.

In addition, be aware that some medications can cause temporary incontinence. These include diuretics (used to treat congestive heart failure or high blood pressure), sedatives, muscle relaxants, and high blood pressure medications. Your doctor may be able to prescribe an alternative drug.

Vaginal Dryness

ex is supposed to feel spectacular. But when a woman experiences vaginal dryness, as about 60 percent of women over the age of 40 do, lovemaking can deliver more pain than pleasure.

Some women avoid the pain by avoiding sex. But this strategy can strain the relationship between a woman and her mate, says Adelaide Nardone, M.D., an obstetrician and gynecologist at the Women's Medical Associates of Westchester in Mount Kisco, New York. The woman feels guilty about avoiding sex and/or awkward about explaining why. The man wonders why she's no longer interested and assumes that it has something to do with him. He may also shy away from sex because he doesn't want to hurt his partner— or because vaginal dryness can make intercourse uncomfortable for him, too.

Vaginal dryness can easily be treated, so there's no reason why your sex life or your relationship should suffer, says Dr. Nardone. Read on to learn the causes of vaginal dryness and how to make sex fun again.

Why You're Dry

Vaginal dryness has a variety of causes. The most common is low levels of the female sex hormone estrogen, says Dr. Nardone. Estrogen helps stimulate vaginal secretions and keeps vaginal tissues moist and supple. Women who have just given birth have low estrogen levels. So do breastfeeding mothers, because the same hormone that promotes milk production suppresses ovulation, which ultimately results in lower estrogen levels. Other, less common causes are certain medications, such as antidepressants, and over-the-counter antihistamines, which dry out the body's mucous membranes, including those in the vagina. Even stress and fatigue can cause dryness simply because they dampen desire, and therefore arousal and lubrication.

Menopausal women frequently experience vaginal dryness, says Dr. Nardone. Waning estrogen levels during menopause can cause the tissue lining the vagina to become dry and thin. Vaginal dryness and thinning can be so particularly bothersome that many women stop making love as often as they used to.

Bringing Back the Pleasure

Regardless of the cause, no woman need put up with vaginal dryness. Here are some ways to replenish our natural moisture.

Hit the pharmacy. There are dozens of over-the-counter preparations that can help ease vaginal dryness, says Dr. Nardone. Vaginal moisturizing lotions, such as Vagisil Intimate Moisturizer, are formulated to relieve dry, irritated tissue on the vulva and labia and can replenish the moisture that's lost. These lotions can be used anytime and as frequently as necessary, she says. Vaginal lubricants, such as K-Y Jelly or Astroglide, offer temporary lubrication and can also make sex more comfortable. It's fine to use both of these products at the same time, says Dr. Nardone.

Caution: Choose a water-based lubricant. An oil-based product can cause condoms to disintegrate and possibly trigger a vaginal infection.

Go to it. Make love frequently, suggests Dr. Nardone. "The vagina and vulva are organs, and if you don't use them, you lose elasticity," she says. Studies have shown that regular sexual activity keeps the vagina healthier.

Ask about estrogen. If the methods above don't ease your vaginal dryness and you're going through menopause, ask your doctor about estrogen medications, suggests Dr. Nardone. These prescription-only medications are applied directly into the vagina. You'll need to wait up to three months to see results.

In some cases, enough of the estrogen in the cream will be absorbed to cause breast tenderness or uterine bleeding, says Dr. Nardone. If this happens, the dose can be lowered or another hormone, progesterone, can be prescribed.

Let him know it hurts. As obvious as it sounds, tell your mate if your vaginal dryness is making sex painful. "He may think you're avoiding sex for some other reason," says Dr. Nardone. He'll no doubt be relieved—and supportive—when you tell him what's going on.

MEN'S
SEXUAL HEALTH

The Male
Body Map

W hen you first start to make love to a guy, you don't give much thought to the inner workings of his genitals. As long as they seem to get the job done, all is well. But stay married a couple of decades, and things change. His penis doesn't get quite as hard, quite as often. His testicles change shape. His plumbing sends him to the bathroom in the middle of the night, and his doctor tells him he has prostate trouble—leaving you wondering, "What the heck is a prostate?"

If you want to help your guy stay healthy sexually, you could probably use a refresher course on the basic workings of the male anatomy. So here goes. (If you're up to speed on male reproductive organs, feel free to skip the anatomy lesson.)

The Brain: His Sexual Control Center

Believe it or not, the workings of the penis start with the brain. A thought, a sensation, or a vision is all that is needed to begin the process of stimulation, erection, arousal, and ejaculation. With a whiff of your perfume or the sight of your legs, a man's brain sends reaction signals to the lumbar region of his spinal cord. These signals then zip along a network of nerves straight to his penis. Time for action, say the signals. Wake up.

The penis comprises a tube and three inflatable cylinders that lie next to each other in a round bunch. (You can distinctly feel them underneath the

Those Amazing Guys

- Unencumbered by a condom, a man's penis is capable of ejaculating semen a distance of 12 to 24 inches.

- In his lifetime, the average guy will ejaculate approximately 18 quarts of semen containing 500 billion sperm.

  It's no wonder, then, that the majority of guys (54 percent) think about sex "every day" or "several times a day." Most women, on the other hand (67 percent) think about sex "a few times a week" or "a few times a month."

skin of the penis, especially when it's hard.) One cylinder is called the corpus spongiosum, and the other two are the corpora cavernosa. They are all made of a spongelike material that gives penises that soft, squishy feeling when they are flaccid.

Flaccid penises can change shape during the day. Penis size is affected by the temperature, what a man is feeling, and what time of day it is. Cold causes shrinkage, heat causes expansion, for example.

The tube inside the penis, the urethra, is contained within the corpus spongiosum. The urethra extends from the bladder to the tip of the penis. It's the hole you see in the head of the penis. Both urine and semen pass through the urethra.

There's another fluid that comes out of the tip of the penis. You've probably noticed it on the tip of a man's penis when he is aroused, but not ready to ejaculate. This seminal secretion isn't the same as semen. It's produced by two pea-size glands, the Cowper's glands, located just below the prostate. The fluid seems to protect sperm by neutralizing the acidity of the urethra. It may also serve as another means of lubricating the vagina for intercourse and conception.

As in all other organs in the body, blood is continually flowing into and out of the penis. When the amount of blood flow changes, so does the size of your partner's penis. During stimulation, the brain tells the arteries in the corpora cavernosa to dilate. When the arousal signal trips, more blood than usual begins to flow into the tiny caverns of the spongy tissue of the cylinders. The expansion of the caverns compresses exit veins within the penis, so the blood becomes trapped. The more signals, the more blood flow, and the harder the penis.

In general, blood flow to and from the penis is a very important sign of good cardiovascular health because it's a sign that the arteries are open and functioning. Scientists believe that the combination of healthy blood flow and brain-signaling (not sexy dreams) is one of the reasons that men of all ages have erections at night. It's the brain's way of making sure the penis is in good working order.

On average, a guy has three to seven nocturnal erections per night. Doctors speculate that it's simply a matter of timing and coincidence when a man wakes up with an erection. His penis will be even harder if his bladder is full because the bladder increases the pressure on the arteries traveling to the penis, trapping the blood more securely. A man's bladder has to empty before the blood will leave the penis.

The Foreskin: So Sensitive

It is the outside of the penis—the skin—that makes it such a sensitive organ. The glans, or head, of the penis is packed with highly sensitive nerve endings. In fact, the penis and clitoris start as the same organ in the fetus, but the penis grows because of testosterone, the hormone largely responsible for male characteristics.

About 60 percent of men in the United States had the foreskin of their penises removed soon after they were born. This is called circumcision. The other 40 percent are uncircumcised, meaning they still have the piece of foreskin that covers the head of the penis. It retracts and rests beneath the head of the penis when a man is erect. The United States is alone in this high number of circumcised men, by the way. Around the world, about 85 percent of men are uncircumcised.

If your husband's (or son's) penis is uncircumcised, then you probably know that he has to take extra care to wash underneath the foreskin, where bacteria can be trapped. Studies have shown that men who don't wash under the foreskin daily are more susceptible to infection.

The Testicles: Live Wires

The sac of wrinkly skin that hangs down below and behind the penis is called the scrotum. It's simply a protective package for the two testicles inside the sac, which feel like two small balls underneath the skin. Testicles are where the body produces sperm and testosterone.

Testicles are simply a mass of stringy tubes all balled up, not unlike a ball of yarn or rubber bands. Sperm is made within the tubes, while testosterone is created in the cells between the tubes. These cells are called Leydig's cells.

The scrotum is very sensitive to both touch and pain; this sensitivity is nature's way of protecting it from injuries that inhibit sperm production. The scrotum holds the testicles away from the body to keep their temperature just a few degrees cooler than body temperature. This is better for healthy sperm because high temperatures kill sperm.

While women are born with a lifetime supply of eggs in their ovaries, men's testicles manufacture 50,000 sperm per minute throughout the course of a man's lifetime.

After it's made, sperm travels through the epididymis, a series of ducts at the rear of the testicles, for about three days from each testicle to another pair of tubes, the vas deferens (or ductus deferens). It is the vas deferens that a doctor cuts and ties off during a vasectomy.

Connected to the vas deferens are the saclike seminal vesicles, where sperm is stored along with other fluids that comprise semen. A man typically ejaculates about a teaspoonful of semen. Ninety-five percent of his ejaculate is seminal fluid, while 5 percent is sperm and nourishing fluid from the testicles. Each teaspoonful, however, is filled with 80 million to 300 million sperm. Each sperm is about 1/1,000 of an inch long, so small that all the sperm in a typical ejaculate can fit inside a space the size of a pinhead.

Once inside the vagina, the sperm travel just one to two inches an hour until they reach the fallopian tubes—a journey that takes up to 48 hours. On the other hand, if a man ejaculates outside of a woman's body, the sperm die any time from two hours to three days afterward. If a man doesn't ejaculate, the sperm are simply re-absorbed by the man's body. So don't believe any stories about it being dangerous for a man to ignore an erection and not ejaculate.

One more thing: One testicle always hangs a bit lower than the other, and in most men it's the left one.

The Powerful Prostate

Because the prostate is the number one area where older men will develop cancer, it receives a lot of negative press. During most of a man's lifetime, however, the prostate is a healthy and respectable little organ. In fact, it's the gatekeeper that determines whether urine or semen will exit the penis.

The prostate is a walnut-size gland that resides at the front of a man's rectum, beneath his bladder and surrounding his urethra. Aside from its job of preventing urine from entering the urethra when a man is aroused, the prostate has another function. It produces, along with the seminal vesicles, the fluid that combines with sperm to make semen. This fluid helps move the sperm along to its destination.

Aside from all of its health-related roles, the prostate is also extremely sensitive to touch and is sometimes called the male G-spot. The only sure-fire way to stimulate a man's prostate is to insert a finger into his anus or apply pressure to his perineum, the area between the scrotum and the anus.

As men age, two things can go wrong with the prostate. It can get larger or it can develop cancer. The enlarged prostate is a much more common occurrence, as it begins growing in all men once they hit their late forties or fifties. The prostate, which, as we said, is normally the size of a walnut, can become the size of an orange. This condition is known as benign prostatic hyperplasia and is not a form of, or precursor to, cancer.

The most common sign that a man's prostate has begun to enlarge is that he has a hard time urinating; either it won't come out, or the flow of urine slows down to just a trickle. Men over the age of 40 and in the higher risk groups for prostate problems—those who are Black; have a father, brother, or uncle with prostate cancer; or experience any of the signs of prostate enlargement mentioned above—should have their prostates checked for both enlargement and signs of other problems by a doctor every year. Your husband will be unhappy about that news, but happy about this piece of information: One of the best ways to keep the prostate healthy is to have regular sex.

Ejaculation: Letting Go

All of the fluids and tubes in the penis make for some mighty powerful hydraulics. Although erections are controlled by the brain, it does sometimes seem as if it's the reverse: It's the erection in control of the man. His penis engorged with blood, semen at the ready in the seminal vesicles, your mate's mind becomes focused on one thing and one thing only.

Once it has gone from flaccid to erect, the average penis is 5½ inches long. The angle as well as the shape of the erection varies from man to man. As he ages, a man's erection won't point as far up as it did when he was young.

While a man's excitement continues to build, the area between his scrotum and anus contracts, closing the neck of the bladder and opening the ejaculatory channels. Both the testicles and the penis continue to grow as they prepare for ejaculation.

No matter its size or shape, the erection will only go away if one of two things happens.

First, a man can stop thinking about, looking at, or touching whatever it is that's providing him with stimulation. If he loses interest, then his brain will signal the penile arteries and caverns to contract. This allows the blood to flow out of the penis again.

Or a man can ejaculate. After a man has an orgasm, the brain sends a signal to the penile arteries to contract and let the blood out.

To ejaculate, a man's level of arousal first must intensify until, quite literally, he reaches a point of no return. As stimulation increases, the prostate, seminal vesicles, and vas deferens all contract, sending sperm and seminal fluid surging into the urethra. These contractions, along with those of the pelvic muscles, propel the semen forward. There is a point where nothing, not even the appearance of your pajama-clad five-year-old at the bedroom door, can prevent your husband from ejaculating.

Orgasms are remarkably similar from person to person. In fact, they involve the whole body and not just the sexual organs. Involuntary muscle contractions and spasms occur in the arms, legs, and back. Nipples may become erect, and much of the body becomes flushed. The heart races, blood pressure soars, skin breaks a sweat.

Men can have orgasms without ejaculating as well as ejaculate without having orgasms. Most of the time, of course, the two arrive hand in hand, so to speak.

What? No Afterglow?

Unlike women, men cool down quickly after ejaculating. After the contractions subside and the stimulation ends, the little exit arteries in the penis open up again, allowing blood to leave the penis, and it promptly goes limp.

Will he want to do it again anytime soon? That depends almost entirely upon his age and the stimulation he receives. A boy in his teens or a young man in his early twenties will have a refractory, or unresponsive, period of a few minutes and be ready to have sex again shortly. A more mature man in his late forties or fifties could probably go unaroused for a few days before he has sex again.

Of course, the most common thing for a man to want to do after sex is fall asleep. After ejaculation, it takes about 2 minutes for a man's body to be completely awash in waves of relaxation. Sleep is just the obvious culmination of these biological changes, which include a slowing of his pulse and a softening of his penis. How long does it take a woman to physically relax after orgasm? About 20 minutes. Just one more hint that Mother Nature has a sly sense of humor.

Impotence and Erection Problems

Were you surprised, too? Certainly much of America was. In April 1998, Viagra, the first anti-impotence pill for men, hit the market with a hoopla rarely seen for a new medicine. Couples went on television bragging unabashedly of their rekindled sex lives. A photo of the pill graced the cover of *Time* magazine. Roughly three million prescriptions were written during its first three months of availability. Who knew that so many men were plagued by erection problems, that so many couples were struggling to culminate their sexual liaisons?

A Drawerful of Solutions

Look at the back pages of any men's magazine, and you'll see ads for gadgets, pills, and potions that are supposed to help a man restore his vitality. Even before the rollout of the anti-impotence drug Viagra, the erectile dysfunction business—both legitimate and illegitimate—was booming.

"Although Viagra seems to be the first pill that does what it claims to do, it's unfortunate that it will stop men from trying other options," says Gerald Hoke, M.D., chief of urology at Harlem Hospital Center in New York City. "A penile implant, for example, is great for many men."

Implants require surgery, so while they are highly reliable, they are considered a more extreme, final solution. Some of the other popular choices include injections (done a few minutes before lovemaking by your partner or you, with the result being a solid erection for 30 minutes or so), vacuum devices (draw blood into the penis, then place a rubber ring at the base to hold the blood in), and pellets inserted into the urethra opening at the tip of the penis (these contain similar medicine as the injection).

Then there are the more bogus remedies—the creams and potions and

---

Well, sex counselors. They knew. They knew that as men get older, any number of health problems can have the side effect of inhibiting them from achieving erections. But if there is ever a private health matter among guys, it's erection problems. What is worse for a man to admit than that he's "impotent"? A guy will talk about his bad heart or his bum knee, but the state of his privates? Forget it. Until Viagra, "erectile dysfunction" was among the most hush-hush of major health problems in America.

Sildenafil (Viagra is the brand name) may or may not be a wonder drug—the number of deaths linked to its improper use is growing, causing some second thoughts about who should or shouldn't use it—but it has served the important function of pushing the topic of impotence out of collective darkness. What follows is even more light on what can cause a man to have erection problems, and how you can help him, and yourself, cope when it happens.

magic pills. The bottom line? "A man should rely on his doctor to be armed with accurate information," says Dr. Hoke, "because what he hears from his friends and what's publicized in advertisements is not always going to reflect the full picture."

Your mate should also consult you—and if he doesn't, you should gently let him know that this decision affects you as well, and that you want to offer your opinion. You may not have the stomach to give him injections, for example. "Women often aren't asked for their opinions on these solutions," says Judith Seifer, Ph.D., a sex therapist and associate clinical professor at Wright State University School of Medicine in Dayton, Ohio. "And many of them aren't happy when their husbands want to make love for an hour or have sex every night."

Another potential problem: Older men who can suddenly remain hard for an hour may start bragging to friends and neighbors about their new abilities. Once again, this is a team issue. Let your lover know what topics you consider private, suggests Dr. Seifer.

The Ups and Downs of Impotence

While it's often difficult to believe this, a man's erection problems are almost never a reflection of his feelings toward his partner.

"Men don't usually blame their partners for their erection problems," says Roger Crenshaw, M.D., a psychotherapist and sex therapist in La Jolla, California. "In fact, I've seen about 10,000 men in 30 years of practice, and off-hand, I can think of 3 guys who did that."

So what's to blame? Maybe he's nervous. Overly stressed about work. Anxious. Distracted. Maybe even a little drunk. And he's wondering why he can't get it up? "Most couples who have been together for a while will experience this situation once or twice over time," explains Judith Seifer, Ph.D., a sex therapist and associate clinical professor at Wright State University School of Medicine in Dayton, Ohio.

The mind plays a crucial role in erections, and when it becomes disengaged or distracted, the result is erection failure. Such cases are usually one-time occurrences and shouldn't trouble a man deeply—or you.

If there is a silent epidemic here, it is with long-term, chronic erection problems that have their origins in physiology, not the mind. As men enter their forties and fifties, any number of things can cause erection problems, among them:

- Major illness. Any problem that affects blood flow, such as heart disease, will also affect erection capability. Diabetes, which affects both the circulatory and nervous systems, also can cause erection problems.

- Excess cholesterol. If too much of the gooey stuff clogs the arteries of the penis, it can't get enough blood for a firm erection.

- Medications. Numerous prescription drugs can cause impotence as a side effect. They include cardiac medicines, antihypertensives, antidepressants, sedatives, and hormonal medications.

- Alcohol. Drinking too much can cause short- and long-term erection troubles. "Even during one evening, alcohol can immediately begin to suppress blood flow to the penis," says Gerald Hoke, M.D., chief of urology at Harlem Hospital Center in New York City. "Long-term alcoholism will change a man's testosterone level and his central nervous system, leading to erection problems."

Long-Term Solutions

So your partner is repeatedly having erection problems. What do you do? Here are several bits of sage advice.

Talk away from the bedroom. Telling yourself (and him, for that matter) not to worry, especially when the two of you are in bed, is a waste of breath, Dr. Seifer says. Instead, suggest that you talk about the problem outside of the bedroom. And remember, no mean-spirited remarks, no matter how you feel inside.

Refocus his thinking. He's hurt and embarrassed. His mind is full of phrases like "failure" and "I can't perform" and "I'm not a man anymore." You need to convince him to stop thinking about erection failure itself, and instead on the underlying cause. Failed erections are almost always a symptom of something else, perhaps as minor as work stress or as major as heart disease. Deal with the underlying issues, and the erections likely will come back, says Dr. Seifer.

Help with the diagnosis. One thing about erection problems is that they're pretty easy to figure out. Does he achieve nocturnal erections? Can he masturbate? Does the meltdown only occur at penetration? If the answer to any of these is yes, the problem is more in his mind than in his body. And the solution to that is obvious: communicating, perhaps some soul-searching, maybe counseling, says Dr. Crenshaw.

Send him to the doctor. If the two of you realize that he suddenly can't get any erections, or if he is wilting during sex for a stretch lasting more than 60 days, don't let him play denial games, cautions Dr. Crenshaw. Let him know that this is about more than just sex; it's about his health and life. Reassure him that the doctor will understand what he's talking about, even if all he mentions is feeling "run down" and "not quite himself."

The doctor will check for all age-related illnesses, such as heart disease and diabetes. If a problem is found and the doctor offers potential solutions, be sure your husband asks about potential side effects. As mentioned above, many medications can contribute to erection problems. But there are always treatment options as well as solutions to medically caused erection disorders, says Dr. Crenshaw.

Feed his penis like he feeds his heart. In the end, the penis is just another blood-engorged organ, quite similar to the heart. It needs to be treated well, just like the heart. And what's good for the heart is also good for the penis. Exercise, a low-fat diet, and a low-stress lifestyle will increase his chances of leading a longer, healthier life as well as his chances of having firm erections until the end of his days.

Take care of yourself. Erection problems likely will become an emotional issue for you, too. "I always tell my male patients that while he worries about his problem 30 to 100 times a day, he doesn't realize that she's also wondering if it's because her breasts sag a little or because her tummy is bigger," says Dr. Crenshaw.

Ultimately, a woman's response to her husband's lack of an erection will depend on her own sense of self-esteem as well as her opinion of their sex life. She may think this takes her off the hook sexually, or she may think it means she has lost her touch. The most important thing? Make sure your feelings about the situation are taken as seriously as his feelings are. "Don't let this haunt you," Dr. Seifer says. "Get it out on the table."

How a couple handles erection problems reflects the strength of their marriage. If there is closeness and openness, blame games get set aside and both partners support each other. But if communication is weak in the relationship, failed erections can magnify the problem. For example, if there are unspoken jealousies or resentments, she might incorrectly think that his limp performance is linked to his dissatisfaction with the relationship, says Dr. Seifer. In other words, the erection problem is going to end up attaching itself to any other problem that bugs you.

When Mind Rules over Matter

Performance anxiety: It's a common, obvious expression, linked most often to fumbling young guys who are so nervous in initial sexual encounters that they can't get it up. But don't believe that it's just a young man's issue, says Dr. Crenshaw. If you've found fault in something your husband has done, or if he feels threatened in some way, performance anxiety can strike anyplace, anytime.

And older gentlemen get it, too. "Sometimes we call it widower's syndrome," says Dr. Seifer. "A man hasn't dated in 30 to 40 years, his wife dies, and suddenly he's on more dates than he can handle. He finally decides to get intimate with Lady Number 7 or 9, and then he finds out that he can't get it up."

Once again, this has nothing to do with the woman he has chosen. "Don't you think his wife is in bed with the two of you?" Dr. Seifer asks her patients. "This kind of erection problem is a sign that you have yourself a good guy. He's still attached to his first partner. Just give him time to get used to the idea of sleeping with someone else."

Remember high school, when you would go out with someone for months (or maybe years) without actually having sex? Sure, you'd do "everything else," and it was great, but you didn't actually do the deed. "Great idea," says Dr. Crenshaw. "Focusing on intercourse puts a lot of pressure on both people, and very often, it's rushed in the beginning of a new relationship." So take a slow, calm, natural path to sexual intimacy—it's the best way to guarantee that when the ultimate moment comes, both of you will be completely ready, mentally and physically.

Male Menopause

It's the subject of daytime talk shows. Magazines. Best-selling books. No longer do men merely go through midlife crises, say the pundits: They experience "male menopause."

We beg to differ. Technically speaking, there is no such thing as male menopause. Here's why: Menopause means a permanent "pause" of the *menstrual* cycle. In other words, the definitive end of fertility for a woman. Men do not necessarily lose their fertility.

Nevertheless, men do experience their own particular change of life. Most medical experts today group these signs and symptoms under the term *andropause*, which means a drop in the body's production of the hormone testosterone, an androgen. Unfortunately, this, too, is a bit of a misnomer, because while testosterone levels decline as men age, the decline is usually slow and often with only mild observable effect on a man. And it rarely takes testosterone levels to zero.

If a man does show symptoms related to andropause, they certainly don't resemble the extreme mood swings and sudden hot flashes of female menopause. Instead, you're more likely to notice that your once active and vital boy-within-a-man has gradually become a bit more grouchy, with a bigger potbelly, and seems more interested in The Weather Channel than in sports, the house, or even sex. Oddly enough, you won't be able to place exactly when this change occurred.

"Hormonally speaking, when men age, they enter a gray zone for a much longer period of time than women do," says Eugene Shippen, M.D., author of *The Testosterone Syndrome*. While a woman's level of estrogen production can change dramatically in a year or two, leading to menopause, a man's production of testosterone can dwindle for a decade or more, he says.

Why Testosterone Matters

Although it's often called the male hormone, testosterone is actually found in both men and women. Throughout their lives, however, women have approximately one-tenth the amount of testosterone that men do. Women's testosterone is created in the ovaries and adrenal glands, while approximately 90 to 95 percent of a man's testosterone is created in the testicles (the adrenal glands supply the rest).

For both sexes, testosterone plays two roles in the body—that of a hormone and that of a steroid. As a hormone, testosterone in men is the blowtorch that starts the fire of sperm production, hair growth, a deepening of the voice, and the development of sexual urges and needs. As a steroid, testosterone helps strengthen bones and build muscles in both sexes (although the effect on muscles is less pronounced in women, since they secrete much less).

"Testosterone is responsible for a man's sex drive," says Roger Crenshaw, M.D., a psychotherapist and sex therapist in La Jolla, California. "It's also considered an aggression hormone, and it plays a part in his energy and intensity level."

During childhood, a boy's body doesn't produce a lot of testosterone, but you can really see the hormone do its job during puberty and adolescence. Throughout his teenage years and early adulthood, an average man's testosterone level will range from 800 nanograms per deciliter of blood (or ng/dl) to about 1,200 ng/dl. Fully grown adult men are considered to be in the normal range if their testosterone levels finally settle down anywhere between 300 ng/dl and 1,000 ng/dl.

So while you may have fallen in love with a mild-mannered, easy-going guy who has cruised through life with a testosterone level of 400 ng/dl, your best friend may have married a high-energy, competitive workaholic who has a testosterone level of 900 ng/dl. These are both typical and healthy adult levels, and no one need worry about these differences. Health and sex drive problems only arise when a man's normal level, whatever it may be, begins to drop.

How to Deal with His Changes

Testosterone levels can fall in three ways. A few guys only notice a difference in their energy levels very late in life, while a small group crash in their younger years (usually because of illness). The vast majority of men, however, experience "an accelerated slow decline," according to Dr. Shippen.

"Most of the changes that we always chalked up to the natural aging process are related to our decline in hormone levels," Dr. Shippen says. For instance, some of the first signs of a change in testosterone level are the appearance of a midlife paunch or a few gray hairs. Then, a man may begin to complain more about aches and pains as he reaches his fifties and sixties.

"The first indication most couples have of a man's serious change in testosterone level is his dwindling interest in sex," says Dr. Shippen. "But we are interested in falling testosterone levels because they can point to other serious problems regarding health, including heart disease. Falling testosterone levels can be a red flag for major diseases smoldering under the surface."

In other words, just as a woman's dwindling hormone levels can signal the increased risk of other serious problems, such as osteoporosis, a loss of testosterone may be a sign that other problems may soon develop in a man.

So what's a woman to do when her man hits his forties and no longer seems his old self?

Follow this advice.

Monitor your mate. According to Dr. Shippen, possible signs of a falling testosterone level that a wife might notice are:

- Irritability or depression

- Decreased spontaneous erections in the mornings

- Weight gain and loss of muscle mass

- Fatigue or shortness of breath

- Frequent urination during the night

- A loss of interest in activities and more sedentary behavior

- Sweating at night

If your husband is experiencing any of these symptoms, encourage him to see a doctor and get a testosterone reading. Remind him that none of these problems are inevitable signs of aging. It may be completely possible for him to regain the lost vitality and vigor of his youth.

"It's very easy to replace testosterone in the body," says Dr. Crenshaw. "Men can wear skin patches, just as women do for hormone-replacement therapy." Other options include injections, pellets, lozenges, gels, and creams.

Be vibrant . . . together. Lifestyle and diet have a tremendous effect on hormone levels. Testosterone decreases with stress, lack of exercise, drinking too much alcohol, and making poor food choices. If you're a woman who strives to eat well and exercise, encourage your partner to join you in these pursuits. It will help his health as well as your relationship, says Dr. Shippen.

"A guy who wants to live a long, sexy life needs to fill his time with healthy, life-improving habits," says Bob Francoeur, Ph.D., professor of human sexuality at Fairleigh Dickinson University in Madison, New Jersey.

Check for crisis. Many people confuse male midlife crisis with male menopause, or andropause. Midlife feelings of frustration can center around a man's job, his relationship with his wife, the children, or anything else that's important to him. "Some men reach middle age and realize they aren't going to meet their life goals," says Dr. Francoeur. "Everyone responds to these feelings differently, but this has nothing to do with the physical changes that go on throughout the body during middle age."

The most important thing you can do for your husband, and your relationship, during this time is to communicate, both verbally and sexually, how much you love him. "Let him know he's valued and attractive," says Dr. Crenshaw. "At this time in his life, a man often feels that he has supported a family for much of his life, but no one appreciates how well he has done his job."

Premature Ejaculation

Here's more proof that Mother Nature has a cruel sense of humor. Despite a woman's relatively slow sexual arousal time, from a biologist's perspective, the man who ejaculates the fastest is the superior male, since he spreads his seed most efficiently. "The premature ejaculation gene has beat the 60-minute-man gene over the course of evolution," says Roger Crenshaw,

M.D., a psychotherapist and sex therapist in La Jolla, California. "It has only been during the last 40 years that a man having an orgasm too quickly has been seen in a negative light."

Truth be told, the only reason premature ejaculation exists, even as a semi-scientific term, is because modern men want to last long enough to please their thoroughly modern partners.

Indeed, there is no agreed-upon criterion for what constitutes premature ejaculation, says Gerald Hoke, M.D., chief of urology at Harlem Hospital Center in New York City. "Any criterion that has ever been set was only used for a certain study," he notes.

In real life, what denotes premature ejaculation is different for each couple. If intercourse is not lasting long enough for you, well, then, it's not lasting long enough for you. And that's a legitimate problem.

Slowing Things Down

In the past, most men have tried to solve ejaculatory problems on their own, while most women have remained politely quiet. This may be why many of the so-called technique solutions haven't worked very well.

"Most men with a lack of ejaculatory control go from zero to 60 without stopping to enjoy the 45 to 50 miles-per-hour zone of sex," says Dr. Crenshaw. "So, for years, men have tried a number of things (wearing condoms, using anesthetic cream, running down the Yankee's lineup) to ignore the rapture they feel from being inside women. This stuff just doesn't work. Let's face it, the whole point is to enjoy the experience, not to shy away from it."

Here's the good news. If the two of you take matters into your own hands (both literally and figuratively), there's a good chance you'll soon be on a mutually satisfying timetable.

Give him time. "Ejaculatory control is most often an issue when a man is young or when a relationship is new," says Judith Seifer, Ph.D., a sex therapist and associate clinical professor at Wright State University School of Medicine in Dayton, Ohio. "Once a man has been in a long, committed relationship, he usually develops ejaculatory control."

So don't put too much pressure on a guy the first few times you are intimate. Remember, he's nervous and excited, too. "One of the greatest pleasures most men have is to see their partners have orgasms," says Dr. Crenshaw. "So give him the benefit of the doubt and let him know what works for you, even if it doesn't involve intercourse. He'll probably be happy to make sure it happens."

Set realistic expectations. Anything more than 10 minutes of vaginal penetration and thrusting is going to make someone, if not both of you, uncomfortable, says Dr. Crenshaw. Let your partner know that you aren't expecting him to last all night.

"Most men have enough control so that they can prolong their orgasms for a few minutes," Dr. Crenshaw says. "Ask your partner to slow down while you're starting to come in order to pace himself to you a little more. Tell him exactly what it is you're looking for in terms of time and technique."

Put him into training. There are many techniques a man can use to learn ejaculatory control, says Dr. Crenshaw. But the most common and effective is the simple "start-stop" method. The bonus of this method is that you can do it together, even make a game of it. Or if he's embarrassed, urge him to do it on his own and then surprise you with his progress. The idea is to stimulate the penis manually, almost to the point of ejaculation, and then stop. After he regains his composure, repeat the process—several times. Over time, he can learn to tolerate longer and longer periods of sexual stimulation. Eventually, switch from manual stimulation to intercourse, doing the same thing—lots of starting and stopping—until everyone's ready for the grand explosion.

Think foreplay and afterplay. In reality, the majority of women don't have orgasms through intercourse, so if he feels he has to prove that he can give you an orgasm through penetration, he might be setting himself up for failure.

Instead, turn your attention to foreplay and afterplay techniques that satisfy you both. Taking the emphasis off of intercourse and thrusting may, in the long run, improve the intercourse and thrusting, says Dr. Seifer.

Go back for seconds. Most men have more self-control the second time around, so take advantage of his refractory period (the time when his erection begins to fade after an orgasm).

"After you've had sex, get up, go to the bathroom if you need to, get some water, come back to bed, and cuddle," says Dr. Seifer. "Then try again in 20 minutes. It will probably last longer the next time."

Consider medication. Not long after the drug Prozac became available to treat depression, a side effect caught the attention of researchers: Prozac seemed to delay orgasm. Today, the class of selective serotonin reuptake inhibitor (SSRI) antidepressants that includes such common prescription drugs as fluoxetine (Prozac) and sertraline (Zoloft) is being prescribed for more serious premature ejaculation cases—usually, when physiology is to blame, says Dr. Hoke. "You take the pill four hours before intercourse," he explains.

The only downers? Having to plan when you're going to have sex and drowsiness afterward (a common side effect of antidepressants). But, hey, how many men don't get drowsy after sex anyway?

Aging

When we were kids, we couldn't imagine our parents doing it. Now that we're our parents' age, it's hard to imagine *not* doing it.

Surveys confirm what most of us have known all along: People over 40 *can* have sex, they *do* have sex, and they *like* to have sex. In fact, many couples report that entering midlife heralds a period of sexual rejuvenation. Midlife and late-life sex, they say, is the best they've ever had.

Maybe it's not as frequent. Maybe it's not as explosive. And, more often than not, it's punctuated by an occasional lost erection, hot flash, or back twinge. But it's more meaningful and satisfying, having been seasoned by years of shared experience, tenderness, and trust.

Midlife partners have new opportunities to explore their sexual relationship in ways that they couldn't when they were younger, says Wendy Kyman, Ph.D., a certified sex therapist and assistant professor of health education at Baruch College in New York City.

"Their kids have left the nest, so they have much more uninterrupted time for sex," Dr. Kyman says. "They're more financially secure, so they can take more weekend getaways and vacations, which are always good times for relaxed lovemaking. And there's no more worrying about an unplanned pregnancy."

Party Hardy—Again

As odd as it sounds, growing older can return you to the carefree days of your youth. "Some couples say that the sex is like when they were young, before the kids. They can spend Sunday afternoons in bed. Remember that?" says Dr. Kyman.

"Too Old for Sex" and Other Stupid Myths

When it comes to sex and aging, studies show that sexual satisfaction depends more on our beliefs about sex than on our bodies' physical changes. Here are three common myths about aging and sexuality. Don't buy into them.

Myth #1: The older we get, the less important sex becomes.

"Sexuality is from birth to death," says Wendy Kyman, Ph.D., a certified sex therapist and assistant professor of health education at Baruch College in New York City. "Broaden your definition of sexuality away from just intercourse. Think of it as holding, kissing, touching, intimacy, and sharing, in addition to intercourse."

Myth #2: If we can't have intercourse, we're not having sex.

Intercourse is wonderful, but so is oral sex and mutual masturbation and kissing and holding hands, says Dr. Kyman—and they count as sex. It's especially important to move beyond this narrow definition of sex if you or your partner has disabilities that prevent you from having intercourse, or if your partner sometimes has difficulty getting or keeping an erection.

Myth #3: It's unseemly for older people to make love.

This is the most damaging myth of all. "We never outgrow our need for love and affection," says Dr. Kyman. "Sex is an expression of intimacy between two people who love and care for each other, regardless of their ages."

That's not to say that aging has no effect on our sex lives. Growing older causes physical and hormonal changes that can affect sexual desire and performance.

As women grow older, they experience vaginal changes triggered by declining levels of the female hormone estrogen. We take longer to lubricate. The lining of our vaginas may become thin and easily irritated. And sometimes, the vagina itself becomes narrower, shorter, and less elastic. These changes can make sex uncomfortable or even painful.

Some women find that their interest in sex wanes. One possible cause: our flagging levels of testosterone, the male sex hormone that fuels sexual desire and arousal in both men and women.

Men may find that they need more direct stimulation to get an erection, or that their erections aren't as firm as they once were. They also experience longer refractory periods—intervals between ejaculations—and take longer to reach orgasm.

But while things may be slower to heat up, so to speak, couples who cope with these challenges with mutual support (and a bit of humor) may be in for the best sex of their married lives. That's because this slowdown has an up-side. Because men take longer to become sexually aroused and to get an erec-tion, there's more of an emphasis on foreplay, says Dr. Kyman.

This is to our advantage. "A woman may have asked her husband for years to slow down. Now, finally, he is," says Dr. Kyman. "And if it takes her longer to lubricate, that slowing down can be wonderful for both of them. They're finally in sync."

Strategies for Endless Love

You can stay forever young between the sheets, regardless of hormonal fluctuations, temperamental hips, backs, and knees, and other aging-related issues. These strategies can help.

Extend "playtime." If you don't lubricate as quickly as you used to, ask your husband for more foreplay, says Dr. Kyman. A few extra minutes of kissing and caresses can give you the extra time you both need to become physically aroused before intercourse. (If he's willing, oral sex works nicely, too.) Another option: vaginal lubricants, which are available at any drugstore.

Remember that variety is the spice of life. Lost that lovin' feeling? Don't accept it—take action. Varying your sexual routine can pique a dulled sexual relationship, says Saul H. Rosenthal, M.D., retired psychiatrist, former director of the Sexual Therapy Clinic of San Antonio, and author of *Sex over 40*. (For tips on how to broach this delicate topic, see Sexual Needs on page 125.)

For example, you may notice that you're too tired to make love late in the evening. The obvious solution: Try some morning (or afternoon) delight. "Making love in the morning has real advantages for men and

**Having Their
Best Sex Ever**

In a large national study of older adults, 80 percent of women and 64 percent of men reported that sex feels just as good as or better than when they were younger.

women over 40, and it can make sex a pleasure instead of a chore," says Dr. Rosenthal.

If these strategies don't fire your desire, you might consider testosterone therapy, says Dr. Rosenthal. Several studies have shown that supplementary testosterone (in patch or pill form) can significantly increase sexual arousal in postmenopausal women, especially in women whose ovaries have been removed, he says. Your doctor can explain the benefits and drawbacks.

Give him a hand. Even men who've opted to take Viagra to overcome erection problems need some kind of stimulation for the drug to work. To help your husband get an erection, manually stimulate his penis with a bit of baby oil, suggests Dr. Rosenthal. (If you're using condoms, use a lubricant made specifically for use with condoms, such as Astroglide.)

Caress his inner thighs with your fingertips. Cup his testicles in one hand as you stroke his penis with the other. Experiment with your caresses, and ask him what feels good. (Pretend you're an optometrist performing an eye exam: Is this better, or is this?) Many men find that long strokes up and down the shaft help the penis become erect, while caressing the ridge below the head of the penis encourages orgasm, says Dr. Rosenthal.

Be a tease. If your husband gets anxious when he loses his erection, try the Teasing Technique, suggests Dr. Rosenthal. Have him lie back and relax. Again, lubricate his penis with baby oil. (If you're using condoms, use a lubricant made specifically for use with condoms, such as Astroglide.) Gently run your fingertips around his penis. Then orally or manually stimulate him until he becomes erect.

When he does, keep playing—but don't let him climax and don't have intercourse. Just let his penis go back down, says Dr. Rosenthal. Repeat the "teasing" several times, with short breaks in between. "You'll both be amazed at how many times he can get erect, as long as he hasn't reached a climax," he says.

Repeat the Teasing Technique at least once a week for three or four weeks in addition to your regular lovemaking, Dr. Rosenthal says. Eventually, if he loses his erection, he'll know you can help remedy the situation.

Position yourself right. Aches and pains—even bad backs or arthritis—don't have to put a crimp in your sex life. Dr. Rosenthal recommends the following positions.

If you have hip trouble: Lie on your side, and have your husband lie behind you and enter you from behind. (Imagine that you're two spoons nestled in your silverware drawer.) For extra comfort, put a pillow between your legs. Alternatively, kneel over a piece of low furniture, such as a small footstool, and rest your knees on a pillow. Or you may kneel on the floor and lean across a bed, resting your weight on your elbows or forearms. The idea is to minimize the degree to which you have to spread your legs. Your partner then kneels and enters from behind.

If he has hip, knee, or back trouble: Have him lie on his back while you kneel over him. He can use pillows to support his knees, if he chooses.

Stretch to stay flexible. Stretching before sex will limber up your muscles, making it easier to vary positions and stay comfortable, says Bob Anderson, a physical education instructor in Palmer Lake, Colorado, and author of *Stretching.* See "Limber Up for Love" on page 404.

Don't drink away desire. While a glass of champagne may get you in the mood, more than one or two drinks can kill it, says Dr. Kyman. Alcohol is a depressant that can dampen desire and affect performance—for women as well as for men.

Check your meds. Before you blame age for your lack of desire (or his lack of erections), check the contents of your medicine cabinet. Drug manufacturers list more than 200 drugs—from antidepressants to blood pressure medications—that can affect sexual desire or performance.

Depression

༈

We all get the blues. But not everyone suffers from depression.

Depression—sadness intense enough to interfere with everyday functioning—has been described as "a soul-crushing sense of hopelessness and despair." And not only for the person who has this devastating condition. Marriages in which one partner is depressed are nine times more likely to end in divorce, says Mitch Golant, Ph.D., a clinical psychologist in Los Angeles and coauthor of *What to Do When Someone You Love Is Depressed: A Practical, Compassionate, and Helpful Guide.*

The divorce statistics are not surprising. The emotional withdrawal that often accompanies depression—the continuous sleeping, the apathetic silences—amounts to a kind of separation or "divorce." "Depressed people crawl inside themselves and hide," says Nancy Gambescia, Ph.D., a marriage and family therapist in Bryn Mawr, Pennsylvania, who teaches at the Penn Council for Relationships in Philadelphia. Other symptoms of depression, such as irritability, agitation, and feeling worthless and empty, may pull a couple farther apart.

Depression also causes a kind of physical divorce: Many people with this condition lose interest in sex. Because sex is a basic way of expressing intimacy, "the depressed partner's loss of sexual interest can leave the other partner feeling that he or she is no longer loved or desired," says Dr. Gambescia.

Mired in despair, people suffering from depression can't see how their condition affects their mates. And spouses witnessing the person they love sinking ever-deeper into despair are likely to feel frightened, frustrated, drained, and powerless to help.

If you or your mate has been fighting feelings of sadness and despair for more than a few weeks, or if either of you is having suicidal thoughts, it's time to seek professional help. And there *is* help: Approximately 80 percent of people suffering from depression get relief from therapy, medication, or both, Dr. Golant says.

If it's your husband you're worried about, don't wait for him to "snap out of it." His health—and that of your relationship—depends on taking action, says Dr. Golant.

Self-Help for the Blues and Depression

The blues are actually fairly normal. Each of us from time to time will experience a setback, a disappointment, or a loss of a loved one that may cause
us to feel sad and less energetic. It is important not to confuse normal sadness
and grief with depression, Dr. Golant says.

Usually the blues are situational and will dissipate in time. But there are
occasions when the blues can lead to depression. When and how that happens often depends on how much you ruminate on your state, Dr. Golant
says. Rumination is repetitive worry—brooding thoughts that fixate on how
poorly you are doing or how sad you are feeling and that often include re-
counting many regrets. Clearly the blues are a mood we should take seriously,
he says.

Are You Depressed?

If you or your mate has five or more of the following symptoms for
more than two weeks, consult a doctor or therapist, says Mitch Golant,
Ph.D., a clinical psychologist in Los Angeles and coauthor of *What to
Do When Someone You Love Is Depressed: A Practical, Compassionate, and Helpful Guide.* Serious depression doesn't respond to
self-help alone, he cautions.

- Feeling sad or miserable most of the time

- Losing interest in things that used to make you happy

- Losing interest in sex

- Feeling apathetic or lethargic (you don't care about anything and
  don't feel like doing anything)

- Having trouble sleeping—or sleeping too much

- Eating far more or less than usual

- Feeling restless or irritable

- Feeling helpless, hopeless, worthless, or empty

- Having difficulty thinking or concentrating

- Thinking repeatedly about death and suicide

The following are suggestions that are helpful for the blues and may also help depression. But if you or a loved one is depressed, it is important to seek professional treatment, Dr. Golant stresses.

Uplift with herbs. A yellow-flowered herb called St.-John's-wort (*Hypericum perforatum*) is considered "nature's Prozac." Several substances in this weedy-looking plant have been shown to reduce mild depression. One, hypericin, protects the brain's natural "feel-good" chemicals, such as serotonin. In studies of 3,250 women and men who used the herb, 80 percent felt improved or totally free from the debilitating low spirits of depression. A typical dosage of St.-John's-wort is one 300-milligram capsule taken three times a day with meals. St.-John's-wort can be taken for up to eight months without harmful effects. If you're fair-skinned and taking St.-John's-wort, avoid direct sunlight, as the herb may cause sun sensitivity. Do not use it with other antidepressants without medical approval. You'll find St.-John's-wort in supplement form at most pharmacies, health food stores, and supermarkets, Dr. Gambescia says.

Get moving. Take a walk or engage in some other physical activity, even if you don't feel like it, suggests Dr. Golant. Aerobic exercise, such as dancing, biking, or swimming, can relieve mild to moderate depression and enhance the treatment of more severe depression, research shows. It may be that exercise distracts from negative feelings or gives a sense of accomplishment, says Dr. Golant. Endorphins—chemicals in the brain that reduce the experience of pain and create feelings of elation—are released during exercise and may help to boost a blue mood.

Curb caffeine and sugar. If you or your spouse drinks coffee by the potful or colas by the six-pack, stop. Research shows that, for some people, a diet rich in sugar and caffeine can cause mild depression. In one study led by Larry Christensen, Ph.D., chairman of the department of psychology at the University of South Alabama in Mobile, 20 people with serious depression cut all sugar and caffeine from their diets. In three weeks, they reported feeling significantly less depressed.

Mutual Support

While the strategies above can help ease mild depression, it's equally important to have the support of a caring partner. Here's how you can help him—or how he may be able to comfort you.

Get to the Cause

Millions of men and women suffer from depression but don't seek help. Many feel that depression is a personal weakness that is best handled alone. But depression is a real medical condition—"just like diabetes," says Mitch Golant, Ph.D., a clinical psychologist in Los Angeles and coauthor of *What to Do When Someone You Love Is Depressed: A Practical, Compassionate, and Helpful Guide.*

There are a number of factors that can send you into a deep black hole, emotionally.

Setbacks and stressors. The loss of a job, a chronic illness, legal problems, or a financial setback are traumatic events that can trigger depression, explains Dr. Golant. For women, the risk factors for depression include an unhappy marriage or dissatisfaction with their roles at home or in the workplace. Men's depression typically centers around their careers, he says.

Use the power of touch. While someone in the grips of depression may avoid sex, nonsexual physical contact can be comforting, says Dr. Gambescia. If your partner is depressed, offer him a full-body massage. Or tickle his back (if he likes it). Or rub his feet. If you're feeling blue, ask your mate to hold or caress you. (It's okay to ask him to avoid touching your breasts and genitals.)

Because depression tends to deaden a person's senses, make the experience as sensual (not sexual) as possible, advises Dr. Gambescia. "Dim the lights," she suggests. "Use scented oils. Put on music that you like."

Say, "We'll get through this together." Use the communication technique of mirroring, in which you repeat what is said to you to show that you understand and empathize, says Dr. Golant. For example, if your partner says, "I'm feeling completely alone," say, "I know it feels that way. Together we can get through this lonely feeling." To a comment such as, "Life isn't worth living. Why go on?" say something like, "I know it feels that way to you right now, but I want you to know how important you are to me and the children. We'll get through this hopeless feeling together." Then steer him toward professional help.

Unresolved childhood issues. A traumatic or turbulent childhood may predispose a person to depression, Dr. Golant says.

Physical and physiological changes. Depression can be caused by inadequate amounts of the brain chemical serotonin, which regulates mood. Certain illnesses, such as thyroid deficiency and multiple sclerosis, or certain drugs, such as blood pressure medication, sleeping pills, birth control pills, and cortisone and other steroids, may also cause depression, Dr. Golant explains. The hormonal shifts following childbirth may also be a cause of depression.

Genetics. People with a family history of depression seem to be vulnerable to developing the condition themselves, says Dr. Golant.

If you or your partner is seriously depressed, you need to figure out why and get help, Dr. Golant stresses. Hoping to just shake it off won't work, he adds.

Give him the facts. If your partner denies the possibility that he's depressed, "present him with evidence," says Dr. Gambescia. "Say, 'It's been six weeks since we've made love. It's been two months since you've been out with the guys. This is hurting us. I love you, I value our relationship, and I want you to get help for us.'"

Then back off. Nagging him to get help "will just drive him farther away from you," says Dr. Gambescia.

Act if you must. If your partner's depression seems to worsen and he continues to refuse treatment, "it's your right and responsibility to get him help if he won't help himself," says Dr. Gambescia.

As a first step, you might enlist the help of your family doctor, clergyperson, or close friends or family members, says Dr. Golant.

Recharge Your Batteries

Dealing with your husband's depression can take its toll on your mental well-being, even if you're not depressed yourself. A relaxation technique like meditation can help recharge emotional batteries drained by a partner's depression, says Dr. Golant. He suggests the following five-minute exercise. (Or show this to your spouse if you're the one who's depressed.)

1. Sit or lie in a comfortable position. Take three deep breaths.

2. Now, note the point at which your breath enters your body. Is it your mouth? Your nose? Pay attention to whether your breath feels warm or cool, heavy or light, gentle or strong. Breathe in and out, staying aware of your breathing. If your mind wanders, don't worry. Just refocus on your breathing.

Secrets of Long-Lasting Love

Surviving Depression Triggered by World War II

Gertrude and Efford Goddard of Adrian, Michigan, spent 50 years together before Efford passed away in 1992. Gertrude says their biggest challenge was the depression Efford suffered after serving in World War II.

Efford and I met on the job in an Alabama textile mill. We were both just 20 years old, and we married a year later, in 1942. Going into marriage, both Efford and I knew that he would have to serve in World War II, but we were assured that it would be at least three months before he'd be sent.

Those three months turned out to be three days—we married on a Sunday, and on Wednesday, Efford received his service call. We didn't even have time to celebrate our marriage before he was gone. And it would be well over four years before we would live together again.

For the first two years, Efford was stationed in the States. We saw each other on weekends only. For the next two years, Efford was sent overseas, so we were limited to writing letters. We wrote each other faithfully each day. Sometimes I wouldn't hear from him for a while, which was tough because I always feared the worst. But eventually, I would get a stack of letters and read through them one by one.

When the war was over and Efford came home, things were still difficult

3. Now, pay attention to any tension in your body. Mentally scan yourself, starting with your chest and the in-and-out movement of your lungs as you breathe. When you find a spot of tension, perhaps in your neck, imagine that your breath can travel to that area of tension and that it is a soothing elixir that softens and eases the tightness in your neck, says Dr. Golant.

4. Continue to scan your head, neck, shoulders, arms, torso, back, thighs, and legs. Again, if your mind wanders, bring it back to your body and your breath.

for us. He experienced a lot of tragedy overseas, which really changed him. He was injured twice, and he saw his best friend get blown out of a foxhole. Our marriage had also changed. Two years is a long time to be apart, and at first we felt like strangers in each other's arms. It must have also been a shock for him to hold our two-year-old son, whom he'd never even laid eyes on before.

Efford certainly was a different man. The happy, easygoing man I married had come back bitter and depressed. A war will change anyone. It took a lot of work for us to get used to being with each other again, but we toughed it out. We made a vow to stay married until the end, so we did the best we could to make things work. We just took things day by day and loved each other.

When Efford died unexpectedly in 1992, I felt totally lost. I don't remember ever feeling as cold and alone as I did that day. I fell into a stupor for quite some time. But now I'm able to look back fondly on the 50 years we had together.

Through my marriage, I learned that it takes a lot of love to keep things working. And if I could offer one piece of advice to newlyweds, it would be to make sure you really love each other, and everything about each other.

Here are some other ways to cope with a partner's depression, says Dr. Golant.

Maintain your friendships. Your partner may be isolating himself, but you don't have to.

Keep a journal. Use a diary to give yourself positive reinforcement or simply vent without hurting your mate.

Keep living. Take a class, take up a hobby, go to movies. Your happiness and well-being matter, too.

Diets
for Better Sex

B y now, virtually everyone can recite the health benefits of eating less fat and more fresh fruits and vegetables: increased energy, a more youthful figure, and an age-defying cardiovascular profile, to name a few.

But what you may not know is that such healthy eating promotes a healthy sex life.

Following a diet that gets 30 percent or less of its daily calories from fat helps keep your arteries (and your husband's) clear of cholesterol, says E. Douglas Whitehead, M.D., associate clinical professor of urology at the Albert Einstein College of Medicine and director of the Association for Male Sexual Dysfunction, both in New York City, and author of *Viagra: The Wonder Drug for Peak Performance*. Plugged-up arteries restrict blood flow and raise blood pressure. They can also keep a man from getting an erection, since blood flowing into the penis causes it to expand and maintain an erection, Dr. Whitehead says. So switching from a high-fat to a low-fat diet can improve erectile dysfunction in some men. "Basically, what's good for the heart is good for the penis," he explains.

But clean arteries are also good for women's sexual parts. Studies show that postmenopausal women with arteriosclerosis (hardening of the arteries) are more likely to complain of low sexual desire and muted orgasms than

women without this condition, says Irwin Goldstein, M.D., professor of urology at Boston University School of Medicine. "Based on these studies, diet could well be an important factor in female sexual response, especially as women age," he says.

Fresh fruits and vegetables would also seem to safeguard our sexual vitality, says Dr. Whitehead. They're a rich source of antioxidants, compounds that protect the body from cell-damaging molecules called free radicals. There's evidence that damage from free radicals accelerates the aging process and contributes to degenerative conditions such as cancer. And the older (or sicker) you feel, the less lusty you're likely to be.

A diet rich in antioxidants, which include vitamins C and E and beta-carotene, may also reduce the risk of heart disease. This is another plus, because a strong heart keeps the body primed for frequent, energetic sex, says Dr. Whitehead.

Truly Romantic Dining

Eating healthfully at home isn't hard; you get to have meals "your way." Not so when you're dining out. Oftentimes, it's the chef's way.

It's especially hard to eat right during a romantic rendezvous at a fancy restaurant. You've entered an erotically charged atmosphere of flowers, candlelight, and long, lingering glances. Rifling through a fat-gram guide while you peruse the menu kills the mood.

But healthy dining doesn't mean forgoing a sensual gastronomic experience. You simply need to order strategically, says Janis Jibrin, R.D., a nutrition consultant in Washington, D.C. "A romantic dinner can leave you energetic and ready for love, not sluggish, gassy, or in a blue haze of garlic," she says. Here are a few of her basic rules.

1. Eat light. Menu items swimming in butter, cream sauce, or cheese can make you sluggish. These high-fat options slow digestion, thereby diverting blood flow from your brain (and genitals) to your gut. Pasta and other high-carbohydrate meals can make you sleepy. Stick to high-protein meals, which tend to increase alertness and energy. Examples: grilled or broiled chicken or fish, minus the high-fat butter or cream sauces.

2. Drink light. If you wish, have a glass of wine or champagne—or two. But no more. Alcohol depresses the central nervous system, which short-circuits sexual desire and performance.

3. Avoid garlic and gas-producing foods like beans. This tip has nothing to do with nutrition. It's just hard to be sexy with garlic breath and a rumbling gut.

Better-Sex Menus

Want to enjoy good food now and good sex later? Here's what to order and what to avoid, starting with the two most romantic of all cuisines—French and Italian, says Lynne W. Scott, R.D., director of the diet modification clinic at Baylor College of Medicine in Houston and coauthor of *The Living Heart Guide to Eating Out*.

French

Best bets: Grilled fish and vegetables. Dishes with wine sauces, such as bordelaise; they tend to be lower in fat. Avoid soaking up rich sauces with bread.

Pass up: Any menu item that contains any of the following phrases: au gratin (topped with cheese and sometimes butter); béarnaise (sauce containing butter and egg yolk); béchamel (sauce of milk, flour, and butter); crème fraîche (a tangy heavy cream); or hollandaise (sauce made with butter and egg yolks).

What to say when you order: "Can I get the sauce on the side?" "For dessert, I'd like the sorbet." (It's 125 calories, compared to crème caramel, which weighs in at 348 calories.)

Insider's tip: Butter is often added to sauces immediately before serving. So ask your server to tell the chef to hold the extra butter, says Scott.

Italian

Best bets: Pasta with chicken and vegetables. (Ask them to hold the garlic. To avoid sleepiness induced by high-carbohydrate meals, don't eat all of the pasta.) Grilled fish or chicken with vegetables. For an appetizer, choose minestrone or Italian wedding soup over the antipasto platter, which tends to feature high-fat cold cuts and cheese.

Pass up: Anything the menu describes as parmigiana (batter-fried and topped with cheese); meats cooked saltimbocca (sautéed in butter); or Alfredo (cream, butter, Parmesan cheese, and sometimes eggs).

What to say when you order: "Instead of a regular white sauce, may I have a light cream sauce?" (Or, "Please cut the cream sauce amount by half.")

Insider's tip: Some Italian restaurants now offer ravioli stuffed with pumpkin or butternut squash, instead of heavy, fatty ricotta cheese, says Jibrin. "Also, veal cutlets in a light wine sauce are fairly lean."

Chinese

Best bets: Wonton or hot-and-sour soup; steamed rice; steamed dumplings; moo goo gai pan (a combination of mushrooms, bamboo shoots, water chestnuts, and chicken, served with rice); a shrimp and vegetable stir-fry or steamed dish. For dessert, have fortune cookies and lychee (fruit in sauce).

Pass up: Egg rolls; kung pao chicken, moo shu pork, or other deep-fried dishes; dishes containing duck or fried cashews or peanuts; and fried rice.

What to say when you order: "Please cook my order with no oil, or as little oil as possible." "This dish sounds delicious. Can I get it steamed instead of stir-fried?"

Insider's tip: Rendezvous at a Cantonese restaurant, if possible. Cantonese food tends to be steamed or stir-fried. Szechuan or Hunan cuisine tends to be higher in fat, says Scott.

Indian

Best bets: Breads and meat cooked in a tandoor (special clay oven). Examples: chicken or shrimp tandoori.

Pass up: Any menu item described as ghee (clarified butter); korma (braised meat with a rich yogurt and cream sauce); malai (heavy cream or

What Makes Chocolate So Hot?

In one survey, 50 percent of women polled said they would choose chocolate over sex. Why the allure? Sure, chocolate tastes good (largely because of all that mouth-watering sugar and fat). But it also makes us feel good. Chocolate boosts levels of endorphins, chemicals that transmit energy and euphoria to our brains. And it contains phenylethylamine, a chemical nicknamed the "molecule of love" because we churn out more of it when we fall in love (and also during orgasm), says Theresa Crenshaw, M.D., in her book *The Alchemy of Love and Lust*.

But why choose chocolate over sex when you could have both? To give your after-dinner lovemaking an extra spark, indulge in one of these decadent desserts or dessert coffees. (They're not on the menu? Then hit a bakery before you hit the sheets.)

Ethnic chocolate delights:

Bittersweet chocolate soufflé, chocolate marquise, chocolate-orange pots de creme (French)

Chocolate-amaretti custard, chocolate biscotti, chocolate gelato (Italian)

Chocolate classics:

Chocolate-covered strawberries

Chocolate mousse

Death by Chocolate cake

Mississippi mud pie

Chocolate dessert coffees:

Belgian chocolate

Chocolate almond

Chocolate caramel truffle

Chocolate hazelnut

Chocolate macaroon

Chocolate orange

White chocolate mousse

cream sauce); or pakora (deep-fried dough with vegetables). Also, avoid the appetizers called samosas (deep-fried pastry filled with meat and vegetables) and poori (deep-fried bread).

What to say when you order: "I'd like the (chicken or shrimp) tandoori. And please ask the chef not to brush it with oil or ghee while it's cooking."

Insider's tip: Avoid entrées with sauces, such as biryanis and curries. Because sauces are prepared ahead of time, they can't be specially made with less fat, says Scott.

Mexican

Best bets: Vegetable burrito (minus the refried beans) on a soft tortilla; rice; soft corn or flour tortillas; red or green salsa; fajitas; soft tacos; grilled or marinated chicken breast without skin; or fish.

Pass up: Tortilla chips; chimichangas; dishes made with sour cream, guacamole, and cheese; chorizos (spicy sausages).

What to say when you order: "Might we get some soft flour tortillas to dip in this salsa, instead of the fried tortilla chips?"

Insider's tip: Ask if the restaurant has "off the menu" items such as grilled fish or chicken breast. Some are willing to make food to order, says Scott.

Exercise for Better Sex

In a woman's quest for ultra-satisfying sex, which outfit is most likely to deliver the goods?

a. A slithery number from the Victoria's Secret catalog

b. A sweaty T-shirt, faded sweatpants, and worn-out sneakers (your usual workout attire)

If you guessed b., you're right (although we'd suggest buying some Odor-Eaters for those sneakers). Research on the effect of exercise on sexual desire suggests that people who work out have more sex and enjoy it more.

Limber Up for Love

Stretching often will give you the flexibility to vary positions and stay comfortable during sex, says Kathleen Berglund, a physical therapist at K Valley Orthopedics in Kalamazoo, Michigan. Perform this quick series of stretches several times a week and before you make love, she suggests.

Quad stretches. Whether it's you or your husband, the partner who takes the top position needs strong, flexible muscles on the fronts of the thighs. To stretch these muscles, kneel on a bed or the floor, with your thighs perpendicular to it. Your legs should be shoulder-width apart, toes pointed behind you, hands positioned in front of your thighs. Lean backward slowly until you feel the stretch in the front of your thighs and in your ankles. Hold for 15 to 20 seconds. Repeat two or three times.

Another way to stretch the quads is to stand, bend one knee, and grasp the ankle of the bent leg. Try to push the thigh behind you. Hold for 15 to 20 seconds. Repeat two or three times.

Groin stretches. Especially in women, the muscles in the hips and around the pelvis need to stay flexible, says Berglund. To keep them loose, lie on your back with the soles of your feet together, knees bent and out to each side. Pull your heels toward your groin. Now, let your knees slowly drop toward the bed or floor. (To help them along, put your hands on your inner thighs and apply slight downward pressure.) Hold the stretch for 30 seconds.

"Sex is a physical activity, so it's not surprising that something that affects our bodies like exercise also affects our sexuality," says Linda De Villers, Ph.D., a sex therapist in El Segundo, California, and author of *Love Skills: More Fun Than You've Ever Had with Sex, Intimacy, and Communication.*

The Sex Lives of the Fit and Sweaty

Exercise helps you to stay in shape and prevent illness. But research shows that it also enhances our emotional well-being and our desire for sex.

Dr. De Villers asked more than 8,000 women ages 18 to 49 about the

To help your husband stretch his groin muscles, kneel facing your mate as he sits in front of you on the floor or bed, your knees barely touching the tops of his ankles to keep them from moving. Now, put your hands on either side of his inner thighs, just above his knees, and apply downward pressure until he feels the stretch in his hips and groin. His knees may move slightly downward. (It shouldn't hurt.) Have him hold the stretch for 30 seconds. To further stretch your groin muscles, reverse roles and positions.

Lower-back stretches. This stretch is especially beneficial for folks who have back problems, says Daniel Hamner, M.D., a physiatrist and visiting lecturer for the department of physical medicine at New York Hospital in New York City. Lie on your back. Hold the back of your bent left knee with your left hand and pull your knee toward your chest. Hold the stretch for 30 seconds. Switch legs and repeat. Now do both legs at the same time. Be careful to let your legs down easily. (If you or your husband has had back trouble, it's a good idea to check with your doctor before trying this stretch.)

To help stretch your mate's lower back, face him as he lies on his back and put your hand on his leg, just below the front of his knee, and gently push his bent knee to his chest, says Berglund. When he feels the stretch, have him hold the position for 30 seconds. Repeat with his other knee. Then push both of his knees to his chest. He, in turn, can help you do this stretch.

effect of exercise on sex drive. Of those surveyed, 40 percent noticed that after beginning a regular exercise program, they became more easily aroused. And 31 percent noticed that they had sex more often. "Exercise gives women a sexual second wind," she says.

Jo Marie Kessler, R.N.P., a nurse practitioner in San Diego and a certified sex therapist, routinely advises sedentary women with low sexual desire to add exercise to their program. "After a while, as the benefits of exercising enhance the rest of the treatment, they find that they're more receptive to sex and might start initiating it themselves."

Among the many benefits of exercise, experts cite these.

It gets the blood pumping. The link between sex and exercise has been studied for years by James White, Ph.D., professor emeritus of physical education at the University of California, San Diego. In a landmark study, Dr. White had 78 men follow a moderate aerobic regimen four times a week. After nine months, the men reported that they had sex 30 percent more often and achieved 26 percent more orgasms. (They also deep-kissed their partners 20 percent more often.) Dr. White says that these findings probably apply to women as well.

Dr. White's research shows that as fitness levels improve, so does cardio-vascular endurance—a prerequisite for the physical rigors of sex for men and women alike. Exercise also increases the circulation of blood to every part of the body, including the genitals. Just as better circulation improves a man's capacity to sustain an erection, it enhances a woman's vaginal lubrication and the swelling of her clitoris, he explains.

It increases desire. Exercise increases the body's production of the sex hormone testosterone, which fuels the libido of men and women. "For women, even a slight increase in testosterone caused by exercise can posi-tively affect arousal," says Dr. White.

It increases self-esteem. Having a strong, fit body gives women a sense of power, self-confidence, and control, says Kessler. "Exercise has also been clinically proven to reduce stress and depression, two common causes of low sexual desire." What this all adds up to, she says, is that the more you like yourself, the more likely you are to enjoy making love.

It helps you love your body. Regular exercise also increases our awareness of our bodies—and increases our respect for what they can do, says Dr. De Villers. In one study of 212 college students, researchers at the University of Arkansas found that women and men who exercised had more positive body images than those who did not. "An improved body image can help women feel more comfortable about being sexual," Dr. De Villers points out.

The Bare-Bones Program

To get the benefits mentioned above, you need to engage in aerobic ex-ercise at least three times a week for at least 20 minutes at a time, says Eric Gronbech, Ph.D., professor of physical education at Chicago State Univer-sity. He defines aerobic exercise as any moderately intense activity that uses the whole body, elevates your heart rate, and works up a sweat, such as jog-ging, cycling, or tennis. Most experts recommend that you exercise in "doses" of 20 minutes at a time.

On the days that you don't engage in aerobic exercise, consider weight lifting, suggests Dr. White. Resistance training is the best and fastest way to build muscle and burn fat, both of which can improve your physical strength and body image, he says.

Before long, you'll find that you have increased energy and desire for sex, says Dr. De Villers. If you exercise in the early morning, you might want to crawl back into bed and give your guy an extra-special wake-up call.

"His testosterone level is at its highest at that time of the day, and by working out, you've just boosted your own testosterone level as well," says Dr. Gronbech. "So early morning can be an ideal time to make love."

Special Exercises for "Love Muscles"

Performed daily, the following exercises can improve the strength and flexibility of muscles used when you're making love, such as those in the hips and abdomen, says Dr. Gronbech.

Power up your pelvis. Your hips power the thrusting motions of sex, so it's important to keep them flexible. Pelvic tilts can help. To do them, lie on your back on a soft mat or towel with your knees bent and your hands be-hind your head. Keep your back pressed to the ground. Tighten your buttock muscles, lift your pelvis without lifting your back off the ground, hold the mo-tion for five seconds, and relax. Repeat 5 to 10 times, eventually working up to 25 tilts, suggests Dr. Gronbech.

Make like a cat. These "cat back" stretches also help keep the hips flex-ible, says Dr. Gronbech. Get on your hands and knees. Slowly let your back and abdomen sag toward the floor. Now, slowly arch your back away from the floor. (Imagine a cat stretching after a long nap.) "You should feel the stretch in the lower part of your abdomen down to the pubic area," he says. Repeat 5 to 10 times, eventually working up to 25 repetitions.

Strengthen your abs. Strong abdominal muscles also power the thrusting motion used during sex, says Dr. Gronbech. (As a bonus, they help hold your belly in.) Abdominal crunches can get your abs in shape. Lie on your back, knees bent, feet flat on the floor and hip-width apart. Be sure to tuck your chin toward your chest. Place your hands on your shoulders, waist, or across your chest. The higher your hands are positioned on your body, the greater the resistance will be. Now lift your head, neck, and shoulders off the floor and slowly curl toward your navel. Hold this position for several seconds, then lower slowly. Start with 10; work up to 20 repetitions.

Do the ultimate sexercise. Some women find that regular exercise of the pubococcygeal (PC) muscles—the tiny muscles that run from the pubic bone to the tailbone—can lead to stronger, more intense orgasms, says Dr. De Villers. To locate your PC muscles (sometimes called the pelvic floor muscles), stop and start your flow of urine. To do the exercise—called Kegels—squeeze the PC muscles for 10 seconds and breathe regularly. Relax them. Repeat 10 times. Next, squeeze the muscles as fast as possible 10 to 25 times. Repeat. You can repeat these slow and fast squeezes two or three times a day.

Men should practice short Kegels by squeezing and then immediately relaxing their PC muscles, Dr. De Villers says. Your guy should do this quick release 15 times twice a day, and gradually increase the number of squeezes to about 75 twice a day. When he can do this comfortably, he can try a variation. Instead of immediately releasing the contraction, he should hold it for three seconds. Since these are a bit more difficult, he should work up to about 50 of these long Kegels. A good approach, then, would be to do one set of quick (as fast as you can) squeezes followed by one set of long (holding for 3 seconds) squeezes each day.

Fatigue

One thing's for sure: You're healthy.

You know this because you've been tested for all the medical conditions that can cause tiredness. Chronic fatigue syndrome. Thyroid problems. Low blood pressure. Multiple sclerosis. Anemia. You even took a pregnancy test.

But still, you're tired. So tired. Especially tired, it seems, any time your husband nuzzles your neck and strokes your thigh—his little preludes to love.

He's tired, too. Tired of hearing you say, "Not tonight, honey."

Time It Right

If a doctor has pronounced you physically healthy but you're still too tired for sex, a simple adjustment or two in your routine can jump-start your sex life. Here's what experts recommend.

Rev your desire. Take a brisk walk with your partner, and chances are you'll *both* be more energetic in bed. Walking briskly for just 10 minutes a day can boost mood and raise energy levels for up to two hours, according to a study by Robert Thayer, Ph.D., professor of psychology at California State University, Long Beach.

Synchronize your schedules. Sometimes all it takes to enjoy wide-awake sex once again is to accommodate one another's body clocks, says Nancy Gambescia, Ph.D., a marriage and family therapist in Bryn Mawr, Pennsylvania, who teaches at the Penn Council for Relationships in Philadelphia. For example, if your partner is a night owl but you're an early bird, take a brief nap when you get home from work or after dinner. By the time you're ready for bed, you'll really *be* ready for bed. Don't nap for more than an hour, though, or you'll throw your sleep cycle out of whack, cautions Dr. Gambescia.

Try some morning delight. If you're an early bird, try making love in the morning. The stresses and demands of the day are still in front of you, and the early-morning silence is a prime time to connect with each other. Set the alarm clock for an hour earlier, so you'll have time to cuddle before and after sex.

Infertility

At 29, Jean Smits married. At 30, she and her husband, John, set out to get pregnant. "We did what everyone does—we stopped using birth control," says the executive director of a women's health nonprofit organization in Philadelphia.

Eighteen menstrual periods later, the couple started infertility treatment. More than six million men and women of childbearing age face infertility,

a problem of the reproductive system that keeps them from conceiving. Infertility is one of the most distressing life crises a couple can face, stirring up
painful feelings of anger, guilt, and depression. Infertility can also cause a
couple to feel isolated, both from each other and from a world seemingly
filled with happy parents and their children.

Jean and John pursued infertility treatment for a year. It was expensive,
time-consuming, frustrating, and—ultimately—unsuccessful. But five months

New Hope for Infertile Couples

Many couples turn to high-tech procedures to make a baby. And in some
cases, they hit the jackpot: a healthy baby of their very own.

These methods don't come cheap, however, and they can cause enormous emotional stress. And, ultimately, they may not work. Only you and
your husband can decide whether the "grand prize"—a longed-for child—
is worth putting your time, money, and emotions on the line.

Here's a brief overview of the most commonly used high-tech procedures.

Donor insemination (DI). Commonly performed when a woman is fertile
but her partner's semen contains little or no sperm, DI is considered the
least expensive and simplest infertility treatment. In DI, sperm from another
man (the donor) is injected into a woman's cervix or uterus near the time of
ovulation in the hope that an egg will be fertilized. This method costs about
$250 to $300 per treatment. Most women who get pregnant using DI do
so in the first three to six cycles. Success rate: 8 to 15 percent per attempt.

A child born using DI will be genetically related to the woman but not her
husband. This can cause emotional repercussions for both. A man's self-esteem may be shaken, or he may fear that his infertility will cause his wife to
leave. A woman may feel anger toward her husband for being infertile. These
issues should be discussed—and resolved—before proceeding with DI.

In vitro fertilization (IVF). This method is often used when a woman
has blocked fallopian tubes or endometriosis, or when her husband is infertile. In IVF, a woman's ovaries are stimulated with drugs. A few days

after her last infertility treatment, they finally got their baby. Their adopted son, Max, was born September 12, 1995—Jean's 33rd birthday.

The pain of being unable to have her own child will probably never completely fade, Jean says. But from the pain came wisdom—and a sense of their strength as a couple. "As painful as the experience was, it taught my husband and me that we could deal with adversity," she says. "Having to work through it—together—was good for us."

---

before ovulation, a doctor "harvests" the ripened eggs using a hollow needle and a suction device. They're then mixed with sperm in a glass dish to fertilize them. If fertilization takes place, one or more fertilized eggs (called embryos) are transferred through the cervix and into the uterus with a long, thin tube. A single attempt with IVF averages $8,000 to $10,000, but more than one attempt is often necessary. Success rate: 10 to 60 percent.

Gamete intrafallopian transfer (GIFT). As with IVF, GIFT begins with fertility drugs to stimulate the ovaries. But unlike IVF, the eggs are collected, mixed with sperm, and injected into the fallopian tube or tubes in one surgical procedure. This way, fertilization occurs in its natural environment instead of in a glass dish. Candidates for this method include women with unexplained infertility or mild endometriosis, or women whose husbands have poor sperm quality. The cost of one attempt is from $8,000 to $13,000. Success rate: about 25 percent.

Zygote intrafallopian transfer (ZIFT) and tubal embryo transfer (TET). In ZIFT, eggs are collected through the vagina and fertilized in a dish. The next day, the zygotes (fertilized eggs that have not yet divided) are surgically placed into the fallopian tubes. In some cases, the egg is allowed to divide before being placed into the fallopian tube, a procedure known as tubal embryo transfer. Doctors recommend these procedures if a woman's egg quality is poor, or if GIFT hasn't worked. The cost is from $10,000 to $13,000. Success rate: about 25 percent.

Unfulfilled "Baby Lust"

Infertility, defined as the inability to conceive after having unprotected sex for a year, is a growing problem in this country, especially for older women. At least 20 percent of women wait until they're 35 to begin a family. The problem is that women (and men) become less fertile as they age.

About 40 percent of infertility problems are traced to causes within the man. Male infertility can result from low sperm count (the percentage of sperm per milliliter of semen), a decrease in sperm motility (the percent of sperm who are good swimmers), or poor sperm morphology (the shape of the sperm, which allows it to penetrate the egg).

Another 40 percent of infertility problems are attributed to causes within the woman. Her fallopian tubes—the pathway from the egg-bearing ovaries to the womb—may be blocked, which prevents her eggs from being fertilized. Ovulation can be affected by hormonal imbalances, thyroid disorders, or chronic diseases such as diabetes. Endometriosis (where rogue bits of uterine lining stray outside the womb) and sexually transmitted diseases can also cause conception problems.

About 20 percent of infertility problems are attributed to both the man and the woman, or are unexplained.

Most couples facing infertility choose to see a reproductive endocrinologist, who specializes in the treatment of hormonal and infertility problems. Between 85 and 90 percent of infertility cases are treated with medication or surgery. But being prepared to cope with the human component of infertility is as important to your relationship as understanding the high-tech treatment options.

When Sex Is Work

Making love is one way a couple communicates. When the relationship is going well, sex is an expression of love and closeness. But the stress of dealing with infertility can turn sex into, well, a chore.

"For both partners, sex can become a mechanical act," explains Andrea Mechanick Braverman, Ph.D., director of psychological services for Pennsylvania Reproductive Associates in Philadelphia. What's more, infertility treatment often means that making love is dictated by charts and timetables, rather than desire. "It takes away spontaneity," says Dr. Braverman. "A couple thinks, 'We have to do it tonight, this is our only chance.'"

Knowing that you or your husband is the primary cause of the infertility can trigger guilt that makes it hard to feel sexual, says Dr. Braverman. "Some people may even think, 'My body can't make babies, so what's the point of having sex?'"

It's inevitable that infertility will affect a couple's sex life to some degree, says Dr. Braverman. But it doesn't have to completely demolish it—if you and your husband take time to enjoy sex for sex's sake. Giving each other a massage, going out for a romantic dinner, or taking in a movie can help make life a little more fun. And having fun together will remind you both that making love can be an enjoyable experience—on a schedule, or off.

Why Won't He Talk about It?

Men and women express their feelings about their infertility, and react to it, in different ways, says Dr. Braverman. So it's important to understand how it can influence the way a couple communicates.

For example, men may avoid talking about infertility or the treatment to protect themselves and their wives from pain. What they don't realize is that women "get a lot out of processing their thoughts and feelings about the situation," says Dr. Braverman. "Women, in turn, assume that because men don't want to talk about the problem, they don't care."

Usually, that assumption is incorrect. "Men were raised to protect and care for and make things happen for their partners," Dr. Braverman says. "And infertility is an area in which men can do absolutely nothing."

Dealing with infertility becomes harder still when a close friend has a baby, or when you hear that a family member is pregnant—or even when you see commercials for baby wipes on television. "When we were trying to get pregnant, most of my friends conceived," says Jean. "At first, I chose not to tell them—or anyone—because I was afraid they wouldn't understand. Most people just don't understand how emotionally difficult it is not to be able to get pregnant."

Men may resent that their wives spend all of their emotional energy on getting pregnant. "John was supportive, and he understood that I was in pain, but he really wanted us to go on with our lives," Jean says. "He kept saying,

'Getting pregnant isn't the only thing in life. We can still create a life for our-selves without having children.'"

As in most situations, the best way to get your needs met is to respect his. This means letting your husband know you need to talk and asking if he can hear you out. But it also means understanding the times your husband needs to *not* talk about the issue—and respecting his feelings. "The goal isn't to make the other partner have the same needs," says Dr. Braverman. "It's to have each of you get your needs met."

Coping Together

As you and your husband struggle with infertility, try the following ex-pert-recommended suggestions. They can help you to stay close, seek other sources of support, and get through the bad times.

Remember the big picture. While you're trying to create a new life, don't forget to live your own. If you think of nothing but getting pregnant, you need to refocus on your relationship and the qualities that drew you to-gether in the first place. "Couples need to realize that they fell in love with each other, not just a set of ovaries or testicles," says Dr. Braverman.

Have just-for-fun sex. If making love according to charts and time-tables has taken the spontaneity out of sex, stir it up a little. If you're sup-posed to do it on a Thursday at 6:00 A.M., do it on the kitchen table—or the washing machine.

Present a united front. Discuss how you and your partner would like to reply to well-meaning but often insensitive comments from family and friends, suggests Dr. Braverman. You can tell the truth or keep it private. For example, to the question, "When are you going to start a family?" or "When am I going to be a grandmother (or grandfather, aunt, or uncle)?" you might say, "We've been trying to have a child, but we have an infertility problem." Or: "We consider ourselves a family now. If we decide to expand our family, we'll be sure to let you know."

Take care of your body. Continue to eat right and exercise—not just to improve your chances of conception, but to protect your self-esteem, says Dr. Braverman. "I see women with fertility problems gain weight to punish themselves," she says. "They think, 'I feel crummy about myself, so I might as well eat.' Don't fall into this trap."

Seek support. Find an infertility support group, suggests Dr. Braverman. "Finding other couples who are struggling with infertility is what helps the most," says Jean, who, with her husband, began attending meetings while they were in treatment. "I could say, 'Sometimes I'm walking to work and I feel like I see 50 pregnant women,' and someone else would say, 'Yes, I've felt like that, too.'" And John? "He was able to hear that I wasn't crazy, that the other women had the same tensions and struggles."

Seek counseling, if necessary. If you have isolated yourself from family or friends, experience ongoing depression or anxiety, or have trouble eating, sleeping, or concentrating, consult a therapist with experience counseling infertile couples, says Dr. Braverman.

When to Say When

You've been trying to get pregnant for a year. Two years. Five years. When do you call it quits?

That's one of the most difficult decisions a couple pursuing infertility treatment can make, says Dr. Braverman. "For each couple, that turning point is different," she says. Some couples find that it's easier, emotionally, to continue treatment and keep hope alive. Others opt to stop their treatments, grieve, and go on.

If you're considering ending treatment, there are steps you and your husband can take to help you finalize the decision.

Set a deadline. You might decide to try for another year—or another three months. Or you might choose to take a short "vacation" from treatment, so you can decide whether you want to continue or stop. Whatever you decide, establishing a time frame can give you a measure of much-needed control.

Find others who've been there. Talk to other couples who ultimately decided to end treatment, especially if you are undecided. Ask them how they made the decision and how they feel about it now.

Consider your options. You may decide to adopt or to remain childless. Either way, expect the pain of infertility to linger for a while, says Dr. Braverman. "It's a process of letting go—you grieve, and eventually you work through it."

Major Health Problems

ouples living with a major illness such as diabetes, heart disease, or cancer often struggle with sexual problems. Sometimes, they give up on sex entirely.

This is too bad, because our sexual feelings and our need for physical closeness don't end when we get sick. If anything, they become more important.

The stresses of coping with a major illness, such as pain, health-insurance hassles, tests or surgery, and the side effects of powerful drugs, can make us feel less than human. Physical intimacy—a touch of the hand, a gentle embrace, the comfort of skin-to-skin contact with the one you love most—breaks through the isolation. It makes us feel human again. It says, "I love you, and you are not alone."

Besides, having a major illness doesn't have to draw the curtains on your sex life. If you can challenge your old assumptions about sex and explore new ways of giving and receiving pleasure, sex can be as passionate as ever, says Jackson Rainer, Ph.D., associate professor of psychology at Gardner-Webb University in Boiling Springs, North Carolina, who counsels couples facing chronic diseases.

It's helpful, for example, to let go of the belief that sex doesn't count unless it includes intercourse, or that being sick causes us to lose our sexuality. "We're raised to believe that our sexuality rests between our legs," says Dr. Rainer. "But actually, it rests between our ears. Sexuality is an energy. It includes any activity that attracts us, that warms us, that feels healing and loving."

Desire Dampeners

Of course, it's not fair to expect that a major health problem will have no effect on a couple's sexuality or level of intimacy.

For one thing, long-term illnesses can cause discomfort or pain. "Pain robs people of their ability to experience sexual pleasure and to connect emotionally with their partners," says Dr. Rainer.

An illness can also cause physical changes that short-circuit the "wiring" needed to have sex or experience sexual pleasure. Some examples:

- Diabetes can cause nerve and blood vessel damage that can dull a woman's genital sensations—affecting her ability to climax—or a man's ability to get an erection.
- Nausea and fatigue caused by cancer treatments such as radiation, chemotherapy, and surgery commonly reduce sexual desire.
- Multiple sclerosis can damage nerves that send signals to the genitals. This damage can interfere with vaginal lubrication in women, cause erection problems in men, and make it harder to reach orgasm in both sexes.

A long-term illness affects our emotions, too. When we're frightened and in pain, we spend our emotional energy on coping. There's just none left for sex. Negative feelings stirred up by being sick or tending an ill partner, such as depression, guilt, and anger, can also dampen desire, says Dr. Rainer.

If an illness causes a major physical change in our appearance—the loss of a breast, testicle, or limb, for example—we may believe that we lose our "right" to be sexual. And so we may stop feeling turned on, or we may turn away from our mate.

It doesn't have to be this way.

Redefine (and Revive) Sex

Typically, we regard the "appetizers" of sex—the kissing and cuddling, bubble baths and pillow talk—as less important than the main dish of intercourse.

But intercourse and orgasm are only one small part of our sexuality, which entails the countless ways in which we experience and express our sexual feelings, says Dr. Rainer. When you give and receive sexual pleasure, you're having sex, and it doesn't matter how.

Don't expect to give up the intercourse-is-best way of thinking overnight, says Dr. Rainer. It will take time. But when you love each other, you make room for other expressions of your love, he says. "Once you do that, you'll want to do it out of tenderness. And when you find that tenderness, you'll find your sexuality."

What follows is a condition-by-condition guide to five major health problems. It explains how each can affect sexuality and offers practical ways to express sexual feelings that don't involve intercourse. Most important, you'll discover that you can keep or regain sexual intimacy in the shadow of chronic illness. (Read the tips suggested for each illness, not just your own. What works for one condition may work for another.)

Arthritis

In osteoarthritis, the most common form of arthritis, the cartilage that covers the ends of bones deteriorates, causing bone to rub against bone. This friction causes pain and swelling of the joints, most commonly in the hips, knees, and back. This pain and swelling also limits flexibility, which can make sex difficult.

Effects on women's sexuality: Many women with arthritis lose interest in sex, says Dr. Rainer. It's not hard to see why: Being in physical pain doesn't exactly get the sexual juices flowing.

Effects on men's sexuality: Same as for women.

Better-sex tips for women: If possible, treat yourself (and your mate) to a hot tub. Water's soothing warmth and buoyancy can relieve joint pain and stiffness. (It's also an ideal place to cuddle, talk, or fool around.) If you have lung or heart disease, diabetes, or high or low blood pressure, or have undergone joint replacement, don't use a hot tub without asking your doctor first.

If you're never in the mood, talk to your doctor. Medications prescribed for arthritis, such as prednisone or muscle relaxers, can affect sex drive and the ability to climax. You may be able to take another medication that works just as well, but that doesn't dampen your libido.

Don't let a negative body image cheat you out of great sex. To feel better about your body, pamper it. Take scented bubble baths. Sleep on satin sheets. Treat yourself to a massage. (Ask your partner if he might serve as your masseur.) And if your doctor says it's okay, exercise regularly. Working out often makes people feel stronger, both physically and mentally.

Plan your sexual rendezvous. Time your medication so that it peaks during the time you're in bed. (If you take pain medication every 12 hours, for example, plan to be 4 to 6 hours into a dose.) Turn on the electric blanket so the sheets are toasty-warm, then unwind with a warm bath or shower together.

Better-sex tips for your guy: If your mate has arthritis and seems angry, frustrated, or embarrassed by its effect on his sexual performance, assure him that there's more than one way to have sex. "Remind him that the brain is the best sex organ and the skin is the biggest," says Dr. Rainer.

Making sex better together: Use a "pain scale" of 1 to 10 to regulate your level of sexual intimacy based on how much pain you're in. "Pain is a subjective experience," notes Dr. Rainer. "If your only choices are yes and no, that's a scale of 1 to 2. On a scale of 1 to 10, you have more room to negotiate. You can say, 'I'm at a 2 today; let's go for it!' or 'I'm at 7, but I'd love to hold and kiss you.'"

If your favorite sexual positions are painful, try new ones. The following positions are suggested for men and women with arthritis.

If you have hip problems: Lie on your side, facing away from your partner. Your partner then enters from behind. For added comfort, put a pillow between your knees.

If he has hip or knee problems: Try straddling your partner while he lies on his back.

If he has back problems: Lie on your side, facing your partner. (He should be facing you, too.) You'll need to supply most of the hip movement.

If you have lower-back or knee problems: Lie on your back, with a pillow under your hips and thighs. Your husband supports his weight on his hands and knees.

Cancer

Being diagnosed with cancer—then living with it—can be emotionally devastating, says Dr. Rainer. Both men and women can experience an emotional shutdown that kills their desire for sex. Cancer treatments such as radiation, chemotherapy, and potent drugs also affect sexual desire and performance.

Effects on women's sexuality: Cancer is a known libido-killer. Worry, depression, and nausea from cancer treatment or medications can cause loss of desire, as can pain from pelvic surgery, radiation treatment, or chemotherapy. If a woman's ovaries are surgically removed or damaged by chemotherapy, the resulting sudden loss of estrogen can cause her vagina to become dry and tight, one symptom of sudden menopause. She may also experience hot flashes and lose all desire for sex.

Effects on men's sexuality: Men, too, are likely to lose their desire for sex, says Dr. Rainer. Men with cancer of the bladder, penis, testicles, or prostate may also have trouble getting an erection, ejaculating, and reaching orgasm, or they may not be able to have intercourse at all.

Secrets of Long-Lasting Love

Magic from Beginning to End

Dottie Zeigler of Zelienople, Pennsylvania, shared 46 wonderful years with her husband Kenneth before he passed away in 1991. From their initial encounter to their last moments together, they surrounded each other with love and admiration. Her two children call it magic; Dottie calls it love.

I remember everything about Ken very vividly. We met outside a hotel in Washington, D.C., on Saturday, October 6, 1945, at 6:00 in the evening. I was meeting a friend, and Ken, who was in the Marines, was leaving to go to a party with some officers. Our eyes met, and he walked over to me and asked me to go to the party. There was something about him, and from that first glance, I was completely taken by him. So I accepted his invitation, and we went to the party.

We spent the next day together. That was a Sunday, and that was also the day that Ken proposed to me. On Monday, we were in his hotel room, and I accepted both his proposal for marriage as well as his proposal for intimacy. It was crazy, but Ken and I knew we were right for one another. We married the following Saturday.

From the beginning, we had complete trust in each other. On the Sunday after we met, Ken and I told each other everything there was to tell about ourselves. Since that Sunday afternoon, we had nothing to hide from each other.

Better-sex tips for women: If the missionary position hurts, try positions that let you control the movement. The woman-on-top position often works well. Or you and your partner can try lying on your sides, either face to face or in a "spooning" position.

If you have had a mastectomy and aren't ready to expose the scar during intercourse, consider wearing a brief nightgown or camisole, or a bra with a prosthesis inside.

The honesty we had at the start of our relationship really set things in place for the rest of our years together. If we had an argument or something was bothering one of us, we talked about it immediately. At times, it was difficult to make up. But we figured that life is too short to waste time and energy being angry and distant with each other, so we dealt with the problem and then moved on.

In 1984, my husband had a stroke that took his sight and left him with numb, prickly pain in his hands and face. Even though this was tragic, believe it or not, our love for each other became much stronger. Our relationship suddenly faced this new challenge, and we had to change with it. In marriage, you have to be willing to change for the person you love, and if you do, the payoff is just wonderful.

It was a difficult time for Ken because he had always been so active, and now his abilities were limited. But we shared in ways that we could. I would read to him, or we would listen to music. Sometimes we would just talk. I had such admiration for this man: He was in constant pain, but he continued to love me and stay positive.

Later, Ken developed cancer in some of his facial glands that eventually killed him. But for both of us, Ken's death was just as beautiful as our beginning. We were together. Our eyes were locked, and he passed away. And even though Ken is gone, I'm still very much in love with him.

Orgasms Survive Cancer

Cancer treatments, including chemotherapy and pelvic radiation, almost never affect a woman's ability to reach orgasm.

If you've had a colostomy, consider buying or making a cover for your colostomy bag. A pretty cover can make the bag look less "medical." Some women sew covers to match their favorite lingerie.

Better-sex tips for your guy: If your mate is having trouble getting an erection, encourage him to talk to his doctor. There are several ways to treat erectile dysfunction, including injections of certain medications into the penis, penile implants, or the FDA-approved oral drug Viagra.

Viagra is taken on an as-needed basis, about an hour before sex. In clinical studies, 50 to 70 percent of men taking this medication said the quality of their erections improved, as did their overall sexual satisfaction.

While it may be against a man's instincts to talk about his problems, especially sexual problems, encourage him to open up. The more openly he can talk about the changes in his sexual functioning, the more likely he is to seek help for the problem, says Dr. Rainer.

Making sex better together: Be patient and flexible with each other. The things you used to do in bed may no longer be possible or practical. If you have always been the more assertive lover, for example, your mate may have to take the initiative, at least temporarily. If you've always enjoyed the rear-entry position but it causes discomfort now, explore other positions. (You may discover a new favorite.) And if you've always had vigorous sex, explore how being a more tender lover feels.

It seems obvious, but when you feel angry, sad, or vulnerable, tell your partner. Learning to express and respond to such negative feelings can strengthen your trust in each other, which can increase intimacy and make it easier to be sexually playful.

Diabetes

With diabetes, the pancreas either doesn't make enough insulin or it makes too much. This hormone helps ferry sugar from food from the bloodstream into the cells, where it's used for energy. Most people with diabetes produce insulin, but it doesn't work normally. Blood sugar—glucose—builds up in the blood, eventually damaging the nerves, blood vessels, heart, kidneys, and eyes.

Effects on women's sexuality: Poor blood sugar control can affect a woman's estrogen levels, causing scanty vaginal lubrication. Chronically high blood sugar can also lead to chronic yeast and urinary tract infections—another cause of painful intercourse—or loss of genital sensation, which can make it harder to climax. Needless to say, such problems can reduce a woman's enthusiasm for sex.

Effects on men's sexuality: Between 50 and 60 percent of men with diabetes over the age of 50 have trouble getting erections, says Stanley Feld, M.D., former president of the American Association of Clinical Endocrinologists. Nerve and blood vessel damage is commonly to blame. Either the penis can't respond to the brain's signals to get hard, or damaged vessels can't get blood into the penis, which prevents it from getting erect and firm.

Better-sex tips for women: If you're having trouble lubricating, invest in a tube of vaginal lubricant, such as Astroglide, Replens, or K-Y Jelly, says Dr. Feld. If you're extremely dry, try inserting a lubricating suppository into your vagina before sex. If you're going through menopause, ask your doctor about prescribing an estrogen cream or ring. Applied around and in the vagina, estrogen can help improve dry vaginal tissues.

If you're having difficulty reaching orgasm, invest in a handheld vibrator. You and your partner can use it as part of foreplay.

Better-sex tips for your guy: If he's having trouble getting erections, convince him to talk to his doctor. If tests reveal that nerve or blood vessel damage is to blame, Viagra, penile suppositories, penile injections, or vacuum erection devices might help.

Making sex better together: Take responsibility for managing your diabetes—or help your husband take charge of his. "Doing everything you can to influence the course of the condition—and there's a considerable amount you can do—will make you feel more powerful and in control," says Dr. Feld. "And those feelings can significantly improve your sexual experience."

Heart Disease

When we're aroused, our hearts beat faster and we breathe more rapidly. That's why many people still mistakenly believe that sex is a no-no for anyone with a heart problem. According to one estimate, between 50 and 75 percent of men and women who have had heart attacks drastically cut down on sex or avoid it completely. People who experience chest pain brought on by heart disease (angina) also tend to avoid sex.

Effects on women's sexuality: Studies suggest that women with heart disease may be more depressed and take longer to resume sexual activity than men.

Effects on men's sexuality: Men who have a heart condition, or who have had a heart attack or heart surgery, also avoid sex, fearing that it will bring on "the big one."

Better-sex tips for women: Don't be afraid to hold, kiss, or caress your mate. While you may fear that these displays of affection will arouse you or your partner, lead to intercourse, and trigger angina or a heart attack in either of you, it's virtually unheard of. In fact, if either of you is depressed, tender touching may actually make you feel better, says Robert DiBianco, M.D., associate clinical professor of medicine at Georgetown University School of Medicine in Washington, D.C., and director of cardiology research at the risk factor and heart failure clinics at Washington Adventist Hospital in Takoma Park, Maryland.

fascinating FACTS

A Heart Attack after Sex?
Slim Chance

- The risk of a healthy 50-year-old man having a heart attack within two hours of intercourse is about two in a million, according to a study done at Harvard of 1,774 people with heart disease.

- Chance of having a heart attack if he abstains from sex: One in a million

- Chance of sex causing a second heart attack: About 20 in a million

There's no one position that will stave off angina or a heart attack, so feel free to use the ones you like. Use those that are comfortable and familiar. If you have still-sensitive surgical incisions from a bypass, however, you may find it less painful to use a side-by-side position.

Warm up the sheets using an electric blanket before your sexual rendezvous. Cold stresses the heart.

Better-sex tips for your guy: All of the suggestions listed above are fine for men, too. In addition, if your partner runs short of breath while lying down, suggest that he try sitting in a chair with you on his lap.

Persuade him with the facts. (Men respond to logic.) And the fact is, if he can walk up a flight of 20 stairs at a usual pace, it's unlikely that having sex will cause chest pains or a heart attack, says Dr. DiBianco.

Making sex better together: Take the pressure off intercourse. Instead, focus on other ways to give and receive pleasure, such as mutual massage, mutual masturbation, or oral sex.

If you take the prescription heart drug nitroglycerin for chest pain associated with exertion, your doctor will probably suggest that you take it shortly before sex to stave off the pain of an angina attack.

Check your medications. Some drugs used to treat heart disease and high blood pressure can leave men unable to get an erection, or reduce sexual desire in both men and women. Consult your doctor if you notice that you're less than raring to go after starting a new drug or increasing the dosage of your current medication. He'll likely be able to prescribe a different, yet still effective drug.

Multiple Sclerosis

Multiple sclerosis (MS) destroys the covering of the nerves (the myelin sheath). Sexual arousal begins in the central nervous system, as the brain sends messages to the sexual organs along nerves running through the spinal cord. If MS damages these nerve pathways, it can affect sexual response, says Randall T. Schapiro, M.D., clinical professor of neurology at the University of Minnesota in Minneapolis and director of the Fairview Multiple Sclerosis Center.

Effects on women's sexuality: Lack of sexual desire is a common sexual problem in women with MS, says Dr. Schapiro. It is estimated that 48 percent of women with MS reported losing interest in sex. Depression, or the medications prescribed to lift it, may play a significant role. Other effects include reduced vaginal lubrication, numbness in the vaginal area, and difficulty reaching orgasm.

Effects on men's sexuality: Many men with MS—even mild MS—have difficulty getting or keeping an erection, says Dr. Schapiro. This may be due to physical symptoms caused by the MS itself, untreated depression, or antidepressant medication. A man may also lose sensation in his penis, making it difficult or impossible to ejaculate.

Better-sex tips for women: If you're having trouble lubricating, buy an over-the-counter vaginal lubricant.

If you experience pain in the vaginal area, ask your doctor about applying a cold pack to the area.

If you've lost sensation in your clitoris and have difficulty reaching orgasm, treat yourself to a vibrator. Explore its possibilities with your mate (or just keep it for yourself).

Be aware that antidepressant medication can quash sexual desire. If you're rarely in the mood anymore, talk to your doctor. She may be able to switch you to an antidepressant that doesn't depress your libido.

Better-sex tips for your guy: Sometimes, men find it easier to get an erection when they masturbate, says Dr. Schapiro. Suggest to your partner that he give himself a hand and then share his erection with you.

If he's unable to achieve an erection, Viagra may help, says Dr. Schapiro. "I'd estimate that Viagra has worked for about 80 percent of the men with MS I've worked with," he says.

Making sex better together: Talk about the changes in your sex life as openly as you can, says Dr. Schapiro. Discuss what feels good and what causes discomfort or pain. Brainstorm different ways of pleasuring each other. Above all, discuss how you can think about sex as a way to give and receive love and comfort, not just orgasms.

Medications

We take medication to lower blood pressure and lift mood, to treat heart disease and heal ulcers, to clear stuffy noses and cope with stress. So the discovery that these drugs—and many others—can affect our sex lives is a bitter pill to swallow.

Men and women who take antidepressants often find it difficult or impossible to reach orgasm, or they find that their sex drives vanish altogether. Blood pressure medications can affect a man's ability to get an erection or to delay ejaculation. In fact, there are over 200 drugs, prescription and over-the-counter, that can affect some aspect of sexuality.

Medication-induced problems "can have major repercussions on a relationship," says William W. Finger, Ph.D., a certified sex therapist and associate professor in the department of psychiatry, behavioral science, at East Tennessee State University in Johnson City.

Women whose medications cause them to lose interest in sex or leave them unable to climax may start to reject their mates' advances. Or they may fake orgasm, a kind of sexual lie that erodes the bond between themselves and their partners. Men whose medications affect their desire or performance may also avoid sex.

Physical withdrawal can turn into emotional withdrawal, says Dr. Finger. Less touching, less talking, less trust—less intimacy.

Of course, medication isn't to blame for every bedroom problem. But when it is, solutions exist.

Drug Offenders

It's impossible to list all the medications that can dampen your sex. Here are the most common.

Antidepressants. Experts aren't sure why, but antidepressants are hard on your sex life. The newer antidepressants, known as selective serotonin reuptake inhibitors (SSRIs), delay orgasm in both women and men. In fact, this side effect of SSRIs is so universal that they're used to treat premature ejaculation. Fluoxetine (Prozac), paroxetine (Paxil), and sertraline (Zoloft) are examples of SSRIs.

Older antidepressants known as tricyclics can cause erectile disorder. Tricyclic antidepressants include imipramine (Tofranil) and amitriptyline (Elavil).

Antihistamines. These drugs help dry up mucous membranes in the nasal passages. They can also leave a woman's vagina bone-dry, which can make sex painful. Lack of lubrication may even lead her lover to think that she's no longer turned on by him, says Dr. Finger.

Blood pressure medications. Most medications used to treat hypertension have been reported to cause erectile disorder, perhaps because they reduce blood pressure in the penis, says Mark A. Slagle, Pharm.D., a clinical pharmacy specialist at the James H. Quillen Veterans Affairs Medical Center in Johnson City, Tennessee. Some classes of blood pressure drugs, including beta-blockers and diuretics, can reduce sexual desire. It may be that these drugs short-circuit signals from the central nervous system that trigger sexual excitement, he says.

Oral contraceptives. Although the Pill freed women from the fear of unplanned pregnancy, and liberated their libidos in the process, it can also reduce their interest in sex. Experts aren't sure why this happens, but one possible explanation is that birth control pills reduce levels of libido-revving testosterone.

Tranquilizers. Alprazolam (Xanax) and diazepam (Valium), to name but two, seem to decrease sexual desire or delay or prevent orgasm the same way alcohol does—by depressing the central nervous system.

Ulcer medications. Many of these medications, particularly cimetidine (Tagamet), work by suppressing the stomach's secretion of gastric acid. But they may also suppress production of testosterone, the male sex hormone that fuels sexual desire in both men and women, says Dr. Slagle. This decrease in testosterone may leave men unable to get or keep an erection.

Rarely, over-the-counter antacids such as Tagamet HB, Zantac 75, and Pepcid AC may decrease desire. More often, they cause erectile disorder.

Sex-and-Drug Strategies

If you suspect that your medication (or your husband's) may be affecting your sexuality, call your doctor. Period. "Never discontinue any medication without your physician's consent," says Dr. Finger. Here's what to do instead.

Start a "sex watch." In the weeks following the start of a new drug or a change in an established medication regimen, pay attention to any changes in sexual desire or function, says Dr. Slagle. Let's say that your partner began to have trouble getting erections a week or two after he started on Tagamet, but the problem improved when he discontinued the drug. Then it's likely that the medication, not his penis, is to blame, and another medication can be tried.

Ask about alternatives. Report any problems to your doctor. She may be able to prescribe an alternative to a drug that's causing sexual side effects, says Dr. Finger.

For example, someone taking a diuretic or a beta-blocker for high blood pressure may be able to switch to an alpha-blocker or ACE inhibitor, "which have been reported to cause fewer sexual side effects," says Dr. Slagle. If medication has muted your desire, ask about a change in product or dosage.

Discuss timing your meds. Taking medication at a different time of day can sometimes improve sexual function, says Dr. Finger. So a man who usually takes a medication with dinner and notices that he has trouble performing a few hours later may be able to take the drug at breakfast instead. Don't reschedule your medications on your own, stresses Dr. Finger. Ask your doctor first.

Or discuss taking time off. The antidepressants Zoloft and Paxil have a reputation as orgasm killers. So if you're taking either of these medications and you've noticed that your sex life has headed south, ask your doctor about taking a "drug holiday."

Researchers at McLean Hospital in Belmont, Massachusetts, had 16 women and 14 men on three different antidepressants discontinue their medication for four consecutive weekends. Specifically, the volunteers took their last dose for the week on Thursday morning and resumed the medication Sunday at noon. During this time, the folks taking Zoloft or Paxil (but not Prozac) reported that sex improved and depression did not return. Prozac takes longer to be eliminated from the body, which may be why the medication-free weekends didn't rekindle desire for those taking it.

Overweight

~~~

hat do a scale, a tape measure, and a set of dumbbells have in common? Any one of the three can make your sex life sizzle or fizzle.

Extra pounds can sap our energy, keeping us from being as energetic in bed as we could or want to be. Overweight is linked to chronic ailments such as diabetes, which can make it difficult for a woman to lubricate and to become aroused and for a man to get an erection. Carrying as little as an extra 15 to 20 pounds can make us shy about sexual adventure and undressing in front of another.

Those pounds can come between a man and a woman even when they're not in bed, particularly if one is overweight and the other isn't. The thinner partner may feel frustrated by the other's weight but feel too guilty to say so—or, worse, nag and make cruel comments. In either case, being overweight can affect a relationship as surely as it affects physical health.

When You're Heavy and He's Not

Generally speaking, when we feel fat, we don't feel sexy. "A woman's sexuality and her body image are intimately related," says Howard Rankin, Ph.D., a clinical psychologist, the executive director of the Carolina Wellness Retreat on Hilton Head Island, South Carolina, and the author of *Seven Steps to Wellness*.

When we dislike our bodies, we may feel that we don't deserve sexual pleasure, explains Dr. Rankin. So we reject our mates' advances. "This withdrawal can affect a woman's relationship with her partner," he says.

It's every woman's right to make love and enjoy it, regardless of her dress size, Dr. Rankin says. And most men would agree. Not only do most men feel closest to their partners when they're making love, but they also simply aren't as critical of our bodies as we are. "There's a tremendous difference between what you may feel about your body and what your partner sees," he says.

If you're okay with your extra pounds but your mate isn't, it's up to him to tell you in a direct but gentle way that your weight bothers him, says Myles

Faith, Ph.D., research fellow at the New York Obesity Center at St. Lukes–Roosevelt Hospital in New York City. It's then up to you to decide how to respond to your partner's concerns, by agreeing to lose the weight or by telling him you're happy just the way you are.

But what if your weight is a constant source of friction between the two of you? If he has become a food cop—passing judgment on what you should or shouldn't eat—or insults or ridicules your body, your weight isn't the problem. The real problem may be his need to control the relationship by controlling you, and his inability to accept you as you are, says Dr. Faith.

Focusing on a partner's weight can be a way to avoid unspoken problems in the relationship, points out certified sex therapist Judith L. Silverstein, Ph.D., professor of psychology at Harvard Medical School and a clinical psychologist in Needham, Massachusetts. Seeing a couples therapist may help you and your partner unearth buried conflicts and resentments, she says. "If these issues can be resolved, weight becomes less of an issue."

When Your Hubby Is Too Chubby

After 15 years of marriage, you're within 10 pounds of your twentysomething weight. Your husband . . . well, let's just say that years of prime-time TV and fat-filled snack foods have left him struggling to zip his relaxed-fit jeans.

If you're miffed that you work at keeping fit and he doesn't, you're not alone, says Dr. Silverstein. Many women feel the same way—with good reason.

"Wanting your partner to lose weight is reasonable," says Dr. Faith. "And it's fine to tell your partner how you feel about his weight, in a kind and sup-

A Fun Way
to Burn Off Calories

During the average sexual encounter, we burn about 150 calories. That's about the amount of calories in three chocolate chip cookies.

portive way." You might say, for example, "I've noticed that you've been putting on some weight. I'm concerned about your health."

What's not okay: to call him a tub of lard and demand that he lose weight, says Dr. Silverstein. If you've told your partner how you feel and he isn't willing or able to shed the pounds, you may have to decide to accept your partner's teddy-bear physique and focus on his positive qualities—his kindness, his quirky sense of humor, the fact that he can still wow you in bed. "Acceptance can enhance intimacy because you're seeing him as he is, not as you would like him to be," says Dr. Silverstein. "Accepting him is a sign of a loving, healthy relationship."

When You've "Grown" as a Couple

Many couples discover that as they approach their 20th wedding anniversary, they're each 20 pounds heavier. Blame the usual suspects: eating more, exercising less, and slower metabolism.

While the "midlife 20" may be typical, it's not inevitable, says Dr. Faith. "Teaming up with a companion who has a similar weight-loss goal—whether it's your spouse, a friend, or a co-worker—can be a very helpful weight-loss strategy," he says.

It's nicest when your weight-loss buddy is the man you love. Small steps that lead to weight loss—poring over low-fat cookbooks together, taking nightly strolls, talking each other through potential cookie binges—bond you and give you a common goal. And working together to reach this goal can foster a renewed feeling of intimacy.

One way to involve each other in your weight-loss efforts is to go to the grocery store together, suggests Dr. Faith. Stroll the aisles. Point out the healthy foods you buy now and those you might like to try. Along the way, mourn the snacks you'll miss—or devise a plan to enjoy them in moderation. Brainstorm new ways to prepare old favorites. (For example, instead of making pan-fried potatoes, you might sprinkle them with salt and pepper and bake them on a baking sheet.) When you've completed scouting the store, return to the entrance and grab a cart. You're ready to shop.

Another way to "buddy up": Arrange your schedules so that you can work out together at least three times a week. It has been shown that people who exercise keep the weight off, while those who merely diet are more likely to regain the weight, says Dr. Faith.

Uninspired by the usual workout options? Sit down together and pick an unusual workout you would both enjoy—judo, horseback riding, fencing, whatever. Then make it happen. You'll trim down, tone up, and break out of your unhealthy (and unsexy) couch-potato routine.

The Ultimate Buddy System

Losing weight and keeping it off is a matter of diet, exercise, and psychological motivation. These expert-recommended strategies can help.

Rediscover the joy of food. *For you:* The next time you head for the fridge when you're feeling down, think, "HALT!" It stands for Hungry, Angry, Lonely, and Tired. Various forms of self-destructive behavior, including overeating, can occur when you're in the grips of any one of these feelings, says Dr. Faith. His suggestions: Eat a nutritious mini-meal every few hours so you never get ravenous. And keep a food journal, in which you write down how you feel during every meal, snack, or binge. "You'll start to see patterns emerge—showing that you may tend to overeat when you're tired, lonely, or stressed," he says.

For him: If your man is a meat-and-potatoes kind of guy, don't harangue him about the evils of sirloin. Like you, your partner is more likely to stick to his diet if he doesn't feel totally deprived of the foods he loves, says Dr. Faith. (And about those potatoes: Make them baked, with a slathering of low-fat salad dressing or mustard. Both taste great on spuds.)

For both of you: Buy a low-fat cookbook or two and start experimenting in the kitchen, suggests Dr. Silverstein. Cooking is an intimate activity, and you're likely to have as much fun working together to slice vegetables and sauté garlic as you will watching the pounds drop away.

Get active again. *For you* and *for him:* Exercise 30 minutes a day, every day, says Dr. Faith. But feel free to break it into 10-minute increments. One example: You might bike to the convenience store to buy milk (10 minutes), park your car in the farthest parking lot at the mall and walk to the entrance (10 minutes), and turn on a music-video station and take a 10-minute dance break.

For both of you: Reminisce with your partner about what you used to do to keep in shape—jogging, cycling, swing dancing—then take it up again, suggests Dr. Rankin. Schedule workout dates. Getting sweaty together can increase a couple's intimacy while it reduces their waist sizes.

Motivate each other. *For you:* Lose weight for the right reason. If your mate is a little too insistent about your losing weight, stay cool. "Get past thinking, 'To hell with him, I'm not going to lose the weight,' when it's in your best interest to do so," says Dr. Rankin. Realize that remaining over-weight doesn't hurt your partner. It hurts you.

For both of you: Sit down together and list all the times in the day when you're vulnerable to overeating—and then make a pact to be there for each other during those times, suggests Dr. Faith. Call each other if you're near a phone, for example.

Sexually Transmitted Diseases

I n our daydreams, we meet a special man, fall in love, and live happily ever after. Contracting a sexually transmitted disease (STD) just isn't in the script.

If you're in a mutually monogamous relationship of long duration, you probably have nothing to worry about. If not, you may be a moving target for more than 25 types of sexually transmitted bacteria, viruses, and para-sites. Many of these diseases show no symptoms, so they're often passed unknowingly—a kind of "silent" STD. And while early detection and treat-ment clear up most STDs, they can have devastating consequences if left untreated.

Generally speaking, women are infected more easily then men because the lining of the vagina is thin and has a large surface area, which makes it vulnerable to infection. Also, women can be exposed to sexually transmitted viruses or bacteria for longer periods of time than men because semen can remain in the vagina for hours or even days—far longer than a man's penis is in contact with vaginal secretions. Moreover, semen contains more infectious viral or bacterial material than vaginal secretions do, making it easier for men to infect women.

If you're sexually active and you're not completely certain the relationship is totally monogamous, you should know that using a latex condom combined with a spermicidal foam or jelly every time you have sex is the most effective protection against STDs, says David Celentano, Sc.D., professor of epidemiology in the infectious diseases program at the Johns Hopkins University School of Hygiene and Public Health in Baltimore. This isn't big news: It's hard to miss the safer-sex public service announcements on TV, or the articles about STDs in women's magazines.

And yet, when the lights are low and the sheet is turned down, many of us choose not to practice safer sex.

Why?

It's Not Just "Condom Phobia"

With STDs, there are two unseen enemies. The first: microbes. The second: human nature.

Many of us refuse to believe that STDs can and do infect nice, clean, decent, hardworking people. Like us. This denial keeps us from taking the actions that can help protect us, such as asking about a potential partner's sexual history or using a condom.

"When it comes to STDs, there's a huge gulf between what people know and what they do," says Susan Lloyd Schulz, a physician assistant and senior clinical consultant for the American Social Health Association.

Apparently, many people infected with STDs can't bring themselves to inform potential partners. According to a survey of 1,500 men and women conducted by the Kaiser Family Foundation and *Glamour* magazine, 97 percent of the women and 96 percent of the men agreed that anyone infected with an STD has a responsibility to tell a potential lover before they have sex. But only 34 percent of women and 28 percent of men who have had an STD did so.

Our beliefs about love and relationships also affect our sexual behavior, says Lloyd Schulz. To women who grew up believing that women are "swept away" and men are the "sweepers," for example, the idea of planning for sex can seem cold and calculating, and asking a man to wear a condom intimidating.

The times in which we grew up can have a huge influence on our sexual behavior. If a woman's last date was 25 to 30 years ago, chances are she carried a comb, a lipstick, and a compact in her evening bag—not a three-pack of condoms. "Older people, especially older women, may be the least equipped to have an open discussion about sex, or to buy or use condoms," says Dr. Celentano.

But as thrilling as pinwheels-in-the-sky sex is, it takes more vulnerability and trust—more intimacy—to talk about sex than to engage in it. Having "the talk," and insisting on safe sex, shows a man that you want a partnership based on mutual trust right from the start. "This is a great way to start a relationship," says Lloyd Schulz.

So is learning the facts about STDs.

What follows is a list of the most common STDs, arranged by estimated new cases per year—starting with the most common. Included are basic facts about each disease and how each affects women as well as information about prevention, symptoms in women and men, diagnosis, and treatment. (You'll even find out if you can get it from a toilet seat.) Be sure to see your doctor if you or your partner experiences any of the symptoms below.

Read on. A woman forewarned is a woman forearmed.

Chlamydia

This STD gets its name from the Greek word for "cloaked." And chlamydia, caused by the *Chlamydia trachomatis* microorganism, lives up to its name: About 70 percent of all women and as many as 20 percent of all men who are infected don't have noticeable symptoms. So it's often spread unknowingly through vaginal, oral, or anal sex.

Can you get it from a toilet seat? No.

What women need to know: Untreated chlamydia puts fertility at serious risk. The bacteria may spread from the cervix (the opening of the uterus) to the fallopian tubes or ovaries and result in pelvic inflammatory disease (PID). Up to 40 percent of women with untreated chlamydia will develop PID, which can cause infertility by scarring and blocking the fallopian tubes. PID can also cause a pregnancy to develop outside the uterus, a life-threatening condition called ectopic pregnancy.

Moreover, women infected with chlamydia are three to five times more likely to be infected with HIV, the virus that causes AIDS, if they're exposed to it.

Women's symptoms: About 70 percent of women with chlamydia don't have noticeable symptoms. If symptoms do occur, they typically begin in 5 to 10 days after infection and include painful intercourse, bleeding after intercourse, abdominal pain, low-grade fever, painful urination or increased urination, and vaginal discharge.

Men's symptoms: Up to 20 percent of men do not have noticeable symptoms. The rest may notice a watery or milky discharge from the penis or pain or a burning sensation when they urinate. If the infection spreads from the urethra to the testicles, it can cause epididymitis, an inflammation of the duct through which sperm travel, which can cause sterility. Symptoms of epididymitis include fever and swelling and severe pain in the scrotum.

Best prevention: Latex condoms (or polyurethane if you or your partner has a latex allergy) combined with a spermicidal foam or jelly (rather than a condom treated with a spermicide). "Spermicides have been shown to be protective against STDs," says Lloyd Schulz. "They also increase the effectiveness of condoms, especially if the condom breaks." Don't rely on natural skin condoms to protect against STDs—they're too porous to protect against microbes.

How it's diagnosed: In women, by culturing a smear from the cervix. Men may have a swab inserted into the opening of the penis, and the extracted fluid is cultured to detect the bacteria.

How it's treated: Antibiotics, most often doxycycline, tetracycline, and zithromax. Erythromycin is often prescribed for pregnant women and other people who cannot take tetracycline.

Don't make this mistake: Unless you're in a mutually monogamous relationship, don't perform oral sex on a man without using a condom: Chlamydia can infect your throat and, rarely, lead to cancers of the throat, says Dr. Celentano.

Trichomoniasis

Spread through all forms of intercourse and through contact with semen or vaginal discharge on towels, washcloths, or sheets, "trich," caused by the bacterium *Trichomonas vaginalis*, is a common cause of vaginitis.

Condom Skills for Women

Never seen 'em? Don't know how to use 'em? Well, practice makes perfect. Here's the correct way to use a condom—both the male and the newer female version.

The Male Condom

Even men don't always know how to use male condoms correctly. One British study found that out of 300 men asked to demonstrate how to put on a condom, 20 percent failed. (They tried to unroll it from the inside out.) Here, then, are the best directions for using a condom the right way—the first time, every time.

1. Check the expiration date before you use a condom. Latex deteriorates over time. Open the packet at a corner, tearing along one of the serrated edges. Use your hands—not your teeth or scissors, which may tear the condom.

2. After opening the packet, look to see which way the condom is sitting, so you can roll it on quickly and avoid putting it on inside out.

3. Hold the condom by the tip to squeeze out the air. Air trapped in the tip during intercourse can cause the condom to break.

4. Unroll the condom all the way down the hard penis.

5. After sex, have your partner hold the condom in place as he pulls out of your vagina. Not holding it may cause it to slip off.

Can you get it from a toilet seat? Yes.

What women need to know: Trichomoniasis may damage the fallopian tubes, leading to infertility.

Women's symptoms: Some women don't have any at all. If symptoms do appear, they typically develop from 3 to 28 days after infection. They include a frothy, white or yellow-green discharge, itching in and around the vagina, and mild pain during urination or intercourse.

Men's symptoms: Men rarely have symptoms. But if they do, the symptoms include a slight discharge before urinating first thing in the morning and itching or a tingling sensation in the urethral tract.

Best prevention: Latex condoms (or polyurethane if you or your partner has a latex allergy) in tandem with spermicide.

If you buy condoms, keep them in a cool, dry place. Use them with a water-based vaginal lubricant that contains the spermicide nonoxynol-9. Never use skin lotions, baby oil, petroleum jelly, or cold cream with condoms. The oil they contain will cause condoms to break.

The Female Condom

It's a strange-looking sight: Six inches long, several inches wide when it is stretched out, with a soft ring on each end. But if used correctly, a female condom offers nearly as much protection as a male condom. The bonus is that you can insert it before making love. Here's how.

1. Add water-based lubricant to the *inside* of the condom. You may also want to add lubricant to the outside to help with insertion into the vagina.

2. Squeeze the inner ring of the condom. Place the inner ring and pouch into your vagina.

3. With your finger, push the inner ring as far into your vagina as it will go. The outer ring should stay outside of your vagina.

4. Guide your partner's penis into the condom.

5. After sex, twist and squeeze the outer ring and then gently pull out the condom before you stand up.

How it's diagnosed: Microscopic examination of vaginal discharge, or a culture of the sample.

How it's treated: Drugs called 5-notroimidazoles.

Don't make this mistake: If you get trich, don't allow your partner to skip out of being treated. If he goes untreated, there's up to a 25 percent chance that you'll become reinfected.

Genital Warts

Caused by human papillomavirus (HPV), genital warts are transmitted by contact with the warts during vaginal, oral, or anal sex or by touching infected towels or clothing.

Can you get it from a toilet seat? No.

What women need to know: Women are extremely susceptible to genital warts because cervical cells divide quickly, which makes it easier for the virus to multiply. This is important, because HPV is the single most important risk factor for cervical cancer.

Women's symptoms: Genital warts may take one month to several years to appear. And while they can show up where you can see them, such as on the outer genitals, they often show up in places you can't, such as in the vagina, cervix, or anus. They're typically soft and flesh-colored, and they resemble tiny cauliflowers. They're usually painless, but they may itch.

Men's symptoms: Typically, warts appear on the penis and scrotum or in the urethra (the tube through which urine is passed) or rectum.

Best prevention: Use a latex condom (or polyurethane if you or your partner has a latex allergy) and a spermicidal foam or jelly every time you have sex. But bear in mind that a condom may not cover all infected areas, like the base of the penis, says Lloyd Schulz. In this case, "there's nothing to be done except to refrain from having sex, since the HPV virus can 'shed,' which means it can be transmitted by contact with his skin even if he has no warts or other symptoms."

How it's diagnosed: A doctor's visual examination.

How it's treated: A doctor may apply one of several chemicals directly to the warts, or he may send you home with prescription medicine that you can apply yourself. A doctor may also choose to freeze them off (cryotherapy), burn them off (electrocauterization), or remove them surgically or with a laser. But results may not last: Warts recur at least 30 percent of the time, which means that you may need more than one treatment.

Don't make this mistake: Never, ever skip a Pap test: It can reveal the presence of precancerous or cancerous cells caused by HPV. Also get checked for HPV if you suspect that your partner is not monogamous. Women whose husbands have other sex partners are 5 to 11 times more likely to develop cervical cancer than other married women.

Gonorrhea

Caused by the *gonococcus* bacterium, gonorrhea is another "silent" STD that is passed through vaginal, oral, or anal sex.

Can you get it from a toilet seat? No.

What women need to know: Left untreated, gonorrhea can cause PID in women and epididymitis in men.

Women's symptoms: Symptoms may appear 10 days after infection and include yellowish, puslike vaginal discharge that is irritating to the vulva, followed by pain while urinating and irregular menstrual bleeding. Often, however, there are no symptoms until PID develops.

Men's symptoms: No symptoms at first, or a thick yellowish discharge from the penis and pain while urinating.

Best prevention: Again, latex condoms (or polyurethane if you or your partner has a latex allergy) teamed with spermicides, or a female condom, says Lloyd Schulz. If you perform oral sex on a man, use a condom.

How it's diagnosed: A doctor examines the genitals and/or tests vaginal or penile discharge for *gonococcus*.

How it's treated: The antibiotics ceftriaxone, spectinomycin, or penicillin. When treated early, gonorrhea clears up rapidly in 90 percent of cases.

Don't make this mistake: Don't ignore mild symptoms, hoping they'll go away. While initial symptoms will fade within a few weeks, untreated gonorrhea may result in permanent infertility or kidney problems.

Pubic Lice

They're not life-threatening. But pubic lice—transmitted through sexual contact or contact with infested bedding, clothing, and toilet seats—cause intense itching that can threaten your sanity.

The Hit List of STDs

Thought AIDS was the number one sexually transmitted disease in America? Surprise: It's chlamydia, which infects four million people a year. Below, the runners-up.

Trichomoniasis: Up to three million

Genital warts: One million

Gonorrhea: One million

Pubic lice: One million

Genital herpes: 500,000

Hepatitis B: About 200,000

Syphilis: Below 120,000

AIDS: 40,000

Can you get it from a toilet seat? Yes. Ditto for infected bed linens and blankets, clothing, and upholstered furniture.

What women need to know: Frantic scratching can cause vulvitis, which is characterized by redness, irritation, and swelling of the vulva (the external female genitalia).

Symptoms (women and men): Within five days of being infested with these critters, intense itching around the genitals or anus will begin. Seen with the naked eye or through a magnifying glass, pubic lice look like tiny crabs (hence, their nickname). They attach to any hairy area—armpit hair, pubic hair, eyelashes, and eyebrows. Their eggs show up in small clumps near the roots of the hair.

Some people notice a bluish-gray "rash" (actually, lice) or white nits that look like dandruff (actually, eggs) that cling stubbornly to the roots of the hair.

Understandably, people with pubic lice also feel irritable.

Best prevention: Limit your number of sex partners. Don't try dousing yourself with over-the-counter anti-lice medications such as Kwell, RID, and A-200 before sex. Theoretically, that may offer some protection, but you won't smell very attractive to your partner.

How it's diagnosed: Typically, people diagnose themselves. And it's not a pretty sight.

How it's treated: The over-the-counter medications mentioned above. (Pregnant women and babies need to use a treatment especially for them, such as Eurax.)

Don't make this mistake: Don't underestimate this parasite's hardiness. To be on the safe side, avoid sexual contact with the infected person until the infestation is eliminated. Also, immediately wash all bedding, towels, and clothing in very hot water, and dry them on the hot cycle.

Genital Herpes

Often called the gift that keeps on giving, genital herpes is caused by the herpes simplex 2 virus. It is often spread by people who don't know they have it, through vaginal, oral, or anal sex, and even kissing. But once you get herpes, it's forever: There's no cure.

Can you get it from a toilet seat? It's unlikely. And touching towels or other objects used by someone with herpes doesn't seem to spread the virus, either.

What women need to know: Over the course of one year, the chance of getting genital herpes from an infected partner with no symptoms is 10 percent. Men pass the herpes virus to women more frequently than women give it to men. Moreover, it's possible for a woman in the midst of an outbreak during childbirth to transmit the virus to her newborn. (To prevent this, doctors commonly perform a cesarean section in pregnant women with herpes.)

Women's symptoms: Symptoms typically begin 2 to 20 days after infection. Red, painful bumps may appear on the outer genitals, inside the vagina, on the cervix, or on the thighs and buttocks. These sores turn into fluid-filled blisters teeming with the virus. These blisters fill with pus, break, and become painful sores surrounded by a red ring. The blisters crust over and heal within a few weeks. (Sores inside the vagina may take 10 days longer to heal.) Other symptoms include fever, chills, headache, and swollen, tender lymph glands in the groin and throat and under the arms.

While the sores typically heal in two weeks, the virus remains in the body, eventually triggering another crop of sores. Some people have no recurrences. Others have mild, brief episodes that become less frequent over time. Stress is a common cause of flare-ups.

Men's symptoms: Men may develop sores on the penis or surrounding area. Otherwise, the symptoms are the same as for women.

Best prevention: Latex condoms (or polyurethane if you or your partner has a latex allergy). But as with genital warts, herpes virus can shed without any symptoms, and sores may be present outside the protective layer of latex.

How it's diagnosed: A doctor inspects the sores and/or cultures a sample of fluid from a sore to detect the presence of the virus.

How it's treated: The antiviral drugs acyclovir, famciclovir, or valacyclovir. Taking small, daily doses of these medications (called suppressive therapy) may reduce the frequency of recurrences for people who have more than six outbreaks a year.

Don't make this mistake: Don't assume that a man doesn't have herpes if he doesn't have sores. The virus may shed even when sores aren't present.

Hepatitis B

Of the four types of hepatitis—A, B, C, and D—type B is most often transmitted through sexual contact (or to babies at birth), and it's 100 times more contagious than HIV. About 30 percent of hepatitis B cases are transmitted by unprotected sex with an infected person or multiple sex partners. Like HIV, type B can be transmitted by sharing contaminated razors, toothbrushes, or needles.

Can you get it from a toilet seat? No. But you can get it if you're in a profession that puts you in contact with infected blood.

What women need to know: There's a 90 percent chance that a pregnant woman infected with hepatitis B will infect her child at birth. From 15 to 25 percent of these children will die of liver problems before they reach middle age.

Symptoms (women and men): Many people with acute hepatitis have no symptoms. Or symptoms may resemble a mild case of the flu: loss of appetite, nausea, vomiting, diarrhea, fatigue, muscle or joint aches, and mild fever. Some people may have whitish bowel movements, tea-colored urine, or jaundice, a yellowish discoloration of the skin and whites of the eyes.

Best prevention: Latex condoms (or polyurethane if you or your partner has a latex allergy) combined with spermicides.

How it's diagnosed: A blood test that can detect the presence of hepatitis antibodies.

How it's treated: Currently, the only approved treatment for hepatitis B is interferon. But only 35 percent of eligible candidates will benefit. Given by injection, interferon can also cause side effects such as headache, nausea, vomiting, depression, diarrhea, and fatigue.

Don't make this mistake: Don't refuse to be vaccinated for hepatitis B if you don't already have it, especially if you have multiple sex partners. You'll need an initial injection, another one in a month, and a third one five months later. The vaccine protects for at least 14 years, and maybe a lifetime.

Syphilis

Increased condom use has dramatically reduced the incidence of syphilis, which is caused by the bacteria *Treponema pallidum*. So have antibiotics. But syphilis is still transmitted the old-fashioned way: through direct contact with a sore, called a chancre (pronounced "SHANK-er"), during vaginal, oral, or anal sex.

Can you get it from a toilet seat? No.

What women need to know: Because the virus can breach the placenta (the life-sustaining organ connected to the fetus by the umbilical cord), a pregnant woman can pass it to her unborn baby, resulting in miscarriage or stillbirth. Congenital syphilis (a syphilis infection present at birth) can damage a newborn's sight or hearing or deform the bones or teeth. The good news: Women treated for syphilis before their fourth month of pregnancy will most likely not pass the virus to their babies.

Symptoms (women and men): Syphilis has four stages. On average, symptoms appear within three weeks of infection. In the primary stage, a hard, round, painless chancre appears at the spot the bacterium entered the body. It lasts for one to five weeks and heals on its own. The secondary stage is characterized by a skin rash; slimy, white patches in the mouth; swollen lymph glands; hair and weight loss; headaches; muscle aches; sore throat; tiredness; and fever. Left untreated, syphilis enters the latent stage, in which the virus can "sleep" for up to 40 years, burrowing into the brain, spinal cord,

New Love Interest? Read This

If there's a new man in your life and you're about to become intimate, the expert-recommended tips below can reduce your risk of contracting a sexually transmitted disease (STD).

Be prepared. Buy a box of condoms and learn how to use them. (Unroll them onto an appropriate-size zucchini or carrot, bedpost, or any other smooth, cylindrical object. Think of this as a variation on a preteen's perfecting her kissing technique on a pillow.) If you're embarrassed, practice buying them until you're not. Broach the subject of STDs to an imaginary first-time sex partner—and practice saying, "No condom, no sex." Condoms are more effective when used with a spermicide that contains nonoxynol-9.

Be realistic. Assume that any potential sex partner is already infected with an STD. As unromantic as it sounds, it will help keep you from being "swept away." Don't pretend that you are immune to STDs.

Be sober. Alcohol and some other drugs increase the likelihood of risky sexual behavior.

Be selective. Carefully choose your sex partner, avoiding anyone who uses drugs or participates in high-risk sexual activities. Just asking about your partner's past isn't enough. You need to be familiar enough with him to be able to tell if you will be given a truthful answer.

Be vigilant. Report any unexplained vaginal discharge, painful urination, lower abdominal pain, foul odors, or irregular bleeding to your doctor, and show him or her any open sores, bumps, warts, blisters, or rashes. The sooner you're treated, the better off you'll be.

Be firm. Don't perform oral sex on a new partner—not even with a condom in place.

Be responsible. If you're not in a mutually monogamous relationship, get tested for STDs every year. If you do become infected, see your doctor as soon as possible and inform all past and current partners. You may keep others from acquiring the infection.

bones, and circulatory system. Finally, in tertiary-stage syphilis, the infection can cause brain damage, mental illness, and death.

Best prevention: Male and/or female latex condoms combined with spermicides.

How it's diagnosed: In the primary stage, by examining and testing fluid from a chancre. A blood test is used to diagnose the later stages.

How it's treated: People who have had syphilis less than a year can be cured with one dose of the antibiotic penicillin. Those who have had it longer will need additional doses.

Don't make this mistake: If primary- or secondary-stage symptoms disappear, you could still be at risk. See a doctor to receive proper treatment for eliminating the infection.

HIV/AIDS

The human immunodeficiency virus (HIV), the virus that causes acquired immunodeficiency syndrome (AIDS), chips away at the immune system, which protects us from disease. AIDS completely destroys an infected person's immunity, leaving him or her vulnerable to a variety of otherwise treatable diseases.

Blood, semen, vaginal secretions, and breast milk all carry HIV. Because of this, it can be transmitted through vaginal, oral, or anal sex, during blood transfusions (if the blood is contaminated by the virus), by sharing needles (during tattooing, ear piercing, or drug use), from mother to child during pregnancy and childbirth, or through breastfeeding.

Can you get it from a toilet seat? No. Nor can you "catch" HIV or AIDS from doorknobs, sheets, towels, clothing, telephones, showers, swimming pools, utensils, or drinking glasses.

What women need to know: Sex between men and women—not men and men—is now the primary route of HIV infection worldwide. Men are more likely to pass HIV to women than vice-versa, because there's more virus in ejaculated semen than in vaginal secretions.

Symptoms (women and men): HIV can lie low in the body for years; as a result, many people experience only mild symptoms, such as swollen lymph nodes and fever. AIDS causes weight loss, fatigue, diarrhea, and the development of opportunistic infections that take advantage of the body's ravaged immune system, such as rare forms of pneumonia (*Pneumocystitis carinii*) and cancer (Kaposi's sarcoma).

Best prevention: Male or female latex condoms teamed with spermicides for vaginal and anal sex. If you perform oral sex, make your partner wear a condom.

How it's diagnosed: The most widely used HIV test, the ELISA (enzyme-linked immunosorbent assay), detects antibodies to the HIV virus in the blood. If these antibodies are found, another blood test, the Western blot, is used to confirm the ELISA. The diagnosis of AIDS (rather than just HIV) is made on the basis of HIV antibodies in the blood, a low count of white blood cells, and/or the presence of other diseases associated with AIDS.

How it's treated: At this writing, there's no safe, effective vaccine against HIV, or a cure for AIDS. But new treatments have raised hopes that, in time, AIDS will be a chronic disease rather than a terminal one. There are currently 13 antiretrovial drugs, including zidovudine (AZT) and protease inhibitors, approved for treatment. Used in various combinations, they work to slow the multiplication of HIV in the body.

Don't make this mistake: If you're with a new partner, don't allow the desire to be loved or "swept away" cloud your judgment. Don't engage in high-risk sexual practices—particularly anal sex—without a condom. And don't have unprotected sex with a steady partner if you suspect that he may be unfaithful.

Snoring

According to one theory, prehistoric men snored to protect their sleeping womenfolk by scaring off night-stalking predators. "Isn't that a tender image?" asks Derek S. Lipman, M.D., an ear, nose, and throat specialist at Emmanuel Hospital in Portland, Oregon, and author of *Snoring from A to Zzzz*.

Not to any woman who has slept with a heroic snorer. To her, snoring is the bane of the bedroom, the robber of slumber, even a cause of a less-than-harmonious relationship. Her mate's rumbles, rasps, and rattles leave her tired. Frustrated. And probably too grumpy for sex.

In fact, snoring loud enough to make a woman (or her mate) flee to a spare bedroom can strain a relationship. "If a couple can't share the bedroom on a regular basis, they have less opportunity for intimacy, whether it means simply cuddling in the same bed or making love," says Dr. Lipman. "Snoring has driven a wedge between them."

But there's more than lost love (and lost sleep) at stake. Loud, habitual snoring can signal health problems. The most serious, obstructive sleep apnea (OSA), has been associated with health problems such as high blood pressure, stroke, and heart attack.

Whether you're concerned for your mate's health or for your own sanity, it's possible to silence even the most heroic snoring. But first, you have to figure out the cause.

Not-So-Silent Nights

Snoring occurs when tissues in the upper airway, taut during the day, relax during sleep. These soft, pliable tissues, which include the soft palate, uvula (the small fleshy mass hanging above the back of your tongue), tongue, and the strips of tissue around the tonsils, partially block the airway. To compensate, we suck in air with greater force. Snoring is the sound of these soft tissues vibrating against each other.

Occasional snoring is usually caused by extreme fatigue or by drinking too much alcohol. Both deepen sleep, relaxing the upper airway more than normal. In addition, allergies can cause tissues in the nose and upper airway to swell, partially blocking the airway. Further, some medications, including oral contraceptives and estrogen replacement, cause hormonal changes that narrow nasal passages. Even being overweight can cause snoring, because a thick neck and a double chin can compress the throat, narrowing the airway.

Snoring that threatens to bring down the roof, however, should be evaluated because it's a sign of OSA, says Dr. Lipman. People with OSA may stop

fascinating
FACTS

He Snores, She Snores

One of every three adults says that his or her mate snores, according to a survey commissioned by Mission Pharmacal, a pharmaceutical company. These folks say their partners' night music affects them in the following ways.

They have lost hearing (5 percent).

They have begun to snore, too (6 percent).

They sleep in separate bedrooms (11 percent).

They're grumpy in the morning (15 percent).

The snoring has gone on so long that it's just "white noise" (52 percent).

breathing momentarily hundreds of times a night. Researchers believe that many of the physical problems associated with OSA, including heart attack, stroke, and high blood pressure, may be caused by a lowered level of oxygen to the heart and brain.

OSA has also been linked to erectile dysfunction caused, researchers believe, by the cumulative effects of chronic fatigue, depression, high blood pressure, and weight gain. (Men with OSA are commonly overweight.)

Snore-No-More Strategies

Sometimes, a few simple tactics can quiet a snorer's nocturnal symphony. See if they work for you—or your bedmate.

Get off your back. People who sleep on their sides snore less than those who sleep on their backs, says Dr. Lipman. To keep off your back, sew a pocket into the back of your nightdress or pajamas and insert a golf ball or tennis ball. "After several months of this, some snorers become used to lying on their sides," he says. "They can then dispense with the ball and sleep comfortably, snore-free."

Change your bedwear. Trade in a soft mattress for a firm one, and multiple high, fat pillows for a single low, thin one, suggests Dr. Lipman. The straighter your neck, the clearer your airway.

Go on a snore-free diet. If you're moderately to severely overweight and you have signs of sleep apnea, try to shed the extra pounds. Sleep studies on seriously overweight men and women have shown that losing from 15 to 25 percent of body weight can significantly reduce apnea, or even eliminate it completely, by reducing the amount of fatty tissue around the neck, throat, and abdomen.

Drink less, or not at all. Alcohol depresses the central nervous system. This is potentially dangerous for those with sleep apnea, since it can cause you to stop breathing more frequently during the night, says Dr. Lipman. Mild snorers should drink in moderation; alcohol also deepens sleep and increases muscle relaxation, which aggravates snoring.

Unplug your nose. Antisnoring nasal strips are designed to open the nasal passages, making breathing through the nose easier. These strips are sold over-the-counter and are about the size of a small adhesive bandage. Basically, you stick the adhesive-backed strip on your nose. As the adhesive dries, the strip gently pulls on the area above the nostrils, opening the passages to let in more air. The strip is applied a few hours before going to bed, and it's recommended that the strip be worn for at least 12 consecutive hours.

Medical Silencers

If snoring doesn't respond to self-help treatments, ask your doctor about the following treatments.

CPAP. Continuous Positive Airway Pressure, or CPAP, is the most common device used to treat snoring or sleep apnea. At bedtime, the snorer places a plastic mask connected to an air blower over his nose. The blower sends air through the nose into the throat, which keeps the throat structures and air passages open. CPAP isn't a cure, so the snoring will start up again if you stop using it.

Mouth appliances. One device, called a tongue retaining device, pulls the tongue forward so it doesn't block the throat. Another, known as a mandibular repositioning appliance, fits over the teeth and holds the lower jaw forward, expanding the airway. Both can be uncomfortable, but studies show that they significantly reduce both snoring and sleep apnea. Only a dentist—preferably one with special training in sleep disorders—can fit these devices. Your local dental society or sleep disorder clinic should be able to help you locate a suitable dental practitioner, says Dr. Lipman.

UPPP. The most commonly performed surgery for sleep apnea, uvulopalatopharyngoplasty is often referred to as a face-lift on the back of the throat. In order to expand the airway, the uvula, the tonsils, and part of the soft palate are removed. The procedure is performed under general anesthesia and requires a hospital stay. Afterward, expect to have a severe sore throat for at least 10 days. Side effects aren't minor: Your voice may take on a nasal quality. And a small percentage of people will have "persistent nasal regurgitation," a polite way of saying that food may flow into the nasal cavity while swallowing. Still, this procedure works about 95 percent of the time, according to Dr. Lipman.

LAUP. Laser-assisted uvulopalatoplasty is the treatment of choice for socially disruptive snorers, severe snorers with daytime fatigue, and snorers with mild or moderate sleep apnea. In this procedure, a laser is used to remove some of the soft palate and part or all of the uvula. It's usually performed in a doctor's office. You'll leave with a sore throat and ear pain, which can persist for up to two weeks but can be relieved with pain medication and gargles that contain local anesthetic. Some people will need a second procedure. It works about as well as UPPP surgery.

Somnoplasty. In this new procedure, a surgeon inserts an electrode into the soft palate, above the uvula. The electrode emits a radio frequency that selectively destroys tissue, shrinking the uvula and opening the airway. The procedure and recovery are virtually painless, says Dr. Lipman.

Stress

In the hurricane of everyday life, great sex should be the eye of the storm, the calm in which a couple can draw comfort from each other. But more often, when stress mounts, sex is the first thing to go.

What's more, sex itself can become a source of stress. That's because men often view sex as a stress-reliever, while stressed-out women tend to avoid sex, says certified sex therapist Judith L. Silverstein, Ph.D., professor of psychology at Harvard Medical School and a clinical psychologist in Needham, Massachusetts.

Talk about a dilemma. If we're too tense for sex, our partners take our disinterest as a personal rejection. Still, feeling pressured to relieve his tension with a session of sexual aerobics when we're not in the mood is just as stressful on us.

Take heart. It's possible for couples to master stress and enjoy sex despite whiny kids, job worries, or endless bills. You can't prevent stress; it's as much a part of modern life as your ATM card. But according to experts, you can change the way you perceive stress and learn to react to it in ways that lessen its damaging effects.

Sex—And Stress—On the Brain

The desire for sex—or the lack of desire—really *is* all in our heads. Emotional stress unbalances brain chemicals that govern sexual desire and arousal, says Mona Lisa Schulz, M.D., Ph.D., a neuropsychiatrist in Yarmouth, Maine.

"You need a certain amount of 'juice' in your brain to want sex," explains Dr. Schulz. That juice comes from brain chemicals collectively known as neuropeptides, which include norepinephrine, epinephrine, dopamine, and oxytocin. "Sex requires all of your neurochemistry to be balanced," she says. "Stress can unhinge any of the four phases of the sexual response cycle—appetite, arousal, orgasm, or resolution—causing neuropeptide imbalances at each phase."

Stress affects a woman's sexual response early in the cycle, dampening appetite and arousal, says Nancy Gambescia, Ph.D., a marriage and family therapist in Bryn Mawr, Pennsylvania, who teaches at the Penn Council for Relationships in Philadelphia. As for reaching orgasm, forget it: Stress hijacks a woman's brain, often making her unable to concentrate on physical pleasure.

Stress typically hits men during the arousal phase, which can prevent them from getting or keeping an erection. This can trigger performance anxiety (a distinct form of stress), which can continue to undermine a man's sexual performance, explains Dr. Gambescia.

Secrets of Long-Lasting Love

Strong Family Ties Help Weather Stress

Eleanor and William Kasenchar of Clifton, New Jersey, met in the summer of 1947. Ellie's best friend from college introduced them. She and Bill clicked and made plans to see each other again. They dated for half a year before marrying on January 24, 1948. In more than 50 years of marriage, they've had to cope with major bouts of stress. What has kept them together through it all, says Ellie, is love and family support.

I remember our wedding day well because the winter of 1947 to 1948 was so bad that there almost wasn't a wedding. There were piles of snow on the ground, and it started snowing again that morning. It took us two hours to get to the church, which was usually a 15-minute drive away!

That rough start foreshadowed our marriage. During the first six to seven years, Bill was plagued with one health problem after another. He had bad arthritis and a hernia that put him in the hospital. But he pulled through, and so did we.

In 1977, our oldest daughter, Patti, was sick with a rare type of cancer that put her in the hospital for an entire month. We almost lost her, but she persevered through months of medical supervision and treatments. All of us—myself, my husband, Patti, our two other children Bill and Barbara, and our son-in-law Brian—thought we'd seen the worst. But about 10 years

The longer stress keeps a couple from connecting sexually, the more damage it can cause in a relationship, says Allen Elkin, Ph.D., a certified sex therapist and director of the Stress Management and Counseling Center in New York City and author of *Urbanese: Stress-Free Living in the Big City* and *Stress Management for Dummies*. "This lack of intimacy becomes just another source of stress, leaving a couple feeling bad about themselves and their relationship."

Discouraging words, indeed. But there are solutions.

later, Patti was diagnosed with breast cancer, and we were right back where we'd started.

Thankfully, Patti recovered completely and went on to raise two adopted children. But the only way we all made it through those trying times was with the love, support, and strength we shared as a family. Bill and I both grew up in close-knit families, and we knew that was what we wanted for our own family. Our main goal as a couple has been to provide a stable and loving home. And we've succeeded. Our family is proof that if you have that love and support at home, you can face anything that comes your way.

We've definitely had our share of rough times, but the good times far outweigh the bad. Plus, I think you need the bad to appreciate the good, and to have more insight into life—Bill and I are much wiser for it. Our experiences brought our family closer together and gave us much more to share with our children.

Our family's health problems also helped us put things in perspective. Bill and I discuss things right away when they bother us so that little things don't build into something larger. Time is too precious to spend it fighting. And now that we've retired, Bill and I have more time to do the activities we enjoy, like traveling and spending time with our children and our grandchildren. We have our family and we have our health, and that's what is most important.

No-Brainer Stress-Blasters

When we're under stress, it's easy to neglect our health. But the way we treat our bodies can ease stress or aggravate it. So if you're in a stress-induced sexual slump, try these strategies first.

Go easy on caffeine. Avoid consuming large amounts of coffee, tea, cola, and other caffeinated substances. A stimulant, caffeine may reduce your brain's stores of norepinephrine and epinephrine, says Dr. Schulz. And it may boost your levels of cortisol, a hormone that increases the body's stress response.

Hold the liquor. If you drink, limit your intake to one glass of wine before you make love, or avoid it completely. Alcohol shunts blood to the vital organs and away from your genitals.

Sweat out your tension. Exercise boosts desire by boosting endorphins, hormones that produce sensations of euphoria. "Taking a brisk walk together a few times a week might facilitate closeness and also relieve some of the stress," says Dr. Silverstein.

Check your meds. If you're stressed out, your doctor may have prescribed an antidepressant or other medication. But some prescription drugs, including antidepressants and blood pressure drugs, can affect arousal, lubrication, and orgasm, according to Dr. Schulz. Ask your doctor if any of the medications you're taking have sexual side effects. If they do, ask him or her if you could take alternative medications that do not have the sexual side effects, she advises.

Easing the Pressure — Together

Sex can be an antidote to stress, says Dr. Elkin. So if your libido (or your husband's) has been hijacked by stress, try this combination of mutual TLC and practical strategies to help liberate it.

Provide adequate ventilation. If you know that your partner is under stress, be his sounding board. "Allow him to vent," says Dr. Elkin. "Don't offer advice. Just let him talk about his stress while you listen." Hold his hand. Nod sympathetically.

If you're the one under stress, tell your husband that you need to vent, and ask if he can hear you out. Often, men offer advice instead of sympathy, which drives most women nuts, says Dr. Silverstein. So be sure to tell him what you need: empathy, not solutions.

Schedule "sex dates." Planning for romance can actually stir up some anticipatory excitement, says Dr. Elkin. You may begin to look forward to these times—and prepare for them—like your high-school self would have prepared for a Saturday night date.

Have amour in the A.M. Most people make love before they go to sleep. For some people, this may not be the best time, Dr. Elkin says. You

Women Need Sugar, Men Need Sex

He's stressed; he reaches for you. You're stressed; you reach for the chocolate bar on your nightstand. Why do women tend to soothe stress with food, while men seek release with sex?

The answer may lie within a tiny portion of the brain called the hypothalamus, says Mona Lisa Schulz, M.D., Ph.D., a neuropsychiatrist in Yarmouth, Maine.

The hypothalamus is a part of the limbic system, a group of brain structures that govern food, fighting, fear—and sex. In most women, the part of the hypothalamus that rules sexual desire is extremely close to the part that controls feeding, says Dr. Schulz. In most men's brains, these two portions of the hypothalamus are farther apart.

That doesn't mean that some women don't get lusty when they're under stress, or that anxious men don't turn to jelly doughnuts. We all have unique ways of soothing ourselves, says Dr. Schulz. "But there's no question that more women than men eat under stress, and there are neuroanatomical differences in how men and women are programmed for sex—at least, in the hypothalamus."

may be too wiped out by the demands of the day to be able to give or receive pleasure. The solution: daytime sex. "In my experience, people enjoy making love in the morning or afternoon because it's more relaxed and they are less tired," he says. "It's waking up with your mate and wanting to be close."

Be touchy-feely. "Touching is a form of physical intimacy that promotes psychological intimacy," explains Dr. Elkin. So give each other a lingering hug, a loving caress, a back massage. Or take a warm bath together. You may find that the tension melts away and you're in the mood after all.

"If you're willing to just cuddle, you may find that it's a transition to sex," says Dr. Silverstein. Even if it doesn't lead to sexual intercourse, cuddling is nice in and of itself, she adds.

Give it a go. If stress has seriously curtailed your lovemaking and you know your husband is frustrated, consider making love anyway—for the relationship. "Just jump in and see what happens," says Dr. Elkin. You may be glad you did. Of course, never make love if doing so would make you resent your partner or if you would feel used, he stresses. This option works only if you give sex wholeheartedly, as a gift.

Tape Over Your "Stress Tapes"

Sometimes, stress traps us in an endless loop of negative self-talk.

"I'll never get all this housework done!"

"My boss is never satisfied with my work."

"I should have gotten that promotion. I'm never going to get anywhere."

Banishing such negative self-talk can make stress easier to bear, says Dr. Elkin. Instead, replace it with a more positive interpretation: Just because I didn't get this promotion doesn't mean I can't get one in the future. Here's how to replace stress-inducing thoughts with more stress-resilient ones, according to Dr. Elkin.

Stressor: It's 8:00 P.M. Your kids have been at each other's throats since after dinner and you have four loads of laundry to do and overdue bills to mail. You're fantasizing about running off to Tahiti with that nice personal trainer at your gym.

Stress-Provoking Self-Talk: Can't-stand-it-itis. (As in: "That's it! I'm going off the deep end!")

Stress Rx: A deep breath and a reality check. Is the situation literally intolerable, or just unpleasant? Will you really go clinically insane? No.

Once you've squelched these irrational thoughts, deal with each stress separately, advises Dr. Elkin. For example, you might send the kids to bed, ignore the laundry, and do the bills. And then you might invite your mate to join you in a stress-relieving bubble bath. You forget all about the personal trainer.

Stressor: Your boss tells you that the report you've spent weeks preparing is disorganized and missing key information. She expects a rewrite in three days.

Stress-Provoking Self-Talk: Ego-bashing. (As in: "I'm a failure. She's going to fire me.")

Stress Rx: Running yourself down will only fuel your stress. Instead, challenge your negative self-perceptions. You're not going to be fired. Your boss doesn't think you're a failure—you've done excellent work in the past. You'll do a better job next time.

Stressor: A promotion opens up in your office, and it goes to someone else.

Stress-Provoking Self-Talk: Should-ing. (As in: "That job should have gone to me. It's all in who you know. Life just isn't fair!")

Stress Rx: Erase the word "should" from your brain. "Shoulds" won't change the facts, and continuing to cling to them only feeds stress, says Dr. Elkin. If you replace your "should" with "I would like to," it will spare you a lot of stress, he adds.

PART SEVEN

Extraordinary
Problem-Solving

Alcohol Abuse

Q: My husband has always enjoyed a beer or two after work, but in the past months he has been drinking heavily in the evenings. I suspect he has a few drinks at lunch, too. I've tried to shrug it off; he says that he's under a lot of pressure at work, and that nagging from me only makes things worse. So far, I've hidden the problem from our families and friends, even calling his office with excuses when he's too hungover to go to work. I have threatened, cajoled, hidden our few bottles of liquor, and once even poured it all down the sink. But nothing helps. What should I do now?

A: In a loving effort to help your husband, you're actually protecting him from the full consequences of his actions, and so you're making it a bit easier for him to continue drinking, says Patricia O'Gorman, Ph.D., a psychologist in Canaan, New York, whose treatment specialties include substance abuse, and author of *Dancing Backwards in High Heels: How Women Master the Art of Resilience*. At the same time, you may be so caught up in his problem that you're overlooking its damaging effects on you, your relationship, and your family.

For your own well-being, and for the future of your marriage, it's time to stop helping him and concentrate on your needs. "The first thing you should do is to stop protecting him, stop cajoling him, and stop rationalizing away the problem when he says he drinks because of work stress," Dr. O'Gorman says. "Instead, you need to get support so that you can take good care of yourself and find more effective ways to deal with your husband."

Your husband's alcoholism can—and will—significantly erode many aspects of your marriage. "The changes are so slow and subtle that you don't realize what's happening," Dr. O'Gorman says. "You may wind up paying all the bills and taking over all the household responsibilities." Sexual intimacy can suffer. While alcohol increases desire, it takes away the ability to function, and it may decrease his capacity to appreciate your needs and feelings.

"The biggest impact of all, though, is loss of trust financially, emotionally, and mentally," says Marla Elmore, a certified addictions counselor at the Prairie Center for Substance Abuse in Urbana, Illinois. "You can no longer count on your spouse for help and support." (Other forms of substance abuse have similar effects, she notes. The steps recommended below for dealing effectively with alcoholism would also be helpful if you suspect your spouse has a drug problem.)

Where to Turn for Help

The best place to begin? Call the nearest chapter of Al-Anon, a support group for family members and friends of alcoholics. This group has chapters across the country, with convenient meeting times that are often publicized in local papers. (For drug problems, call Nar-Anon, which is dedicated to supporting the families and friends of drug users.)

While family, friends, clergy, and psychotherapists can listen and offer a shoulder to cry on as well as give you important insights, both Elmore and Dr. O'Gorman say that Al-Anon excels at combining emotional understanding with practical, immediate strategies for dealing with the unique problems in a marriage touched by alcoholism. Think of Al-Anon as the true experts—the people who, like you, love and choose to live with a spouse who has an alcohol problem, Elmore says. "People attending these groups do not spend their time focusing on the alcoholic, complaining about their behavior. Their purpose is to help families and friends deal with the effects of alcoholism on themselves and what they can do to stay healthy. They get down to the business of what works for them, not on how to fix the alcoholic."

Why start with yourself when your spouse has the problem? "You have to be selfish and take care of yourself, or you and your family will be dragged deeper and deeper into the problem," Dr. O'Gorman says. In a support group, you will learn to stop seeing this as your shameful problem, and therefore to stop hiding it. You will learn new behaviors (such as not making excuses for him when he can't go to work) that place responsibility for his actions where they belong—with him. And you will also learn how to address the issue of alcoholism with your children, if you have any.

There are no guarantees that by changing your behavior, your husband will automatically see the light. But it does increase the odds, Dr. O'Gorman says. "When you stop covering up for him and hiding the problem from friends and family, he'll feel the natural consequences of his actions," she explains. "That may help wake him up. It can be a powerful tool for change."

The Road to Recovery

Once you quit running interference with his boss, pouring the scotch down the kitchen drain, telling little white lies to your friends, and treating him with kid gloves because he says he's under stress, what's left to do? Be honest. Tell him how his drinking is hurting you, your marriage, and your family. And ask him to get treatment, says Elmore. (Options include public and private outpatient or inpatient substance-abuse treatment centers, hospitals, and self-help recovery groups such as Alcoholics Anonymous.)

Don't make the mistake of expecting him to change his attitudes just because you are. Your recovery is yours. "The hardest thing to accept is that someone with an alcohol- or substance-abuse problem can only decide on his own to change," Elmore says. "Your most heartfelt words may not lead to recovery. People with substance-abuse problems usually strongly deny that anything is wrong. So you have to talk about it because it helps *you* and keeps things honest in your relationship."

If he continues to drink, you may want to talk with your doctor about the problem and then bring your husband in for an office visit. Ask the doctor to seriously discuss the consequences of alcoholism, and to tell your husband specifically how booze is already harming his body. "Sometimes, that's enough to frighten someone into seeking help," Dr. O'Gorman says.

You may also want to consider organizing the kind of large-scale confrontation that trained professionals such as addictions counselors call an intervention. "A good intervention takes a lot of time and a lot of planning," says Dr. O'Gorman. "It can be a very powerful experience, but you have to remember it's not foolproof." Organized with the help of a treatment center or with a trained professional suggested by your support group, an intervention brings together in one room all the significant people in the alcoholic's life—from his employer to his children to close friends and neighbors. "You go around the room, and everyone shares how the person's alcoholism has affected them," Dr. O'Gorman says. "Then you insist the person get treatment immediately. I attended one, for a man who was not moved by anything anyone said. Finally, his young granddaughter simply said, 'Granddad, you stink when you're drinking.' He broke down. You never know what, or who, will get the message through."

It's important to have treatment arrangements already in place—such as at an outpatient or inpatient treatment center—so that recovery work can begin as soon as the intervention ends, Dr. O'Gorman says.

It's equally important to keep on seeking support for yourself during your husband's recovery. "Many aspects of your life together will have to be re-negotiated," Dr. O'Gorman says. "He will have to reassume responsibilities around the house, adjust to sex without alcohol, and find new ways to socialize and celebrate. All of these changes will affect you and your relationship. The two of you will learn to build a new life that doesn't include alcohol."

Domestic Abuse

Q: My husband and I lived together before we got married. Two times, he got really angry and hit me during an argument. In both cases, he had been drinking. He always felt bad the next day, and I forgave him. He would alternate between being really sweet and loving, and highly critical and demeaning.

Now that we're married, his outbursts seem to be getting worse as well as more frequent. And he forced me to have sex on his terms. I've considered leaving, but when I bring it up, he gets really contrite and promises he'll change. But the last time he hit me, I had to go to the emergency room. I'm really scared. I'd like to believe he'll change, but I don't want to live the rest of my life this way.

A: First and foremost, congratulate yourself. Recognizing that you don't want to live your life this way is the first and most important step in helping yourself, and possibly your husband and your relationship, says Richard Meth, Ph.D., director of the Humphrey Center for Marital and Family Therapy and coordinator of the domestic violence program at the University of Connecticut in Storrs.

Unfortunately, what's happening to you is typical of the abuse cycle— your husband has assaulted you verbally and physically; he feels guilty and apologizes for his violent behavior; you want to believe that it won't happen again, so you accept his apology. But quite likely, the abuse cycle will repeat itself unless you or your husband takes definite steps to interrupt it, says Dr. Meth.

In the early stages of an abusive relationship, the abuse can be difficult to recognize because it often begins with subtle verbal attacks. "When people think about male to female violence, they usually think about physical aggression, with visible marks such as bruises or cuts," says Dr. Meth. "But abuse also includes any psychological or emotional threat of physical aggression to intimidate, manipulate, or control you."

When a relationship first becomes physically violent, it isn't unusual for you to accept his apology in the hope that it was a one-time incident, or for you to "excuse" his behavior because it happened when he was drinking, says Dr. Meth. It also wouldn't be unusual for you to blame yourself and attempt to alter your behavior in the hope that if you are a "better wife," he won't hit you again. "But it's a tremendous mistake for a woman to think that she can change an abusive situation on her own," says Dr. Meth. "Abuse is too pervasive and deep-seeded for that, and both you and your husband need professional support and counseling."

Though abuse can occur for lots of different reasons, men primarily use violence as a method of power and control. Many men feel they need power in relationships to regulate the degree of intimacy, says Dr. Meth. In addition, many men learn that abusive behavior is acceptable in intimate relationships because they were abused as children or they observed their own fathers abusing their mothers.

Learned behavior may also be a reason why you have decided to stay in your relationship. If you grew up in a violent home, you may think that you

Can an Abusive Man Change?

You've laid it on the line: If your marriage is going to have a future, your husband's abusive behavior needs to change. But will it?

Maybe, maybe not.

"It's amazing how motivated some men are to change when they feel threatened with losing someone they care about," says Richard Meth, Ph.D., director of the Humphrey Center for Marital and Family Therapy and coordinator of the domestic violence program at the University of Connecticut in Storrs. So some men can change their behavior if they are committed to it, says Dr. Meth. But most abusive men stay abusive.

If your husband (or any man you live with) fits all or most of the risk factors for abuse listed below, your relationship may not stand a chance, says Dr. Meth.

His abuse is regular and uncontrolled. Incidents of abuse may start out seemingly infrequent and minor, but they generally repeat and escalate into greater violence over time. If his violent outbreaks are regular and uncontrolled, it may be dangerous for you to stay. But even a single isolated incident is cause for concern.

He blames you for his behavior. Many abusive men blame their partners in an attempt to justify their violence. For example, they might say, "If you hadn't nagged me so much, I wouldn't have hit you."

deserve abusive treatment, or that violence is part of normal family dynamics. Women may also stay in an abusive situation out of fear or economic necessity. But, according to Dr. Meth, most women stay in abusive relationships because of the positive interactions they share with their partners when they are not abusive. "For outsiders who see only the abusive nature of a relationship, it's easy to say that a woman should leave," he says. "But for the woman living with the man day in and day out, there may be positive aspects to the marriage—aspects she often takes into consideration when deciding whether to leave or stay."

He abuses alcohol or drugs. Use of alcohol or drugs can only exacerbate your husband's emotional instability and intensify the conflicts between you. It's likely that abusive men will use alcohol and drugs as an excuse for their violent behaviors.

He doesn't take your feelings seriously. If he dismisses your concerns about his abusive behavior, he probably doesn't care about changing it.

He grew up in an abusive family. It isn't unusual for men who are abusive to have grown up in violent homes. If your husband's father hit his mother, he may have a distorted view of what constitutes a loving relationship.

He has a history of abuse. If your husband's previous relationships with women ended because of abuse and he has continued his abusive behavior, it's not likely that he will change for you.

If your husband truly wants to change, he needs to get counseling—specifically anger management therapy and support group counseling, says Dr. Meth. "Men who are abusive need to learn new ways of thinking about masculinity and male/female relationships." At times, it may be a good idea for you and your husband to separate while he works on changing his attitude and behavior.

Only you can determine if and when it's time for you to leave your abusive relationship. If you aren't ready to leave, it's important that you, your husband, and your children, if any, go to counseling. It's also important that you have a safety plan should you need to leave a violent situation quickly: Have a change of clothes packed with an extra set of car keys; set aside some money; gather important papers such as birth certificates; have a safe place you can go to, such as family, friends, or a local shelter. And if you are ready to leave, you can get specific information about resources in your area from the human or social services pages of the phone book.

Infidelity

Q: My husband had an affair for six months with a former co-worker. I confronted him after his behavior became suspicious—he was working late a lot, avoiding me at home, growing distant in the bedroom. The final piece of evidence was a handful of crumpled restaurant receipts, for places we'd never been, stashed in the glove compartment of his car. He says the relationship is over and that he never loved her. He wants me to forgive him and move on with our life together. But I can't. I feel hurt, betrayed, extremely angry—and scared that he doesn't love me. I'm afraid he had the affair because I didn't satisfy him in some way. I'm so upset that I just want to walk out and end our marriage. Is there any hope for us?

A: "Discovering your mate's infidelity can be devastating," says Janis Abrahms Spring, Ph.D., a clinical psychologist in Westport, Connecticut, and author of *After the Affair: Healing the Pain and Rebuilding Trust When a Partner Has Been Unfaithful.* "Women, in particular, tend to blame themselves for their husbands' affairs and fall into the trap of believing that they are unlovable or somehow not good enough."

His unfaithfulness may have little to do with who *you* are—and everything to do with his own feelings and responses to issues in his own life and in your marriage, says Dr. Spring. You must now decide whether or not you will attempt to rebuild your marriage—an extremely difficult choice when you're not sure you can even trust your husband.

Your husband seems to want quick forgiveness and a return to "normal" life—perhaps hoping both of you can bury your feelings and forget that the affair ever happened. Meanwhile, you're contemplating divorce. These are normal responses, but neither will allow the two of you to reconnect in a healthy way.

Marriages Can Mend

It may or may not be of any comfort to know that infidelity is common—and that many couples recover. Estimates vary widely. One report found that one-third of married men and one-fourth of married women had been unfaithful to their spouses, while another national study found that 20 percent of married men and 10 percent of married women had had affairs. Psychologists like Dr. Spring suspect that the true numbers are higher, because many of those surveyed refuse to answer the question. "Plus, there are other kinds of infidelity that aren't even measured, such as anonymous sex on the Internet and emotional infidelity," she points out. "The true definition of infidelity goes beyond sex—it's really about secrets and a breach of trust in a committed relationship."

Which couples survive? "Nobody has reliable numbers," Dr. Spring says. "Certainly, both partners have to be committed to staying together and learning from what happened. The work can take at least a year, and there will always be echoes of the affair. So, in a sense, it takes a lifetime. The positive side is that you can both become stronger individuals and intimate partners. Your marriage can be better." If the marriage was once good, the odds of reconnecting are higher, she adds.

How can you tell if your marriage is worth fighting for? "You're in a lot of pain. So rely on your head—and not your feelings—to make this crucial decision," Dr. Spring advises. "Look at your past. Was your marriage happy and intimate in its early years? Did you have shared values, a vision for your future, activities you enjoyed together, a satisfying sex life? Any or all of these are strengths you can build on now." (If, on the other hand, you look back and see a string of affairs or one-night stands, dishonesty, distrust, hostility, or a lack of love and support, you may decide not to stay, she adds.)

First Steps

With the facts in mind, you can make a commitment to work on your marriage even though you feel devastated and ambivalent right now. "I've found that the couples who recover after affairs are those who work on their marriages even though there are still strong feelings of hurt, mistrust, and bitterness between them," Dr. Spring says. "If you wait until you feel motivated or absolutely certain or in love before rebuilding, a reconciliation may never happen."

Will the good feelings ever return? By choosing to treat each other in ways that build tenderness and intimacy, you may be able to work through the bad feelings and bring love back into your relationship, Dr. Spring says. You can confirm your commitment—say, by writing a pledge together. You might promise to

Eight Warning Signs of Infidelity

Receipts for hotel rooms you've never seen, let alone slept in. Credit card bills for roses you never received. Mysterious hang-ups when you answer the phone. Some clues to a spouse's infidelity are nearly impossible to overlook. Other signals, listed below, are less obvious.

Irregular hours. He is in a pattern of coming home later than usual, being away from the office for unusually long lunches, or suddenly "working weekends."

Broken promises or vagueness about his whereabouts. He says he'll be home at a certain time, but he shows up hours later. Or he won't say exactly where he has been.

Flashes of temper. He overreacts when you confront him about where he has been and what he was doing.

A new look. He is suddenly spending more time on grooming, has a new hairstyle, has changed his taste in apparel, or wears a new cologne.

Surprising interests. Out of the blue, he has a new hobby that doesn't reflect any interests you were aware of. (Why is he suddenly playing squash? Showing an interest in jazz? Reading poetry?) It could be an interest of the other woman's.

look at how you both have contributed to any problems in your relationship and agree to take each other's grievances seriously, she suggests. At the same time, each of you can take important steps that will help your marriage recover.

As the hurt spouse, you can:

- Provide hope for your husband. "Unfaithful partners worry that they will never be forgiven and will be punished for life," Dr. Spring says. If you see that your husband is working hard to be accountable to you, let him know how much his efforts comfort you.

- Try to believe him when he says it was "just sex." As the hurt partner, a woman is likely to worry about the emotional connection between her husband and the "other woman," and she may believe she can't offer the same intense bond. But the truth is that men often seek sexual playmates more

Stronger interest in you. He displays more generosity, takes you out for unaccustomed dinner dates, provides extra help around the house. All this seems great, but it may indicate he's feeling very, very guilty.

Or a growing chasm between the two of you. His guilty secret may, instead, prompt withdrawal and evasion. (During an affair, some spouses alternate between lavishing extra attention and withdrawing, notes Jane Greer, Ph.D., a marriage and family therapist in New York City and author of *How Could You Do This to Me? Learning to Trust after Betrayal.*)

Changed sexual behavior. Your mate may want to make love more often, or less often, than usual. Or he may suddenly display new lovemaking techniques. Unless you've been reading sexual self-help books together, you may wonder, "Now, where did he learn how to do *that*?"

Don't assume your husband is having an affair, says Dr. Greer. Some changes may be prompted by other factors. But if something seems odd, do find out what's going on, she says. Denying that your mate has changed in some way is in itself a sign that something might be strained within the relationship.

than soulmates when they have affairs, Dr. Spring says. "It can be hard to believe if your husband tells you the affair was about sex, not love," she notes. "But he could be telling you the truth." (You'll want to insist that you both be tested for sexually transmitted diseases.)

Your husband must begin restoring your trust, Dr. Spring says. To heal the relationship, an unfaithful spouse should:

- Stop the affair immediately
- Demonstrate that he feels compassion and remorse for the pain he has caused
- Be able to listen to your point of view respectfully
- Show willingness to take responsibility for the affair, and to help repair problems in your relationship

Restoring Intimacy

Rebuilding your relationship is a journey through new emotional territory. Couples who recover try to understand why the affair happened. They also try to build more satisfaction into the marriage. You may want to seek couples counseling to help understand and manage the difficult emotions that can arise, Dr. Spring suggests. A therapist can also act as a referee, ensuring that both of you speak up and get a fair hearing.

Taking responsibility for how you have each made room for a third person to come between you is key, Dr. Spring says. "When nothing is learned and nothing changes, the problem remains and so does the temptation to stray."

You may wonder if you can ever really trust him again. Finding out the truth—"Where were you on that night you said you were working until 1:00 in the morning?" "Did you give her any gifts?" "Have you seen her at work this week?" "Will you tell me if she calls you or tries to see you privately?"—can help by lifting the damaging veil of secrecy. But be careful: Women often get stuck obsessing about the "other woman" instead of focusing on their marriages.

fascinating FACTS

Is It Cheating?

In the wake of President Bill Clinton's affair with former White House intern Monica Lewinsky, Time/CNN polled married men and women about what they believe constitutes cheating in a marriage. Here's what they found.

Contact	Women (%)	Men (%)
Kissing	75	59
Casual flirting	38	32
Holding hands	49	40
Sexually explicit phone conversation	74	64
Sexually explicit Internet conversation	72	62
Fantasizing about sex with another	43	39

Other trust-building strategies include asking your husband to share more of his daily feelings and experiences with you, to spend more time with you (by coming home on time for dinner, planning a get-away vacation, or making time for sexual intimacy, for example), or to attend more closely to your emotional and physical needs. "Be as specific as you can be in your requests, and be prepared to make changes he asks for, too," Dr. Spring advises.

Don't be surprised if you find that reconnecting physically brings up new fears and concerns. This is a normal reaction. You may worry that your husband won't find you as desirable or satisfying as his former lover, or fear that he's still cheating if he's not interested in sex when you are. Your husband may worry that if he doesn't satisfy you, you'll assume he's still interested in his lover. "Try to distinguish fact from fear," Dr. Spring suggests. Your husband may be tired, feel pressured to perform, or fear a confrontation if you make love. There are lots of explanations that don't implicate you and that are probably the right ones. Talk about your sexual relationship in a nonjudgmental way, and let your husband know that what's most important to you is connecting again.

As you work on your relationship, also try to enjoy each other as best you can, Dr. Spring suggests. Take a walk. Go out to dinner. Make love. Rent a movie. By generating good feelings instead of expressing bitterness or doubt, you may find that your marriage can blossom again.

Midlife Crisis

Q: For years, I was happy with my home life, my job, my friendships, and my marriage. But ever since my 50th birthday, I've felt more and more discontent. I regret some choices I've made, and I even feel a little disappointed in my marriage. I suddenly crave more substance in my life. My children aren't at home anymore, and I want to branch out—travel, maybe get a new job. Yet I worry that by making changes, or even paying attention to this restlessness, my marriage might never be the same. Am I having a midlife crisis? What should I do?

A: Welcome to the growing pains of midlife. After decades of contentment at home, at work, and with family and friends, you're heeding a sudden urge to re-evaluate your life from top to bottom. This can feel disconcerting, but take heart: Reviewing your life at its midpoint and making changes is a normal, healthy process, says Janice Levine, Ph.D., a clinical psychologist and director of the Couples Health Program in Lexington, Massachusetts.

"Midlife doesn't have to be a crisis," Dr. Levine says. "It's an opportunity, a transition to a new phase of life, a time to reclaim yourself as an individual."

You're right about one thing: Midlife change can potentially affect your marriage. "Midlife questioning, doubts, and re-evaluations usually begin with one partner or the other, but inevitably they end up involving both partners," Dr. Levine says. "One individual can't change without affecting the dynamics of the relationship." If the two of you can talk together about the experience, and try not to blame each other for personal disappointments, your relationship will likely be enhanced, not torn apart. "Growth and change are the lifeblood of a healthy marriage, not things to be feared or resisted," she notes.

Why Now?

Many events can trigger midlife angst, from a milestone birthday to the death of a parent, from the arrival of menopause to your youngest child's departure for college, leaving you alone in an empty nest. "At these times, we face our mortality. We start to see that time is limited and precious," says Carol Landau, Ph.D., clinical professor of psychiatry and human behavior at Brown University School of Medicine in Providence, Rhode Island, and coauthor of *The Complete Book of Menopause*. "The good news is that you also have a second chance at happiness. At age 50, you may have 30 or 35 more years ahead. There's still plenty of time."

Trigger events can bring long-held feelings of discontent into sudden, sharp focus. "For example, you may have stayed in a job for years, not because you liked it but because it kept the family afloat financially, was close to home, or had a convenient schedule. You weren't happy in it, but you pushed aside the frustration," Dr. Levine notes. But when a trigger event such as turning 50 occurs, you may suddenly see that job in a new light. "Now you may see that you've been postponing your desire to put your own needs first," she says. "And you may feel a strong need to do something about that."

A trigger event will only prompt deep questioning if you're already experiencing a mismatch between what you most deeply desire and what you're actually getting out of life, Dr. Levine says. If you're not fully aware of that mismatch, then you might not recognize the wake-up call. In that case, a trigger event can prompt a true crisis—you may find yourself desperately unhappy without knowing why, and you may even mistakenly blame others for your dissatisfaction.

Financial security—and insecurity—can also prompt midlife re-evaluations. If you and/or your spouse have had good jobs, bought a home, and saved for retirement, now you may be saying to yourselves, "Is this all there is?" Hap-

---

Real Crisis, or Just Midlife Growing Pains?

A landmark birthday, an illness, an emptied nest—any one of a number of major life events can trigger restlessness at midlife, says Janice Levine, Ph.D., a clinical psychologist and director of the Couples Health Program in Lexington, Massachusetts. Other classic triggers of midlife change include:

- Death of a parent, spouse, or close friend

- Your child reaching adolescence

- Menopause

- Male sexual problems, such as erectile problems or impotence

- Realizing that you're not as young or attractive as you used to be

- Economic security (You're set for the future and wondering what to do now.)

- Financial insecurity (You realize you can't retire when you would like, or you have to stay in a job you don't enjoy.)

"These trigger events can bring to the surface discontent you might not have realized was even there," Dr. Levine says. Dealing with what's really bothering you can help prevent a full-blown crisis and, instead, prompt positive change.

pily, you may now have the means to make new dreams come true. If, on the other hand, you or your partner has faced layoffs, business setbacks, or health problems that curtailed earnings, you may feel nervous about the future as your hoped-for retirement years approach. You may feel stuck in a job and see no way out. And if you have become the family breadwinner, you and your husband may feel uncomfortable in new economic roles that give you more financial power and seem to diminish his traditional position in the family.

Put Yourself First

"At midlife, many women begin thinking about autonomy and individuality, about expressing who we really are," says Dr. Landau. "I see women becoming more assertive, in a positive way, and more active. We move beyond our traditional roles as nurturers and begin putting ourselves first." That could mean speaking up more at home and at work, pursuing a more meaningful career or doing volunteer work, choosing new hobbies, or making new friends—or taking other steps that bring new meaning to your daily life.

At the same time, a woman may also look more critically at the quality of intimacy in her relationships with her spouse, her children, and her friends and feel a need for a deeper connection, Dr. Landau says.

Among the feelings that may surface now are discontent ("I don't want to stay in this job forever!"), doubt ("We've never had the perfect marriage. Did I make the right choice?"), and regret ("I haven't seen the family and friends who really matter to me often enough. I've missed some important times together. I wish I had been there.")

Do feelings of discontent mean that you've made all the wrong choices, or that to be happy, you need to file for divorce, lose 20 pounds, color your hair, sail to Hawaii, take a handsome young lover, and learn to cliff-dive into the blue Pacific? Probably not. A strong sense of discontent is a loud signal that it's time to pay attention to your inner needs, but not necessarily a sign that your life needs a complete overhaul. Small or gradual changes may make all the difference, according to Dr. Levine.

To help you sort out your discontent and decide what to do, experts offer the following advice.

Let the big questions simmer. Dr. Levine asks herself questions about her life and then lets the answers rise to the surface. "I ask myself if I'm doing what I really want to be doing. If I'm still happy with my marriage, my job, my social life," she says. "The questions just simmer in the back of my mind. I notice that little red flags go up if I find I'm doing things that I really don't want to be doing." In the same way, little green flags may go up when you are doing what pleases you most. If you pay attention to the red and green flags, you could have an "Aha" moment, when you recognize choices that are working for or against you.

Select a confidante. "For most women, the single most important help at midlife is having a close friend you can confide in," Dr. Landau says. "Choose someone who can listen without having her own agenda. For instance, if you are married and need to talk over doubts about your relationship, do not confide in a woman who is in the midst of a separation herself."

Put regret in its place. At midlife, many women feel at least some regrets. Some point you toward important actions, such as making peace with your parents or siblings, Dr. Landau says. But others can take on a life of their own, with no resolution. If you find yourself spending lots of time ruminating about the road not taken, it may be time to forgive yourself for simply being human. (After all, if you decided to raise three children and work part-time instead of becoming a research chemist or a concert pianist, remind yourself that you made a great choice. No one can do everything. Put superwoman to rest.)

Clue Him In

Trying to hide midlife questioning from your partner won't work—and could be dangerous for your marriage, experts say. "He will probably see changes in your behavior before you do," says Dr. Levine. You may start acting distant, lose interest in activities you've shared for years, stop seeing old friends as often, even change your wardrobe or your hairstyle. He's bound to notice and wonder what's up.

More important, resisting change out of fear that your marriage will be altered shortchanges both you and your relationship, Dr. Levine says. "If you hold back in an effort to keep everything the same, your need for change may express itself in unhealthy ways. You might grow to resent your husband, become depressed, even spend money recklessly or have an affair," she notes.

So speak up. For all you know, he may be experiencing similar feelings. "A lot of couples go through midlife changes at the same time," Dr. Landau says. "The kids have left, the mortgage is paid, and they decide together what they'd like to do next."

How women and men deal with change is different, though. While a man might distract himself, a woman may be more likely to want to talk things out. Try talking with your spouse in a nonthreatening way about your hopes and frustrations, suggests Dr. Landau. Pick a time when the two of you are relaxed, not tired or rushed. And be specific about what you want from him. If

---

Handling His Midlife Crisis

Suddenly, something has gotten into your man. Perhaps he's criticizing you more often. Or opening up in surprising ways. Maybe he's more withdrawn. Or he has declared war on stodginess—and has swapped his sensible four-door sedan for a red roadster, updated his wardrobe, even made some risky investments.

Ah, men at midlife. No two experience this season of change in exactly the same way. But you can take actions to help yourself—and your marriage—thrive while he re-evaluates his life, says Carol Landau, Ph.D., clinical professor of psychiatry and human behavior at Brown University School of Medicine in Providence, Rhode Island, and coauthor of *The Complete Book of Menopause.*

First, understand that midlife change isn't a crisis—it's healthy, a time when men and women alike seek greater fulfillment. For men, this sometimes means looking beyond traditional sources of satisfaction. "A man who has defined himself by his work may feel a new need for relationships, or a new need to express his emotions," Dr. Landau says.

Here's how you can help your guy, according to Dr. Landau.

Listen openly. Marriages thrive during midlife if partners talk together about their new wants, needs, and dreams, Dr. Landau says. Encourage conversation by talking about your own experience and listening attentively when he talks about his.

And keep on listening. Be prepared: Rightly or wrongly, he may be critical of you or your marriage. "It's very hard to listen to criticism, but try to do so without getting defensive or overreacting. Listening doesn't mean

the two of you have spent every weekend for the last 18 years doing something with the kids or doing household chores, maybe it's time for something new. Be ready to suggest some alternative activities.

Talking is especially important if your midlife hopes and dreams don't seem to match up, Dr. Landau says. You may be ready to dive into a new career, for example, while your husband is interested in pursuing new leisure-time activities.

---

you agree with everything he says," Dr. Landau notes. "Your husband may be right—just as your husband's behavior affects you, you may be contributing to a situation he no longer likes in your marriage."

Set limits. Don't be a doormat—you don't have to fix everything that's bothering him. "Just because he's unhappy in some part of his life doesn't mean it's your fault or that you need to fix it," Dr. Landau says. "Women often take on a big emotional burden by making our husband's happiness our job. You don't have to do this."

If you have made changes at his request but the criticism continues, be assertive. Remember, it's tempting, and very human, to blame others for our own unhappiness. "Tell him you've tried his suggestions, but something's still not right. Ask if something else is bothering him," Dr. Landau suggests.

Stay alert for stealth tactics. There's nothing wrong with a sporty new car, a wardrobe update, or a new hairstyle—for the guy in your life, or for you. But if your spouse is taking unwarranted risks with the household savings, drinking more than usual, taking up a dangerous sport, or suddenly making radical changes in his physical appearance, these may be signs that he is caught in the throes of a midlife crisis but doesn't know how to identify it or think it through. Acting out brings temporary relief but won't address his real concerns. What can a spouse do? Try gently describing the patterns you see, and suggest that he may be grappling with larger issues. Be aware, however, that you cannot go through his midlife transition for him.

Think through your frustrations before starting a conversation. If you feel bored with your marriage, don't simply blame your husband. Ask yourself why. Perhaps you always imagined married life would bring a certain kind of excitement, but that hasn't materialized. And so it may be time to give up an unrealistic expectation. Or perhaps the two of you are stuck in old routines—maybe you've made love the same way for years or done the same things every weekend, for example. It may be time to try something new.

"If the two of you keep sharing with one another, keeping each other abreast of the shifts and growth you're experiencing, then your marriage will be enriched," Dr. Levine says. "When partners keep their needs secret, it creates distance."

In truth, not all marriages survive midlife changes. The divorce rate among middle-aged people is second only to the rate among younger couples who've been married seven years or less, Dr. Landau notes. "If one partner has felt alienated for years and has only stayed to raise the kids or out of economic necessity, then midlife can be an opportunity to leave a bad situation and start over," she notes.

Happily, that's the exception, not the rule. "We hear a lot about failed marriages at midlife—the affairs, the couples who divorce," Dr. Landau says. "But in reality, most people's transitions work out just fine."

Rebounding after Divorce

Q. Two years after my divorce, I still don't feel completely healed. Sometimes I feel very angry with my ex-husband, yet other times I long for a reconciliation. Sometimes I savor my independence, at other times I long for a new, committed relationship. My friends are encouraging me to date again, but I'm not sure I'm ready. How can I get on with my life?

A: Divorce and its aftermath can change a woman—or man—dramatically, says Sandy Plone, Ph.D., a licensed psychologist in Santa Monica, California, whose treatment specialties include divorce recovery, couples counseling, trauma recovery, and life transitions. "If you allow yourself to experience and work through the full range of emotions that the end of a marriage brings, then you'll have new energy for all that life offers, including dating and new relationships with men," she says.

For the moment, however, "it is quite normal to feel the type of ambivalence you describe about dating and socializing," Dr. Plone says. It may be too soon to date or consider a committed relationship, but you may be ready to venture out socially with a group of close friends or with a male friend you trust and enjoy on a "just-friends" basis. Going slowly, so that you can rebuild trust in yourself and in the people around you, is an important part of the divorce-recovery process. "With the courage to go through the feelings and risk new attachments and challenges, a divorced woman can emerge as a stronger, wiser, more creative person," she says.

Ready to Play the Dating Game?

When it comes to dating after divorce, trust your instincts, says Denise Prefontaine, R.N., a licensed psychotherapist and mental health counselor in Boston. "Don't buckle to the pressure of friends or family, who may be saying, 'Oh, you should get out more.' Instead, focus on what it is you really need, and try to achieve that. Follow your own interests."

Ask yourself why you want to date, says Prefontaine. "Is it to have fun? To find a committed relationship? Or as revenge against your former spouse?" If you're dating just to prove you can, because your ex-husband has a new girlfriend, or to fill a lonely gap when you're still having a strong emotional reaction to your divorce, it may be too soon.

Not sure you're ready? Then give yourself more time. Dating too soon could set you up for negative experiences, Prefontaine says. "If you're just not feeling ready, you may still be hurt and angry, vulnerable and feeling weepy," she explains. "If you go on a date and you really don't feel confidence in yourself about socializing and interacting with a man who may be interested in you, then you're going to give off a negative aura." You may not even be aware that you're being negative or condescending, but a man will likely pick up on these

For a Fresh Start, Buy New Bedsheets

"The first thing a lot of women (and men) do when they get divorced is buy new bedsheets," notes Denise Prefontaine, R.N., a licensed psychotherapist and mental health counselor in Boston. "And some don't stop at new sheets. Some of my newly divorced clients buy new mattresses, new beds, and new bath towels. Some even redecorate the whole house."

Replacing intimate household goods is an act of cleansing, a way to begin anew. "It's a concrete way of creating a new life," says Prefontaine.

Small wonder. Sheets, mattresses, and towels can hold memories, almost the essence, of an ex-spouse. "It's as if the smell of the other person were still there somehow," Prefontaine says. In contrast, she has also worked with former wives and husbands who hold on to these marital reminders, which become symbols of their hope that a former spouse will return.

While it can be refreshing and a relief to get rid of the old things, such external change won't bring about the much-needed emotional changes that really will allow you to lead a new life, Prefontaine adds. Ultimately, sheets are just sheets.

---

subtle signs that you're still feeling badly about yourself or about relating to men. "He'll respond, perhaps by being cool to you," Prefontaine says. "And so you may get the message that you're somehow a failure, somehow not good enough. You'll feel badly about yourself, when all you really needed was to work out your own feelings a bit more before beginning to date."

What if you think you're ready, but you feel a little scared and vulnerable? Relax, says Prefontaine. Nearly everyone out there in the adult dating world is a little bruised by now. "Most people who are dating in their forties or later, or after divorce, have been hurt or disappointed in one way or another," she points out. "If you've been left by your partner, certainly you were hurt. But it's also true that if you left somebody, you felt disappointed, too. I tell women this all the time. It's really an even playing field out there." Once you have worked through all the emotions that divorce brings and feel comfortable as a single person in the world, you'll feel more of an interest in the dating world.

From Shock to Serenity

There's no road map for rebounding from divorce; the experience is as unique as each person who journeys through it. Still, according to Dr. Plone, each person goes through similar stages that are reminiscent of the stages of grief after losing a loved one. "Divorce is, after all, the death of a relationship, the death of a marriage. The whole process may take time—perhaps several years—and doesn't move in a straight line. It's normal for grief and anger to re-emerge sometimes years later. Divorce recovery is often two steps forward, one step back."

In some ways, it's never completely over. Certain events—perhaps the re-marriage of your ex-spouse, a child's graduation, or the sale of the family home—may trigger old feelings, according to Dr. Plone. So be patient with yourself. The route may be difficult at times, but if you want to heal and move on with your life, it's a journey you would be wise to take. Here's what to expect along the way.

Stage One: Emotional Ups and Downs

You may feel worn down or angry after years of an unhappy marriage, betrayed and abandoned if your spouse left abruptly or had an affair, exhausted by months of legal or financial negotiations, or relieved that the whole thing is behind you. In any case, you've just experienced a traumatic loss, and you may feel as if you're on an emotional roller coaster, angry one minute, fearful the next, regretful another, and grief-stricken at yet another time.

Beyond losing your mate, divorce can have many practical impacts: Your lifestyle, friendships, child-rearing arrangements, and economic circumstances may change dramatically when your marriage ends, requiring you to make all sorts of adjustments at a time when you're already feeling vulnerable.

Stage Two: Your New Identity

As feelings of shock subside, you begin to face the world again—this time as a single woman. It may help if you venture out socially by taking small, comfortable steps, perhaps starting with something as simple as signing up for a class with a friend or joining a tennis club. "Look for the support and encouragement of trustworthy friends and family members to do this. Pick activities that you feel comfortable doing and places you feel comfortable going. Start slowly, and you'll feel better about yourself as you accumulate more and more positive experiences," Dr. Plone says.

Stage Three: Emotional Balance

"Gaining emotional equilibrium may take time, as each woman works through her issues and her own unique set of problems," Dr. Plone says. You will gradually rebuild trust and self-confidence as you pay attention to your feelings and make thoughtful choices about all aspects of your new life, from who you date to where you live to the kind of work you do.

"Before, during, and after divorce, it's important to seek support to help you express and understand your emotions—and to help you make sense of what went wrong in your marriage," Dr. Plone says. "You might want to join a support group, find a counselor, or talk with your pastor, priest, or rabbi. Feelings of anger and grief will not magically disappear. These feelings need expression. Feel them, talk about them, learn from them—and you will heal."

Separation and Reconciliation

Q. My husband and I love each other deeply, but we're constantly fighting. We've talked it all out, even tried marriage counseling, but nothing seems to help. We seem stuck in patterns that we just can't change. I need a break, but I'm not ready to consider divorce. Could a temporary separation help me regain my sanity, and help us re-evaluate our relationship and improve our marriage? Or is separation always a prelude to divorce?

A: "You're frustrated and the two of you are fighting all the time—hardly experiences that make you feel hopeful about your marriage," says Michele Weiner-Davis, a licensed psychotherapist in Woodstock, Illinois, and author of *Divorce Busting: A Step-by-Step Approach to Making Your Marriage Loving Again* and *A Woman's Guide to Changing Her Man—Without Him Even Knowing It!* But you can dare to hope: Both of you are still willing to work things out. That alone is a good sign your relationship can improve.

While you truly need a break, don't pack your bags just yet. Setting up separate living quarters may not be the best route to a better marriage. "When partners separate, it does give them a breather. Sometimes, they realize how much they miss each other, and they gather themselves up and deal with the issues," Weiner-Davis says. "But in general, living apart can be a disincentive to piecing your marriage back together."

To be sure, living apart enables you to avoid dealing with the small but thorny day-to-day issues that can make or break a marriage. But eventually, you'll have to face them. At the same time, you'll miss out on the fleeting good times that nurture your bond. In addition, you'll never know if your husband is really making significant changes if you're not living with him. And if moving out gives you a strong sense of relief, you may associate that good feeling with being alone—and want more of it.

Go or Stay?

Sometimes, of course, leaving is the only option. "If there's danger, such as ongoing substance abuse, domestic violence, or emotional abuse, then it is time to go—and quickly," Weiner-Davis says. For your own safety, only reunite if your husband can demonstrate that he's in recovery and the two of you have found a way to work on your relationship, through therapy or a support group or a 12-step program.

If the problem is less drastic, you may still need to break free for a while. "If a woman feels that there's no way she can go on another day in the same home with her husband and she needs some time alone, then a separation is better than nothing—it's kind of a last-ditch effort," notes Weiner-Davis.

Secrets of Long-Lasting Love

Separation Made Their Marriage Stronger

Marilyn Bauman, an artist, was immediately attracted to her husband Donald, a chemist, when they met in their coed graduate school dorm. Although they didn't appear to have much in common, the two of them clicked, and they started dating that fall. Exactly one year later, on September 6, 1964, they married. Today, the Baumans live in Wilmington, Delaware. Marilyn says their marriage has survived over the years, even through a separation, because of their ability to forgive and their commitment to make their marriage work.

Don and I come from such different backgrounds that sometimes I am amazed we were able to find any common ground. He grew up on a farm in Colorado, I grew up in New York City. He prefers time alone, I prefer social gatherings. He's rational, I'm creative. But I guess the differences don't matter much when you both feel good about each other.

Don and I did feel good about each other, and our marriage, until I was about 40. It was then that I came to realize that at some point over the years of our relationship, I had lost myself. I wasn't sure who I was anymore, and I needed to give myself some emotional distance to learn where Don stopped and I began. We were fighting so much that separation seemed to be the only answer. So I moved into the basement of our home.

"Actions—such as leaving—speak louder than words," says Weiner-Davis. "Sometimes, guys take women's intense desire for a good relationship a bit for granted. It can take a strong action to wake them up, make them realize what they're about to lose."

Reconciliation after a separation is most likely if both partners still want to work on the problem. Prospects are less bright if one partner denies that the marriage is troubled or has privately decided that the relationship has no future.

Simply leaving won't improve your marriage. Boost the odds that the two of you will get back together again by seeing each other frequently during your separation. Go on dates so that you can enjoy each other. Early in the

It may sound silly, but just being in my own space to concentrate on my painting and myself was enough. Don and I needed a break to see if we still liked each other, and if we would still choose to be with each other. Those few months were painful for both of us as well as for our three children. But it was good for me and my need for self-discovery, and it was good for us because Don and I affirmed that we still wanted to be partners.

Deciding that we wanted to be together again was easy, but asking Don to forgive me for the pain I caused him as a result of our physical separation was difficult. Don felt he was doing the best he could, and my need to separate had crushed him. Because my explanations could never resolve the separation, Don had to find it in himself to forgive me if our marriage was going to work. I also had some forgiving to do: I had to forgive Don for being him. What I mean is that I had to say, "I accept you, and I love you for who you are, and I want to work at our marriage."

All that pain seems so distant now. Don and I have come a long way, and we're committed to making our marriage work. As a matter of fact, our relationship is better now than it was before our separation. We're a lot closer, we've grown to be very much alike, and we both feel good about each other again.

separation, you may want to take a vacation from worrying about your marital troubles. But once you feel more refreshed, try to open a new conversation with your husband, says Weiner-Davis. (For advice on how to broach difficult issues with your spouse, see Conflict and Anger on page 13.) To repair a damaged relationship, read on.

Time Out without Moving Out

If you decide to stay, you'll avoid a lot of messy details: signing a lease or camping in a friend's spare bedroom; setting up separate telephone and utility accounts; arranging child care and visiting times; forwarding your mail (or going home frequently to retrieve it); moving your clothes, your books, your favorite coffee mug and sauté pan. "The mechanics of separation are similar to the mechanics of divorcing," Weiner-Davis says. "The danger is, these things can sort of take on a life of their own. You become separate in more ways than one."

If breathing space is your most immediate need, consider establishing separate arrangements without leaving home. Move into a spare bedroom for a while. Declare a two-week timeout, when you won't discuss your marital problems. Spend time pursuing your own interests, even if it means going to the movies alone. (The smallest acts—like having all the popcorn to yourself—are a nice indulgence in the midst of turmoil.) Spend a weekend visiting friends or simply get away to a spa, bed-and-breakfast, or inexpensive cabin overnight.

"Get him to watch the kids, or get a babysitter," Weiner-Davis suggests. "Try a massage. A concert. Get your car washed. There are many ways to pull yourself away without really leaving." Think big and small—and make a habit of it. Chances are, you've invested so much time, brain power, and emotional energy in fixing your relationship that you have neglected yourself. Whether it's a job change, socializing with friends, getting your finances in order, taking daily walks, or just making time to do your nails and smooth on some moisturizer, attending to your own needs on a regular basis could reduce some of your frustration, she says.

This alone won't fix your relationship. But a recharged, happier you will better deal with the problems at hand—and see the situation in a more positive light, points out Weiner-Davis.

Patching Things Up

If you and your husband have done plenty of talking and are still locked in frustrating patterns that perpetuate your problems, Weiner-Davis suggests an action-oriented strategy that can help you change these patterns and learn a new dance of togetherness.

Learn from the good times. For a moment, focus on the times when the two of you get along well. Think about what happens then. "You might find that things go well when you spend more time together, have sex more often, or go out without your children once a week, for example," Weiner-Davis says. "Often, couples find they've stopped doing the things that make them feel close. Then, tension and conflicts develop."

Catch yourselves in the act of getting along, then re-create those good times. "The beauty of this approach is that you get a solution that's uniquely tailored to your marriage," Weiner-Davis says. "You already know it works. You'll also see that there are exceptions to the troubled times. That's hopeful news."

Abandon "fixes" that don't work. If your spouse behaves in predictable and frustrating ways when you try to make things better in your marriage, then it may be time to change your own behavior, Weiner-Davis says. Think over your last few arguments to see if your actions fall into a pattern. Imagine how your spouse sees that pattern—perhaps he'd say that you nag, or keep your thoughts to yourself, for example.

Then, even if you think your behavior has been the right thing to do, try something new the next time you're tempted to say or do the same old thing. Do anything at all (provided it's not intended to trigger an argument), as long as you break your old pattern. "It's amazing how quickly novelty stops nonproductive interaction patterns," Weiner-Davis says.

Reschedule your arguments. Think back. Do your arguments happen at the same time of day, or in the same place (such as your bedroom at 11:00 P.M., or the kitchen at 7:00 A.M.)? "When a typical argument starts, move it to a room where you never argue, such as the bathroom, the garage, or the living room," Weiner-Davis says. "This can seem very humorous and can jolt both of you into having a discussion instead of a fight."

If time of day is part of the pattern, make a point of dealing with tough issues at a new date and time. (For example, talk about your finances on Saturday morning instead of Sunday night.) Choose high-energy times, and avoid touchy subjects late in the evening, when one or both of you are at work, or when you're already doing something, such as preparing a meal, getting the kids ready for bed, or getting the house ready for guests.

Learn to communicate all over again. "We take courses to learn to improve our businesses, work on our homes, pick up foreign languages or new sports," Weiner-Davis says. "But few people bother to take the time to learn how to run a good relationship. Today, there are plenty of ways to do that." (To find out how, see Communication on page 8.)

Choose the right counselor. Couples who decide to see a marriage counselor, or who are considering a return to couples counseling, should find a therapist who specializes in relationship skills, Weiner-Davis suggests. "My experience, from dealing with thousands of couples, is that people know exactly what the problem is," she says. "They don't need to spend weeks or months looking at their emotions, discussing their upbringings. When a couple is in crisis, you need hope. And you can get hope from having concrete skills to work on."

Set a deadline. It's normal to feel cautious and to doubt whether your marriage can be saved, Weiner-Davis says. "Tell your husband that you are close to leaving and it's time to get serious," she says. Then, set a reasonable deadline, perhaps a few months, in which you must see improvement in order to stay. "Promises aren't enough. You need to see proof of improvement. You can find new ways to relate to each other and stay together."

Sex Addiction

Q: Lately, my husband seems obsessed with sex. We make love four, five, or six times a week—and some nights he wakes me up again for more, whether I'm interested or not. He spends hours at the computer, usually in Internet sex chat rooms. And I've discovered pornographic magazines, which I find disturbing, in his closet. Does he just have a stronger-than-average sex drive? As long as he's not being unfaithful, should I ignore his new "hobby"?

A: "There's a big difference between a strong, healthy sex drive and sex addiction," says Deborah Corley, Ph.D., a psychotherapist and certified addictions specialist and clinical director of the Santé Center for Healing, an addictions treatment center in Argyle, Texas. "If your mate's desire for sex is out of control—if he spends so much time at night in sex chat rooms that he can't wake up for work or misses family functions; if he spends an inordinate amount of money on pornography; if he demands sex from you and doesn't take your feelings into consideration; if he can't stop himself from engaging in these behaviors, despite the consequences—then he may have an addiction problem."

And it is a serious problem. Like alcoholism or drug addiction, sex addiction can wreak havoc in all areas of a person's life, from physical health (there's a greater risk of getting a sexually transmitted disease) to finances, employment to emotional well-being, Dr. Corley says. And even if your husband isn't unfaithful, the addiction can also undermine important aspects of a marriage other than sex, including open communication, emotional intimacy, spending time together, parenting, and planning your future.

Facing the problem can be difficult for both partners. "Often, the spouse of a person with a sexual addiction denies the problem vigorously for months or even years," says Dr. Corley. "It's a natural instinct to protect the partner and to maintain the semblance of a normal life. But couples who go this route become more and more estranged. It becomes increasingly difficult to talk about the things that matter. And so the spouse becomes part of the problem, actually enabling it to continue. The sooner you get up the courage to address the problem, the better."

Break the Silence

Why do men—and women—find themselves drawn into compulsive sexual behavior? In many cases, they were sexually abused as children and may be reliving this deeply painful experience in an attempt to undo the damage to themselves. But this kind of out-of-control sexuality also becomes a way to numb themselves against feelings of loneliness, grief, anxiety, or a fear of intimacy, Dr. Corley says. Over time, a sex addict may seek bigger and bigger thrills to achieve the same high feeling. "It becomes like an affair, secretive and thrilling," she says. "At first, a person with a sexual addiction overlooks all the signals that this is wrong because it feels good. But over time, it will do damage."

Understanding the emotional needs that drive this kind of addiction can help you talk with your husband, Dr. Corley says. "When you're ready, approach your husband in a way that holds him accountable and at the same time describes your own feelings. Propose some solutions that involve the two of you," she suggests. "You might say something like, 'Joe, I've read some articles about sexual addiction, and I'm seeing some indicators here—you're spending hours every night on the Internet viewing pornography, and you've gotten angry at me when I haven't wanted to have sex. This scares me and makes me wonder if something is wrong with our relationship. I don't want that to happen. Would you be willing to talk with somebody about this, or for the two of us to gather more information about this?'"

Be ready for a long haul—and a stormy trip. At first, your spouse is likely to deny there's a problem. In that case, consider letting the issue drop for the moment. But stick to your guns: The next time you see behavior that looks like sex addiction, bring it up again in a nonthreatening way. "If he won't get help, you may have to take serious action and even threaten to separate," Dr. Corley says. "This is a tough step to take, but the problem isn't likely to go away on its own."

Treatments for sex addiction include 12-step programs, similar to Alcoholics Anonymous, called Sex Addicts Anonymous; support groups run by trained therapists or addiction specialists; and individual therapy, couples counseling, and family counseling. Drug therapy using antidepressants can also help in two ways: by lifting the depression that can accompany the problem, and by quieting the imbalance of neurochemicals in the brain that helps fuel the addictive behavior, Dr. Corley notes. "Many people combine several forms of treatment," she says. Occasionally, if the problem has become severe, in-patient or residential treatment at an addiction-recovery center may be necessary.

In the first three to six months after seeking help, the two of you are likely to weather strong emotions, including relief, anger, grief—and hope. The couples who best succeed are committed to recovery, respect each other, and reach out for support, counseling, and information.

Sex Therapy

Q: Our sex life has never been as pleasurable as I would like. I don't think I've ever had an orgasm, and lately intercourse hurts. I've tried to focus on other parts of the experience, such as kissing and touching, but we don't do much of that. To his credit, my husband is concerned, but we don't know what to do. Would sex therapy help? Would we have to make love in front of—or with—the therapist?

A: Increasing pleasure and eliminating discomfort are excellent reasons for a couple to seek the help of a qualified sex therapist, says Averil Marie Doyle, Ph.D., a certified sex therapist and educator in Kansas City, Kansas, and author of *The Sexually Disturbed: Treating Psychosexual Disorders.* "And don't worry," she says. "Clients do not disrobe or become sexually intimate in the presence of the therapist. Nor is there any touching between therapist and client."

Nor will you spend countless hours on a couch, delving into your distant past, as you might in traditional psychoanalysis. As you might expect, you'll learn new techniques or coital positions to try. But you'll also explore surprising factors that could be influencing physical intimacy between you and your husband—including medical conditions, medications, your relationship outside the bedroom, your upbringing, and early sexual experiences. Along the way, you'll find ways to overcome barriers to a satisfying, sexually intimate relationship. "Every couple is different, and so therapy is always individual," Dr. Doyle says. "But relationship factors are almost always involved, especially if a woman isn't feeling pleasure or desire."

This results-oriented brand of sex therapy has a high success rate: A study at the University of Minnesota found that 77 percent of couples who sought professional guidance reported improvement. Issues that respond well include lack of orgasm, impotence, premature ejaculation, erection problems, boredom, sexual slumps, fear of intimacy, performance anxiety, feelings of shame and guilt, and the effects of sexual traumas such as rape and abuse.

While many marriage counselors claim to incorporate sex therapy into their work, it's best to look for a trained therapist who's accredited by the American Association of Sex Educators, Counselors, and Therapists (AASECT) or by the American Board of Sexology. Sessions can cost $75 or more per hour (a fee rarely covered by insurance). Some couples report improvement in three months, while others may need a year to uncover and correct the patterns that stand in the way of a mutually satisfying sexual relationship, says Dr. Doyle.

More Pleasure, Less Pain

The first few sessions of sex therapy cover the basics. You and your husband will be asked to describe the problem that brought you to therapy. You'll also be asked about any medical conditions you may have, and any prescription or over-the-counter medications you're taking. Some problems have physical causes, and so a woman may need a gynecological exam as well. (A man would be examined by a proctologist.)

"I also ask clients about their sexual history," Dr. Doyle says. "If a woman doesn't experience sexual pleasure, I would want to explore any negative associations with sexual contact, including whether she had witnessed or been the victim of sexual abuse, or had even been the perpetrator of abuse."

As therapy continues, you will probably be given "homework" assignments. "At first, I would focus on the woman in this case, so that she could build knowledge of her own body, her own sexuality, what feels good and what doesn't," Dr. Doyle says. "I might, for example, ask her to explore her genitals while looking in the mirror, so that she gains familiarity and can find out if and how she experiences pleasure."

Later, focus would shift to the two of you, and to your relationship in— and out—of bed. "I would want to explore how the couple touches and kisses as well as what type of touching occurs before genital contact and penetration," Dr. Doyle says. "Women need and want more arousal before intercourse—more touching, more foreplay, more kissing—than men do. When a woman is aroused, she will likely be lubricating enough. When she isn't aroused, intercourse can be painful."

You and your husband may find that you enjoy sex more if you feel comfortable discussing what you like and dislike, what is and isn't happening. "Couples spend time in every session talking with each other about their sexual experience," Dr. Doyle says. "If you overcome shame and embarrassment, learn what you like, and learn the words for the areas of the genitals you're discussing, it helps a great deal."

So does understanding the dynamics of your relationship. Issues like anger, resentment, lack of emotional intimacy, and insecurity may prevent you from feeling free to let go and enjoy physical sensations during lovemaking, Dr. Doyle says. "If there's no friendship, no intimacy, no shared feelings, then a woman may not want sex," she says. "When a couple discovers what each other needs and enjoys, a satisfying sexual relationship is possible."

Temptation

Q: I met an old flame while away from home on a business trip. We had dinner together—with lots of wine and dancing. At the end of the evening, we shared a passionate kiss. I flew home the next morning. Now we have long, frequent phone conversations with a romantic, sexual edge. Sometimes I want to see him again and sleep with him. But at other times, I want to call it off and tell my husband. Things just aren't the same with my husband. I feel bored and guilty at the same time. Have I been unfaithful to him? What should I do about it?

A: "Technically speaking, you haven't broken your marriage vow, and so your actions can't be described as infidelity," says Jane Greer, Ph.D., a marriage and family therapist in New York City and author of *How Could You Do This to Me? Learning to Trust after Betrayal*. You are, however, siphoning a lot of emotional and sexual energy out of your relationship with your husband and into your flirtatious relationship with another man.

No wonder you feel guilty, confused, and stressed: You're straddling the fence—not stepping outside the marriage to have an affair, yet not directly addressing issues in your marriage or your own life that may be pushing you to look elsewhere for intimacy, passion, and excitement.

The temptation to have an affair is great if you're bored with your spouse—and if you feel energized and attractive with your former boyfriend. There's some chemistry with this old flame. But think hard before you act on it: Do you want your marriage to survive and thrive? If so, the smartest move would be to use your recent experience to help get your relationship with your husband back on track, says Dr. Greer. Take a deep breath and focus on your future happiness.

"Trust is the glue that binds lasting, meaningful relationships together. Having an affair would betray that trust," points out Dr. Greer. And while an affair might distract you from problems in your marriage or in your own daily life, it will only increase the emotional distance between you and your spouse as your sense of guilt and the need to keep a damaging secret both grow. At the same time, an affair will not solve any problems or adequately fill gaps in your life or your marriage, though you may hope it will.

If your marriage matters, resist temptation. Politely but firmly end the flirty phone calls, and look homeward. You have important work to do.

Lessons of a Near-Affair

After the last goodbye, don't give in to guilt and simply dismiss your phone relationship with your old flame as a terrible mistake, Dr. Greer says. The truth is that this clandestine relationship contains valuable information that could help improve your marriage, a road map for re-creating extraordinary togetherness at home. To read the lessons hidden in a near-affair, ask yourself two questions.

- How does this relationship make me feel about myself that I haven't felt in a while? "You may be feeling desirable, attractive, sexy, and just plain wonderful," Dr. Greer says. "And you may realize you haven't felt that way on your own recently."

- What is happening in this relationship that isn't happening in my marriage? Perhaps your husband hasn't been listening to you as much as you'd like, or perhaps you feel he hasn't been supportive or caring. Maybe you wish he would make you feel special and important, or just that the two of you would be more in sync and excited about being together. Perhaps your sexual relationship has become routine, or sex is infrequent.

"Think honestly about what you're getting from this new relationship," Dr. Greer says. "Then think about ways to bring those feelings into your own life and into your own marriage." Ask yourself what has kept you from feeling wonderful and desirable in your own right. Then pursue it. And ask yourself what's standing between you, your husband, and marital bliss. Then get ready: It's time to have an important conversation.

"Honey, We Have to Talk . . ."

Don't rush home and spill all the intimate details of your near-affair to your spouse, Dr. Greer says. "That's very high risk," she explains. "A confession will most likely spark insecurity and anger, when you're really trying to

The Innocent Side of Flirting

A mild attraction. A short, teasing conversation. A quick smile. Provided light-hearted flirtations go no further, they can actually bring zest into your marriage, says Jane Greer, Ph.D., a marriage and family therapist in New York City and author of *How Could You Do This to Me? Learning to Trust after Betrayal.*

"We're human. We're bound to feel attracted to other people even after we're married," Dr. Greer says. "Flirting can make you feel more alive, vital, and desirable, and it can give you a sense of yourself as an independent, attractive woman. Just remember to bring that energy and sexual desire home with you. Flirt with your husband. Jump into bed. Rekindle the flames that really matter."

achieve more intimacy with your husband." Resist the temptation to tell all, either in an effort to be totally honest or as a cloaked way of shocking your spouse into a jealous passion or as a punishment for not treating you as you would like.

"Be honest by talking about the truth of your feelings," Dr. Greer says. "Focus on what you would like to have in your relationship with your husband. Talk about missing the romance you had early in your time together. Of being lonely. Of needing more affection." Keep hurtful details, such as the two bottles of wine, the slow-dancing, the long kiss, to yourself. "Be considerate," she says.

Should you mention your old flame at all? "An indirect mention is best," Dr. Greer says. You could share with your husband that you find yourself fantasizing about old romances with old lovers because you wish there were more romance in your life right now. If it's true, you might even say that you're frightened that if things remain as they are, the growing gap between the two of you could lead you to try to fulfill your fantasy.

If your husband pushes for more information, tell the truth. "But always frame your answers in terms of your own feelings and in terms of shedding light on your marriage," Dr. Greer suggests. If he wonders who you're thinking about, say that an old boyfriend has been in your thoughts. If he wants to know more, share that you did have a chance encounter that brought up feelings from the past. You could even say that your old flame has made overtures that left you feeling vulnerable and susceptible—and those feelings are the very reason you want to talk and improve your marriage. If your husband is the jealous type, ask yourself if he really needs to know the details. Make sure you are not motivated by spite. Think carefully and fully consider your comments before the conversation, cautions Dr. Greer. (If your husband overreacts and expresses extreme jealousy, see Jealousy on page 32 for coping advice.)

Talking about your feelings and desires is vital now. Your near-affair is a sign that your marriage needs to be tended. Simply forgetting about your old flame and settling back into married life as if nothing ever happened won't help your relationship. "Take the risk. Speak up," Dr. Greer says. "Value your marriage enough to be truthful about your feelings. Don't wall yourself up when your true desire is to feel more closeness. Share the struggle to be happy and satisfied."

Index

Underscored page references indicate boxed text. Prescription drug names are denoted with the symbol Rx.

A

Abdominal crunches, for improving sex, 407–8

Abuse
    alcohol, 463–66
    domestic, 466–69
        characteristics of men committing, 468–69
        lack of emotional safety with, 128
        leaving, 469, 487
        from live-in lover, 273
    drug, 464, 469
    sexual
        harmful fantasies after, 165
        from live-in lover, 273
        sex addiction after, 493
        sex therapy for, 119, 496
        sexual anxiety from, 116

Acquired immunodeficiency syndrome (AIDS), 447–48

Acyclovir (Rx), for genital herpes, 444

Addiction
    alcohol, 463–66, 469
    drug, 464, 469
    sex, 492–94

Ads, personal, 221–24
    benefits of, 221–22
    characteristics of placers of, 222

composing, 224
    on Internet, 195, 197, 223
    placing, 222–23
    responding to, 223–24

Adventure, 147–50
    for preventing boredom, 147–48
    vacations for, 148–50, 149

Aerobic exercise, guidelines for, 406–7

Affairs. *See also* Infidelity
    during independence phase of marriage, 22
    temptation to have, 497–500
        lessons from, 498
        talking about, 498–500

Affection, for re-romanticizing relationship, 288–89

Afterplay, 53–54
    ejaculatory control and, 384
    importance of, to women, 126

Aging, sex and, 386–90
    changes affecting, 386–88
    myths about, 387
    statistics on, 389
    strategies for, 388–390

AIDS, 447–48

Al-Anon, for families of alcoholics, 464

<u>Underscored</u> page references indicate boxed text. Prescription drug names are denoted with the symbol Rx.

Boredom
  as cause of divorce, 40
  overcoming, with
      adventure, 147–48
      vacations, 41
  sexual, 69–70
  temptation to have affair from,
      497
Brain, in male sexuality, 367
Breast cancer
  mastectomy for (see
      Mastectomy)
  risk of, from oral contraceptives,
      311
Breastfeeding
  low sexual desire from, 360
  using contraception during,
      360
  vaginal dryness from, 365
Breast reconstruction, after
      mastectomy, 333
Breasts
  as erogenous zone, 60, 62, 294
  massaging, 101
Buttocks
  as erogenous zone, 61
  massaging, 102

C

Caffeine
  avoiding, to reduce stress,
      455–56
  depression from, 393
Calendar method of birth control,
      323, 324, 325

Cancer
  breast
      mastectomy for (see
          Mastectomy)
      risk of, from oral
          contraceptives, 311
  cervical, from human
      papillomavirus, 440, 441
  endometrial, oral contraceptives
      for preventing, 311
  ovarian, preventing, 311, 316,
      326
  prostate, 371
  sex affected by, 417, 419–22
Cancer treatment
  affecting sexual pleasure, 333,
      417, 419–20
  capability for reaching orgasm
      after, 422
Candlelight, for sex, 131
Car, sex in, 171
Carbohydrates, complex, for PMS,
      349
Careers, dual, in marriage, 251–58,
      252–53
Ceftriaxone (Rx), for gonorrhea,
      441
Cervical cancer, from human
      papillomavirus, 440, 441
Cervical cap, 307–8, 307
Cervical mucus, in natural birth
      control, 323–24
Cervix, 297
  removal of, with hysterectomy,
      326, 327
Chamomile, for insomnia, 341

Underscored page references indicate boxed text. Prescription drug names are
denoted with the symbol Rx.

Underscored page references indicate boxed text. Prescription drug names are denoted with the symbol Rx.

Underscored page references indicate boxed text. Prescription drug names are denoted with the symbol Rx.

Underscored page references indicate boxed text. Prescription drug names are denoted with the symbol Rx.

Underscored page references indicate boxed text. Prescription drug names are denoted with the symbol Rx.

Underscored page references indicate boxed text. Prescription drug names are denoted with the symbol Rx.

Underscored page references indicate boxed text. Prescription drug names are denoted with the symbol Rx.

Underscored page references indicate boxed text. Prescription drug names are denoted with the symbol Rx.

Knees, as erogenous zone, 61
Kwell, for pubic lice, 442
K-Y Jelly, for vaginal dryness, 366,
    423

L

Labia, as erogenous zone, 62
Labia majora, 294
Labia minora, 294
Laser-assisted uvulopalatoplasty
    (LAUP), for treating
    snoring, 452
Lavender, for insomnia, 341
Learning vacations, as adventure,
    150
Legs, massaging, 102
Letters, for long-distance
    relationships, 174–75,
    176–77
Levsin (Rx), for urinary
    incontinence, 364
Leydig's cells, in testicles, 370
Lice, pubic, 441–43
Lidocaine, for painful sex, 353
Light, during sex, 130–32
Lingerie
    choosing, 169–70
    for preventing night sweats, 340
Lips, as erogenous zone, 293
Lipstick, for allure, 152
Listening, in preparing for
    marriage, 264
Living together, 272–77, 274–75
Long-distance romance, 173–77,
    174–75

Love
    chemistry of, 4–5
    at first sight, statistics on, 259
    maintaining, in relationships,
        37–42, 38–39
    in readiness for marriage, 262–64
    stages of, 19–22
    statistics on, 212
Love maps, 5–6, 7, 134
Loveplay exercises, 64
Low-fat diet, better sex from,
    88–89, 398–99
Lubricants, vaginal, 352, 366, 423
Lumpectomy, for breast cancer, 329
Lust, purpose of, 39
Lysistrata, as sex comedy, 67

M

Marijuana, sexual problems from, 115
Marriage
    children affecting, 239–46,
        240–41, 242–43
    cultural differences in, 246–51,
        248–49
    deciding on, 258–64, 260–61
    determining readiness for, 259–64
    dual careers and, 251–58, 252–53
    fear of committing to, 262–63
    infidelity in (see Affairs;
        Infidelity)
    in-laws and, 268–72, 270–71
    interfaith, 247, 249–50
    living together instead of,
        272–77, 274–75
    money issues in, 278–84, 282–83

Underscored page references indicate boxed text. Prescription drug names are
denoted with the symbol Rx.

Underscored page references indicate boxed text. Prescription drug names are denoted with the symbol Rx.

Underscored page references indicate boxed text. Prescription drug names are
denoted with the symbol Rx.

<u>Underscored</u> page references indicate boxed text. Prescription drug names are denoted with the symbol Rx.

Underscored page references indicate boxed text. Prescription drug names are denoted with the symbol Rx.

hysterectomy, 326, 327–28
menopause, 337–38, 342
multiple sclerosis, 425–26
low
from arteriosclerosis, 398–99
from breastfeeding, 360
from fatigue, 408–9
hormones and, 59
masturbation for, 70
medications affecting, 427–29
menstrual cycle and, 343,
344–45, 346, 347, 350
after pregnancy, 358, 360
during pregnancy, 355–56
stress and, 452–54
in women vs. men, 119–20
Sexually transmitted diseases
(STDs), 434–48
failure to protect against, 435–36
incidence of, 442
infertility from, 412
lack of discussion about, 440
preventing, with
female condom, 304
male condom, 142–43, 300,
302
risk of
reducing, 446
in women, 434–35
sex on the beach and, 108
testing for, after infidelity, 473
types of
AIDS, 447–48
chlamydia, 436–37
genital herpes, 443–44
genital warts, 439–41

gonorrhea, 441
hepatitis B, 444–45
HIV, 447–48
pubic lice, 441–43
syphilis, 445, 447
trichomoniasis, 437–39
Sexual needs, 125–30
exercise for communicating, 127
of men, 128–29
satisfying, 129–30
of women, 126, 128
Shoulders, massaging, 101
Shower, sex in, 105–6, 107
Sildenafil (Rx). *See* Viagra (Rx)
Silent types, dating, 227–28
Singles' bars, 228–29
Singles' network, 201–2
Sleep apnea, 449–50, 451
Small talk, in flirting, 167
Smiling, in flirting, 168
Smoking, urinary incontinence
and, 362
Snoring, 448–52
causes of, 449–50
effect of, on partner, 450
medical treatment of, 451–52
self-help for, 450–451
Snow, sex in, 172
Solitude, importance of, 49
Somnoplasty, for treating snoring,
452
Soy products, for preventing hot
flashes, 339
Spectinomycin (Rx), for
gonorrhea, 441
Sperm, production of, 370

Spermicides
    allergy to, 351
    for contraception, 308–10, 309
    diaphragms and, 305, 306, 307
    for preventing
        chlamydia, 437
        genital warts, 440
        gonorrhea, 441
        hepatitis B, 445
        HIV, 448
        trichomoniasis, 438
Spirituality, for building intimacy,
    31
SSRIs, delayed orgasm from,
    427–28
STDs. See Sexually transmitted
    diseases
Sterilization
    with tubal ligation, 316–17, 317
    with vasectomy, 317–20, 320
Stomach, massaging, 101–2
Storm-chasing tours, as adventure,
    149
Stress
    coping with, 454–55, 455–56
    dual-career couples and, 254–56
    male vs. female response to, 457
    from negative self-talk, 458–59
    sexual desire affected by, 452–54
    remedies for, 456–58
Stress incontinence, 363, 364
Stretching exercises, for better sex,
    390, 404–5, 407
Striptease, as Valentine's gift, 185
Substance abuse, 463–66, 469
Sugar, depression from, 393

Support groups
    Al-Anon, 464
    breast cancer, 332, 334
    after divorce, 486
    infertility, 415
    Nar-Anon, 464
    for sex addicts, 494
Syphilis, 445, 447

T

Tagamet (Rx), sex drive affected
    by, 428
Tagamet HB, erectile disorder from,
    428
Talk, erotic, 109–11
Talking. See Communication
Temperature method of birth
    control, 323, 324
Temptation to have affair, 497–500
    lessons from, 498
    talking about, 498–500
Testicles, anatomy of, 370
Testosterone
    exercise for increasing, 406, 407
    function of, 380
    loss of
        with aging, 388
        in men, 379, 380–82
        during menopause, 337–38
    medications reducing, 428
    in menstrual cycle, 343, 344,
        346, 347, 348, 350
    purpose of, 296
    sexual desire and, 57, 59, 120,
        328

Underscored page references indicate boxed text. Prescription drug names are denoted with the symbol Rx.

Underscored page references indicate boxed text. Prescription drug names are denoted with the symbol Rx.

Vulvar vestibulitis, painful sex from, 351, 353
Vulvodynia, painful sex from, 351, 353

W

Walking
communication during, 11
for increasing sex drive, 409
for stress reduction, 456
Wardrobe, for dating, 201
Warts, genital, 439–41
Weekend getaways, 186–91
planning for, 188–90
purpose of, 187–88
signs of needing, 190
strategies for, 190–91
suggestions for, 188–89
Weight loss
program for, 432–34
for sleep apnea, 451
Western blot, for confirming HIV diagnosis, 448
Whitewater rafting, as adventure, 148–49
Withdrawal, for birth control, 324
Work. *See* Careers
Workaholism, signs of, 255
Workplace romance, 232–36
allure of, 234–35
rules for, 235–36
telling boss about, 234

Worries, interfering with sexual desire, 123–24

X

Xanax (Rx), sex drive affected by, 428

Y

Yeast infections
from diabetes, 423
misidentifying, 352
painful sex with, 351
Yoga, for preventing night sweats, 340

Z

Zantac 75, erectile disorder from, 428
Zidovudine (Rx), for AIDS, 448
ZIFT, for infertility, 411
Zinc, sources of, 156
Zithromax (Rx), for chlamydia, 437
Zoloft (Rx)
for depression, 428
orgasms affected by, 429
for premature ejaculation, 385
Zygote intrafallopian transfer (ZIFT), for infertility, 411

Underscored page references indicate boxed text. Prescription drug names are denoted with the symbol Rx.